YEATS, ELIOT AND R. S. THOMAS

YEATS, ELIOT AND
R. S. THOMAS
Riding the Echo

A. E. Dyson

First published 1981 by
THE MACMILLAN PRESS LTD
*London and Basingstoke
Companies and representatives
throughout the world*

ISBN 0 333 13027 8

*Typeset by Computacomp (UK) Ltd,
Fort William, Scotland.
Printed in Hong Kong*

For Julian Lovelock

                         Nature bandaged
Its wounds. Healing in
The smooth sun, it became
Fair. God looked at it
Again, reminded of
An intention. They shall answer
For you, he said. And at once
There were trees with birds
Singing, and through the trees
Animals wandered, drinking
Their own scent, conceding
An absence. Where are you?
He called, and riding the echo
The shapes came. . . .

                         (R. S. Thomas, 'Echoes')

Contents

Preface

This book proceeds mainly by way of practical criticism, and depends entirely upon the poems discussed being *heard*. I should like to make an urgent plea to every reader to heed the words of Yeats on this topic:

> If they are to read poetry at all, if they are to enjoy beautiful rhythm, if they are to get from poetry anything but what it has in common with prose, they must hear it spoken by men who have music in their voices and a learned understanding of its sound. There is no poem so great that a fine speaker cannot make it greater or that a bad ear cannot make it nothing. (*Samhain*, 1906; in *Explorations*, p. 212)

Whether this account is being read in a study, or used as the basis for group or seminar discussion, I would ask readers to *read aloud the poems discussed and to hear them read aloud*. Personal reading is essential, whether one's voice 'has music' in it or not. For the student, there is no investment more valuable than a simple tape recorder, on which he can hear his own reading, rub it out, try again, and so continue until the music and meaning of the poem come across as best he can manage, given the voice he has. In a group, several people should read, listening to each other, making constructive suggestions, and entering the poem first in this way.

With Eliot, we are fortunate enough to have his own recording of *Four Quartets* (as well as of other poems), and several other recordings made by men with fine voices. Ideally, these too should be heard (though not before the personal reading has been attempted: and duly remembering, of course, that copyright laws make this a strictly personal exercise). The poet's own reading has peculiar authority, in that it reveals how *he* heard it; but it is not definitive, as Eliot was the first critic always to insist. There are maybe as many 'good' performances possible, for poems of this kind, as there are of major symphonies. Each performance may have something new to teach, some new pleasure to give.

My own comments have been based on reading, hearing and discussing the poems with many students, and are offered simply as insights, to be accepted or rejected by readers against their own considered response. If they add to understanding and pleasure, then I shall have succeeded; if not, the personal reading and discussing of the poems will have at least been worthwhile.

It will be seen that, though outstanding debts are acknowledged when I come to them, I make no attempt to list every debt. The bibliographies – on the first two poets in particular – are extensive, and it is impossible to do justice to the amount of insight I have myself received, over many years. Debts to students – at the University of East Anglia, the University of Connecticut and the University College of North Wales in particular – are still more extensive: if I have unwittingly assimilated their thoughts, I hope they will regard this as the debt it is, and not as deliberate theft.

This said, two further points remain. The first is that the ideas expressed here are my personal responsibility. The second is that certain handbooks have proved invaluable to me, as they must to all students: notably A. N. Jeffares, *A Commentary on the Collected Poems of W. B. Yeats*, and B. C. Southam's *A Students' Guide to the Selected Poems of T. S. Eliot*.

I have not used, while actually writing, either Jon Stallworthy's two fine books, tracing the evolution of Yeats's poems through various drafts, or Helen Gardner's more recent work of a similar kind on *Four Quartets*. This approach to literary criticism, by way of scholarship, is uniquely valuable, and complements criticism of all other kinds. It offers insights available in no other way into both creative intention and creative process, and cannot fail to have an authority peculiar to itself. Even so, I think there is still room for creative readings (or performances), based on the finished text, and approached as one might a musical score, as it stands. The dividing line may be a thin one (particularly in the case of Yeats, where some knowledge of his life, imported from outside the poems, is essential equipment), but it does, I think, exist.

We are extremely fortunate to have so many aids to the understanding of Yeats and Eliot. It is greatly to be hoped that the ten volumes between *Song at the Earth's Turning* and *Frequencies*, and other private collections, upon which R. S. Thomas's reputation so far rests, will soon be available in a *Collected Poems* – the most important so far non-existent literary work of the century. Tapes and recordings of the poet can be obtained, and are immensely helpful, but I hope that, like Eliot, he will also be far more extensively available, on commercial recordings, before long.

Note that books mentioned in the text are listed in section 1 of the Select Bibliography (p. 327). In section 2, I list a small selection of the other books which I particularly recommend.

University of East Anglia, January 1980   A. E. Dyson

Acknowledgements

The author and publishers wish to thank the following who have kindly given permission for the use of copyright material:

William Collins, Sons & Co. Ltd and Pantheon Books, a division of Random House Inc., for the extract from *Memories, Dreams, Reflections* by C. G. Jung, edited by Aniela Jaffé, translated by Richard and Clara Winston.

Faber & Faber Ltd and Harcourt, Brace, Jovanovich Inc., for the extracts from T. S. Eliot's 'Tradition and the Individual Talent' in *Selected Essays*; and the extracts from *Four Quartets*, *The Hollow Men* and 'Gerontion' from *Collected Poems, 1909–1962*; USA © 1936 by Harcourt, Brace, Jovanovich Inc.; © 1943, 1963, 1964 by T. S. Eliot; © 1971 by Esme Valerie Eliot.

Penguin Books Ltd, for the extract from *Tao Te Ching* by Lao Tzu, translated by D. C. Lau.

Routledge & Kegan Paul Ltd and Harcourt, Brace, Jovanovich Inc., for the extracts from *Modern Man in Search of a Soul* by C. G. Jung.

R. S. Thomas and Granada Publishing Ltd, for the extracts from his poems, published by Hart-Davis MacGibbon Ltd.

A. P. Watt Ltd, on behalf of Anne and Michael Yeats, and Macmillan Publishing Co. Inc., for the extracts from *Collected Poems*, © 1956; *A Vision*, © 1937 by W. B. Yeats, renewed 1965 by Bertha Georgie Yeats and Anne Butler Yeats; *Autobiographies*, © 1916, 1935, renewed 1944, 1963 by Bertha Georgie Yeats; *Essays and Introduction*, © 1961 by Mrs W. B. Yeats; *The Letters of W. B. Yeats*, edited by Allan Wade, © 1953, 1954 by Anne Butler Yeats; and *Explorations*, © 1962 by Mrs W. B.Yeats.

Every effort has been made to trace all the copyright-holders, but if any have been inadvertently overlooked, the publishers will be pleased to make the necessary arrangements at the first opportunity.

Introduction:
Riding the Echo

I

'Riding the echo' – I choose this phrase, from one of R. S. Thomas's poems, for a subtitle, since it indicates one of the points where the three poets who are to be considered here share common ground. Though all, in differing ways, are masters of syntax (Eliot more consistently so than critics always acknowledge), all share also a striving towards meanings beyond any that syntax can contain. Language is pushed towards, and beyond, the boundaries of discursive intellect, seeking not the negation of known experience, but its extension. All are explorers of inner and complex consciousness, through the medium of verbal artefacts instinct with unusual power.

Every poem, every song or symphony has its autonomy – but, in the realm of art, the works of major creators set up resonances and echoes among themselves. In this manner, we come to recognise a distinctive 'world' of Beethoven, Mahler, Yeats (a long, but finite roll-call). And for those whose depths are stirred by such artists, especially through the course of a lifetime, no basic defence of their power and authenticity has to be made.

In this book, I shall be considering works of three outstanding modern poets, pioneers of human consciousness in the medium of words. All are different, all are religious; all offer a major exploration in their art as a whole. All present the fruit of a sustained and vulnerable preoccupation with the realm where religion, art and personal consciousness converge. All seek, through continuous interplay of image and resonance, the 'status' of human existence and creativity, opting for 'hints and guesses / Hints followed by guesses', not for dogma, as their continuing mode.

In literary terms, all are heirs (again in differing ways) of the symbolists, but I shall not be concerned with literary theory in this current approach. My aim rather is to offer critical readings of individual poems, allowing comments on poetic method and tentative 'meaning' to emerge in this way.

My subtitle comes, as I have said, from R. S. Thomas, but very similar words will be found near the opening of Eliot's 'Burnt Norton' (and are considered in that context later, where they belong). It may be in order also to quote two passages from Yeats's prose with a direct bearing, passages which shed a light, as if from opposite directions, on the main aim of this book. The first is from 'A People's Theatre', dated 1919, and can be found in *Explorations* (p. 255):

> I desire a mysterious art, always reminding and half-reminding those who understand it of dearly loved things, doing its work by suggestion, not by direct statement, a complexity of rhythm, colour, gesture, not space-pervading like the intellect, but a memory and a prophecy: a mode of drama Shelley and Keats could have used without ceasing to be themselves, and for which even Blake in the mood of *The Book of Thel* might not have been too obscure.

The other is from 'Modern Poetry: A Broadcast' (1936) and can be found in *Essays and Introductions*, pp. 502–3:

> I think profound philosophy must come from terror. An abyss opens under our feet; inherited convictions, the presuppositions of our thoughts, those Fathers of the Church Lionel Johnson expounded, drop into the abyss. Whether we will or no we must ask the ancient questions: Is there a reality anywhere? Is there a God? Is there a Soul? We cry with the Indian Sacred Book: 'They have put a golden stopper into the neck of the bottle; pull it! Let out reality!'

Yeats's prose has a tantalising beauty so close to his verse, in theme and rhythm, that I was tempted to insert a chapter on it here. This would, however, too greatly unbalance the project; so I shall hope to write on the prose independently, elsewhere.

In contrast, T. S. Eliot's prose was, by conscious choice, removed from poetry. He saw it as a wholly different medium, and to quote from it would throw little light on *Four Quartets*. Just occasionally however, he permitted himself prose evocations akin to poetry, and I quote a passage from *The Use of Poetry and the Use of Criticism* (1933) where we can catch the origin of a famous image in 'The Journey of the Magi' at its inception:

> . . . only a part of an author's imagery comes from his reading. It comes from the whole of his sensitive life since early childhood. Why, for all of us, out of all we have heard, seen, felt in a lifetime, do certain images recur, charged with emotion, rather than

others? The song of one bird, the leap of one fish, at a particular place and time, the scent of one flower, an old woman on a German mountain path, six ruffians seen through an open window playing cards at night at a small French railway junction where there was a watermill: such memories may have symbolic value, but of what we cannot tell, for they come to represent the depths of feeling into which we cannot peer.   (p. 148)

II

In their basic technique of resonance, these poets owe debts to the Symbolists, but resemble also most of the great poetry, and art, of the world. Much of the theory evolved by the Symbolists was not only a new direction for poetry in the later nineteenth century (though it had immediate influence as such), but more basically, a discovery of the way in which the greatest art always has, and will, work. Our understanding of the books of Job and Revelation, of Greek tragedy and of Shakespeare, is now deeply indebted to it; so, still more, is our understanding of music. 'All art aspires to the condition of music' is a precept that underlies most of the best modern criticism, as well as most of the best modern art.

There is one further general matter I wish briefly to touch on, which gives Yeats, Eliot and Thomas particular centrality to our own times, and lives. Until the early nineteenth century, various dogmatisms – religious, philosophical and, later, scientific – had great power in Europe and, for many reputable thinkers and artists, were the main road to 'truth'. Since then, a combination of circumstances has combined to 'fragment' our culture and, though the younger Eliot lamented this, many will regard it chiefly as gain. Today, there are still dogmatists in plenty, notably in religion and politics: but they operate from widely differing premises; and they are always prone to appeal for their sanctions to some forms of naked authority which, unless backed with powers of life and death, are increasingly rejected. Most are seen to be ill-informed, illiterate or egocentric, in the sense that they would try to cram the whole world into tiny moral or intellectual structures where they can either find, or escape from, themselves successfully, and to which they are prepared to sacrifice, if allowed, the freedom, dignity and diversity of all their fellow men. Unless we turn our back on knowledge, the movement away from dogma is irreversible, and the doctrines announced by Blake, Wordsworth and other early nineteenth-century prophets, based on belief in individual uniqueness and celebration of individual creativity, are doctrines by which man's future will be shaped.

If so, then all sensitive men face various converging quests, none without tensions – the quest for self-knowledge; the quest for religion (or orientation to external reality); and the quest for some workable hypotheses that make sense of their lives. The strain in this commitment has been acknowledged by many moderns; I think, for instance, of Stephen Spender's *The Struggle of the Modern* (1963) and Frank Kermode's *Sense of an Ending* (1967). Even so, the exploration, whether one calls it romantic, psychotherapeutic or transcendental, involves strains from which honest, not dishonest, knowledge and dignity are born. I believe that increasingly all men and women who are seriously concerned with the quest (unless I am wrong, the overwhelming majority) will seek personal wholeness or healing based on honest openness to their particular tensions; and that, in formulating whatever views of man's cosmic significance come to seem most 'true' for themselves, they will offer these as insights, not as dogmas, when they share them with their fellow men.

Whether Eliot the Anglican fits this pattern, I am by no means certain; but the author of *Four Quartets* most certainly does. So, without reservations of any kind, do Yeats and R. S. Thomas. It is for this reason that I shall tacitly be regarding them as major prophets and pioneers of our human future, even though my emphasis falls, as is right in a critical book, on their art.

But it should be recalled that, if this situation is 'modern', it is also 'ancient': the European episode spanning the period from the conversion to Christianity of Constantine to the impact of evolutionary theory and the 'higher criticism' of the Bible is by no means the whole story of man. The Greek tragic writers conducted explorations remarkably similar in kind (though not of course in cultural concepts) to those of my three present poets, and in my experience as a teacher I find them as challenging and relevant, in the response of today's students, as they must have been to their original Athenian audience so long ago. The same openness is to be found in the surviving art of many non-European civilisations, and increasingly, under the accelerating cross-fertilisation of cultures, we recognise that the ancient writings of India and China, and the spontaneous vitality and honesty of negro writing, have wisdom and energy to add to the common store. A visit to the Sainsbury Collection at the University of East Anglia also brings this home forcefully; the recognition may even be implicit in those 'hints of earlier and other creation' which run through *Four Quartets*, though Eliot's explicit references are usually to natural, not human relics, when he peers beyond Europe.

My personal contact with Christianity has eventually persuaded me that the teaching of Christ himself, and also I would argue of the later Old Testament prophets and of the major New Testament writers, rests on a mixture of witness, enigma and vivid personal experience which – if, and when, the dogmas of the surviving 'visible' churches are ignored and the texts looked at afresh – is closely akin to the explorations of our finest modern writers (ironically, to the allegedly 'post-Christian' era).

A final word on *In Memoriam* before I leave these general reflections. Tennyson was once called, in my hearing, the most 'stupid' of our poets; I think he could be seen rather as one of the most forward-looking and intuitive, even though his art is, unhappily, flawed.

If we are to locate the time when recent European 'intellect' ceases to find God in Nature, and starts rather to find intellect an obstacle to faith, then the 1820s and 1830s are the place to look. Wordsworth's *Prelude* had been completed in its original version by 1805 and is optimistically religious, and, though Wordsworth went on revising during his lifetime, there were no alterations to the basic celebration of faith. Tennyson's *In Memoriam* is another story. The famous stanzas LIV–LVI were written in the mid 1830s, a full quarter of a century before *Origin of Species* was published (1859) and when evolutionary theories were still in their infancy; but they already held the full anguish of doubt which was to become so common later, among the Victorians. Tennyson's doubt was no mere intellectual dabbling, as far too much eighteenth-century philosophising in verse had been, but was an anguish of his whole being, precipitated by bereavement. Arthur Hallam's death opened an 'abyss' which forced him back on what Yeats called 'the ancient questions', in his double need both to understand the nature of his love for his dead friend, and to assess the prospects of an after-life that might vindicate and even fulfil it. Like Eliot later, in many key sections of *Four Quartets*, he found his quest leading not through light, or logic, but through darkness. In the course of the poem, he finds power to throw himself

> Upon the great world's altar-stairs
> That slope through darkness, up to God

and records that this upward gesture of man, humbled and prostrate, is later met more by the intimation, than by any certainty, of an answering downward gesture from God:

> And out of darkness came the hands
> That reach through Nature, moulding men. . . .

This *via negativa* of anguish is, further, linked with an exploration of the status of poetry and language as media for 'truth', and to sections such as the remarkable fifth one, in the final arrangement of the poem, where preoccupations we shall meet time and again in Yeats,

Eliot and Thomas receive one of their most potent expressions in modern times:

> I sometimes hold it half a sin
>   To put in words the grief I feel;
>   For words, like Nature, half reveal
> And half conceal the Soul within.
>
> But, for the unquiet heart and brain
>   A use in measured language lies;
>   The sad mechanic exercise,
> Like dull narcotics, numbing pain.
>
> In words, like weeds, I'll wrap me o'er,
>   Like coarsest clothes against the cold:
>   But the large grief which these enfold
> Is given in outline and no more.

The notion that style and metre themselves might be a 'sad mechanic exercise', effecting only temporary forgetfulness, is sufficiently striking, as indeed is the perception that language can as much evade or obscure, as reveal, 'meaning', by its very laws. In linking 'words' and 'Nature' as he does here, Tennyson is on ground not too distant from that of R. S. Thomas in some of his most recent poems. We may remember too that if he sounds 'romantic' in an older sense when he writes lines such as 'My heart stood up and answered, "I have felt" ', there are other phrases in *In Memoriam* which look forward uncompromisingly to modern tentativeness:

> There lives more faith in honest doubt,
> Believe me, than in half the creeds. . . .

The section of the poem which now functions as its prologue, but was written as late as 1849, is on the surface a profession of recovered faith. But the language is so drenched in qualification, and the tone so marked by uncertainty, that it seems, at best, a kind of whistling in the dark. Throughout, however, Tennyson remains an explorer, open to the reality of powers which may exist, though he cannot fully express or appropriate them. He is determined to do justice to the mingling of delight and despair, doubt and faith, hope and enigma in life, whether he is thinking of personal love, or personal bereavement. Words written by T. S. Eliot in 'East Coker' seem highly apt as a description of the enterprise started in *In Memoriam*, and continued (though with diminishing power) through Tennyson's later life:

> the fight to recover what has been lost
> And found and lost again and again: and now, under conditions
> That seem unpropitious.

If *In Memoriam* is for the most part inferior, as poetry, to the work that will now concern us, this is due more to flaws in artistry than to any failure in honesty. The habit of philosophising in verse, inherited from the eighteenth century, mars the poetry, precisely because Tennyson is so often unable, or unwilling, to 'ride the echo' in his quest. As various critics have said, those sections in which he does allow images to take control are among the finest (Eliot himself picks out part VII, 'Dark house . . .', for special praise).

With this major reservation, I would suggest that Tennyson should not be written off, either as a minor lyricist, or as an intellectually conventional poet, but allowed his rightful place as a forerunner of the modern consciousness as we shall encounter it here. T. S. Eliot is, of the two, much the finer artist, but in temperament and development he had more in common with Tennyson than he ever acknowledged. Both were driven by inner crisis and melancholy, not by abstract reasoning; both were haunted by cultural breakdown, experienced as a highly personal threat. Both show evidence of strong impulses to suicide, coloured by some sickness associated with guilt and with sex. Both capture moments of self-doubt and grief with memorable precision; both were driven by the need to 'construct something / Upon which to rejoice' against very frightening odds. Both, as artists, produced from their inner needs and agonies images that became recognised as central to their age. I have often wondered if it is wholly accidental that one of the most perceptive comments ever made on *In Memoriam* is Eliot's; and that the words could almost as fittingly be applied to *The Waste Land*: 'It happens now and then that a poet by some strange accident expresses the mood of his generation, at the same time that he is expressing a mood of his own which is quite remote from that of his generation' ('Tennyson', in *T. S. Eliot: Selected Prose*, p. 180). In writing this book, I have been acutely aware that these three poets, all highly idiosyncratic, all in many ways very untypical of their century, seem none the less near its spiritual centre. Of the three, R. S. Thomas has so far received less than his due acclaim during his lifetime, even though the highest praise of his work has repeatedly been made by many critics of note. I have no doubt at all that he belongs with the other two in stature; and in time will be seen as the outstanding poet, to date, of the second half of this century.

A last word may fittingly be given to Yeats, who in his own prose justifies creation and even criticism more frequently and persuasively than any other writer I know. This comes from *Samhain* (1903) and will I hope still be the justification for schools of English, and the study of literature, long after more allegedly 'scientific' defences (or attacks) have had their day:

> Literature is, to my mind, the great teaching power of the world, the ultimate creator of all values, and it is this, not only in the sacred books whose power everybody acknowledges, but by every movement of imagination in song or story or drama that height of intensity and sincerity has made literature at all. Literature must take the responsibility of its power, and keep all its freedom: it must be like the spirit and like the wind that blows where it listeth; it must claim its right to pierce through every crevice of human nature, and to describe the relation of the soul and the heart to the facts of life and of law, and to describe that relation as it is, not as we would have it be; and in so far as it fails to do this it fails to give us that foundation of understanding and charity for whose lack our moral sense can be but cruelty. . . .(*Explorations*, p. 117)

1 Yeats's Poetry: the Major Phase, 1916–39. No Enemy but Time

Dear shadows, now you know it all,
All the folly of a fight
With a common wrong or right.
The innocent and the beautiful
Have no enemy but time. . . .

('In Memory of Eva Gore-Booth and Con Markiewicz')

Introductory Note

In the Introduction I mentioned certain ideas which were formulated by Yeats in his prose writings, and span his life. Now, I want to consider the verse, starting with 'The Wild Swans at Coole', and moving through a commentary attached to selected poems written from that period until his death.

Yeats has no single poem of the 'magnitude' of *The Waste Land* or *Four Quartets*, yet his poems, though autonomous, live together in a manner not dissimilar, in final effect, to a major *oeuvre*. Certain themes weave in and out of the poems, as they do in the prose, each time achieving a complete 'image' which may seem to imply finality; and I have no wish to deny this autonomy. Indeed, the sense of completeness in most of Yeats's finest poems is so marked, that many stay in the mind as if the entire ordering of words were inevitable. We know from Yeats's own testimony that this was far from the case; and Jon Stallworthy's invaluable studies enable us to follow the evolution of many important poems from comparatively unpropitious beginnings to the remarkable achievements we now explore.

My own procedure will be to discuss the poems as they exist in their final form, approved by the poet. Inside this framework, I shall be emphasising that the dialectic set up between the poems, which in fact forbids us to take any single one of them as a final statement from the 'poet himself' (as opposed to 'the poem itself'), is at the core of our teasing sense of some major *oeuvre* waiting to be unearthed. Perhaps I can add, to allay certain natural fears such a statement might generate, that I do not believe the poet himself either did achieve, or would have expected to achieve, a definitive philosophy. Like most major poets he was an explorer and one who would have recognised death as the one bitter irrelevance beyond his control. I am aware too that my own selection of the poems, like those of any other critic, must be subjective. I justify this partly on pragmatic grounds; there is neither world enough nor time, nor publishing patience, for more. But also, the justification is in my own concept of poetic criticism, and maybe of the criticism of the poets this book concerns itself with especially. There is a place for the reader, undoubtedly: the obvious place, necessitated by recreation, which the poet can more easily release than control, though he points the direction; and the less easily defined place, where 'life' intervenes. All readers are as much men of their time, and of their personal temperament, as are the authors they study; all will contribute to any insight, or even synthesis, they impose. The effort not to 'read into' a poem is literary discipline; but the urge to explore for oneself is that tribute to art without which it would wither and fade. The reader's response is part of 'tradition'; and 'tradition' complements 'individual talent', as Eliot says, in the life of art. No doubt, Eliot was thinking more of the artist's problems and challenges than of the reader's, but increasingly, these two aspects seem to me to merge into one. We live at a time when certain Marxist critics assault or deny the autonomy of art, seeking to identify with class or social mores a fullness of effect that is far more deep, and universal, in its ultimate source. The linguists and structuralists pose a parallel threat, no doubt partly in innocence, if they deflect attention too much from the human sources of art to art's structures *per se*. My own stand as a critic remains firmly in the tradition of Arnold, the Symbolists, T. S. Eliot, the Geneva critics, A. C. Bradley – with whatever modifications of emphasis any grouping of such essential individualists must, by its nature, imply. During the 1970s I have come to see ever more clearly that this tradition is ultimately European and American, and will stand or fall with the destiny of the matured, fragile humanism of these two great continents. I believe that art is revelatory – though the revelation is complex, and dark with enigma – and that the *life* of art is more central to a sensitive humanism, than most people yet see. It is art which most rescues us from all moralisms, all dogmatisms, all illusory certainties, pointing us back rather to that anguish of uncertainty, tolerance, understanding, which is a rich soil for love.

Of course, there are other soils propitious for love (I would not deny it), nor would I claim that love is the only fruit in the garden of art. Yet the chorus in *Agamemnon* was surely right in its insight, 'men must suffer and grow wise'; nor is there any reading of art that does not draw upon, and refine, human suffering. What follows may be taken then as one reader's selection and exploration of Yeats's poetry; one map to a territory as rich in suffering and wisdom as it is in joy.

One further generalisation before I start. Among the artistic qualities of these poems that may cause difficulties is one which *reading aloud* can most effectively solve. In many poems it will be noted that, while the forward march of syntax presents an illusion of assured progress, prophetic statement, the resolution of complexity, this is balanced, almost always, by its telling counter-truth. A continuing play of unsolved ambivalence, conflicting directions, opposed possibilities, exists in flux with the apparently simpler and grander effects that may remain in our mind. Only when the poem's complexity is grasped can it be *read* successfully; and the reading alone reveals metre, tone, mood in their unified power. Occasionally, some reader will doubt Yeats's metrical skill and find it clumsy; always, this is a sign that the 'meaning' has yet to be fully explored.

Each reader, of course, has his own voice only, when tape-recording; though he may become aware of richer and deeper possibilities than this will produce. The important thing is to record, and rerecord, until the reading satisfies, whilst remaining alert also to verbal effects which a different voice might transform. It is my experience that this exercise of reading, and listening, is the best first approach to criticism, since without it no degree of intelligence can be sure of engaging with the poem itself. I have recommended readers of this book to have a tape recorder at hand, and to explore the poems through personal reading alongside my commentary, since agreements or disagreements will be sharpened in this way. This advice applies equally to Eliot and to R. S. Thomas, and for similar reasons. It can be understood that such readings are intended only for the student's private use, as a teaching method; and that a single tape, reused, is all that one needs.

'The Wild Swans at Coole'

The Wild Swans at Coole (1919), published when Yeats was fifty-five, will be my starting point. The title poem is, at first sight, akin to Yeats's earlier mode. It is sharper, of course, than Yeats's earliest work, which reveals his original debt to the pre-Raphaelites and Morris, but it might still be mistaken, at a casual glance, for one of the better poems of the Georgians. Very quickly, however, we notice that the transitions are oddly elusive, and that certain lines stand out with a force only partly explained by their context. It was in 1897 that Yeats first felt totally at home in Coole Park, home of his patroness and life-long friend Lady Gregory. Her great house hidden in trees, with the strangely beautiful lake in its grounds, was profoundly satisfying to one side of the poet's nature. Aristocratic, Protestant (and therefore remotely English, though Lady Gregory delighted as much as Yeats in Ireland's magic and folk-lore), it symbolised everything gracious, ancient, outstanding that attracted his loyalty. Maybe everything in him which loved beauty, revered heroes, celebrated high achievement, cultivated friendship, hated vulgarity, found a mirror here. 'We were the last romantics', as he wrote much later, in another poem from Coole – and 'the last romantics' carries connotations that were not specifically English (though Yeats admired and learned from Blake and Shelley), but those of a 'romanticism' related to medieval, Celtic and still older traditions, where courtesy flourished, openness to wonder nurtured the mind and spirit of man, and patronage, such as Lady Gregory provided for Yeats and his peers, was not an anachronism half-dreamlike to contemplate. Coole Park appealed also to the feeling for genetic purity which haunted later plays such as *Purgatory* and even seduced Yeats to the first stirrings of political fascism, though conceivably it sensitised him also, at a level we can now see as more fruitful (certainly less disturbing, fifty years later), to some of the insights of Jung.

There were, naturally, tensions between these aspects of the poet and his no less passionate republicanism, occultism and rejection of all forms of Christian and English influence other than any which could be seen to contain some remote debt. Christianity provided an occasional image, however changed by context; Shakespeare, Spenser, Shelley and other English poets receive Yeats's homage, as masters of the language in which his own work was felt and conceived. 'The Wild Swans at Coole' is typical in its total exclusion of irrelevant tensions and its use of the central image to explore a particular, complex mood.

The first stanza suggests a ritual re-enactment, attuned to 'autumn', as also to the poet's acceptance of the last phase of life. The word 'their' establishes a truth cyclical in nature, yet new to the poet. (Maud Gonne had rejected his proposal of marriage for the final time – a proposal made after the execution for treachery of her husband, John MacBride; Maud Gonne's illegitimate daughter had likewise rejected his proposal. After this bizarre episode, Yeats had surprised in himself relief at the refusals and, accompanying this, confirmation of the truth so long resisted, 'Oh, who could have foretold / That the heart grows old?'). A mood of melancholy coloured his momentous decision to marry Georgie Hyde-Lees, and to make Thoor Ballylee his home. From now on, an autumnal mood colours most of his verse, along with increasing energy, as if some charm to recall the spring, or stabilise eternity, is the unfailing quest.

'Mirrors' in l. 4 combines momentary calm with a hint of illusion. In this temporary stasis, we are led on to the more personal ritual described in the final lines, an annual counting of swans. The memorable 'nine-and-fifty' is highly distinctive of the poet's predilection both for the meticulous and the capricious. We have it on Lady Gregory's authority that George Moore had once forgotten 'Yeats ... and everything else in the delight caused by a great clamour of wings and the snowy plumage of thirty-six great birds rushing down the lake, striving to rise from its surface'. Yeats, now making *his* 'nineteenth' count, uses similar phrases, but a different number. Is it possible to count up to fifty-nine exactly, as the graceful creatures float and maybe interweave, with no margin of error? The need for exactness is perhaps a precondition of the 'All' in l. 4 of the second stanza, and the 'All's changed' in l. 3 of the third, as well as of the apparent concreteness of the poem's conclusion, concealing (as it artlessly does) the sudden transposition of birds and man. On the other hand, the difference between George Moore's even number, and Yeats's odd, may signify the importance that there *is* one swan not included in the pairings ('lover by lover' – stanza iv). I think of 'The swan has leaped into the desolate heaven' (floating, out of context, from 'Nineteen Hundred and Nineteen'); of the exquisite image of the dying swan, alone, in the third section of 'The Tower'; and of the one swan of power in 'Leda and the Swan' – along with the reference to 'daughters of the swan', tacitly identifying one of Leda's two tempestuous daughters with Maud Gonne, the solitary swan who never paired with Yeats, in 'Among School Children'. It is impossible to know Yeats without cross-references of this kind acquiring a powerful, if elusive, suggestiveness across the poems; and here, certainly, the man himself is left solitary at the poem's end, when no swans remain.

In the second stanza, the phrase 'before I had well finished' emphasises, now, the contrasting theme of flux and inevitable confusion, casting doubt back upon the exact numbering. Yet 'All suddenly mount', with its powerfully rising cadence, places the power of the swans decisively inside time and change; and the last two lines of this stanza, as well as offering visual brilliance, yoke together 'clamorous' with the inescapable price of action – 'scatter' underlining the necessary end of harmony, even as harmony forms itself ('great *broken* rings' – my italics).

The conjunction of 'great' and 'broken' is precisely the poet's response to this ritual, the contradiction in his empathy. The third

stanza moves from 'brilliant' to 'sore'; and though the first word
describes the 'creatures', and the second the poet's 'heart', the two
come together in 'All's changed': a phrase redolent of much to
come. We sense that it is the poet who has changed and that,
surreptitiously, the birds are now excluded from the process, so that
the 'bell-beat of their wings' can acquire a mythic changelessness
(akin to Keats's transformation of his nightingale into an undying
symbol, for the central and visionary episode in the 'Ode to a
Nightingale'), against which the poet's 'tread' succumbs to the
depredation of time. In the fourth stanza, the birds are fully mythic –
and note that, achieving the humanly unattainable 'Unwearied',
with the fidelity of 'lover by lover' (equally inaccessible to mere
men ?), they also take on something of 'cold'. In fact, the marvellous
placing of 'cold', causing the reading voice to pause and register,
before it passes on to the qualifying 'Companionable', allows the
poet a strangely effective device. This is not the transformation *back*
from myth to reality, so powerfully heralded by the same word ('Cold
pastoral') in Keats's 'Ode to a Grecian Urn'. Rather, 'cold' can, after
the pregnant pause, become allied to 'Companionable' and 'climb'
– and can then co-exist with 'hearts have not grown old', 'Passion or
conquest, wander where they will' – a potent accumulation of the
heart's desires which the heart of man, at least, will never achieve.

We might feel that the birds are left with the best of both worlds:
the world of reality where, in each of nineteen years, actual swans
have known their moment of beauty and fullness; and the symbolic
world, where this freedom is a permanence possible only in myth.
We should recall also, however, that the word 'cold' is usually a good
word in Yeats. In 'Cat and the Moon' it goes naturally with the
affinity of feline grace and lunar light; often, it is associated with
creative austerity (cf. the stanzas about John Synge in 'In Memory of
Major Robert Gregory'): nor can we forget the end of 'Ben Bulben',
inscribed for perpetuity on Yeats's own tomb, 'By his command'.
The line 'Attend upon them still' is, in strict syntax, descriptive, but I
cannot resist the feeling that it has something of the force, too, of the
poet's blessing. No doubt, these powerful cross-currents prepare the
way for the final stanza, where the transposition of birds and poet is
completed, but without any apparent change of mood or reference.
'But now they drift' – and the 'now' is forever since, in their
eternalised state, they will continue to 'build' and 'Delight men's
eyes' beyond all reach of change. Even so, the conjunction of 'drift'
and 'still' serves, beyond its visual clarity, to underline paradox:
'Mysterious, beautiful' may suggest not simply the birds, but the
equivocal status of eternity itself. The poet remains in time, and
'when I awake some day / To find they have flown away?' *is* an
ending finely judged to tease. We conclude not with the poet, grown

older, remembering swans of yesteryear, but with swans of his own transforming, outlasting himself. The final triumph, I think, is that he casts the ending in the form of a question – forcing us to envisage the reality of the future men (and so of the undying swans), even though the 'lake's edge or pool' not only will not, but cannot, exist. 'Awake' could refer to the poet's return from art to life, and from dream to reality; or it could here be a direct synonym for death. Either way, we are left with the prevailing mood of melancholy – almost as if this were the simple Georgian poem that a first glance suggested. But a new dimension of greatness appears in Yeats's art.

'In Memory of Major Robert Gregory'

This poem is dated 14 June 1918, just less than six months after the death of Lady Gregory's son.

In appearance, it is two poems merged into one. Robert Gregory's death had clearly shocked Yeats profoundly, though not, one senses, at the deepest level of friendship. The memorable phrase 'that discourtesy of death' in stanza vi at once introduces a social, and even courtly element into the lament, and perhaps underlines the sharing of grief. Gregory had been very generally regarded in his circle, we learn, as a new Sir Philip Sidney: a Renaissance ideal, skilled in the arts, aristocratic, a superb sportsman and scholar; one of the perceived hopes (alongside that of Irish culture) of revitalising Europe, in the twentieth century, as Greek culture had done two-and-a-half-thousand years earlier. His death therefore seems a slap in the face for hope, an omen perhaps of the conviction, to grow rapidly upon Yeats from this time, that the decay of civilisation was now irrevocable. Maybe men of Gregory's stamp almost belong to the past, to death, by the logic of history. In the strategy of the poem, Gregory is compared with three of Yeats's other friends, also dead, who in varied ways had failed, each in aspects where Gregory was a natural model. This somewhat uneasy strategy coexists with the poem's more immediate purpose – the source, no doubt, of its sombre and undeniable power – which is to celebrate the final stages of Thoor Ballylee's reconstruction with a kind of house-warming party of the dead.

Three times again in major poems, and often in passing references, Yeats was to use the eerie strategy of a confrontation with the dead ('The Tower', 'All Souls' Night', and 'The Municipal Gallery Revisited'). When he wrote this poem, his recent marriage had sealed him off for ever from Maud Gonne, and from whatever promise of youth was inalienably vested in her by the poet himself. Many of his closest associates were dead, and maybe one of the

profound psychological adjustments of life's final phase, which Eliot
also evoked memorably ('As we grow older / The world becomes
stranger, the pattern more complicated / Of dead and living' – 'East
Coker') is his major dynamic. The Tower, Yeats's new home, which
was also to become a major symbol, had been suggested to him, as
his place of settlement, by Gregory. The conjunction of Gregory's
death with the Tower's completion, and the awareness that many
fine touches which Gregory might have added are now lost, with the
man himself, must have sharpened many fears. Apart from this
poem, most of us would not have heard of Gregory, since he left
promise, not lasting achievement, locked in the minds only of
friends. The poem itself therefore offers the immortality it
celebrates; yet Yeats must have wondered whether Gregory's fate
was to involve all art, including his own, in a final triumph of death.
The exuberant recreation of Gregory's life is the artist's defiance of
death, yet the poem he intended to write is not written (last stanza).
This paradox, too, recurs in later poems, an embryo of further
explorations of the delicate status and balance of art with 'life'.

The poem is dedicated to Gregory, and has magnificent lines and
stanzas in it, yet again and again I have found it is a surprising poem
to teach. It provokes more diverse reactions, even from students
most closely attuned to Yeats, than almost anything else in the
canon. Stanza ix, for instance, opens with five lines of undoubted
magnificence, which then give way to a conclusion in decidedly
lower key. Stanzas x and xi, with their somewhat mechanical
repetition of 'Soldier, scholar, horseman he', seem to fail at the exact
moment when most of Yeats's poems would reach some memorable
climax. Gregory's pre-eminence is asserted in Renaissance terms,
but scarcely demonstrated; the powerful eighth stanza, where the
horsemanship, at least, is vividly imaged is matched by no
comparable images of the other qualities. Rather, Yeats's attention
to 'The Tower', and its elemental environs, provides the finest lines;
and these link with more generalised reflections on art than one
might expect. The eleventh stanza, with its fine conclusion 'What
made us dream that he could comb grey hair?', opens with an image
more 'metaphysical' than Yeats would normally use (l. 2, notably);
the stanza is a variant on the Greek theme, 'whom the gods love, die
young', and it is hard to doubt that Yeats's own 'grey hair', which
was greatly to preoccupy him, might be more central than Gregory
to his hopes and fears for the achievement of art that *will* 'live'. I have
heard students decide, with conviction, that the poet is projecting his
own fear of death into an apparently disinterested expression of
bereavement. Occasionally, but not always, this can be further
clarified into some general mistrust of heroism, at least in the form
which this poem presents it.

In my view, such criticisms have some validity, in that the poem, for all its grandeur, is somehow flawed. Yet criticism of too dogmatic a kind makes me uneasy; criticisms can too casually simplify both the poem and its genre. No doubt Yeats did not love Gregory as much as Tennyson loved Hallam, if we choose *In Memoriam* for comparison; moreover, Hallam's potential for achievement does not rest for its witness on Tennyson alone (as, arguably, Gregory's does on Yeats?). Yet *In Memoriam* is no doubt the exception not the rule among elegies, in most of which personal fears and obsessions very normally mingle with, and even overshadow, personalised grief. We may think of Milton and Edward King, Dryden and Mrs Anne Killigrew, Pope and the 'unfortunate lady', Shelley and Keats ('Adonais'), Arnold and Clough ('Thyrsis') – the list could be extended; we neither doubt the sincerity in such poems, nor imagine that the elegiac poet thinks solely of one lost person's fame. 'Sincerity' is notoriously a difficult test, in life as in literature, and must be the more so when emotions as complex as grief, death, art, and the poet's own power, are at stake. Gray's 'Elegy' could be instanced as perhaps a still more striking enigma; Gray neither knew the peasants he wrote of, nor in life would have known them; nor were they generally considered (this is one main theme of the poem) a fit subject for elegy at all. In every instance (except for that of Keats) the person elegised remains a more shadowy figure than the poet who celebrated him; such poems must be at once more personal, and more universal, than their surface concerns may proclaim.

My own hunch (it can be little more than this) is that Yeats was indeed profoundly affected by Gregory's death, even as grief on Lady Gregory's behalf also merged with this, together with the allied oppressions, already alluded to, of his own. The poem's concluding stanza is undoubtedly mysterious, and might be too readily read at face value, unless we take care. Its opening lines concern Yeats's earlier self ('All those that manhood tried, or childhood loved / Or boyish intellect approved') and the symbolism of 'bitter ... wind' may seem to involve the poet, and the poetry, alike. In other poems, he 'sends imagination forth' with less sense of failure; here, 'imagination' appears to have been waited upon in vain. The phrase 'some appropriate commentary on each' points to diminished creative intensity in the poem; the 'fitter welcome' awaited has failed to appear. The concluding words are bitter, and also surprising: 'took all my heart for speech' seems a depressing enough critique.

Yet speech there *has* been; and poetry: need we regard the ending then as more significant than any other mutation familiar in the annals of grief? The place of 'heart' (and 'mind') in verse is to become a major theme in Yeats later; could this be why the elegy seems deliberately seminal, rather than complete? The formal ending which refuses formality is itself an artifice, maybe especially appropriate (if we think again) to the always unfinished business of grief.

If we return to the start (to check the conclusion for literal accuracy), we must admit to very different impressions, since the first lines have unmistakable, even magical, power:

> Now that we're almost settled in our house
> I'll name the friends that cannot sup with us. . . .

We know that Yeats conjured magically, in séance and ritual; one quest of his life was power to call back the dead. 'I'll name' has all the force of invocation – names have power, if used with sufficient art and lore. Yeats's art is pre-eminently close to magic, as I shall have occasion to stress time and again as we proceed.

The 'narrow winding stair' is already a symbol – that stair which runs from door to roof of Thoor Ballylee, without a break. The friends to be summoned were all seekers for 'forgotten truth', like Yeats, if not all 'Discoverers'; now, 'All, all are in my thoughts to-night being dead'. Yeats's 'thoughts' are a common haven, the place where all our dead gather; it is for the poet, the magician, to give thought substance and form, returning the dead to life.

In fact, Robert Gregory is the chief ghost to be summoned; it is he who is to be left alive, in the poem, when Yeats, and his thoughts too, are gone. But first, other friends must be conjured to the house-warming and, by the laws of art, summoned on Yeats's terms. Stanza ii outlines a commonplace sadly familiar – yet, for Yeats, this too is subject to *his* power:

> But not a friend that I would bring
> This night can set us quarrelling,
> For all that come into my mind are dead.

'. . . into my mind' – so the meetings, like the commentaries, will be on Yeats's terms, and the terms will be those (if the poem succeeds) of his art. A line from Keith Douglas comes to me: 'Simplify me when I am dead'; and who has not sometimes felt the force of this, as a dearest wish? Yeats was later to simplify himself – dramatically – for his tombstone, leaving a three-line enigma as key to all the rest. In 'Easter 1916' friends and foes alike are simplified – off with the motley, on with the heroic mask – 'Wherever green is worn'.

Yet, in other moods, who will not resent such simplification bitterly, knowing that no poet, not Shakespeare or Pope even, could offer more than a fraction of the truth? How can art dignify and keep alive, except in parody: even if the parody is to be conjured with, and revered for the art's sake, for the rest of time?

Perhaps we must accept the distortion (as Yeats does in 'The Municipal Gallery Revisited') as the price, and indeed the tact, of successful art. 'This is not the dead Ireland of my youth', he affirms, confronted with other men's portraits: yet the portraits are, after all, the place we must come to, if we want to seek Yeats; and myth may have a kind of truth, after all, which 'the past' could not hold.

In later poems, Yeats's own process of selection and distillation grows ever more astringent, as his art discovers yet further laws of compression for the exact 'truths' he needs.

No doubt the portraits offered in 'In Memory of Major Robert Gregory' are too simplified: perhaps they are too idiosyncratic, too self-indulgent even, for the greatest art. There is a slight feeling of random selection, deliberate exaggeration, wilful inclusion and omission – certainly in stanzas iii and v (though stanza iv surely gives promise of the far greater things that are yet to come). The whole strategy conceivably is distorted by Yeats's attempt to compare unlike with like, and he would have done better to concentrate on the one friend, for this solemn night.

We should not forget, however, that he was one of the first modern poets to bring personal friends into his poems, and to give them something of the status associated with public figures and public myths. The European properties – Caesar, Helen, Michaelangelo – coexist with new Irish heroes; and Irish heroes with Maud Gonne, the Gregories, the people from Yeats's own life.

Maybe only a great poet can or could get away with this, since the highest powers are required to *make* a myth. There are, of course, precedents – Shakespeare's golden boy, Pope's Belinda, Smart's cat Joffrey – and all three poets knew they had the *power* for such an attempt. Yeats is, I fancy, the first poet to turn such power into a strategy, thereby demanding some knowledge of his personal life for the fullest understanding of the art. More recently, the technique has been called 'confessional' and – if we except Robert Lowell and Sylvia Plath – has become devalued through too many failures, too little disciplined artistic control. If Yeats succeeds, it is not only because he is an outstanding poet, but because his own friends are taken in the fullest degree seriously in life *and* art, distinguish though he will – and must – between the two. As a result, they become genuine myths. They are universalised in a manner to touch us all.

This, to my mind, is why stanza vi is so important to this poem, and, notably, the images in its first four lines. There is little doubt that we all have our own friends, people, cats, dogs or other loved creatures to enrich us – little doubt that without them neither life nor art would be one tenth part as rich as it is. The greatest artists will always be those who remain faithful to their own originals, yet in a manner which releases them, also, with precision, into *our* lives. Shakespeare's golden lad, Pope's Belinda, Smart's cat Joffrey, live in art, as their creators predicted, chiefly because they live also in us. It is not that we loosely 'read in' to the poems overriding particulars; rather, it is that we offer our own emotional resources to make them dance. Later, Yeats will explore this more precisely – 'Those images that yet / Fresh images beget' ('Byzantium'); later still, he will define the dance between creator and perceiver – 'And I / Delight to imagine' ('Lapis Lazuli') – as the very life of art. An original person or scene; an artist's consciousness, culminating in an artefact; *then* ourselves, the readers, and the actual dance of the art.

Stanza vi seems to me very finely to capture the manner in which our own major experiences, taking on mythic qualities in memory, can then be reanimated and enriched through the further dimension of art. The process includes, indeed, idealisation, or how could it happen? – yet idealisation which may 'simplify' towards, not away from, celebratory truth:

> They were my close companions many a year,
> A portion of my mind and life, as it were,
> And now their breathless faces seem to look
> Out of some old picture-book. . . .

Perhaps it is no accident that, just as in the first half of the poem the stanza concerning Synge stands out, so, in the second half, stanzas vii, viii and the first five lines of ix are the ones that remain in the mind. Clearly, it was this image of Gregory riding – and the image of Clare and Galway as the eternal background – which really haunted Yeats as he recalled his dead friend. The tenth stanza is comparatively trivial – trifling, and lacking conviction; the eleventh is not fully adequate to the immensity of its own truth.

So, maybe stanza xii does embody the poet's stern self-criticism, whilst failing to do justice to the poem as a whole. For me, this poem belongs in the canon of Yeats's great period not for its total success, but for its promise; its hints of many themes later to develop more fully; above all, for certain lines, images and stanzas that cannot be exorcised. It is also the first poem in which we encounter so closely Yeats's great gift for friendship – one of the elements which make him so splendidly accessible, for all of his quirks.

'An Irish Airman Foresees His Death'

The pared-down syntax and diction introduce us definitively to late Yeats, all adornments banished; words so controlled that the poem might seem more like one extended word, unalterable as marble, than sequence. Clusters of statements and images, undercut with exquisite precision by counter statements and images; and above all, in the artefact, an aloofness of art more seemingly inevitable than spontaneous – some grand illusion of an artefact outsoaring time, to take its place in some order beyond.

The poem is said to be inspired by Robert Gregory, but this I prefer to ignore. Here, the original occasion is concealed, and the marvellously judged equations are allowed to float. The entire effect is distanced and impersonal, leaving the reader maximum scope (and seminar discussion, in depth, shows how far this extends). Most readers will be likely to identify the poem with someone known to them, or with a state of mind, or in more extreme cases with a mood personally familiar, though with widely diverse connotations.

In appearance, the poem is virtually mathematical; an equation deceptively moving towards the unacceptable solution, nought equals nought. Alternatively, it is an unusual assertion of will-power, freedom, exhilaration – a technique in which a train of logic, already sufficiently familiar to the speaker to be no more than scaffolding, releases passionate acceptance of life and death. Leaving aside the first two lines for a moment (though they hold the key to alternative readings), one can admire the marvellous economy of ll. 2–8. What are the classic causes of human conflict? Every single one is touched on and dismissed, in balance with its own opposite. Love and hate vanish – the personal motives, whether inspired by people, countries or ideas, which must have accounted for half the heroic commitment of the world. Then 'fight' and 'guard', linked with these opposites, vanish also: along with the siren hope that conflict may avert some disaster, or win some gain, for anyone loved. Finally, the poet moves to the remaining normal causes of conflict, grimly familiar in 1916 to English conscripts, dying in the mud of France for that 'war to end all wars' which was, in fact, that war to end all civilisation, the supreme folly of Europe's needless suicide as we now see it to be. Not that Yeats seemed unduly bothered by the Great War – or, a little later, by the Russian Revolution. Ireland remained his microcosm for doom as it had once been for hope, his obsessive dream. 'Law' vanishes – the ritual enlistment for slaughter of a whole generation, dragooned into dying, by elderly hypocrites, before they could live. 'Duty' vanishes – that perennial con-trick of priests and philosophers, turning men into fodder, replacing the sweetness of love and youth with the bitter folly of death. And finally glory, 'fame is the spur', vanishes – the glorious homecoming to the plaudits of a grateful nation, which some expected; or, if not that, a cold name graven in perpetuity on a marble tombstone, that most men would shun, or once a year 'honour' on 'remembrance day'.

The Irish Airman, pondering and dismissing these things without comment, allows these comments from one reader (different comments from others) to drift through the mind. *His* mind, emptied, is now beautifully opened, so that 'A lonely impulse of delight' may make all of his fate. In the final four lines, past and future are balanced – 'the years to come', 'the years behind': again vacuum, where a further moment of fate hangs, finally, against a moment's delight. Note the mastery with which 'waste of breath' is repeated from the end of one line to the beginning of the next – adding some further power to the final, and rhyming, word, 'death'.

What is the mood of the poem? It seems a stuff for the making of saints, or of suicides; can we know for sure if it the final logic of depression or the momentary lift of a youthful heart? Undoubtedly, 'delight' acquires immense colour in the context as the word coupled with 'tumult', both as cause and effect. This, surely, is the peculiar mystery and success of the poem – its sustained neutrality of tone, as mighty opposites balance, and fail. Read one way, it might mirror the despair of Hardy's Jude, or the vacuum of Camus's Meursault: an arrival at the place where, all meaning lost, there is one choice only to make. Read another, it might be closer to the fierce exhilaration of Donne's union of present and eternity in some inviolable ecstasy: 'I wonder, by my troth, what thou and I / Did, till we loved?' Line 11, certainly, leaps out, as a great surge of energy – demanding also, it seems, its balance – one lonely moment of death.

The last line of the poem, resonating against the first, hints at an allied mystery, also familiar (if more rarely experienced, in most of our lives). Both lines suggest some kind of fatalism, but where it comes from, why it is weighty, is less easy to see. The final line undeniably appears as a final equation, an assertion required to complete things, when all else is gone. It is as if a pair of Olympian scales hung in delicate suspense, impeccably accurate, and governing the poem's dynamics with impersonal sway. 'Love' in the one scale, 'hate' in the other; then, 'guard' and 'fight', 'loss' and 'happier', 'law' and 'duty', 'public men' and 'cheering crowds', 'years to come', and 'years behind'. Each time, the left scale falls, as the new factor is added; each time, the right returns to perfect balance, when evened up.

Is it any wonder then that, if 'delight' has been dropped into the scales a little earlier, 'death' must be added ('delight' now equated with 'life') for the final effect? If 'delight' makes us immortal, the gods must repay it – either by taking life, or by punishing hubris, as we choose.

Indeed, what force has 'know' in the first line; what *kind* of knowledge is asserted, and so implacably upheld? This is not the 'know' of empirical philosophy or of mathematical demonstration;

but neither is it the 'knowledge' presented by craven fear. Perhaps it seems closer to the 'know' which announces a premonition (though not all 'premonitions' come true, in real life). Perhaps it is the 'know' of vision, or of some desire too strong to be ousted – the propensity we may call 'self-fulfilling prophesy' as we seek for a name. Maybe it *is* something in Gregory that Yeats was thinking of; that 'something' which emerged in 'What made us dream that he could comb grey hair?' in the previous poem. A reader will be free to think of Amy Johnson, or Glenn Miller, or the Battle of Britain pilots, or wartime suicide missions – or to depart from the visual image to some inner world of his own. What we cannot escape is the pervasive image of solitary flying – that 'up and away' which only air pioneers may know. Undeniably, again, a marvellous archetype for total escape, or oblivion; for an end to all tension that, momentarily, makes all tension worthwhile.

Without the mighty opposites, no balance; without the balance, no cancelling; without the cancelling, no totally satisfying final equation, the single moment when life and death join the balance, and perfectly hold. I conclude with some words from the final pages of Jung's *Memories, Dreams, Reflections* – lines associated there with age (as this poem is not) yet, it seems to me, pertinent; and not to this poem only, but also to Yeats's later work:

The world into which we are born is brutal and cruel, and at the same time of divine beauty. What element we think outweighs the other, whether meaninglessness or meaning, is a matter of temperament. If meaninglessness were absolutely preponderant, the meaningfulness of life would vanish to an increasing degree with each step of our development. But that is – or seems to me – not the case. Probably, as in all metaphysical questions, both are true. Life is – or has – meaning and meaninglessness. I cherish the anxious hope that meaning will preponderate and win the battle.

When Lao tzu says: 'All are clear, I alone am clouded', he is expressing what I now feel in advanced old age. Lao tzu is the example of a man with superior insight who has seen and experienced worth and worthlessness, and who at the end of his life desires to return into his own being, into the eternal unknowable meaning. The archetype of the old man who has seen enough is eternally true. At every level of intelligence this type appears, and its lineaments are always the same, whether it be an old peasant or a great philosopher like Lao tzu. This is old age, and a limitation. Yet there is so much that fills me: plants, animals, clouds, day and night, and the eternal in man. The more uncertain I have felt about myself, the more there has grown up in me a feeling of kinship with all things. In fact it seems to me as if that alienation which so long separated me from the world has become transferred into my own inner world, and has revealed to me an unexpected familiarity with myself.

'Men Improve with the Years'

The quotation immediately above would not have been endorsed by Yeats, amazingly akin though he and Jung seem. Perhaps this is why the 'Irish Airman' does not wait for old age before meeting his destiny; perhaps it is why Yeats more than half envies the death.

In this poem, the title is ironic (as it would not be for Jung), and as if, in deliberate contrast with the 'Irish Airman', a touch of savage self-mockery drives it along. The opening presents a familiar paradox, 'weather-worn, marble triton' surviving, grotesque if fascinating, the erosions of time. (It is worth contrasting 'Lapis Lazuli' – a later and, of course, far more substantial poem – for a complementary response.) If 'all day long' is life, 'this lady's beauty' is Maud Gonne and ll. 8–11 clearly assert the facile hope that beguiled him: 'Delighted to be but wise, / For men improve with the years'.

Underlying this, no doubt, is an image akin to Tennyson's 'Lady of Shalott' – the sacrifice of 'reality' to shadow-show, love to art, life to a dream. Its very falsity makes 'And yet, and yet' burst out with a curious pain – the pain which always attends Yeats's doubts about sacrificing life to art. But the next lines make a slight retreat from honesty (I am taking this poem very personally – maybe wrongly?): of course the poet *had* met his own *femme fatale* when he had his 'burning youth' – it is not in the irony of external circumstance that his own deep pain resides. 'I grow old among dreams' has nothing, therefore, of Pre-Raphaelite escapism, in this context – especially with 'Is this my dream, or the truth?' as the anguished context leading up to it. 'A pictured beauty' may cast doubts even on Maud Gonne: where, except in the poet's picture, is *she* to be found? But there is little consolation for the poet, even here; pictured or real, it has been all 'in a book'.

The phrase 'Among the streams' occurs twice and indeed closes the poem, but is little more than a picturesque touch. There is no symbol of regeneration in these waters. The Triton itself, man in the upper half, was dolphin below: a hybrid born of Poseidon and Amphitrite, yet maybe a sport of the gods. As image of the artist, it suggests divine sport more than divinity; and maybe Yeats recalled also Scott's teasing image from *Pirate*: 'The group of old men who looked on, bore no inconsiderable resemblance to a party of aged tritons, engaged in beholding the sports of the sea-nymphs'.

'A Song' and 'To a Young Beauty'

'A Song' and 'To a Young Beauty' are two of those slighter poems, often juxtaposed for deliberate effect, in which Yeats uses ballad or lyric for a momentary perception or mood. The complexities are less calculated than in the more substantial poems, but seldom absent. Maybe it is the sheer quantity of these small gems – most of which space forces me to ignore – which contributes to our sense of Yeats's *richness* as poet. They tend to stay in the mind, and often to reappear glancingly, as we wrestle with (say) 'Byzantium' or 'Lapis Lazuli' – not as elucidations exactly, but as reminders of the range of attitudes, and momentary clarities, throughout his work.

'A Song' is memorable chiefly for the refrain, with its gnomic appearance, yet it has calculated variants in each stanza. Stanza i is a statement of youth's optimism – or, more apparently, a calculatedly shallow myth of one aspect of this. Yeats had indeed included 'keep fit' exercises among his innumerable phases, but would scarcely have expected of them this particular miracle. The second stanza makes erotic love the one honest good, which all other quests ('many words' notably) become little more than a trick to evade. This notion, equally superficial, yet at moments profoundly tormenting, haunts his entire *oeuvre*: hatred of aging and regret for lost sexuality were major themes, likely at times to overshadow all else, however aware he also was of their incompleteness, even triteness. They coincide with the period now known as the 'male menopause' – an authentic phenomenon, which the present critic, and any other writer of his age would play down only at some risk of hypocrisy. The fact that this poem coincided also with a marriage made possible only after the belated exorcism – maybe by age, as much as anything – of Maud Gonne and her daughter Iseult from his system, may lend it the peculiar force which transcends its apparent trifling with profundities. Or, more probably, the force is generated by the last stanza, with its ironic yet intensely bitter admission that the second stanza no longer raises the regret which it manifestly *has*. From now on, the notion of 'losing the heart' as a prelude to achieving peace and serenity will often reappear, in poems where the theme is belied (happily for us – and for Yeats the poet) by the sheer intensity of lust, rage, regret, longing for barely possible panaceas, out of which negatives an immense, creative achievement was to flow.

'To a Young Beauty' was written to Iseult Gonne, and in a note in his invaluable *Commentary* Jeffares glosses 'every Jack and Jill' as follows: 'Yeats disapproved of the Bohemian company Iseult Gonne was keeping in Dublin'. Even so, the poem strikes me as being written to a child ('Dear fellow-artist' might come from Marvell's exquisite 'To Little T. C. in a Prospect of Flowers', though there is no question of Yeats's lyric attempting the range and subtlety of Marvell's). 'Jack and Jill' reinforces this notion, since the nursery-rhyme context, pursued throughout stanza i, is surely appropriate rather to a very young beauty than to a mature one. (If Iseult was indeed the inspiration, I suspect that Yeats had for some reason been reminded for a moment of her childhood – as he is, also for a moment, reminded of her mother's childhood in the infinitely more complex 'Among School Children'.) As in the later 'A Prayer for My Daughter', one plea is for dignity. 'Choose your companions from the best', 'Be passionate, not bountiful / As common beauties may' are two commands, playful in tone, which evade the risk of elitism or even snobbery (attitudes admittedly familiar in Yeats) only because the child neither can, nor needs, to understand them as the poet does. *Her* art is artless; and the opening salutation, along with the immediate warning in stanza i and the more sophisticated one at the end of stanza ii, which neither child, nor normal reader could follow without a footnote, no doubt reflects Yeats's awareness of the irrevocable difference between the arts of innocence and those of experience. The last stanza leaves the child behind, and returns to the mature poet's consciousness. And here the culmination is not self-mocking bravado, as in 'Men Improve with the Years', but adult dignity, to balance the child's. The first three lines ring true, as if in counterpoint with the preceding poem: 'The winters gone' can be praised, as well as mourned, despite beauty's bitter 'wages'. The exhortation to the child is likewise balanced again, by an adult's pride in elitism. In the end he too will bê with his peers; and we need not probe here for a religious meaning, I think, but may regard the conclusion as the artist's hope of enduring posthumous fame in his work:

> There is not a fool can call me friend –
> And I may dine at journey's end
> With Landor or with Donne.

Yeats's ambiguous attitude to folly is notorious, but here he is surely thinking not of archetypal fools but of his own threatening folly, the loss of dignity in bitterness as old age draws on, and the many others who have become engulfed in it. Jeffares's note (in the *Commentary*) elucidating the appearance of Landor by a quotation from Yeats's 'Anima Hominis' (1917) is very helpful here: 'A poet, when he is growing old, will ask himself if he cannot keep his mask and his vision without new bitterness, new disappointment. Could he if he would, knowing how frail his vigour from youth up, copy Landor who lived loving and hating, ridiculous and unconquered, into extreme old age, all lost but the favour of his Muses?' '. . . the favour of his Muses' is, of course, one supreme reality, which Yeats will never forget; yet, whether the frailty of vigour in youth really can help old age – particularly when it can now be, only too late, regretted – ensures that the resolution of this short lyric will be anything but Yeats' last word on the theme.

'Ego Dominus Tuus'

I include a note on this poem somewhat reluctantly, and only because some of Yeats's critics cannot let it alone. With the exception of odd lines, the poetry is more akin to that in his plays than to that in his verse (that is, almost uniformly inferior), and maybe Yeats's impatience with his unsatisfactory invention Michael Robartes has something to do with a purely artistic lack of weight. It is good to know that in 1925, ten years after this poem was written, Yeats himself noted, 'I can now, if I have the energy, find the simplicity I have sought in vain. I need no longer write poems like "The Phases of the Moon" or "Ego Dominus Tuus".' This is from *A Vision*, where he also wrote, 'I had invented an unnatural story of an Arabian traveller which I must amend and find a place for some day because I was fool enough to write half a dozen poems that are unintelligible without it'. In this poem, 'Hic' defends the objective, 'Ille' the subjective. There is a gloss on the theory of the mask (for example, 'I call to my own opposite . . .') in Yeats's essay in 'The Death of Synge':

> I think that all happiness depends on the energy to assume a mask of some other self; that all joyous or creative life is a rebirth of something not oneself, something which has no memory and is created in a moment and perpetually renewed. We put on a grotesque or solemn painted face to hide us from the terrors of judgment, invent an imaginary Saturnalia where one forgets reality, a game like that of a child, where one loses the infinite pain of self-realisation. Perhaps all the sins and energies of the world are but its flight from an infinite blinding beam. (*Autobiographies*, pp. 503–4)

Certainly, this theory helps explain the poem before us – but, by and large, I am avoiding too many references to Yeats's theory of masks (as to *A Vision*), since I regard them as less important to his poetry, except through incidental references, than he often imagined. Yeats later himself said that once he had formed the idea of the mask he became over-allegorical and his imagination became sterile, for nearly five years, and he only escaped by mocking his own thoughts. Maybe the putting on of certain obvious masks – the bard ('Easter

1916'), the prophet ('The Second Coming'), the fool (numerous later poems) and so forth *is* important, but usually because it is a technique unencumbered, in the major poems, by too close a reference to Yeats's excursions into allegory and dogma. Of all our poets, he is one who is not only instantly recognisable as 'himself' (in tone), whatever the mask or disguise adopted, but also most continually personal, in the very obvious sense that he transforms the people and circumstances of his own life for use among his stock of central myths. Moreover, in the major poems his genius, like Jung's, is precisely in enigma and elusiveness – the frustration of dogmatism – however tempted towards dogmatic directions he was, by occult and other promptings, throughout his life. One final word on what may seem a wilful playing down of this side of his work: in literary criticism, Richard Ellmann and Frank Kermode, two of our major critics, have already examined these aspects with great thoroughness and almost definitively. And, if one is willing to move a little from the strict realm of literary criticism, I would argue that a reading of Jung's major writings is more fruitful to an understanding of Yeats's central archetypes than too much puzzling over his own more theoretical and occult imaginings can ever be.

In 'Ego Dominus Tuus' the inner tension between conscious and unconscious is associated, notably through the continual references to Dante, with the older religious notion of the *bellum intestinum* (the old Adam versus the new). Essentially, the poem turns on the poet's defence of being still 'Enthralled by the unconquerable delusion, / Magical shapes', even though he had 'passed the best of life'. Hic's accusation has in it a real sting, as we know – but in this poem Hic functions as little more than a stooge. There may be a certain defiance (dishonesty?) in 'Ille's' claim

> By the help of an image
> I call to my own opposite, summon all
> That I have handled least, least looked upon

but Hic's reply 'And I would find myself and not an image' is brushed aside with predictable brusqueness:

> That is our modern hope, and by its light
> We have lit upon the gentle, sensitive mind
> And lost the old nonchalance of the hand.

It is perhaps odd that Ille, while essentially rejecting the world of action for the shadow-self, produces a line reminiscent of the Renaissance ideal, and of Robert Gregory as depicted in his elegy; also, that Ille should risk finding Dante's inspiration in hidden sin,

Keats's in open vulgarity, whilst also adducing them as instances of
true art, which 'Is but a vision of reality'.

In that use of 'but' one readily detects Yeats's blarney (never
entirely absent, even at the most serious moments) – or his defiantly
overreaching exaggeration, if one prefer to describe it that way.
Hic's final remarks about style (at best, a fairly trite half-truth) are
met by Ille's reiterated claim 'I seek an image, not a book'. In a
manner not easy to pin down, I feel that what could have been a
profound poem about the artist's split self becomes confused with
the naïve 'sedentary toil' versus 'inspiration' argument about 'art'.
The lines

> Those men that in their writings are most wise
> Own nothing but their blind, stupefied hearts

strikes me as interesting far more because of the long debate about
'heart' that will be pursued through 'Sailing to Byzantium', 'Among
School Children' and many other fascinating explorations, up to
'The Circus Animals' Desertion' and 'Ben Bulben' itself, than for
anything actually realised *here*. The rest of the poem, I freely admit,
eludes me (had Yeats been dipping into his more obscure occult
oracles again?), though the concluding image is a promise of far, far
better things to come (notably, the marvellous close of 'The Tower').

'The Cat and the Moon'

Certainly one of the finest cat poems ever written, whatever we make
of the moon. In his notes to the play of the same name, Yeats drives
his own reflections on the moon to the verge of anarchy (some might
think, well over the verge); but 'black Minnaloushe' had the
happiness to be Maud Gonne's cat and, that apart even, Yeats
captures the quintessence of felinity. Only Smart's cat Joffrey stands
up to this, in any cat-literature known to me. (*Old Possum* is, *qua* cat
poetry, a non-starter – though the concealed cat in 'The Love Song of
Alfred J. Prufrock' deserves an honourable mention.)

The poem turns on the regal polarity of Minnaloushe as at once
'kindred' of the moon and erotic slave. Yet animal dignity turns lust
to dance – and 'sacred' encompasses the two strange creatures in
their nightly ritual. The final twelve lines transcend any consciously
literary symbolism so completely that the poem seems charged,
rather, with the mysterious symbolism of creation itself. The intense
life of two creatures both technically 'below' man in the scale of life,
yet in grace, relationship and mystery so decisively other and higher,

culminates in an ending which might be the view of the god who created, wholly at ease for once with his own work:

> Does Minnaloushe know that his pupils
> Will pass from change to change,
> And that from round to crescent,
> From crescent to round they range?
> Minnaloushe creeps through the grass
> Alone, important and wise,
> And lifts to the changing moon
> His changing eyes.

It is because Yeats can offer such indisputable, if novel, truths on territory known to me that I trust him (for the most part, at least) on his own stranger grounds. The verse – lucid, delicate and subtle in rhythm as late Beethoven, in observation exquisitely and almost magically precise – is pure joy to read. As a teacher, I tend to regard this as a test poem. Any student who isn't enchanted will probably never like Yeats.

'Easter 1916'

The young Yeats had glorified Ireland, finding in its myths and poetry the seeds of possible European renewal. Just as the small nation-state Greece had been the chief source of two and a half millennia of European culture, so now, when the rest of Europe was sacrificing this priceless heritage to mechanised vulgarity, Ireland might prove rich soil for the resurrection of beauty.

In 1916, at Easter, a far uglier side – or maybe simply the necessary polarity, which Yeats had not allowed for – entered Irish politics. The rhetoric of hatred had been building for years, and Yeats himself had been aware of it. How uneasy it had made him, or how seriously he had taken it, is hard to assess. But the occupation and burning of the Dublin Post Office, an abortive rising which led, in due course, to the punishment by death and imprisonment of the ringleaders, introduced into Irish politics the modern note of bitterness that requires no footnotes. No need, for present purposes, to rehearse the long debate on Home Rule of the late nineteenth and early twentieth century – or the older bitternesses, spanning centuries, which have uniquely bedevilled English–Irish politics. I say 'politics' advisedly, though personal emotions are scarcely irrelevant. Maybe the fact that so many of my closest personal friends are Irish; and that I am writing about an Irishman whose linguistic and other debts to England were always acknowledged handsomely, must just be touched on, to suggest a perspective which these poems, by their nature, often fail to include. It seems a paradox that the English and Irish have much in common and often form the closest of personal friendships, yet in public attitudes remain subject to insoluble political tensions and seemingly endless civil war. Irish writers have produced a fair proportion of the greatest literature written in English, and are less prone to resent the language as such (in my own experience this is true) than are many of the Scottish and Welsh. Yeats wrote as naturally and with as little resentment in English as an American would, yet the underlying conditions are far from the same. Most Americans no longer feel bound to England for anything except its language – which, in the New World 'melting pot', has become distinctively their own. Yeats was able to emulate this in practice, but not wholly in theory; a multivalence of attitude to England haunts him, as it seemingly does all of his fellow-countrymen, appearing in ways too numerous and shifting to chart.

The 1916 rising introduces a split attitude on the political issue itself, for the first time; we shall come up against this more strikingly, before very long. Technically, the poem is a celebration of the dead men, and a monument meant for them; it is poetry becoming part of the war that they fought. More personally, the framework records the initiation of a diverse group of men, whom Yeats had thought of as 'ordinary', into a pantheon of the mighty, and now symbolic, dead. They are translated from the everyday world, the world of fools, of 'casual comedy' where we gossip in motley, into the unchanging world of 'the glorious dead'. The whole life they once led is transcended, in this heroic transposition, this 'terrible beauty' – yet, by the same token, it is also cancelled out, for good or ill. Horsemen, thinker, beautiful women, 'drunken, vainglorious lout' – in life, that is what Yeats made of them (the last, of course, Maud Gonne's husband), but all are 'changed, changed utterly' by their final destiny: they are to be remembered as heroes, by generations who never knew them, not gradually forgotten as most of us are, as the years erode memory and history steals for oblivion all that we were.

'. . . terrible beauty' – this fused image (very much a forerunner of many similar fusions in the later poems) is more of a question, at heart, than the simple assertion that syntax would make it appear. Not the 'beauty of the Medusa' perhaps – though even that is hinted at – but 'Enchanted to a stone' ('The stone's in the midst of all').

The central section, starting 'Hearts with one purpose alone', is meltingly lyrical, and moves in delicate suggestion against the poem's apparent main march. Can the poet who only one year before was writing (through 'Ille'),

> Those men that in their writings are most wise
> Own nothing but their blind, stupefied hearts

now see the death of the heart as a condition of wisdom itself? The
lyrical beauty of 'living stream' – horse, moor-cocks, cloud-changes;
the precise, delicate rhythms of life 'minute by minute' – is a beauty
radically at odds with the static repose of the mighty dead.

> Too long a sacrifice
> Can make a stone of the heart

– and when this final section opens, we have already had, chillingly
forlorn in context, 'The stone's in the midst of all'. At best, the
'enchantment' of terrible beauty will 'trouble the living stream', but
not arrest it; 'trouble' may be deflection (water swirling round the
rocks in its course); or it may be a moment's pause made uneasy by
its very artifice (am I the only man – English, Irish or simply human –
who hates that two-minute silence on Armistice Day?). Flesh-and-
blood life is not 'casual comedy' here, but free-flowing loveliness;
while 'heroism' turns back, in implication, to death. There is death *in*
death – names deeply graven, by sculptor or bard, because death is
their meaning; there is also death in life, the needful preliminary for
such a death itself.

> That woman's days were spent
> In ignorant goodwill,
> Her nights in argument
> Until her voice grew shrill.

this was Constance Gore-Booth, later the Countess Markiewicz,
whose sentence of death was commuted to life imprisonment,
though she was later released (and see, of course, 'In Memory of Eva
Gore-Booth and Con Markiewicz' for a later perspective). Was *that*
life in death really worth it? And then we note, of another 'martyr' (I
return to section ii),

> He might have won fame in the end,
> So sensitive his nature seemed,
> So daring and sweet his thought'.

This poem exists to say that he *did* win fame in the end – yet the
crucial phrase 'might have' hints at a different, more elusive fame,
now permanently lost. In the final section, 'Was it needless death
after all?' is therefore a question anything but rhetorical in its actual
impact, though, once again, the syntax is apparently intended to

reduce it to such. And even the qualifying clause ('For England may keep faith / For all that is done and said') is not the heart of the matter, since the poem drives on, far deeper, to the realm of 'dream', 'love' and 'death':

> We know their dream; enough
> To know they dreamed and are dead;
> And what if excess of love
> Bewildered them till they died?

The word 'dream' may be good or bad in Yeats, or just occasionally neutral; a dream is an image with power; but what is its end? The same ambivalence intensifies in what follows: 'dreamed and are dead' will surely strike no one as a simple, or an unanguished, idea. The phrase 'excess of love' deepens the dilemma, whatever scope we allow it. Love, whether heroic, or erotic, or self-sacrificing, or merely illusory, will always hold 'the world well lost?' in balance with its ecstasy – a question pointing all ways. Finally, 'Bewildered' clinches the ambivalence; would not 'exalted', or some similar word of three syllables, lead into the poem's conclusion with simpler effect?

Nevertheless, that patently equivocating 'enough / To know' serves the poet's bardic purpose, and the finale rises gladly from it – as if there were no enigmas – to the heroic close. 'I write it out in a verse', says Yeats, and we cannot ignore this: the role of bard may indeed override whatever other notions have clamoured to get in. Even so, the rhythmic exhilaration of the climax, with its reassertion of transforming heroism for the 'green' of Ireland, still has something of the suggestion of names carved, bleakly and coldly, onto stone. And, though it is not declared, I would wager that Yeats was identifying bard and hero (as Cowper did in 'The Castaway') in his exploration of the sacrifice of 'life' to some greater end. 'Enchanted to a stone / To trouble the living stream' might describe not the heroes alone, but the poet who sings them. It may describe all art, with its inbuilt power to trouble, when the creator is dead (as in 'Long-legged Fly').

Yeats would have been aware also, however, of the poet's power to influence events; to inflame real anger, perhaps cause real death, in the world of 'life'. Later, there are signs that these thoughts had power to disturb him – though the two most famous references are both in contexts of debate, of unfinished business. I have in mind lines from 'Vacillation', from the period 1931–3:

> Things said or done long years ago,
> Or things I did not do or say
> But thought that I might say or do,

Weigh me down, and not a day
But something is recalled,
My conscience or my vanity appalled

and, still more pertinently, lines spoken by 'Man' from 'The Man
and the Echo', where as late as 1938 he considered the possibility that
his own play *Cathleen ni Houlihan* (1902) might in some sense have
sparked off the 1916 rising itself:

All that I have said and done,
Now that I am old and ill,
Turns into a question till
I lie awake night after night
And never get the answers right.
Did that play of mine send out
Certain men the English shot?
Did words of mine put too great strain
On that woman's reeling brain?
Could my spoken words have checked
That whereby a house lay wrecked?

Normally we stress, rightly, I am sure, Yeats's awareness of art as its
own realm, with power to set vibrating not immediate actions, but
more timeless archetypes. A poem so immediately related to politics
as this cannot be contained in such terms, however. I am conscious
as a teacher that when I read and discuss 'Easter 1916' with students
in the late twentieth century, to me it is a different poem from the
one I taught as a young man. The literary critic in me seeks to deny
this, pointing to an 'order of words', arranged unchangingly on
paper, and to ambivalences carefully balanced in the poem itself. Yet
most readers are less interested in ambivalences than in more
'obvious' meanings, and notably when the poem relates to
bloodshed still going on. I have seen this poem, set alongside other
revolutionary declarations from its period, displayed with honour in
the homes of present-day Irish patriots – some of whom find it still a
living indictment (though none, I am certain, would consciously
perpetuate terror or set off a bomb). Naturally, Yeats continued to
celebrate Irish heroes to the last month of his life (he was granted the
great mercy of avoiding senility, for all the fears he held of this) – nor,
as a rule, would he believe that whatever was alleged against Irish
victims by the English had any substance. As for his hope, it
remained in the 'indomitable Irishry' to the end.

'The Second Coming'

This poem is among Yeats's most famous despite its obscurity; possibly because ll. 3–8, either in selection or as a sequence, lend themselves to all-purpose quotation. Their apocalyptic intent is too clear to be doubted, though its direction can be made to serve almost anyone's book. Is this an instance of continual and wilful misquotation out of context; or is the poem adapted to such flexibility by design?

This was the period when Yeats's metaphysical gloom deepened, assisted by personal, political and occult promptings. The cycle of the 'gyres' in *A Vision* moves towards chaos, as the age presided over by Jesus and associated with love give way to nightmare (though the two lines starting 'That twenty centuries . . .' seem to me to evade exact understanding). Yeats's marriage must also have seemed a mixed blessing, with its farewell to hopes of Maud Gonne, and to youth. Thoor Ballylee was to be a final home for him, but also a defiant reversion to the past, as if for a last stand against whatever might come. Politically, the Irish situation still looms larger than the Great War it seems – though Yeats showed his awareness of those other events in Russia in a letter written to George Russell, probably in April 1919: 'What I want is that Ireland be kept from giving itself (under the influence of its lunatic faculty of going against everything which it believes England to affirm) to Marxian revolution or Marxian definition of value in any form. I consider the Marxian criterion of values as in this age the spear-head of materialism and leading to inevitable murder. . . .'

The title suggests, of course, a Christian reference, and it would be possible to find enigmas in Revelation not unlike this talk of the age of the Beast. But, as always, Yeats seems to me to assimilate Christ to his own mythology, and 'the second coming' of Christ, as envisaged in Christian tradition, has little connection with Yeats's vision of 2000-year cycles of history giving place one to another, with the expectation of antithesis as the most evident sign of change.

To complicate matters further, there is a suggestion in the Introduction to *The Resurrection* that Yeats was haunted, at this period, by an 'imagining' which might have suggested the image of the beast in this poem. Yeats's 'imaginings', poised between dream and vision, or even conscious artifice, tend to offer no obvious clues that a critic can legitimately use: 'I began to imagine, as always at my left side just out of the range of the sight, a brazen winged beast which I associated with laughing, ecstatic destruction'. In a footnote, Yeats himself noted that this beast was 'afterwards described in my poem "The Second Coming" '. The obvious image is of the Sphinx and, as Yeats calls it 'a vast image out of Spiritus Mundi', we are naturally led to think of it as an archetype connected, perhaps, with actual revelation.*

* How far Jung's notion of the Collective Unconscious impinged on Yeats's thought it would be fruitless to speculate. Jung's notion of 'universal symbols' was articulated most sharply when he broke with Freud, about 1913, though his own most fruitful work came later. Readers with a particular interest in the connections between Yeats and Jung – mostly, it seems, non-causal – will certainly wish to read chapter 8 of Jung's *Memories, Dreams, Reflections* (1961). It is called 'The Tower', and describes how in 1931 Jung, too, turned a house which he had bought, at Bollingen in 1922, into a tower – eventually finishing the construction as late as 1955, after his wife's death. For Jung, too, the Tower took on important, and shifting, significances. After the 1931 extension, he remarks that 'the second tower became for me a place of spiritual concentration'. During the years, in a room kept secluded for his own use, he painted on the walls, so expressing 'all those things which have carried me out of time into seclusion, out of the present into timelessness'. After 1955 (when Yeats had been dead sixteen years) he added

> an upper storey ... which represents myself, or my ego-personality. Earlier, I would not have been able to do this; I would have regarded it as presumptious self-emphasis. Now it signified an extension of consciousness achieved in old age. With that, the building was complete. I had started the first tower in 1923, two months after the death of my mother. These two dates are meaningful because the Tower, as we shall see, is connected with the dead. From the beginning, I felt the Tower as in some way a place of maturation – a maternal womb or a place of maturation in which I could become what I was, what I am and will be. It gave me a feeling as if I were being reborn in stone. It is thus a concretisation of the individuation process, a memorial *aere perennius*. ... It might also be said that I built it in a kind of dream. Only afterwards did I see how all the parts fitted together and that a meaningful form had resulted: a symbol of psychic wholeness. At Bollingen I am in the midst of my true life, I am most deeply myself.

Jung does not indicate explicit debts to Yeats, but it is interesting to note that both were deeply immersed in the study of alchemy from the early nineteenth century (or even before). They shared the same occult and eastern sources of religion. They would both have known the Tarot pack, as reconstructed by Pamela Colman Smith, a fellow member with Yeats of the Golden Dawn Society. In A. E. Waite's commentary on the Tower symbol in that pack (*The Key to the Tarot*, 1910), the occult meanings – presumably ignored by Yeats and Jung alike – are far from propitious:

> 'The Tower' (i.e. the sixteenth Trump in the Major Arcana): Occult explanations attached to this card are meagre and mostly disconcerting. It is idle to indicate that it depicts ruin in all its aspects, because it bears this evidence on its surface. ... I see nothing to warrant Papus in

The opening eight lines of 'The Second Coming' tend to remain in the mind, offering (as I have already noted) words that mean many things to many men. A paraphrase would be absurd – enough to note that, whatever we make of them, they mark the time when Yeats's own earlier optimism is ended. We shall find more concrete (some may think, somewhat naïve) commentary on this when looking at 'Nineteen Hundred and Nineteen'. The view once widely held that optimism was rudely shattered by the 1914 war is maybe strained: one could point to many writers and politicians who sounded a note of coming doom at least from the middle of the 1870s (ironically, during the period when the British Empire started to rise to its grand expansionist phase, which lasted for the remainder of Yeats's lifetime). With the line 'Surely some revelation is at hand', we arrive at the more dramatic and mysterious part of the poem. What sort of 'Surely' is this? Yeats's revelations tended to come personally, rather than in cosmic oracles. Presumably, he refers to the specific cycle of change indicated in *A Vision*, meeting his human sense that, for good or ill, the old order was passing irrevocably. 'Surely the Second Coming is at hand.' This more Christian notion is swept away immediately, in a mood which replaces traditional hope with foreboding: 'Troubles my sight' (and one might add again, 'what sort of "sight" is this?').

I cannot pretend to plumb the following images, but certain features can be pointed to. The phrase 'somewhere in the sands of the desert' is vague yet definite: the exact place unknown, the location 'desert'. A little later, desert would be used by Eliot, in *The Waste Land* (1922) as one prevailing image of the post-war period. The 'shape' must be the sphinx (given the personal associations already touched upon), but, if so, two paradoxes are fused into it. 'A gaze blank and pitiless as the sun' appears to remove the sun from the cycles, and give it inherently sinister connotations. This differs markedly from Yeats's normal use of sun (and moon), so maybe we have to associate the sun with its 'desert' role, as killer rather than

---

supposing that it is the fall of Adam but there is more in favour of his alternative – that it signifies the materialisation of the spiritual letter. Christian imagines that it is the downfall of the mind seeking to penetrate the mystery of God. I agree rather with the Grand Orient that it is the ruin of the house of life, when evil has prevailed therein, and above all that it is the rending of the house of doctrine. It illustrates also in the most comprehensive way the old truth that 'except the Lord build the house, they labour in vain that build it'. (pp. 89–90).

It seems certain that Yeats, like Jung, preferred intuitive insights – often founded on dreams – to such formal occult lore, but the importance which a tower home came to have for both of them indicates a similar cast of mind.

giver of life. At the same time, a work of art (or a stone artefact) is
coming independently alive. This, again, lies outside the usual
complexities of Yeats's thinking about the relationship between art
and life. Once more, the suggestions are sinister. The moving of the
'slow thighs' suggests a belated but monstrous birth (all the grimness,
none of the glory of Leda's labour), and the line 'Reel shadows of the
indignant desert birds' appears to suggest that even the preying birds
thrown up by the present era are overthrown by the greater horror
now threatening.

'The darkness falls again; but now I know' – This line encapsulates
much that fascinates, and occasionally infuriates, in Yeats's work.
'The darkness' might refer to many frames, and it is hard to guess
which; nor does that Yeatsian 'know', with its appearance of clarity,
greatly help. The next two lines have been variously elucidated by
critics (and by my own students) until occasionally I have felt almost
at ease with them:

> That twenty centuries of stony sleep
> Were vexed to nightmare by a rocking cradle. . . .

The 'stony sleep' is, presumably, the slumber of the 'rough beast'
during the Christian centuries, and the 'rocking cradle' the cradle of
Christ's birth. Does this mean that 'vexed to nightmare' was, in these
centuries, *contained* – in the uneasy sleep of the monster waiting its
own moment – or does it suggest that in some sense, the night-side of
the Christian age has been conscious of the terror now to come to full
birth, to full daylight consciousness, in the coming millennia?

The concluding lines are a question, clear enough again in general
import, but obscure in detail. 'Bethlehem' is not, I suppose, to be
taken literally; it stands for the birth of the two preceding millennia,
but, since the poem has so thoroughly evaded a Christian
framework, presumably Yeats uses it to signify the still uncertain
birthplace of the coming antithesis. '. . . slouches' captures one of his
pet hatreds – the replacement of 'courtesy and ceremony' with
slovenliness: and in much of the rest of the poetry, up to and
including the exhortation to 'Irish poets' in 'Under Ben Bulben',
there will be a powerful rearguard action against the onset of decay,
which, in this poem, seems prophetic and certain.

'A Prayer for My Daughter'

Yeats is a religious poet to whom the word 'prayer' comes seldom.
There are other exceptions ('Prayer for My Son'; 'A Prayer for Old
Age'), but Yeats is more often inclined to invoke than to intercede.

Some students object to this poem as 'authoritarian', an attempt to map out a child's whole destiny while she is still helpless. They feel as if the spirit of Blake's 'Experience' is stifling 'Innocence', literally at birth. Of course, the word 'prayer' raises problems, but I feel that this reading of the poem is subtly mistaken. I say 'subtly', though I almost mean 'radically': can any parent really assess the freedom proposed, for whatever creature he has helped to birth? 'Prayers' come involuntarily (art such as this is the record of them), and doubtless as he writes Yeats is thinking of personal experience far removed from his daughter. Can one learn from experience? Or can one fantasise – trying out a formula cast in the image of personal wishes and fears? The baby is a bundle of unknown potential, not yet a being; doubtless Yeats is wondering whether, if cast as Fate, he might do the job well. Parental musings – fears, regrets, might-have-beens – are hardly avoidable; nor can Yeats be planning a life, for his child, in any spirit akin to the elder Mill.

At the age of fifty-five, old-age nearing, what can one honestly hope for a daughter, in a season of gloom? What blessing is best envisaged – if blessing is possible; could Yeats, or indeed any adult, miss the irony of the attempt? If asked for the ground of his prayer, might he not offer something like Jung's words in *Memories, Dreams, Reflections* (p. 391),

I am astonished, disappointed, pleased with myself. I am distressed, depressed, rapturous. I am all these things at once, and cannot add up the sum. I am incapable of determining ultimate worth or worthlessness; I have no judgment about myself and my life. There is nothing I am quite sure about. I have no definite convictions – not about anything, really. I know only that I was born and exist, and it seems to me that I have been carried along. I exist on the foundation of something I do not know. In spite of all uncertainties, I feel a solidity underlying all existence and a continuity in my mode of being.

For Yeats, as for Jung, images, visions, archetypes continually emerged from the flux, along with definite statements reflecting now this side, not that, of ambivalent hope. In this poem, Yeats will experiment with the blessing that might have come if he had enjoyed his ideals without enduring his genius: or, maybe, if he had transposed his ideals to the impossible soil of art.

In fact, Yeats naturally knew that destiny is complex for all but the unfortunate, and that to sing defiantly with Piaf 'Non, je ne regrette rien' is the only realistic prayer for himself (whatever superficial moments of contrition certain blows of fate will bring). His essential dignity belongs with acceptance – as, I imagine, any totally objective prayer for his children would also have done. But children are helpless; parents yearn to protect them; a poet is entitled to explore possible reshapings of his own life's pieces, especially if 'the sort of beauty' he has approved (or vainly hoped for) still prospers little.

This poem, in its mingling of ideal and illusion, has a peculiar place in the canon of Yeats's work. I can think of few others where certain of his escapist hopes yearn more nakedly, and of no others further removed from his serious beliefs, or his deeply real hopes.

Not that the word 'prayer' is used cynically; how could it be? There is prayer for what *might* have been for 'the loveliest woman born' (not Mrs Yeats, alas). Nor could it have escaped Yeats's attention that, had his prayer been answered, this would have been his last as well as his first poetic tribute to his daughter. Just as 'the loveliest woman born' does, indeed, steal much of the poem intended to exorcise her, so it is of heroes, of poets, of the tormented and the beautiful, that Yeats will continue to sing. The poem is written in stormy weather, Yeats reflecting it, as that still stormier weather of 'The Second Coming' ran in his mind. Little wonder if the lure of some lasting youth, untroubled gaiety, hidden springtime of happiness should throw up images (images evading the categories – not antithesis, not vision, not mask). In the end, Maud Gonne no doubt ignored the poem, as usual; possibly Mrs Yeats settled, still more thoughtfully and dutifully, at the planchette. As for Yeats, he would have recognised, not without some deep twinge of (what?), another 'real' poem; ready now to dance among the rest.

Yet, when this is allowed for, as I believe it must be, the poem retains validity of a special kind. Maybe the instinct for blessing attends all great artists (recently, Ted Hughes identified it as one mainspring of poetry itself). And, if the project is difficult, Yeats of all men knows this. There will be memorable lines enough to carry him, and the poem, through.

Note the sombre opening. Yeats, on the roof of the tower, is not elated, but driven – his mood half reflecting, half capturing the unchecked 'Once more' storm. Stanza ii counterpoints the prayer with the elements which, of course, answer no prayers. But two elisions arise: 'excited reverie' and 'murderous innocence'. In the first, Yeats does justice to the Apollonian and Bacchic elements in the creative process, defining also that strange mingling of contemplation and turbulence peculiar to this occasion. '. . . murderous innocence' reaches several ways. Is the sea 'innocent' because its shipwrecks and killings are purely impersonal? If so, 'murderous' may describe elements elusive to prayer. And is 'that great Queen, that rose out of the spray' also casually murderous? In Greek literature, all the gods share the amorality or super-morality of elemental powers. Aphrodite ruled Yeats at the child's conception;

ruled him more wildly, too, in other passions, less subject to 'ceremony and order' either in fact or in wish. The 'Horn of Plenty' is an image as unexpected as it is disconcerting. The phrase suggests abundance, excess even, if taken literally, yet here, it is yoked to that possible assimilation of passion to order, beauty to homeliness, which the prayer invokes. This ambivalence is further extended – maybe against the poem's apparent intention also – by the powerful image 'Dancing to a frenzied drum'. In context, this is bound to remind us of the conjunction 'excited reverie', but syntactically it becomes allied to 'the future years' – which, for better or worse, are to be shaped by the 'rough beast' slouching towards Bethlehem to be born.

Stanzas iii–v might be thought of as straightforward, whatever we personally make of them, and to contain a sequence of undeniable, if unexciting truths. 'Courtesy' is a key word, foreshadowing the climax, and signalling the internal balance this poem will achieve. For Yeats, 'courtesy' is always a good word. It belongs with aristocracy, tradition, friendship, artistry – though always, naturally, in tension with other qualities, various in kind. Sometimes, 'courtesy' and 'heart' are in opposition – though in this poem reconciliation is hoped for, the marriage of formal culture *and* spontaneous growth in one, hidden, life. There is a progression also from 'murderous innocence' in stanza ii to the equally elusive 'radical innocence' of stanza ix; and the memorable yoking together of 'innocence and beauty' at the poem's end. Clearly, 'innocence' has to be achieved in some manner – and, if neither in nature, nor in instinct, is the quality unequivocal, some civilised formula has to be devised.

Yeats's choice – for moderate beauty, 'natural kindness', 'heart-revealing intimacy', the charm that earns friendship – translates, in stanza vi, to organic growth. There is no play of wit here – nothing in the least to remind us of Marvell's 'The Garden', despite the metamorphosis of possible passion to amorous green. We are more likely to think of Wordsworth's Lucy:

A violet by a mossy stone,
Half-hidden from the eye. . . .

For a moment, there is a real, even simple, craving for bliss without stress, harmony without competition, 'business' without society. The girl is to be 'a flourishing hidden tree', 'a linnet'. She is to dispense 'magnanimities of sound' (perhaps in direct contrast with 'discourtesy of death' – that striking phrase thrown up, equally fitly as the poet reluctantly conceded, by the entirely different life and destiny of Robert Gregory). She is to assimilate all, quarrel and love alike, to 'merriment'. Stanza vi seems to swell with blessing, as if detaching itself momently from the poem, attaching itself entirely to the simple, deep core of love for a baby who is still nothing – still all to become:

> O may she live like some green laurel
> Rooted in one dear perpetual place.

'Rooted' is, of course, another great word for Yeats – little though we think of him as a 'nature' poet. Consider the force of the word in 'The Municipal Gallery Revisited':

> And here's John Synge himself, that rooted man,
> 'Forgetting human words', a deep grave face.

Recollect also the obsessive search for roots, among so many soils, so much wandering: Irish roots (the ancient culture, seed of another flowering for Europe); Coole Park roots, where art might flourish –

> I meditate upon a swallow's flight,
> Upon an aged woman and her house,
> A sycamore and lime-tree lost in night
> Although that western cloud is luminous,
> Great works constructed there in nature's spite
> For scholars and for poets after us,
> Thoughts long knitted into a single thought.
> A dance-like glory that those walls begot.

> ('Coole Park', 1929)

Thoor Ballylee, roots for himself, after fifty years restlessness; then finally (and here the comparison with T. S. Eliot and 'East Coker' is striking) the rooting back of himself, at death, into Irish soil, the place of the Butlers – attended by those directions and sonorities, dated 4 September 1938, and fulfilled by Georgie Yeats, years after his death and original burial in France, as he would surely have wished.

Why 'laurel'? Maybe Marvell's jest in 'The Garden' is recalled, however remotely – though I suspect that the simple fact of shade, and evergreen, explains enough.

This stanza stays in the mind, as if insulated, yet it is but a moment's rest in the poem's odder flight. Stanzas vii to ix, by becoming so directly personal again, project a suspicion of wishful thinking (even casual thinking) back upon the imaged ideal. The anger is all for Maud Gonne's self-immolation in politics and – more particularly, no doubt – for her continued rejection of him, even as O'Brien's successor. That too-simplified phrase 'By quiet natures understood' would signal this, even if the projection of 'let her think opinions are accursed' upon his daughter (and so on all woman) did not clinch the matter. Yeats well knows that 'intellectual hatred' is not confined to one of the sexes; his own 'hatred' flourished – in poems that now make him faintly uneasy – even while he tried to cure Maud Gonne of hers. The final three lines of stanza vii,

> If there's no hatred in a mind
> Assault and battery of the wind
> Can never tear the linnet from the leaf

offer themselves as a simple moral reflection, at least in tone, yet, on any showing, it is a partial truth at best. Can an inner sweetness wholly defeat circumstance? – can the wind, still 'haystack- and roof-levelling', truly be deflected from every 'linnet' on its leaf? Fairly obviously, this attempt to return to the main poem is an irrelevance, given the potent but hidden springs now guiding the verse. I doubt whether the phrase 'an old bellows full of angry wind' can be detached from Maud Gonne's life, Yeats's love, O'Brien's memory ('This other man I had dreamed / A drunken, vainglorious lout') or function at all successfully, as the syntax makes it do, for introduction to the poem's conclusion.

The penultimate stanza is, however, inherently complex: or conceivably 'muddled' is for once the correct word. 'Considering that' is hard to read aloud – as Yeats very occasionally is – for reasons I have never managed to resolve. There is the ambiguity in syntax. Arriving here, one imagines that the opening follows from the rhetorical question preceding it, and is intended to amplify – at some remove – 'An intellectual hatred is the worst'. Yet, if you give it this emphasis, the stanza later disintegrates, since we see that the phrase is in fact a new start, preparing for the 'She can . . .' in l. 6.

Unfortunately, the whole of the opening of this stanza depends on one's choice of emphasis, and to keep two meanings going would be hard – even if one knew precisely their force. If you make 'Considering that' a reference backwards, then the stanza before becomes a formula, releasing one into the solution: 'all hatred driven hence . . .'. But, if it is a new introduction (as I think it must be), 'all hatred driven hence' and the following clauses are far more floating – a set of possibilities, or conditions, which will lead eventually to the final extravagance, 'be happy still'.

To keep both possibilities open is, I find, impossible (though maybe an extremely neutral, or ritualistic, reading might do the trick?). But the phrase 'all hatred driven hence' is a further complication, since it postulates a state hardly to be attained by humanity (not by Yeats; or Maud Gonne; or his daughter, unless she is to become 'hidden' indeed). The difficulty of the condition in turn affects 'radical innocence' – a striking phrase, in balance it seems with the earlier 'murderous innocence', since both notions are memorable, but far from easy to grasp.

Lines 3–5 are surely particularly elusive. One could imagine Blake writing them, or maybe other early romantics – maybe anyone who asserts that all life is conditioned within. Nowhere else in Yeats does his thought accord with this, and I cannot feel that the poem lends them any strong support. In fact, Yeats's personal assertions of spiritual autonomy are usually far more defiant (cf. 'A Dialogue of Self and Soul', particularly the magnificent second section), and arise from no frame of mind of the kind wished, on his daughter, here. Even so, 'radical innocence' sticks in the mind, maybe because the final stanza – surely one of Yeats's finest – becomes attached to the words – at least when one thinks back.

In this stanza, however, the opposites come together – custom and innocence, ceremony and beauty – and the conclusion seeks to unite tradition and spontaneity, through a yoking of the poem's major organic images together with 'a house / Where all's accustomed, ceremonious' (Coole Park?) – and, of course, with marriage. Marriage is doubly appropriate here – Yeats's own marriage, whose first fruit *is* this child, and the poem's occasion; also the 'happy ever after' marriage of all prayer and blessing, such as this.

I am left with a sense that Yeats has somehow also tried to assert that elemental forces (howling storm; flooded stream; untamed sea; future years; frenzied drum; choking hate) can be cured, by the blessings invoked here; and that he knows, as well as we, the untruth. No doubt he knows equally that if 'murderous innocence' and 'radical innocence' *can* hang in balance, his own genius, and destiny, are closer to the first.

It will be apparent (I hope) that this is not hostile criticism; as I have already said, I think 'A Prayer for My Daughter' has a peculiar place in the canon of Yeats's work. The only clumsiness (if I am right) is the transition from stanza viii to stanza ix, to which I have drawn attention. Otherwise, I assume that the ambiguities were fully apparent to the poet, and that that poem belongs, with the others, in the major dialectic of his art.

'To Be Carved on a Stone at Thoor Ballylee'

'I, the poet William Yeats': magnificent panache! – and of a piece with those other moments when Yeats, assuming bardic robes, allows personal magnetism to infuse force where he will (for instance, 'I thought it out this very day, / Noon upon the clock'; 'I

heard an old religious man / But yesternight declare'; and so forth).
A touch of blarney, but which reader of Yeats would wish it away – or
deny some real celebration of life in mere verbal exuberance?

Here, as in many other poems ('I write it out in a verse . . .', for
instance), the *gravitas* rings true since the theme matches it. Yeats is
writing both of his wife and of his tower. His helpers in the
restoration included 'the local carpenter and mason and
blacksmith', as well as 'the drunken man of genius, Scott', from
whom designs 'for two beds' arrived.

The Yeatses spent summers in the Tower until 1929, when the
rigours of old age at last forced the poet to move again to his last
earthly home (cf. 'An Acre of Grass'). The Tower did fall, once more,
into decay. More recently, it has been restored – at far greater
expense than Yeats might have expected – as a tourist attraction, and
these words are indeed carved on it as the poet wished.

Although short, I find this vintage, and am glad that Georgie Yeats
got a look in, after all, in Yeats's best verse.

'The Tower'

This poem was written in 1926, before 'Sailing to Byzantium'. It is
the title poem of a major volume, but was placed second, not first, in
Yeats's final ordering. I imagine that he wished to leave the other
poem afloat on its ambiguous symbols, and to prevent readers from
prematurely simplifying them – as one is tempted to, if 'The Tower'
becomes too powerful a presence first.

At first sight, 'The Tower' seems simpler than 'Sailing to
Byzantium' – though this results, no doubt, from a structuring
designed to produce such an effect. In fact, though superficially like
those other poems which invoke the dead, it makes an indelible
impression all its own. When reading Yeats's prose, I find that 'The
Tower' comes to mind more often than any other of his poems, and
suspect that it is nearer his true centre (supposing there to be one)
than even the 'simplicities' of his short, sharp poems – or that
Minotaur's maze, 'Byzantium' itself.

Part I is the scene setting – sheer, unadulterated anger at old age.
No sailing away here, to Byzantium or anywhere – only a statement,
fusing anger and dignity in apparent defeat. The words appear
unambiguous also – 'absurdity', 'caricature', 'Decrepit age' – and
likewise the images: a can tied to a dog's tail; 'A sort of battered
kettle at the heel'. The poem does not, however, run to 'foul rag and
bone shops' (as 'The Circus Animals' Desertion' will do later). The
'heart' is still valued, if troubled: valued, *because* troubled by its
foreseen defeat.

The lines starting 'Never had I more . . .' are an interesting half-truth. Yeats knows that bodily and mental realities cry out against him – yet maybe the mind can be trained, beyond the body, to heroic feats? He asserts here, I take it, a truth of consciousness, however qualified. We should remember also that his greatest verse exists mainly between this volume and the last lines he wrote.

I have heard many elderly people make the similar claim that they still feel young. They discover the objective truth only when this feeling risks, if it does, some test. In essence, the illusion depends, no doubt, on forgetfulness, which notoriously makes 'the past' more fiction than history, try as we will. For Yeats, the major sting related to the body – revealed mercilessly in mirrors ('Old clothes upon old sticks to scare a bird'), as well as in fading powers (not least the sexual); and in the mirror of eyes (even those summoned back, as he is now to summon, from the dead). His main fear, even so, is of the mind's failure – and the challenge implicit in this was to drive him, perhaps, to his greatest creature heights. In the later work, the torments of age veer between mind and body – different panaceas tested, different ironies let loose to lacerate, or appal.

That old age might think itself young again can be powerful illusion, in counterpoint (this not its least anguish) with the half-remembered illusions, and sufferings, of youth. Maybe most of us learn the art of being young only when the occasion has vanished, inheriting our bitter might-have-beens along with all life's residual dross. Yeats is rare in declaring his anger so fiercely and passionately, as he is rarer, of course, in achieving the almost impossible, at least in his work. The energy of creation burnt all the brighter from this time onwards, allowing the poems to hang, in balance, against whatever within them speaks of (even, is made from) despair. Not that this solved the personal problem, in most of its torment: the sacrifice of life to art was one of many ironies. Even so, Yeats knew that his poems were 'masterful images', ensuring him dignity – along with the qualified immortality of those destined to be known and loved, for their surviving achievements, after their death. As it happens, he was to be granted also the mercy of writing at his best until a few days before his death. The importance of this as a boon can be gauged from the beautiful conclusion of the poem before us.

When registering this opening section, I always feel tempted to substitute Aristotle and Locke for Plato and Plotinus, who in their finest moment dealt p urely in 'argument' and 'abstract things' as little as Yeats. (It may be worth recalling that Yeats made partial amends to these ancients in later poems; also, that in 1926 Mrs Yeats's spirits were dictating his reading to rigid lines.) I wonder also whether, to 'ear and eye', one should not mentally add penis, since few poems, including this one, lose sight of *that* betrayal, in age. The section's verbal vigour extends no less to recreated boyhood than to present anger; what is clear is that Byzantium will play no part here in the equations to come.

The poem's second section seems almost to start a new poem, designed to modify the first. Stanza i finds him on the roof of the Tower, as in 'A Prayer for My Daughter', and the form in this section is a subtle variant of the verse he used there. Now, he is pacing to more purposeful effect, a magician about to conjure again for the dead:

> I pace upon the battlements and stare
> On the foundations of a house, or where
> Tree, like a sooty finger, starts from the earth;
> And send imagination forth
> Under the day's declining beam, and call
> Images and memories
> From ruin or from ancient trees,
> For I would ask a question of them all.

'Imagination' will be sent forth while he still possesses it (the kick-back at part I is almost defiant). 'Images and memories' yokes together two of those many modes of being where, as a poet, he seeks truths not anchored in time. One could add to the roll-call ghosts, shades, fictions, dreams, wishes, visions – all those many enigmas displaced from temporal reality which haunt his work, seeking their kinship and validity

> Where blood-begotten spirits come
> And all complexities of fury leave,
> Dying into a dance,
> An agony of trance,
> An agony of flame that cannot singe a sleeve.

> ('Byzantium')

This time, it is mythical and fictional beings he chiefly calls – an odd assortment, yet handpicked for his 'question' – the nature of which we, like they, must wait to learn. His 'real' people (notably Maud Gonne), exist here by proxy – mingled, with Helen of Troy, in a legend of local origin (fiction with some slight base in fact?).

What are we to make of them? And why Mrs French first? Does he admire her for her independence, or for her aristocratic ruthlessness? The force of 'most respected lady' doesn't fully declare itself, while the later jest 'Gifted with so fine an ear' will be offensive to different readers in varying degrees. We cannot be sure exactly why 'insolent' is the one adjective earned by the farmer, or know

whose viewpoint it is; the pun on 'fine an ear' for music is likewise
unexplained. Possibly the link between art and destruction is all
Yeats needs for the poem; but his 'image' is singularly vivid, and
disturbing, if so.

The next stanzas (iii–v) start from a peasant (to balance the
aristocrat?), along with her victim (if someone unknown to her can
be called her victim – a delicate point). We know that the incident
concerning Mrs French was being read aloud to Yeats at about this
time by his wife, in a version written by Sir Jonah Barrington, and
that the legend of Mary Hynes and 'blind Raftery' (to give them the
names not put into this poem) had been recorded by Yeats himself in
Celtic Twilight. These episodes have therefore the force of historical
events, known chiefly through legend – and known of course locally
(most of Yeats's readers, as he would realise, would be lost without
notes). The 'peasant girl' is, however, the stuff of more general
legend, and no doubt Yeats relied on the archetype to have its effect.
In essence, we have a peasant girl whose real (or fabled) beauty has
powers of destruction – a local Helen, or Maud Gonne. In later
poems, we shall find Yeats claiming to have brought

> Everything down to that sole test brought again,
> Dream of the noble and the beggar-man
>
> ('The Municipal Gallery Revisited')

and also noting:

> For even daughters of the swan can share
> Something of every paddler's heritage. . . .
>
> ('Among School Children')

In 'The Tower', Mrs French's interest would seem to reside in one
dramatic action, vividly remembered, while the girl's is created
around her by legend and song. The power of art is asserted, at least
as much as its source in natural beauty, for destruction:

> Music had driven their wits astray –
> And one was drowned in the great bog of Cloone.

Moreover, in speaking of men 'maddened' by 'rhymes', Yeats
appears to be rebuking the folly of mistaking art for life (though in
the two poems following, his own uneasy conscience, in the different
sphere of politics, can't fully settle for this). The girl's victims

Rose from the table and declared it right
To test their fancy by their sight;
But they mistook the brightness of the moon
For the prosaic light of day –
Music had driven their wits astray. . . .

The majestic austerity of the verse is so resonant – and the whole episode so apparently peripheral to invocation – that any commentator must tread with care. Yeats is no Locke, warning us against 'false wit' or 'fancy' in the interests of 'reason': nor is he even concerned to focus on the evils of drink. Though the episode seems wasteful, the tone is triumphant – as if art is, after all, vindicated (and Raftery was blind). The word 'Strange', at the start of stanza v, picks up these paradoxes, linking them to the 'blindness' of Homer himself. Although (it seems) *en passant*, the power of art is very central here – nor can the cumulative force of 'blind', 'betrayed', 'mad' be a mere aside. Is there the suggestion that an artist might – in his moon's sphere – be ignorant of sunlight, and unaware of (or not responsible for) any harm that he does? The word 'tragedy' is, again, carefully balanced by 'triumph', and, in his final line, the poet fairly clearly drafts in himself, and his work. Perhaps we need feel no surprise, then, that his immediate transition is from legend to his own earlier fiction – but the deeper transition relates to this section's main strategy, which is not yet declared. The final question – reserved for his own creation Hanrahan – is as important as the first more expected one; and Yeats (Maud Gonne now surely unmasked, and central) symbolises an artist's power also to blind, and maybe ruin, *himself.*

In immediate context, however, 'For if I triumph I must make men mad' sufficiently rounds up the ambiguities for Yeats now to conjure for Hanrahan, and introduce his personal fiction into the company of Mrs French and Mary Hynes. Fancy and sight, life and art, sun and moon stay in tension, unclarified; but Yeats is able to rely on his construct, now, to carry him through.

Hanrahan (interestingly) is yet another user, sometimes a destroyer, of women, but it is drunken lechery (far from Yeats's real-life choice) which earns him his place in this poem. The whole movement of the next two stanzas is hectic and odd: an excited recital of the plot of a play, reaching a near climax, then switched suddenly off: 'O towards I have forgotten what – enough!' Why does the poet become almost feverish and then wearied – as if disgusted by some lurking falsity, or shame? Is it that his well-known scorn for drunks (Lionel Johnson, for example) – which co-existed with a furtive attraction and even envy that he characteristically admitted to – reminds him, suddenly, of some lie in his *art*? This would indeed be

serious. Or is it that 'horrible splendour of desire' is a quality he is
not yet ready or able to glorify, since Byzantium still has to be
explored before he can arrive at Crazy Jane and the later verse? For a
moment one wonders whether the poet has driven Hanrahan, or
himself, the crazier in inventions where the dionysiac has been only
uneasily (and for middle age perplexedly) explored. 'I thought it all
out twenty years ago' – the sting lurks here. 'Bliss was it in that dawn
to be alive' (with reservations); and the changes in himself, in Coole
Park and his other loved places and people, release emotions that
threaten to burst this particular, highly-wrought frame. The heaped
up humiliations of stanza vi, culminating in 'broken' and 'horrible',
(notice, too, that 'drunk or sober' appear to be equated), followed in
the next stanza by a display of lying, again with a massive
undercurrent built on 'shuffled', 'bewitched', 'changed', 'frenzy'
(words that might apply as much to art as to drunken juggling),
appear to be pushing the poem towards something compulsive, yet
counter-productive. But no doubt this is precisely the effect
calculated – leaving the dramatic break at 'enough!', and our
reactions to it, as intended transition to the next and final figures –
this time real, if violent and also half-fabulous; Yeats's predecessors
in the Tower itself.*

Stanzas viii and ix draft in further necessary complications. The
first 'figure' is said to have lived in the tower about a hundred years
before. The word 'recall' suggests that the poet will now move from
'calling imagination forth' to bodying out folk memories. (In the last
stanza of 'In Memory of Major Robert Gregory', it will be
remembered, there is the assertion that the poet has 'brought to
mind' dead friends, then adding 'some.appropriate commentary on
each', while waiting for 'imagination' to bring 'a fitter welcome'.
The literal meaning seems to be that 'imagination' that time failed
him, and the real poem has not been written; but 'took all my heart
for speech', though a moving conclusion, does not fully explain the
actual presence of the poem in the collection, nor give us ground for
denying it 'heart'. I make this aside since such distinctions are always
to be looked for in Yeats's poems – and, while they are clearly
important, the quality of calculated elusiveness should not be
overlooked. I do not think that Yeats intends deliberate confusion –
maybe a reminder of subtle distinctions that his art exists to point to
rather than resolve). In stanza viii, the phrase 'neither love, / Nor

* We shall find that Yeats needs Hanrahan very particularly for this
poem. But I find it interesting that in 'Tales of Red Hanrahan', as they now
exist, the rogue is an outcast, unsuccessful in love, its victim almost, in life
and death. We know that Lady Gregory rewrote these fables, in a style that
seems very much hers – but it is maddening that Yeats's publishers (or his
heirs?) still make the changes in his prose writings so hard to chart.

music nor an enemy's clipped ear' yokes three previous episodes together, stressing their destructiveness, yet turning them into possible sources of 'cheer'. Yeats's predecessor in the Tower remains, however, more shadowy in the popular mind (despite the word 'recall') than the other half 'fabulous' locals. The word 'dog's day' evokes none of the feverish glamour of Red Hanrahan. The final comment 'An ancient bankrupt master of this house' is morally neutral, though resonantly linked, through ownership of the Tower, with Yeats himself. Stanza ix moves back to the earliest inhabitants, now well lost in legend. Once more, Yeats offers a different perspective on the creative process, returning to 'images', but now images 'in the Great Memory stored'. Whether the 'Great Memory' is Plotinus's Anima Mundi, or Jung's Collective Unconscious, remains teasing. Yeats had written, in his general note on the poem, 'The ghosts have been seen at their game of dice in what is now my bedroom, and the old bankrupt man lived about a hundred years ago. According to one legend he could only leave the Castle upon a Sunday because of his creditors, and according to another he lived in the secret passage'. As readers, we have to recognise that, whatever we make of Yeats's mood when he writes in this manner, it is the stuff of his poetry; and that 'ghosts', as *A Vision* progressed, were apt to drift in and out of objective reality: 'We have come to give you metaphors for poetry' (*A Vision*, p. 8).

Part II of 'The Tower' moves now to its final four stanzas, which appear to justify the invocation – and, as the capricious cast assemble ('As I would question all, come all who can'), we are reminded at once (stanza x) of the original purpose of the summoning ('For I would ask a question of them all'), and of their inherent ambivalence ('beauty's ... celebrant' qualified by 'blind rambling'; 'juggler', 'God-forsaken', 'mire', 'mocking' – not to mention the pun about the ear – somehow contribute to an exotic, rather than a depressing, rehearsal). We might recall that several times in the prose, Yeats toys with the idea of finding someone who might answer 'all my questions'. These not-impossible creatures range from some 'old tramp' in Sligo, through some equally old medium in the back streets of London, to one who would have been fresh in his mind (I quote the famous passage from *A Vision* (p. 279) which, in fuller form, relates very closely to the Byzantium poems):

> I think if I could be given a month of Antiquity and leave to spend it where I chose, I would spend it in Byzantium, a little before Justinian opened St Sophia and closed the Academy of Plato. I think I could find in some little wine-shop some philosophical worker in mosaic who could answer all my questions, the supernatural descending nearer to him than to Plotinus even, for

the pride of his delicate skill would make what was an instrument of power to princes and clerics, a murderous madness in the mob, show as a lovely flexible presence like that of a perfect human body.

In 'The Tower', the questions are not answered; but Yeats does rise, in the asking, to one of his moments of ineffaceable power:

> Did all old men and women, rich and poor,
> Who trod upon these rocks or passed this door,
> Whether in public or in secret rage
> As I do now against old age?

The only 'answer' is found in eyes 'impatient to be gone' (why call us back here, for foolish questions?) and, with the exception of Hanrahan, all are dismissed in two words. The rhetorical fury of the question answers itself: here, at least, neither images, ghosts, visions, nor art will make up for lost youth (the youth he never had; and perhaps no man did?).

It seems as if the supplementary question is to be as significant as the original, though addressed now only to the 'mighty memories' of one fashioned by the poet himself. The penultimate stanza is particularly important, and in some ways pivotal in Yeats's development. While 'rage at old age' is not new (despite its very special force here), this open if forlorn praise of the erotic is. Byzantium has still to be explored before we reach Crazy Jane and the remarkable syntheses of the *Last Poems*, but the powerfully erotic, in Yeats, still waits for release. Rage at old age mingles with rage at lost love, lost opportunity – yet there is evasiveness, and tenderness, in this section's close. It seems as if Yeats's reticence (part of art's discipline; or simply cowardice?) torments him now, with the thought of 'a great labyrinth lost'.

Precisely here, we encounter one of those effects most strange in Yeats's writing – verse that is clear, open, memorable in image and syntax, yet oddly elusive in terms of the poet himself. Here Hanrahan is the fulfilled man (whatever he was in the play; or in *Celtic Twilight*) and erotic daring opens, to him, what the poet has missed:

> For it is certain that you have
> Reckoned up every unforeknown, unseeing
> Plunge, lured by a softening eye,
> Or by a touch or sigh,
> Into the labyrinth of another's being. . . .

This knowledge is, however, preceded by the lines

Bring up out of that deep considering mind
All that you have discovered in the grave,

so that the 'Old lecher with a love on every wind' might, after all, be
more posthumous phantom than one truly summoned back from
death to speak of life.

The second question (introducing the final stanza) has also to be
quoted fully, since there seems no comment that can bypass or
replace the words themselves:

Does the imagination dwell the most
Upon a woman won or woman lost?
If on the lost, admit you turned aside
From a great labyrinth out of pride,
Cowardice, some silly over-subtle thought
Or anything called conscience once;
And that if memory recur, the sun's
Under eclipse and the day blotted out.

Why does this have to be asked of Hanrahan? Maybe the poet needed
his extreme antitype, as if to emphasise that Hanrahan (thus
represented) can no more give an answer, than can the poet himself.
The first two lines pose a speculation that few readers alive have not
pondered, though not only convention but also some deep instinct
for civilisation (even survival?) usually keeps it repressed. I am
reminded of the concrete, floating mysteries of Marvell's 'Definition
of Love' ('Magnanimous Despair alone / Could show me so divine a
thing') as the only kind of comment possible (maybe Shakespeare's
'Phoenix and the Turtle' also). Language, like definition, stops with
the question; it is not for life, or art, to expect clarities beyond. In
l. 3, I assume that 'you' is not Hanrahan but the poet (at the very
least, both held in extreme tension together), and that the rhetorical
'If' (does one doubt its answer?) acts mainly as a brake upon fruitless
regret. But, if the various shades *have* reassembled now as Maud
Gonne (and I suppose this could be doubted), Yeats seems, for once,
to be blaming not her but himself. Did she perhaps offer herself to
him once (though not in marriage); and did he refuse? If so, the
refusal was no doubt right (or at least inevitable), whatever ll. 2–6
refer to, or rationalise, from his own life. Maybe 'if memory recur'
was as much as anything the seed of this poem. The conclusion is
freed to resonate for us (sun against memory) as it will:

And that if memory recur, the sun's
Under eclipse, and the day blotted out.

In the poem's third part (a section of great lyricism, bearing the same kind of technical relationship to 'Easter 1916' as the second section does to 'Prayer for My Daughter'), anger and regret seem cast aside, and the mood of vigorous acceptance and power comes into its own. Part II started as invocation, we remember – and, though cast down towards the end, the Magus is still in control. 'It is time that I wrote my will': this is the dignified response to age, and Yeats is not without princely gifts to bequeath.

> I choose upstanding men
> That climb the streams until
> The fountain leap, and at dawn
> Drop their cast at the side
> Of dripping stone. . . .

Youth and action – another antitype (very different from Hanrahan?) – rather, I think, a recreation of what he was, and *is*, since his work is always conceived in pride and action, whatever the cost. The main gift, then, is pride – which is associated equally with his country (maybe the roll-call of Irish patriots from earlier days determined this metre), and with natural beauty. The section starting 'Pride, like that of the morn . . .' proceeds from youth to age quickly, through the fate of the swan. Yeats confessed to being influenced by Sturge Moore's 'Dying Swan', which he had often recited during an American lecture tour – but his own lines are far finer, and the image itself, fairly general romantic property, is more likely to take our minds back to 'The Wild Swans at Coole'. The dying fall anticipates the poem's actual conclusion, but in a manner asserting the enigmatic triumph of art. The swan's 'last song' is that strange turning of death into beauty which will always be one ineffaceable symbol of the mystery of art.

Immediately, the poem again becomes vigorous, moving now from 'pride' to 'faith', the second of Yeats's two testamentary gifts to young men, though it has first, however, to be declared. This process is somewhat obscure. Plato and Plotinus appear to have reverted to their first role, as symbols of rejected abstractions, those 'images in the Great Memory stored' notwithstanding. 'Translunar Paradise' certainly refers to *A Vision*, and 'dream' (yet another concept now linked with 'create') is perhaps associated here with the 'shiftings' and other processes undergone by souls between bodily death and reincarnation. In appearance, the statement is one of extreme subjectivism (even solipsism), but, if so, I am not clear why it is from man's 'bitter soul' that both 'Death and life' come. The lines are written in a manner which enables one to read them aloud with considerable pleasure and every nuance of conviction, and are not in fact, therefore, the obstacle that closer scrutiny makes them appear. 'I have prepared my peace' brings us back to familiar, and moving, experience, so that the exact meaning of 'superhuman / Mirror-resembling dream' is unlikely to trouble readers overmuch. These memories, whether carried into 'Translunar Paradise', the 'Great Memory', some new incarnation, or even oblivion, yield to the inset image of life *going on*, in nature's rhythms, whatever the fate of the individual soul.

One might expect Yeats's last testament to include also his genius (though maybe the phrase 'But all is changed' with which 'Coole Park and Ballylee 1931' will end already haunts him, and he expects 'that high horse' which Homer rode to remain rideless in the millennia of the beast). In fact, he chooses here to reduce art to one of his bitter comments upon it, and perhaps this is why 'art' is not part of the legacy. 'This sedentary trade' can scarcely be the aging process itself – which needs no art to help it – more likely, it is a reminder that youth was itself sacrificed to art.

As most commentators note, 'Now I shall make my soul' is an Irish expression, meaning 'Now I shall prepare for death'; here – and with Byzantium in mind – it possibly retains its more normal meaning as well. The ending is exceptionally beautiful. Rage at old age returns, in images as fierce as ever (a little reminiscent of the 'gifts reserved for age' passage in Eliot's 'Little Gidding'), yet also softened by a suggestion of inevitable ritual. It is immensely characteristic that Yeats should so beautifully evoke the joys of love and friendship, even in images portending their final negation. The 'dying fall' at the end, so gloomy as prophecy, is sweet as swan-song. We may be glad (it is hard not to return to the personal comment) that 'Cuchulain Comforted' is dated 13 January 1939, and 'The Black Tower' 21 January 1939. It is extraordinarily moving to look at Jon Stallworthy's reproduction of, and commentary upon, this poem written on his death bed. The infinite labour and revision of composition are still to be seen, in eleven loose-leaf sheets of manuscript, worked upon by a dying man, and in the single corrected typescript bearing that date. On 28 January 1939, seven days later, the poet died. 'The Black Tower' lacks nothing of the vigour of his prime.

'Sailing to Byzantium'

This poem and 'Byzantium' have been so often commented upon that I almost hesitate to start. Jon Stallworthy's comment on the many versions in *Between the Lines* is indispensable; so are articles by Professor Jeffares, Curtis Bradford, G. S. Fraser, Richard Ellmann and many more critics. For young poets – discouraged, no doubt rightly, by their own early attempts – there can be few better exercises than studying the evolution of this present poem from pedestrian beginnings to its present form. As usual, I propose to base this reading on the finished version and my own critical response to it – ignoring the genesis, and relating the artefact chiefly to its place among Yeats's other works. Innumerable debts may be taken for granted.

'That is no country for old men. . . .' This poem is a far cry from 'The Tower', even though it shares old age as a major theme. It seems closer, in technique and poise, to Keats's Odes (the 'Grecian Urn' especially). Like Keats's major odes, it is a self-contained artefact, continually recalling other words and contexts, yet always transiently. My impression is that, whereas many of the other poems seem momentarily illuminated by cross-references to this one, 'Sailing to Byzantium' has a unity peculiar to itself. For reasons which will become apparent later, I do not link it as closely in my mind with 'Byzantium' as possibly the majority of critics do. The work of Jon Stallworthy, in particular, cannot be ignored, for the opposite view; and to deny close similarities would clearly be absurd. But I certainly cannot see 'Byzantium' as a second attempt to handle this theme as a result of dissatisfaction with 'Sailing to Byzantium' (even though one of Yeats's own innumerable asides gives grounds for such a view). 'Sailing to Byzantium' seems to me highly wrought, complete in itself, highly successful. Like 'Byzantium', it is a most carefully constructed unity, somewhat more accessible than its successor, though scarcely less complex, and ultimately deriving, I should judge, from a different genesis and intent.

Jeffares's *Commentary* offers valuable background material, but, as very often in that indispensable book, interpretative problems are mainly bypassed. Obviously, Byzantium established itself in Yeats's mind as a symbol of mind and spirit, art and religion, enjoying rare harmony. It speaks of eternity, perhaps through all of these connotations, and particularly through their conjunction. Jeffares offers us in addition a useful Irish connection, in a quotation written by Yeats for inclusion in a broadcast of his poems (BBC Belfast, 8 September 1931), though subsequently omitted from the script:

> Now I am trying to write about the state of my soul, for it is right for an old man to make his soul, and some of my thoughts upon that subject I have put into a poem called 'Sailing to Byzantium'. When Irishmen were illuminating the Book of Kells [in the eighth century] and making the jewelled croziers in the National Museum, Byzantium was the centre of European civilisation and the source of its spiritual philosophy, so I symbolise the search for the spiritual life by a journey to that city.

The opening sentence of the poem, which I began by quoting, points in three different directions – as I think the whole of the poem, following this, then also does. At the heart of the triumphant artistry there exists, if so, a remarkable tonal neutrality – which a reader may either seek to maintain throughout, thereby underlining one of the three possibilities, or slant *slightly* in emphasis (though only slightly; since the ambivalences must not be closed), in order to underline instead either one of the remaining two. Any reading must make its decision at the start, and then seek consistency, bearing in mind that the three closely parallel poems contained here are, also, one. Undoubtedly, the poem has tremendous verbal energy – closely connected with Yeats's belief, or his wish to believe, in the symbolic validity of Byzantium – which carries the reader along, making the 'problem' of reading less difficult, in practice, than I have suggested. There is a tide of rhetoric which belongs with this poetic experience, however we interpret, which is itself resilient and triumphant.

'That is no country for old men.' I disagree with Jeffares in his comment that Ireland is intended (the use of 'This' instead if 'That' in the manuscript version is irrelevant, since clearly all changes were made towards the effect of the work as finally printed.) I have never doubted that the 'country' is a symbolic island or continent of 'the young', allegorised in the first stanza, and akin to the islands which 'The Wanderings of Oisin' (1889) pioneered. It is an emphatic start, even if the first reading, as I have said, might seek to achieve neutrality. In other words, the statement will be made to sound in essence a commonplace, a truism, requiring matter-of-fact recognition, without special emotion.

In the act of saying this, however, the other possibilities necessarily appear – however much we choose to restrain them. Statements of this kind are not scientific axioms or equations; they are the stuff of life and of deep responses. One of these (and which reader coming first from 'The Tower' would forget it?) is rage and anger – so the reading slanted *that* way will start with a suggestion of one total interpretation. The words 'no' and 'old' will be infused with regret: we shall sense that, though the old man sails away, knowing his exclusion inevitable, he does so with unhealed bitterness of heart, seeking to find (or maybe rationalise) a second-best. That this will be done with panache can be expected; that a poet of Yeats's temperament will not be entirely sceptical of the spiritual – and allegedly superior – alternative must also be agreed. But his rage at old age is also not in question (as I have already suggested, I think he probably placed this poem *before* 'The Tower' in great part to prevent resonances of the second poem from too directly swaying our reading of 'Sailing to Byzantium'). This, in turn, is a reminder that the idea of life as a pilgrimage from inexperience to wisdom is ancient and widespread; the basis of most religious, and perhaps of most adult, quests. In 'East Coker' we shall encounter Eliot's 'quiet voiced elders', whose claim for the superior wisdom of age is found to be spurious, so that the eventual exhortation old men must be explorers, brings us on to one recurring theme that Eliot shared with Yeats. Both poets were, and remained, religious – which indicates that the recognition of possible evasion and complacency was in no sense, for either, a final word. Both believed in 'tradition' not only as a kind of monument of the past – a remarkable yet dusty museum – but as a dynamic concept, interwoven in cultural, and perhaps religious continuity, beyond the 'individual self'. Maybe Eliot's 'Mind of Europe' was more purely metaphorical than Yeats's 'Great Memory' (though Eliot's assertion that new works of art alter the *total* order of the past brings us to ground where literary intuition threatens to burst the thin bounds set by many between art and religion). Once again, we can usefully recall Jung's Collective Unconscious – together with the fact that Jung himself managed, far more successfully than either Yeats or Eliot, to come to terms with each stage of life, including old age, even though his exploration has much symbolism in common with these literary peers.

I have already said that the ambivalences are intended to be held in tension, and I shall return to this structural triumph at the end. Before that, I want to run through the three possible emphases in reading the poem aloud, as I have mentioned them – pointing to the particular features of each and the ultimate need to keep all choices open.

I shall start from the notion that the poem is essentially a choice of old age against youth – even a condemnation of youth – since this *has* been presented by some critics as 'the obvious' or even as 'the only' meaning, strange though anyone familiar with the poet must surely find it. How does this guide our reading? The emphatic rejection will first appear maybe in an intonation of the word 'old' in l. 1, implying superior wisdom in age, and even the right to a little scorn. The rest of the stanza will include some puritan (or quasi-puritan) rejection of the world depicted. In 'dying generations' we shall take a hint that, while the old man sees truth in 'dying', the young miss it, so that their 'song', unperceived by themselves, is illusion. Even 'all summer long' will suggest illusion – a world of sensuous withdrawal, overlooking the tragic sting in life, mortality itself (l. 5). In this reading, 'Caught' will imply men trapped, or ensnared (erotic sin, or folly), a reading that the word 'neglect' might seem easily to support. The 'Monuments of unageing intellect' will indicate a settled preference, whether the puritan's for spiritual rather than fleshy things, or the intellectual's for the supremacy (inherent, or in the quest for 'truth') of the 'mind'.

The second stanza has now to be read subtly, if this interpretation is not to be wholly undermined. The best one can do is to treat ll. 1–2 (up to 'stick') as almost throwaway, and to bring 'unless' as close to 'until' in its apparent force as one can. No doubt old age *seems* paltry to thoughtless youthful spectators, but it has a different and far superior 'song' of its own. The 'song' of the young was, after all, illusion; the 'song' of the old is based on a surer hope. So, the frailty of the body (very powerfully evoked in l. 4) can be taken as a light price to pay for wisdom: besides, 'body' has already been downgraded by 'sensual' (penultimate line of the first stanza), which will be taken, again, as puritanical dismissal of the flesh. The words 'Nor is there' will be infused with a sense of impending triumph, as far as possible; 'studying' will counterbalance 'sensual', carrying moral approval; the last three lines will ring out with the force of an arrival which, for once, fully justifies hopeful travelling – the word 'magnificence' fully savoured, and 'the holy city of Byzantium' carrying as much as possible of *A Vision* at its highest peak:

> I think that in early Byzantium, maybe never before or since in recorded hisory, religious, aesthetic and practical life were one, that architect and artificers – though not, it may be, poets, for language had been the intrument of controversy and must have grown abstract – spoke to the multitude and the few alike. The painter, the mosaic worker, the worker in gold and silver, the illuminator of sacred books, were almost impersonal, almost perhaps without the consciousness of individual design, absorbed in their subject-matter and that the vision of a whole people. They could copy out of old gospel books those pictures that seemed as sacred as the text, and yet weave all into a vast design, the work of many that seemed the work of one, that made building, picture, pattern, metalwork of rail and lamp, seem but a single image; and this vision, this proclamation of their invisible master, had the Greek nobility, Satan always the still half-divine Serpent, never the horned scarecrow of the didactic Middle Ages. (pp. 279–80)

The word 'therefore' can ring out, in this belief, with the triumph of wisdom not only aspired towards, but at last achieved.

The third stanza is, then, exalted invocation, not unlike the kind practised so often by Yeats in the *making* of art. This invocation is prayer, however – or, if not prayer, at least recreation, of the kind we experience when bringing any work of art alive for ourselves. Sages and saints are summoned from mosaic stillness to inspire the old man with a song not anchored to time. The whole inheritance of art and religion is to be personally appropriated, with self already preparing to merge or transcend itself in whatever may come.

At this stage, there is a further tricky point in the reading, possibly the hardest of all to get round. Is 'heart' really to be sacrificed so readily, that mortality may be put off and the immortal put on? The best we can do again is to make 'heart' function, as far as possible, as a symbol of both 'sensual' and fleshy things, and so a small price to pay, since it belongs with the illusions of youth. The powerful words 'fastened to a dying animal' can be seen, maybe, as the Platonic assertion that 'soul' is merely trapped and imprisoned, as long as it remains in mortal incarnation. This would further be supported by 'It knows not what it is' (the soul itself bemused, if it succumbs to the snares of the senses). The works of great men – great artists and religious mystics especially – can spiritually 'gather' the poet into an 'eternity' where 'artifice' rescues him from mere nature (the life at one remove from 'Reality' itself).

The last stanza reinforces this idea, or can seem to – though here a more serious complication (for *all* interpretations, maybe) sets in.

Let us allow, for a moment, that the word 'nature' is, in this sense, expendable, so that even an artist can dispense with 'heart' and 'nature' alike, and feel only relief. (Let us forget, this implies also, who is writing the poem; or let us assume that Yeats, the occultist and mystic, is in total ascendancy, for the moment at least.) Even so, we can hardly fail to notice that he is now, further, giving up *consciousness*: the choice is to become, himself, an artefact, a golden bird. So, mysteriously, the release, the new song of 'eternity' is immediately frozen, and the poet chooses, for reincarnation, the form of gold.

A very determined critic might find this, I suppose, a symbol of transcended individualism – that merging of the 'self' back into the One (the single wave back into the ocean) which certain platonic and other mystics have always sought. Even so, we are unlikely to forget Hans Andersen's fable 'The Emperor's Nightingale', or to accept, without question, this apotheosis into a toy. 'To keep a drowsy Emperor awake' – is this really the eternal fulfilment celebrated, with so much élan, in the foregoing stanzas? One need not be a devout egalitarian to feel some qualm. We notice that the poetic rhythms are now drowsy – nearer to the early Yeats, or the Pre-Raphaelites, than to the foregoing stanzas – as if to underline illusion, rather than reality, as the prevailing mood. We can further wonder whether 'The lords and ladies of Byzantium' are the safest anchorage for 'eternity' (even without cross-reference to 'Meditations in Time of Civil War' – dated 1923, though placed later). The last line, referring back, as it clearly does, to stanza i, l. 6, establishes that art, however 'eternal' in appearance, needs the world of youth for its material, its passion. It is a poem which swallows its own tail: you can pause after the last line and then begin again at the first. To do this is to discover the uncannily effective insulation of the artefact and the calculated impossibility of allowing *any* subsequent readings entirely to coincide with the first. With this as a clue we can then move on to the problems of reading the poem, if the apparently opposite interpretation is now held chiefly in view.

This time the wistfulness, regret (even bitterness – though this should not be sufficient to unbalance the whole reading) which is infused into the first sentence gives place to felt love for the country which is being left behind. Now the old man sails away from youth because he no longer belongs there, but with every bitter regret that makes the first of his two questions in 'The Tower' so unforgettable still potently at work in him. The phrase 'those dying generations' speaks to us not of the folly of the young, understood with hindsight, but of the tragic, lacerating reality of time. Its resonances link with the words I have taken as the title for this Yeats chapter, and with that whole exquisite poem ('In Memory of Eva Gore-Booth and Con Markievicz') from which they come. The words 'commend all summer long' invoke all we have known of youth and love most sweetly, celebrating the abundance of fleeting, transient beauty while it lasts. In so far as the country is lost to the poet, it is as the wild swans at Coole were lost – yet he recognises that somewhere (in other swans, other human observers) the experience continues, and he is glad of it:

> Unwearied still, lover by lover,
> They paddle in the cold
> Companionable streams or climb the air;
> Their hearts have not grown old. . . .

In this reading the last two lines of stanza i turn inside out. 'Caught' is not ensnared, or trapped in illusion, but 'caught up in' rapture (love, friendship, heartsease, 'the music while it lasts', 'excited reverie'). The 'Wisdom' of Ecclesiastes was not to confound, but to name, the seasons, equally accepting each – the season for living, the season for dying – as it comes. The conclusion of 'Among School Children' also floats into my mind (strange though *that* is, in its context):

> O body swayed to music, O brightening glance,
> How can we know the dancer from the dance?

We recognise now that 'sensual' is a good word (as of course it is, for all except puritans; how can it not be, for lovers or artists?) and that rapture may often be spontaneous blessing, flowing from heart to heart.

What of 'neglect'? We may assume that this word always contains censure, yet is this not also part of a puritan taint? To neglect things that are not worth attending to – or, still more importantly, that are irrelevant – may be one of the highest and rarest modes of wisdom. One remembers Father Time's remark in *Jude the Obscure*, that he would like the flowers so much if he did not keep reflecting that in a few days they would all be withered – and Hardy's 'sure, if bitter, placing of this as pathological morbidity. If we are to live at all, it is well to neglect obsession with death in the season of life.

In this reading, 'Monuments' takes on a more sombre sound, suggesting dead relics listed and contained in a museum, or the chilling shapes of cenotaphs 'to the glorious dead'. It therefore becomes natural to activate, by the barest intonation, the paradoxical notion of 'unageing intellect'. This typical elision of opposites can slip past, here, more obtrusively than some of the others in Yeats ('terrible beauty', 'murderous innocence', and so on), but it is no less challenging if looked at closely. Man's 'intellect', if associated with the brain, is as mortal as his body; its works may last longer, but they outlive consciousness (perhaps the 'golden bird' is prepared for, slightly more ironically than is often thought). If 'intellect' is equated with soul, however, and with 'eternity', then 'Monuments' (twice repeated) can scarcely be dissociated from the force of 'artefact' when it comes.

Continuing, it is now natural to allow much fuller bitterness into the first two lines of stanza ii (again up to 'stick'), with phrases such as 'A sort of battered kettle at the heel' fully activating *this* familiar region of Yeats's art. The word 'unless', far from being pushed unobtrusively towards 'until', will be lingered upon, so that the extreme effort required for what is to follow will not be missed. Lines 3–4 will be seen to exist (even apart from the peculiar effectiveness of 'tatter'), on the borderline of wishful-thinking, if not somewhat beyond. The 'Nor' will come with some edge of desperation, and 'Monuments of its own magnificence', whilst undoubtedly full of vigour on any reading, will again release suggestions sombre as well as grand. Naturally enough, 'And therefore' will ring out, now, with less unqualified triumph; rather, regret for the inevitability of the journey, and its doubtful outcome, may set the tone.

The invocation in stanza iii, ll. 1–4, will remain potent, but with more than a hint of rhetoric known, or feared, to be false, even as it makes its effect. Maybe the old magician is conjuring, now, beyond the limits where his, or any, magic could pull off the trick. 'Consume my heart away' can then take on a degree of the maybe total bitterness which surely must attend an image expressed in this particular way.

As I said earlier, I more normally find echoes of this poem arriving as I read Yeats's other works than the reverse process, no doubt because this artefact *is* so marvellously controlled and complete in itself. But some of the many uses of 'heart' in Yeats are bound to lurk somewhere ('Oh, who could have foretold / That the heart grows old?'; 'What shall I do with this absurdity, / O heart, O troubled heart . . .?'; 'Hearts with one purpose alone / Through summer and winter seem / Enchanted to a stone / To trouble the living stream'; 'Hearts are not had as a gift, but hearts are earned / By those that are not entirely beautiful' – and on, of course, to 'Maybe at last, being but a broken man / I must be satisfied with my heart' in 'The Circus Animals' Desertion', where the word 'heart' controls the development throughout). The words 'sick with desire / And fastened to a dying animal' very readily point to one of the main, and most bitter dynamics, of Yeats's later work. If so, 'It knows not what it is' will be taken not as a philosophical statement (the soul beset, during earthly bondage, with illusion) but as a bitter cry direct from Yeats's own heart.

In this reading, the word 'artifice' insists on the irony which is always difficult to deny it, particularly since a word closer to 'dance' would be easier to cope with in the 'positive' reading. It may be a linguistic oddity (or yet another concealed triumph of puritanism?) that most of the words connected with 'art' are, in normal English usage, tainted or bad. 'Artful' should be, in theory, at least ambivalent, but invariably it means lying, deceitful, devious, cunning or downright treacherous (*something* to give good cheer to Plato's ghost). 'Artificial' should also be ambivalent – but when is it ever used with any suggestion of acceptable art? In manners, it implies the stilted, affected, pretentious (even false pretences); elsewhere, it is doomed to such spheres as fabrics or flowers. (Still worse, to birds, one might add, with the next stanza looming.) 'Arty' is slang and invariably dismissive, managing to yoke 'showy' and 'phoney' neatly into one.

Finally, our word 'artifice' here is scarcely healthier ('artefact' itself only marginally escapes a pejorative intention, because it is so little used in everyday speech). 'Artifice' almost always implies some intent to conceal or deceive, whether it is mind, body or soul that we have in view. Even at best, it makes 'eternity' seem an alarming construct (akin to Borges's Labyrinths, or Kafka's logic, or Einstein's unfinished quest). Beyond this, we are aware that it clinches the distance from youth, heart and nature which the poem has courted – like one of those treacherous wishes, in fairy tales, that always come true.

The final stanza again fits more naturally into this reading, since the languorous music can be openly savoured, now, for ironic intent. Who in truth would prefer death to life, even in the guise of a bird of rare craftsmanship? Which poet would prefer the most exquisite artefact to the song of the humblest flesh-and-blood bird? (Both of these rhetorical questions have alternative answers; and I have not forgotten the third stanza of 'Byzantium' itself.)

The problems in the two proposed 'alternative' readings can usefully return to the strategy of the poem itself. My first suggestion was of a 'neutral' reading, the attractions of which may seem enhanced by perceived complexity. What, then, are the problems here? The challenge, no doubt, is to leave the emphases of both readings so far rehearsed possible, and even active, whilst making the temptation to 'close' the poem either way appear naïve. This may be helped if the poem is almost chanted (a solution favoured, in various asides, by Yeats himself). If so, the images and rhythms are sufficiently sumptuous, exalted and at the same time sensitive, for this to seem the most natural reading of all. We take such a solution for granted with Keats's major odes: analysis shows how rich Keats's complexities are (in some aspects also, how similar), but the reading experience transposes all to a higher key. The verbal and sensuous pleasures of 'Nightingale' and 'Grecian Urn' are not ends in themselves (as they were later debased to being by some Pre-Raphaelites), but a mode of encompassing opposites with minimal artistic strain. They are a triumph of what Keats himself called 'negative capability', and look forward, perhaps, to Jung's famous technique with dreams.*

---

* Dreams proceed, Jung tells us, from our temporarily inaccessible conscious mind (or maybe, from the Collective Unconscious), and are imbued with compulsive symbolism that defies 'understanding' at the time. Yet, if he is right, they positively demand critical analysis later, from the waking consciousness, if the things they warn of, or hint at, are to be properly grasped. For this exercise, the help of a trained analyist may be helpful, even indispensable, since such a person realises his potential for healing, or reintegrating, the 'self'.

It seems to me that the critical attention which literary critics give to poems, though it may appear to some cold-blooded or posthumous, can be justified in much the same way. In fact, all reading of great literature should be recreative, and the potentiality for healing (as well as breakdown) in this should be more clearly kept in mind than it often is. The Geneva critics reminded us that great art, if understood sensitively, is nothing less than a history of human consciousness itself. No doubt dreams proceed from unconsciousness, and great art from consciousness – both raised to a high pitch of intensity, though dreams are widespread and involuntary, while great art is the comparatively rare product of trained wills and minds. But both dreams and art produce symbols potent with meaning – and the correct understanding of both may be necessary to personal wholeness in the adult, rather than pre-adult, phase of life. I would be prepared to argue that the analysis of great art must at least be accompanied by some degree of

I have already suggested that the poem 'swallows its own tail', and even runs the danger of trapping us, as reflections between two walls of mirrors are trapped. Art may 'transcend' life, but only by enacting it; and the enactment demands recreation (that is, more 'life', more consciousness) from ourselves. Likewise, art may become assembled, if approved, in its own order of 'Monuments', but these are invariably made more from the passions of youth (or of suffering age) than from passive repose. This poem draws us, therefore, into one of the poet's major preoccupations: how are old men to remain fully and wholly alive? It is 'unageing intellect' which is the illusion, and 'song' the reality: the songs of youth and age, though apparently polarised, are in reality one.

To notice this is to notice the blatant simplification which Yeats has to adopt to make his complexities work. This, very simply, is the entirely stylised and evidently false polarity between 'youth' and 'age', as developed here, which is, however, inseparable from the poem's success.

Yeats knows as well as anyone that the young are not 'in one another's arms' eternally. Perhaps most of them are less often there than they should be; less often than, with luck, they will be, in later life. All too often, they are in lecture rooms, or examination rooms, or in shabby lodgings, worrying about essays and deadlines; or suffering the pangs of unrequited, rather than requited, love. Again, old men are not perpetually hobbling along on sticks or transfixed in libraries (not, that is, unless they are like the 'Scholars' in Yeats's splendid lampoon of that name). With luck, they are actually *writing* poems like 'Sailing to Byzantium', or brooding frenziedly on lust and rage (and damn the world).

Likewise, the young do not universally 'neglect' great art and music; Yeats knew about Proms, even if he was born too early for pop. It is likely that most of us appreciate certain great art with

---

self-analysis, self-enlightening – and that the risks of subjectivism, which I patently always run myself, as a critic, are the real challenge to cultivate some balanced discipline (close attention to word, rhythm, structure in their unique reality) without which literary criticism can so easily become mere self-indulgence, or merely a game. The corollary it that studying any art includes very particular possibilities, both for breakdown and healing, which make literary critic and psychotherapist near kin (though always different in role). Thus, in studying poems, or dreams, the psychotherapist will always be considering primarily the subjective – and be consciously involved in healing – while the literary critic will be probing poem and poet and remain consciously detached. I would like to see closer co-operation between literary critics and psychotherapists, for their mutual benefit – not the least of which might be a closer understanding of the scope and limits proper to each other's roles.

greater intensity, if not necessarily with greater discernment, in youth and early adulthood than we normally will much later in life. (What could English Literature be, this apart, but a torture-machine?). It seems likely also that those who do not appreciate at least some art deeply at seventeen or eighteen will be unlikely to appreciate any, ever; there is little hope for it merely in growing old.

This poem works by setting up images of 'youth' and 'age' that are stylised fantasy, weaving its spell round this tenuous ground. Yet it works because its major tensions are real and beautifully realised; they concern the voyage for self-integration, for selfhood, from youth to age. At every stage, the archetypes will have differing connotations and differing functions, which is precisely what the ambivalences so splendidly convey.

This poem strikes me as a more complete success in itself than the later 'Byzantium', fascinating though that is, too, in its use of similar images for a different end.

'Nineteen Hundred and Nineteen'

I propose to discuss this poem and 'Meditations in Time of Civil War' again chronologically, rather than in the order Yeats eventually chose for them. In these poems the Irish theme is uppermost, and Yeats's fears of civil unrest were now deepening year by year.

As with most of Yeats's poems, we can point to lines which stick in the mind and seem to live out of context ('Man is in love and loves what vanishes, / What more is there to say?'), but, despite, such lyrical beauty (and, of course, he *did* say more), this poem is unusually harsh in its total effect. The Irish dream was gone, the Irish reality was rapidly turning to nightmare:

> a drunken soldiery
> Can leave the mother, murdered at her door,
> To crawl in her own blood, and go scot-free. . . .

The form of the poem is also new and disconcerting, with its jumps between sections and its symbols more than usually difficult to place. Was Yeats anticipating the technique of *The Waste Land* (half a decade later), or maybe already learning from early Eliot and from Pound? But there is no close analogy, or even influence; only in odd images, taken from context, could Yeats and Eliot ever be remotely confused. The mood in this poem is fairly constant, despite the shifts of viewpoint, and a common thread of logic runs through the whole.

The poem is difficult in parts, but absurdly simple in others;

almost it seems vulnerably naïve. Yeats confesses that he and his closer associates had forgotten that evil exists.

Confronted with this, I am tempted to a digression; or at least, to an attempt to plunge back, for a moment, to my own earlier life. The immediate critical reaction is slightly sceptical: surely Ibsen, Strindberg, Chekhov, Dickens, Dostoievsky, Hardy, James, Conrad, Kipling (one could continue the list) knew of 'evil', and cast long shadows before the crises of 1914, 1916, 1917 and 1919 occurred? The notion that war descended, unheralded, from a world of blue skies and honeysuckle, sunlit euphoria, Edwardian cricket flannels and innocence, must surely be overstrained – particularly if proposed by a man as subtle as Yeats?

Yet to foresee and to experience are, and remain, different. Henry James, who lived to see the Great War, was depressed and horrified, despite that profound sense of betrayal and evil which haunted so much of his art.

How possible is it to 'believe' in a catastrophe before it happens – particularly one as decisive, in the event, as 1914? If that war had not happened, perhaps there would have been no Marxist revolution, no 1916 Easter rising, no Hitler and genocide, no cold war, no collapse of the British Empire, no escalating pollution of the environment: how could such results have been remotely foreseen even by earlier prophets of doom? In retrospect, one may feel that Europe committed suicide, for no known reason, and that world culture (or anarchy) has since moved into other paths. Did it have to happen? If not, would things have been all that much different? Would the evolutionary hope of 'progress' have seemed more perceptive today than, say, the gloom of Yeats's 'Second Coming' in January 1919?

I was born in 1928 and am at a loss for insight: these pre-natal 'ifs' are so many blind alleys, meaningless circles, in the labyrinth of thought. Clearly, Yeats's 'two thousand years' started with Herod killing the children (if we believe Matthew); with Nero crucifying Christians upside down and burning them for sport (if we believe Tacitus) – just as they have culminated, since Yeats's own death, in Belsen, Hiroshima and a particularly grim opening to the 1980s, if we believe our own senses. We know that 'Europe' kept evil sufficiently at bay for 2000 years for 'Christendom' to flourish. What the slaves thought of their lives, we guess at; what the deposed monarchs, states, institutions thought of it is stuff for historians to play with. Somehow, an impression of stability, continuity, growth was maintained, and not least by the arts.

Even one's own experience helps little: in what sense do we 'believe' in a nuclear holocaust, or in totally poisoned air, earth, fire and water, even now? In 1944 I was taught that Jane Austen was a more 'realistic' writer than Dickens and Kafka, and I recall half-believing it, because it was said. Should I have noticed that my own home and street were peopled almost wholly by posthumous creations of Dickens; and that the nightly bombing, burning and killing which dominated London in 1944 were as far removed from Jane Austen's 'realism' as were *The Castle* and *The Trial*? At this period, I heard Churchill's war speeches live, and the resonances haunt me: 'If the British Empire and its Commonwealth last for a thousand years, men will still say, "This was their finest hour".' Well, thirty-five years later, no Empire; no one saying this at all. For me, Churchill *is* the greatest Englishman of my lifetime; but I have no way of communicating this to the students I teach with the faintest hope of being understood. As long ago as 1960, one student said to me, 'But wasn't Churchill a fascist?'

How can we cope with this century? How can a critic look at this poem, 'Nineteen Hundred and Nineteen', and call it – as I did just now – naïve? Yeats had lived in a fool's paradise, he tells us, and now sees it for what it was. Isn't this the story of most of our lives?

'Nineteen Hundred and Nineteen' refuses to remain stately and isolated in a world of 'unageing intellect'; it is as far as possible from the marvellous artifice, the self-sustaining glory, of 'Sailing to Byzantium' and similar poems still to come. It is as if Yeats opens up his own bewilderment, and Ireland's, leaving us either to identify with 'the multitude', or to back decorously away, as a first response:

> Many ingenious lovely things are gone
> That seemed sheer miracle to the multitude. . . .

Immediately, he continues with the lines

> Protected from the circle of the moon
> That pitches common things about.

Yeats's 'moon' symbolism at this period is difficult; a comparison should be made no doubt with the mysterious relationship between Sato's sword (part III in 'Meditations in Time of Civil War', and 'A dialogue of Self and Soul') and the moon. Here, the moon seems closer to the medieval symbolism of 'sublunary' – the sphere of change, as opposed to the immortal world beyond. Like Pope in *The Rape of the Lock*, Yeats draws attention to man's own wilful contribution to the curse of mortality (for example, 'What Time would spare, from Man receives its date; / And Monuments, like Men, submit to Fate'). Yeats's words 'multitude', 'common', and even perhaps 'seemed' may suggest elitist scorn, but the poet is including himself in the more relevant folly which this merely introduces:

We too had many pretty toys when young;
A law indifferent to blame or praise,
To bribe or threat; habits that made old wrong
Melt down, as it were wax in the sun's rays;
Public opinion ripening for so long
We thought it would outlive all future days.
O what fine thought we had because we thought
That the worst rogues and rascals had died out.

Jeffares's *Commentary* reminds us, at this point, of a speech made by
Yeats at the Tailteann Banquet, 2 August 1924, as recorded by
Torchiana – and these words, taken alone, would suggest the
'naïveté' I have already postulated: 'Everyone, certainly everyone
who counted, everyone who influenced events believed that the
world was growing better and better, and could not even help doing
so owing to physical science and democratic politics, and that dream
lasted for many years.' At this point, Yeats was apparently referring
to the 1880s (his own late 'teens and early twenties), but it is hard to
believe that the poet could have been indulging more than his taste
for rhetoric, in a passage so removed from reality. And noticing the
precarious history, we perhaps notice all the more the syntactical
problem which characterises a number of his poems, in this volume
particularly. In the first stanza, the word 'Protected' follows on from
'seemed', not from 'multitude', as one readily perceives when the
meaning clarifies, though anyone attempting to read the poem
aloud for the first time would almost certainly be thrown. 'There
stood' inculcates a deliberate vagueness, both about the historical
period and about the status of art. (Yeats's occasional preoccupation
with lost art – cutting across the distinction between mortal man and
'Monuments of unageing intellect' which 'Sailing to Byzantium'
partly depends upon – will not receive its major treatment until the
splendid 'Lapis Lazuli' in the final volume). The words 'And gone'
pick up the sense from 'are gone' in l. 1, but, given the intervening
complexity, again present a slight problem of syntax for the reading
voice.

In the second stanza, it is hard to say whether the problems set by
ll. 2–4 are essentially due to syntax, or imagery, or meaning, or a
fusion of the three. The word 'indifferent' is presumably a
throwback to the 1662 Prayer Book usage ('Indifferently to
administer justice' – that is, impartially), though by opting for this
archaismYeats casts some doubt on whether he *is* asserting the
assumed integrity of 'law', or whether he is activating, through the
modern meaning of 'indifferent', something of the doubt and
bitterness of Irish feeling about England. The word 'habits' is vaguer
than it might be, particularly when it is linked with the only slightly

concealed Icarus image. He is asserting the beliefs (whether we do indeed think them naïve or otherwise) which culminated in the notion that 'the worst rogues and rascals had died out'. But 'habits' is more personal, less substantial, than more robust words like 'custom' and 'ceremony' (in, say, 'A Prayer for My Daughter'), and the unusual transposition in the image may seem to link back with 'pretty toys'. If so, then 'old wrong' was thought by 'We too' to have taken an Icarus-flight (overreaching, and meeting nemesis?) but such a notion maybe declares its childishness. Does Yeats reflect that as a young man he might himself have been excusably deceived, but that the older optimists (Morris? Shaw?) ought to have seen through 'Public opinion' more readily. If so, the word 'ripening', juxtaposed with, though not perceptibly acting upon, 'wax in the sun's rays', further disorients any simple exegesis of the stanza.

The next two stanzas are more straightforward, though an anger which seems generated almost equally by the new atrocities, and by the old 'philosophy' which failed to anticipate them, keeps judgment open. The bitter last line of the fourth stanza may, when one reaches it, seem sheer self-condemnation, but could also be attached to 'the world' which has evaded 'a rule' of progress so spectacularly ('dragon-ridden', 'nightmare', 'drunken', 'murdered', 'crawl', 'scot-free', 'sweat with terror').

The final two stanzas of this opening section continue the uncertainty, particularly since sinking 'unmanned / Into the half-deceit of some intoxicant / From shallow wits' was not one of Yeats's 'habits': I am tempted to think that the 'We', which so far has seemed to include him so firmly among old illusions, declares itself a persona, behind which the poet can unobtrusively slide in or out in ways left undeclared. 'He who can read the signs' is a better place to look for him; but this leads us on to a qualification of rare pessimism (which is dated however, we should again remind ourselves, nine years earlier than 'Sailing to Byzantium'):

>   who knows no work can stand,
> Whether health, wealth or peace of mind were spent
> On master-work of intellect or hand,
> No honour leave its mighty monument. . . .

On this reading, we may take the 'he' which starts the stanza as the poet – in which event, however, the syntactically long-delayed verb, and its sequel, are scarcely less disheartening:

> Has but one comfort left: all triumph would
> But break upon his ghostly solitude.

I am by no means certain that I understand these lines. The two 'buts' (followed by another, more conventionally conjunctival, as the next stanza opens) both, in this context, are synonyms for 'merely', or 'only'. Is the 'triumph' to be taken as reading the signs, or as making the doomed art? If so, Yeats has done both now (and I think it most likely that he has art in mind, his own especially). In later poems, the assertion of his own 'masterful images' as triumph, for all the perplexities of life and transience, will loom large. Perhaps 'ghostly solitude' is the momentary state of gloom which precipitates this particular mood, and poem: though both 'ghostly' and 'solitude' can be words of hope for Yeats at other times.

The second and third lines of the last stanza contain, as I have said, a rarely beautiful phrase, which surely transcends the context that throws it up. 'Man is in love' has its own powerful comfort, as an assertion; which the classically tragic formula 'and loves what vanishes' can, in contemplative moments, enrich and enhance. The stanza immediately plunges us back, however, into political events, so that these resonances possibly move us more when memory floats them into our mind ('where did I hear that?') than they are allowed to do on the spot. As we know from external sources, Yeats was thinking of real atrocities, immediately brought home to him in Galway and Gort. Already, the contrast between these and former hopes has carried the poem; the poet must be wondering whether the terror and fear would have been possible, but for earlier rhetoric and poetry such as his own. 'None dared admit' could come very closely home to him: in which event, that closeness of creation to destruction which he has already written of, and will explore yet more deeply later (in 'Long-legged Fly', for instance), must have, here, a political and personal, as well as an aesthetic and psychological, charge:

> That country round
> None dared admit, if such a thought were his,
> Incendiary or bigot could be found
> To burn that stump on the Acropolis,
> Or break in bits the famous ivories
> Or traffic in the grasshoppers or bees.

'Romantic Ireland's dead and gone' – and in how many places, except Yeats's youthful art, was it fully alive? As I write this in 1979, the poem's power does not diminish. News that Mr Airey Neave had been blown to pieces in the Palace of Westminster precincts by Irish terrorists reached me as I was writing on 'Sailing to Byzantium'. Lord Mountbatten was blown to pieces shortly after the publisher received the typescript.

The second section I shall not linger over, since it could lead us more deeply into *A Vision* than we need go (too far away from the Swiftian 'savage indignation' which will return in the last three sections, and which is already spilling over, in Yeats's own poetry, from specific broodings on beautiful women grown shrill with polemics, old age *per se*, maybe even the notorious enigmas and 'frustrators' of Mrs Yeats's ghostly oracles, to the Irish situation itself and thoughts of apocalypse). Loie Fuller, an American, danced at the Folies Bergère in the 1890s 'in a whirl of shining draperies manipulated on sticks'. Mallarmé wrote about her, Toulouse-Lautrec painted her, Yeats would have been fascinated, no doubt, by her troupe of Japanese dancers. The 'Platonic Year' is expounded at length by Jeffares in his *Commentary*, but the main image appears to be of the Platonic dance become frenzied (as in the vision of 'future years' in 'A Prayer for My Daughter'). The symbolism makes clear that no ringing out of wild bells can really improve things (could it for Tennyson?). Old and new 'right and wrong' give place to each other in turn, as the apparently 'progressive' view of history, operative in section I, yields to Yeats's more familiar cycles and gyres:

> All men are dancers and their tread
> Goes to the barbarous clamour of a gong.

The poem's third, and pivotal, section strikes me as beautiful but elusive, even though its concluding quatrain brings it back sharply enough to present disgust. The image of the swan recurs, symbolic less of art's beauty (it now seems) than of those who have falsely trusted to such symbolism in a darkening season. The words 'I am satisfied with that' are both brooding and tentative: the reading voice can, and I think should, linger, as if on a final statement, then allow 'Satisfied if' to pick up the thoughts still to come. Swan and poet are closely identified, but through a curious paradox. The 'troubled mirror' is no doubt the poet's art reflecting back truths to the poet. The promise contained in 'An image of its state' now includes transience ('Before that brief gleam of its life be gone') but with little irony. In 'The Tower', the poet's 'pride' was one of his two legacies 'to young upstanding men'. Here, maybe, the swan's 'pride' is very similar, except that the threat of death now extends beyond personal destiny and rage gives way to stoic celebration (as in the 'swan' passage in 'The Tower' itself):

> The wings half spread for flight,
> The breast thrust out in pride
> Whether to play, or to ride
> Those winds that clamour of approaching night.

The central stanza returns to 'A man', and the image of labyrinth returns (this time presaging powerful final stanzas of the central section of 'The Tower'), associated now not with love but with 'art or politics'. The following lines are difficult, but clearly important, since they hark back to that equally difficult image in the first section ('all triumph would / But break upon his ghostly solitude'). The phrase 'Some Platonist' is intentionally careless (or so I suppose). In *A Vision*, we hear of the processes men undergo between incarnations, and the danger they run of having to relive the cycle they have just finished if they have seriously misjudged its rules. In Buddhism, the enlightened human aim is to live with such detachment from the passions that the wheel of human suffering can be finally escaped at death and Nirvana achieved – but this seems a notion alien to *A Vision*, and is encountered in Plato himself, and in most of his followers, in different terms. 'The ancient habit' appears to be the habit of selfhood. I take it that 'our works' include all works – those judged good, or that have become habitual, as well as those repented as evil – and that 'lucky death' must refer to escape from reincarnation. The syntax is once more baffling, seemingly by intention. The poet is not necessarily committed to agreeing with his 'Some Platonist', yet the word 'For', opening the last line, draws an apparent deduction from the foregoing argument which the virtual self-quotation is made to bear out.

Does this mean that 'triumph' is illusory ('For if I triumph, I must make men mad') or, at the very least, that it is won at too great a cost to be bearable ('if memory recur, the sun's / Under eclipse and the day blotted out')? Much depends upon the meaning to be attached to 'our solitude'. The word 'mar' places 'solitude' as an apparent good; earlier in the poem, the word was qualified by 'ghostly'. Whether the sombre 'All Souls' Night' (which concludes the collection *The Tower*, as it also concludes *A Vision*) helps to elucidate it, I am by no means certain.

Immediately, however, the next stanza opens with one of Yeats's most memorable swan images – another line to be lingered on when read (and another line, in my experience, which is apt to reappear in one's memory out of context, with some autonomous power): 'The swan has leaped into the desolate heaven'. 'The Wild Swans at Coole' and the last line of 'Coole Park and Ballylee 1931' are certain to haunt this – along with the 'dying swan' passage from 'The Tower', and, of course, the more brutal departure of the swan in 'Leda and the Swan'. The transposition of 'desolate' from 'swan' to 'heaven' is marvellously effective, yet too multiple in allusion to pin down. From the poet, it precipitates lines of almost suicidal anger:

That image can bring wildness, bring a rage
To end all things, to end

What my laborious life imagined, even
The half-imagined, the half-written page. . . .

These lines also escape the context, and the poem – they belong to
our whole sense of 'Yeats' – yet, as if by magic, they plunge us back
directly into the purely political anger of the poem's main theme.

Part IV is an entracte designed, I take it, to confirm the return to
the main theme and to prepare us for the poem's closing
movements. Jeffares glosses the line 'We, who seven years ago' with
the note, 'these lines measure the decline in British morality since
1914 from the sentiments then expressed and those which later
favoured the activities of the Auxiliaries and the Black and Tans'.
This is no doubt good history (if poor mathematics). Even so, it is
striking to notice how extremely insular Yeats still is, if he can
overlook events such as the Great War, or at least ignore them, in
assessing England's reaction to Ireland: moreover, I am not entirely
sure that the 'We', recalling the emphatic 'We', at the start of the
second stanza in part I, can be simplified into 'British morality'. In
fact, this isolated quatrain seems to introduce the still more bitter
indictment in part V, where the 'Come let us' has a floating, ironic
quality, inviting the reader into a trap, but without letting the poet
himself off his own hook.

This section is, I fancy, complex in some rather off-beat ways, as
well as in its obvious thrust. At first sight it might seem to contradict
the opening, perhaps referring back to those who were associated
with the cult of destructive satire directed against 'eminent
Victorians' (*fin de siècle*, Bloomsbury?), in contrast to those others who
had believed in a forward and irreversible march of enlightenment.
Or possibly Yeats sees this kind of destructive irony as one of the
fruits of the recent violence that disturbs him. The invitation to join
this dance of mockery isolates 'great', 'wise' and 'good' as a pathetic
minority, yet there is real irony left over for them, as for their
detractors, despite the turnabout at the end. The 'great' are mainly
(presumably) politicians who hoped to perpetuate themselves (as well
as artists?): their failure to see 'the levelling wind' (*does* this refer to
the egalitarian spirit chiefly?) was a real flaw. Likewise, 'the wise'
have much in common, at least in this depiction of them, with the
'Bald heads, forgetful of their sins' earlier satirised in 'The Scholars'.
Even 'the good' have ambiguous status. In Yeats, 'gay' is a good
word (it is, of course, the key word in one of his greatest late poems,
'Lapis Lazuli', where it becomes humanity's hope of salvation). Even
so, the word 'fancied' here qualifies it – either the cost was not
counted, or 'gay' was debased to frivolity: it seems that 'the good'
have been swept away by the 'Wind' as well.

The conclusion is therefore ambiguous, rather than merely a

reversal. Doubtless, the mockers – most of us – *are* our own best targets; but could even we have barred 'that foul storm out', had we tried? As we have seen, the majority slumbered, no hint of storm to rouse them; the devastating indictments at the start of 'The Second Coming' were not foreseen.

In the final section we encounter Yeats at his most capricious, stirring syntax and imagery to mime the 'labyrinth' of the unleashed wind. Residual grace dissolves, in 'Violence . . . violence': 'All break and vanish, and evil gathers head'. 'Thunder of feet, tumult of images' throws men of action and poets alike, into tumult: 'purpose' passes out of the sphere of reason and control. The lines spanning 'crazy', 'amorous', 'angry', 'blind' are of bacchic intensity, though the intrusion of 'dare' suggests that the poet keeps some other perspective (his own, as father in 'A Prayer for My Daughter'?) intact. The imagery of the ending recalls, in words like 'lurches', the beast from 'The Second Coming' but Yeats delves for more exotic and unfamiliar images from the Irish past. Jeffares has reminded us that, even in early days, Yeats had written that 'Sidhe is the Gaelic for wind and that the Sidhe had much to do with the wind'. He had also written 'They journey in whirling winds, the winds that were called the dance of the daughters of Herodias in the Middle Ages, Herodias doubtless taking the place of some old goddess.' The 'love-lorn Lady Kyteler' is Dame Alice Kyteler, 'a member of a good Anglo-Norman family that had settled in the city of Kilkenny for many years', according to St John D. Seymour in *Irish Witchcraft and Demonology*, (1913). Living in the early fourteenth century, she allegedly had four highly reputable husbands, the first three of whom she is suspected of murdering, before a visiting bishop found, by means of the Inquisition, that she was in fact the head of a 'band of heretical sorcerers'. Further, it seems that 'That insolent fiend Robert Artisson' was Lady Kyteler's incubus, who had carnal relations with her under various forms, including that of a cat, a hairy black dog, and 'a negro . . . accompanied by two others who were larger and taller than he, and of whom one carried an iron rod'. In a note in *The Dial* in September 1921, Yeats himself asserted that the 'country people see at times certain apparitions whom they name now "fallen angels" ' and, in identifying Robert Artisson as one of these, he characteristically, if somewhat wildly, adds, 'Are not those who travel in the whirling dust also in the Platonic Year?' The poem's final line stirs in the peacock – always a sign that Yeats's rhetoric is at its most baffling – while the phrase 'red combs of her cocks' seems to me to clinch the spate of phallic, if obscure, allusions that have been building up.

Presumably Yeats chose to end with references that would amaze most readers, either to satisfy some obscure violence in himself, or to reinforce the symbolism of unleashed chaos. It strikes me as an instance of the technique to which he was later to give words, in a yet more baffling poem, 'Byzantium':

> Those images that yet
> Fresh images beget. . . .

This formula is a clue to many of the greatest, as well as to some of the most difficult (to some minds, infuriating) moments in Yeats's art; and cuts across his occasional merging of frames of reference ('Symbol', 'emblem', 'shade' and so forth), which may also confuse.

'Meditations in Time of Civil War'

With this poem, I had a stroke of luck. When teaching a graduate class in the University of Connecticut, 1976, Michael North was in the seminar, and presented an account of this poem that was published in *Critical Quarterly* in spring 1977. This opened my eyes to much that had puzzled me, and is among the best critical commentaries I have seen. My own comments, attuned to this book, naturally differ, though they owe a considerable amount to his work. I propose to quote a few general points which he made about symbolism and syntax, since they may be found suggestive of wider trains of thought:

> W. B. Yeats made his early poetry deliberately vague. He seems to have believed in and abided by a principle derived by Arthur Symons from the poetry of Mallarmé: 'To name is to destroy, to suggest is to create.' Any power the early poems have comes from their suggestiveness, from the intimation that they speak of matters too hallowed and remote to be fully identified. But this kind of power did not always satisfy Yeats, who came to believe that his early poetry had been ruined by 'an element of sentimentality through my refusal to permit it any share of an intellect I considered impure.

I suppose I would quibble with 'ruined' (though Yeats's early poetry would not, in my view have earned for him his major stature, I would rather have it than most other poetry from the period, if I had to choose). Yeats's recorded mistrust of his 'intellect' is interesting, but has as usual to be taken with a pinch of salt, as Michael North also says:

> An understanding of this deliberate vagueness is important,

though, because it is linked to certain ideas that Yeats never abandoned. When Yeats first read Villiers' *Axel*, he was convinced that it was a profound book because it was so obscure. This identification of obscurity and profundity may have come from Yeats's belief in the occult, from the kind of belief that bring Symons to write, 'The oracles have always had the wisdom to hide their secrets in the obscurity of many meanings, or of what has seemed meaningless. . . .' A poet who attempts to achieve this kind of profundity will fit Symons' definition of 'a self-respecting man of letters', one who can say 'even after the writing of many books: I have kept my secret, I have not betrayed myself to the multitude'.

As Michael North goes on to say, Yeats was sufficiently impressed by this cult of the obscure to maintain at times that literature is distinguished from more 'ordinary' discourse by its inexplicitness. In 'The Moods' (1895), in a sentence indebted to Mallarmé, he had written, 'Literature differs from explanatory and scientific writing in being wrought about in a mood, or a community of moods, as the body is wrought about an invisible soul; and if it uses argument, theory, erudition, observation, and seems to grow hot in assertion or denial, it does so merely to make us partakers at the banquet of the moods.'

These reminders of one aspect of Yeats's early thinking are undoubtedly pertinent, as we remember not only the conclusion of 'Nineteen Hundred and Nineteen' and the poem now concerning us but also 'Among School Children', 'Byzantium' and one or two of the most difficult of all his poems, now looming up. Nevertheless, it is clear that, however influenced he was by occultism, Yeats's instincts were always for clarity – even if for the kind of clarity which rejoices in exaggerations, riddles, ambivalences, Irish blarney as their mode. His early poetry is more wedded to a 'banquet of moods', albeit in the realms on fancy or wish sometimes, than could be said of most Pre-Raphaelite poets in whom one can indeed feel that the sound is itself at times a spell, lulling towards sleep or hypnosis, and almost designed to deflect attention away from any plain meanings in the words and ideas. The influence of Pound and the Imagists on Yeats, when his early phase was long finished, was to accentuate, if anything, an understanding that prose sense, exact communication, heightened and hard-fought-for precision are ingredients not opposed to, but ideally acting in co-operation with, the Symbolist attempt to evoke particular moods, unique states of consciousness, complex and one-for-all intimations.

In the poems so far discussed, these qualities have been uppermost; only exceptionally, if at all, has 'difficulty' existed for its own sake. My feeling is that Yeats does now pass through a period where syntax undergoes oddities hard to account for rationally; and where certain symbols have levels that are perhaps designedly opaque. I shall bear this in mind, at least, as a possibility, but fall back on it only when otherwise at a loss. Even so, I am well aware that the fault may be in my personal reading, or in simple ignorance (which may be excused, on occasions, by the notably inaccessible references to which the poet sometimes resorts. Even so, this flaw – if flaw it is – could be called endemic in early Eliot, late Joyce, and Pound *tout à fait*. My distinct impression is that the difficulties in Yeats are almost always connected with the material he wrestles with; and that his success in capturing experiences that may be in equal measure complex, elusive, and yet personal as some forgotten childhood memory is not the least of his claims to be among the handful of outstanding poets from any century or place).

When he wrote this poem (the date appended to the whole is 1923) the Irish situation had again darkened, while his own marriage had settled down to a new routine. In a somewhat odd fashion, he combines personal reflections on the Tower with more public (though still anguished) responses to the civil war; and one of his periodic reappraisals of aristocratic tradition interweaves with both of these themes.

1. 'ANCESTRAL HOUSES'. Michael North has conjectured that the brief episode described in the fifth section may be the seed of the poem; but 'Meditations' begins with a poem seemingly complete in itself. Yeats's personal debt to Coole Park and to Lady Gregory's patronage and personal friendship, has always been apparent; we know from the two exquisite later 'Coole Park' poems that in this he had not changed. 'Homer had not sung' will send us back to a familiar later context that has already been quoted: 'But all is changed, that high horse riderless/Though once in that saddle Homer rode . . .'

This poem envisages the devastating possibility that much aristocratic tradition and patronage might be falsehood: not only concerning the present (where its relevance diminishes), but equally concerning the past itself. The immediate force appears to be that such patrons created culture from tainted motives, alien values, sweated labour – and that the values neither softened *them* nor reflected any social, religious or artistic 'truths'. We then find that the actual artists might be involved in this complex betrayal – though how far, how consciously, how devastatingly cannot be pinned down. Both image and syntax seem deliberately designed to puzzle – or, if not to puzzle, to keep open escape-routes from the decided bitterness of mood and tone.

Perhaps a tour through the poem, with the problem of reading it aloud once more as a point of focus, is the easiest approach. Let me pick out the obvious difficulties first. The opening word 'Surely' is difficult. Often an unemphatic word, it here demands emphasis – as if its dogmatic, not its tentative, aspect is to be stressed. 'Surely' – surely, beyond doubt or question: this, I think, its placing demands of us as we read it – especially since the whole stanza, unqualified, flows from the word. None the less, to read it in this fashion is not easy, especially as we become aware of the complex sentence to be navigated before the full stop. The actual statements would seem to allow a resounding 'Surely' full scope in development – the apotheosis of the tradition, all doubts laid at rest. The 'flowering lawns' speak of fullness: 'rustle' suggests ease, 'overflows' abundance; 'ambitious pains' are denied, and the 'rains' are waters of life, not destruction or death. With 'dizzy high' we appear at a peak (not 'dizzy' to falling?): certainly 'choose whatever shape it wills' has the promise of freedom, so that we scarcely notice the qualifying 'As though'. The last two lines further exalt freedoms won by wealth, leisure, power for their lucky possessors, yet 'stoop', 'mechanical', 'servile', 'beck and call' hint another tale. The apparent plenitude depends on slavery: does 'mechanical' cast some dark shadow back even on 'flowering lawns', 'planted hills' and the other beauties, with a suggestion not of paradisal freedom, but of drudgery, in gardening itself?

The second stanza sweeps the first away peremptorily: 'Mere dreams, mere dreams!' – or, if one *has* managed to give force to the reservations in the first stanza while reading, despite the initial 'Surely', it confirms any notion that 'Surely' was, in the larger strategy, neither dogmatic (though it *had* to function as such?) nor tentative, but ironic. (In fact, possibly an attempt could be made to read the first stanza with some definite inflection of irony – or some gentle questioning? – infused into the 'Surely'; but I have never managed this successfully myself). Nevertheless, the direction does not change as rapidly as this emphatic new start would suggest. The next sentence, 'Yet Homer . . .' continues to keep a reader alert for surprises. The image of water as creative energy returns, associated now not with the patronage which made art physically possible, but with some quality in life itself, released through the art. A modern reader is bound to be puzzled, on first reading, by 'The abounding glittering jet', since an image of Concorde or a jumbo-jet at take-off refuses to go away, even though this is a complication Yeats could not have guessed at. That apart, however, it is a difficult image (if it were not, the distraction of a modern irrelevance might obtrude less). One has to imagine no doubt a vast, aristocratic fountain, which has undoubtedly appeared in the first stanza, though not in words that assist the visual imagination. But we have not finished: 'though now

it seems' introduces a further reservation, which a newcomer will
have to guess at until it clarifies; and, with a puzzling turn, we are
back with the fountain as a symbol – now seen to be misleading – of
'the inherited glory of the rich'. Once again, 'As if' adds a doubly
tentative note (cf. the 'As though' in stanza i), and it appears as if
Yeats's main attitude to disillusionment is one of regret, not
satisfaction; so that the notion, if it has struck us, that the aristocratic
tradition itself – rather than its loss – is to be criticised, may appear to
crystallise as a false reading. The word 'Shadows' identifies a menace
hanging over the aristocracy (perhaps not perceived in time – or only
now materialising) but, even so, the 'empty sea-shell' which presents
itself, now, as a fitter emblem is still 'marvellous' (I take it that the
voices heard in the shell, by a child listening, retain their magic, even
if they are thought to mean nothing).

More could be said about 'the obscure dark of the rich streams',
but only, I suppose, by way of underlining ambivalence. The third
stanza may come, then, as a further surprise – particularly since its
own direction shifts and changes in so bizarre a manner. On the face
of it, we are told that the aristocrat who commissioned palaces and
gardens was 'some violent bitter man, some powerful man', and, by
implication, that the result, though caught up in 'sweetness', in no
way represents a culture symbolising the real life of such a man. In
itself, this is easy to follow: the contrast between, say, Venice and the
ruthlessness of the doges (and similar examples from most nations
and centuries) must have often teased minds bent on making 'the
Mind of Europe' convincing – whether as reality or myth. But notice
that, when the concept 'Bitter and violent men' reappears, now in
the plural, in l. 3, it *could* apply as much to the artists as to their
patrons, in terms of strict syntax. Is this a momentary clumsiness
(Homer nodding for once) or is it intended? Later, Yeats was
certainly to explore the ineradicable mix of creation and destruction
in art, and in artists themselves. Even so, the fourth line turns in
another direction, suggesting *some* universal longing for 'sweetness'
(presumably not only in the artist but also in the patron – in all of us?
– however contradictory this sounds). Lines 4–5, taken together, are,
however, complementary. Presumably 'gentleness' can be taken as
almost a synonym for 'sweetness'. If so, the assertion that we all long
for a beauty we never achieve – which could, in a Christian poet,
point to original sin – presumably points, here, to something a little
harder to pin down. The 'sweetness' is commissioned; it appears in
works of art; it expresses human longing (and, therefore, it must
exist at least in the artists who produce it – with whatever
modification from impulses of an opposing kind). To this degree it is
real, a fact of history: yet the general effect is to cast some bitter
doubt, of a floating kind, on its 'truth'. We all long for it; one

tradition produces it: but 'violent' and 'bitter' preside, in the verbal force. All the more startling that the final three lines turn away to yet another theme: the possibility of the aristocratic tradition being true in its origins, but deteriorating through genetic degradation later. As we know from *Purgatory*, Yeats could be bitter about high-born or talented people making ill marriages. (The connection with Maud Gonne and MacBride has already been mentioned; later, Yeats's fascist sympathies hint that the bitterness remained unhealed. Even up to 'Under Ben Bulben', curses are reserved for Irishmen, and for his own family, if they breed beneath them. That Crazy Jane would have been ill-received by Yeats as a daughter-in-law – however potent her symbolism – is a case not requiring much proof.) Even so, the degenerated (putative) heir is described as a 'mouse' ('Wee, sleekit, cowrin', tim'rous beastie'); so, doubling back, one assumes that the 'Bitter and violent men' are supposed better than that.

Maybe this is making the going heavy; but 'Ancestral Houses' is too central, and too puzzling, to ignore. The final two stanzas, hinging on the two 'O what if' phrases in stanza iv, and the further two 'What if' phrases in stanza v, are again very hard to read smoothly. Maybe once more this is merely a challenge: Pope, after all, offers a difficult passage of a not dissimilar kind in one of his finest poems ('Elegy to the Memory of an Unfortunate Lady', ll. 55–68), and this can be read delicately and effectively, though extraordinary voice control is needed for full success.

In this poem, I am more dubious about the possibility of a successful reading. Many of the images are beautiful, though also odd: why, I wonder, is the naked statue of Juno said to be displayed 'Before the indifferent garden deities'? Jeffares identifies the 'peacocks' as coming from Yeats's memories of Lady Ottoline Morrell's house; if so, maybe this explains the 'garden deities' as well? But there is no clue to such private memories in the poetry, and the implied clash between two different orders of pagan deities, all presumably in stone, is scarcely clear in itself. One cannot even suggest that it means that the gardens are now deserted by humans, since the unexpected drift into allegory – 'slippered Contemplation', 'Childhood' – precludes this. The last lines of the stanzas undoubtedly clinch the prevailing ambivalence; 'But take our greatness with our violence' and 'But take our greatness with our bitterness'. The mingling of opposites brings us to familiar ground (both in Yeats, and in normal human experience), but there is still some uncertainty of effect. Is the poem saying – as it appears to be – that the 'haughtier age' which produced this magnificence was better than our own age? This would accord with 'The Second Coming', and with one possible interpretation of T. S. Eliot's contrasts between present and past in *The Waste Land*; but it would appear to conflict with the start, if not the conclusion, of the third stanza, and also to leave 'the greatest of mankind' floating very uneasily. As we know, 'famous portraits', and 'the greatest of mankind' still existed for Yeats in Coole Park, if merely as a remnant (the last romantics). I think I am forced to conclude that maybe there is a muddle here, and, that for all its touches of excellence, 'Ancestral Houses' is less good than any poem we have yet considered. Curiously, the form looks as well-wrought as Yeats ever does; the statements are pregnant with his familiar and important themes, taken seriously. But he appears not to have resolved the complex material with his usual sureness. The effect is not as complete, in itself, as Yeats's artefacts normally are. If so, however, I would be reluctant to accept that Yeats was courting deliberate obscurity for the reasons Michael North gives: I suspect that he was attempting to introduce the longer poem, of which this is the opening; and that he is not fully successful.

II. 'MY HOUSE'. This is surely much stronger – a new start, rooted in himself. In essence, Yeats is describing Thoor Ballylee, and his own poetic mission. The reference to Milton in the second stanza is more fully explained by reference to 'The Phases of the Moon', where Yeats's fictional Michael Robartes and his friend are depicted as looking up at Yeats's window, from outside, and likening it to Samuel Palmer's illustration for an 1889 edition of Milton's shorter poems, called 'The Lonely Tower'. Like Milton, Yeats is a poet whose life is dedicated to art, though shot through with political and revolutionary episodes; characteristically perhaps, it is Milton's Platonism that he identifies with more readily than the Christianity. On the other hand, the vision that Milton is said to be 'shadowing forth' sounds perceptibly more like Yeats than it does Milton, and the general impression is chimerical: the end of the stanza strikes me as 'The Scholar Gipsy' arrived at by way of 'The Tower'. The granite-like first stanza foreshadows the style Yeats will increasingly favour – pared down, elemental and suggestive of autumn. Interestingly, 'An acre of stony ground' moves our mind forward to Yeats's final home (cf. 'An Acre of Grass'), while 'the symbolic rose' appears to evoke the past.

    Maybe the third stanza is the crucial one. It links most obviously with 'Ancestral Houses', though the themes are personalised and simplified, as befits Yeats himself. Thoor Ballylee is not in the high aristocratic tradition, but one of its offshoots – knights, men-at-arms, war: suggestions of chosen loneliness to offset action (note the apparently simple transition from 'this tumultous spot' to 'Forgetting and forgot', reinforced by rhyme). The vision of his own heirs and their inheritance is bleak: no longer ancient Ireland renewed, or revolutionary Ireland liberated, but solitude, exaltation of 'a lonely mind' ('Sailing to Byzantium' maybe lurking), and the final choice of 'emblems' rather than 'symbols' to befit 'adversity'. Part v has still to come, but already one senses Yeats's desire to be detached as well as implicated in tradition and, more notably, in the eruption of violence in place of vision and peace.

III. 'MY TABLE'. Here, the table is occasion, rather than subject. 'Sato's gift' dominates (it is an important image in 'A Dialogue of Self and Soul' and 'Symbols' also) though it, in turn, mingles with images from *A Vision*, and once more picks up themes from 'Ancestral Houses'. As Jeffares's *Commentary* tells us, Yeats wrote to Edmund Dulac on 22 March 1920,

> A rather wonderful thing happened the day before yesterday. A very distinguished looking Japanese came to see us. He had read my poetry when in Japan and had now just heard me lecture. He had something in his hand wrapped in embroidered silk. He said it was a present for me. He untied the silk cord that bound it and brought out a sword which had been for 500 years in his family. It had been made 550 years ago and he showed me the maker's name upon the hilt. . . .

Yeats added that he was embarrassed to receive so handsome a gift, even though Sato (the name of the donor) said he had 'many swords': he felt it should remain in the original family, and wrote to Sato saying that, if he married, he must vow to let Yeats hear of the birth of his first child, so that the gift could be willed back to its ancestral home.

In this poem, the sword is already assimilated to Yeats's home, and to his personal symbols – 'a changeless sword' makes it Byzantine, yet fuses this particular 'monument of unageing intellect' with the transient and destructive purpose of its making. At first, Yeats's response is almost languid: he puts it, 'By pen and paper', that 'it may moralise / My days out of their aimlessness'. The word 'moralise' seems weaker than emblem or symbol, and 'aimlessness', unless pure throwaway, indicates that the poet will not be engaged at any deep level. The ensuing description is also low key, if attentive (and, as Jeffares has reminded us, not good mathematics, since, if the sword were really made 550 years before 1920, Chaucer would have been about twenty-seven at the time).

It is now, however, that Yeats's imagination takes fire, and we plunge into yet another of these 'Meditations' characterised by mingled precision and vagueness:

Curved like new moon, moon-luminous,
It lay five hundred years.
Yet if no change appears,
No moon; only an aching heart
Conceives a changeless work of art.

These lines are memorable (unforgettable, I find) though elusive. One assumes the sword is curved, though surely not crescent. 'Moon-luminous' suggests that, under the embroidered wrapping (though also protected by this *from* light) it has a quality which catches light (even generates light: maybe, the spark of creative energy locked in an artefact). We return to 'Sailing to Byzantium' ground, and to the paradox that, though art may be, or appear, 'changeless', it comes from 'an aching heart' ('whatever is begotten, born, and dies'). Also, the moon is supremely changing – so that its association with 'art' inevitably brings waxing and waning to mind, with 'unchanging' as the hypnotised illusion of, maybe, one serene night.

The lines scarcely explain themselves, though the conclusions of 'Among School Children' and, even more, 'The Cat and the Moon' come to mind. The 'dance' evades these structures (as it evades all others). Minnaloushe and moon move in secret harmony, intensely living, cat's eyes enacting, nightly and constantly, the monthly rhythms of his 'nearest kin'. There may be a lurking thought that the sword, in contrast, arrests 'moon' by its very perfection, making 'change' impossible: and, since, unlike Minnaloushe, it exists in arrest, not motion, this could be oppressive (in *A Vision* the moon presides over the perfection of man's disincarnate phase, at furthest remove from the sun; but this is a point of stasis in the real, complex dance).

Now, Yeats turns back to the ancestral theme, foisting off on 'Our learned men' (whom he will approve or disapprove of as he chooses) the theory of proper inheritance. In the first meditation, enough ambiguities exist to confound the notion. Here, though the idea that families may regard 'marvellous accomplishment, / In painting or in pottery' as personal possessions is neither criticised nor affirmed (Yeats's exacted 'vow' from Sato, recorded in his letter, could have been mere politeness, and most probably was), the word 'seemed', attached to 'unchanging like the sword' points, once more, to illusion.

The poem now becomes more openly ambiguous. With a further shift, we are presented with apparent clarity of statement:

Soul's beauty being most adored,
Men and their business took
The soul's unchanging look. . . .

This could be the Byzantine ideal again, as expressed in passages quoted from *A Vision* – but this context alone, all others apart, has set it in dialectic with change. Yet the poet pins the idea here on some unspecified

> most rich inheritor,
> Knowing that none could pass Heaven's door
> That loved inferior art. . . .

(a dubious statement at best). Now, instead of 'Some violent bitter man, some powerful man' – or even such a person's putative mouse-like descendant – we have a shadowier concept: aristocratic, since 'a country's talk / For silken clothes and stately walk' attend him; yet living artist, since he has 'aching heart' and 'waking wits': phrases that might mean anything. Characteristically, Yeats rounds off the poem with an image colourful, melodramatic and baffling: 'it seemed / Juno's peacock screamed'. Michael North conjectures that this image intentionally shocks every reader, and relates it to one of Yeats's conversational methods. Citing Richard Ellmann as authority, he quotes from him, 'Frank O'Connor has described how, in the midst of an argument with George Russell in later life, Yeats would suddenly pull an image from his private phantasmagoria such as, "But that was before the peacock screamed", and puzzle and overbear his opponent.' We can, if we wish, feel referred back to the fourth stanza of 'Ancestral Houses', the calm garden where 'the peacock strays / With delicate feet' near Juno's statue, and assume that this peace is broken (naturally?). Jeffares does his best in the *Commentary*, citing yet another passage from *A Vision* for possible illumination:

> A civilisation is a struggle to keep self-control, and in this it is like some great tragic person, some Niobe who must display an almost superhuman will or the cry will not touch our sympathy. The loss of control over thought comes towards the end; first a sinking in upon the moral being, then the last surrender, the irrational cry, revelation – the scream of Juno's peacock.

It would be possible to link this both with 'The Second Coming' (and some general sense of cultural ending) and also with the poem's other main theme, announced in its title. Even so, my main impression is that the sword has been explored (as the honey-bees are later) as a tentative symbol, but found useful only as one piece in the larger mosaic.

IV. 'MY DESCENDANTS'. This is the strongest, most accessible and most personal section, centrally placed and homing in on himself. Yet it has its problems. At face value, Yeats is now the originator, and fears degeneration through his children: the second stanza comes near to a parental curse (kept provisional, by the further 'And what if' which controls). An arrogant notion, even for Yeats? Yet notice that his own 'vigorous mind' has been inherited 'From my old fathers'; and, though he hopes to pass it on through 'a woman and a man' (surely his daughter and son?), the qualifying 'I must nourish dreams' could reach many ways. If 'dreams' is a synonym or near-synonym for creation, or vision (as it sometimes is), then the responsibility rests squarely on him. But the next images evoke transience, and surely oddly: a very common image of loss ('torn petals', natural ravages) cannot be detached from riddles of parts I–III. Is the poet indeed saying that there is now to be a special decline, fated by gyres; or that 'common greenness' is almost bound to be sequel to his own special gifts? To put it like this is to risk the brutal; yet one knows that all such thoughts were haunting Yeats at this time almost as his personal 'fatal Cleopatra'. The second stanza, all tentativeness notwithstanding, has an energy verging on prevision, or despair. The phrase 'natural declension of the soul' would be positively ruthless, if it referred to 'descendants' only, and not at all to self. Lines 3–4 revert to now familiar anxieties, which may be alternative hazards to 1t2, or may be suggested modes of its fated fulfilment.

This section in no way directly connects with 'Ancestral Houses', where ambiguities in aristocracy, and art, are acknowledged. Maybe 'the laborious stair' (the famous winding-stair of multi-reference) functions here as felt tiredness in himself? Labour of art; labour of rejected love, late marriage; labour foreseen in old age; labour of ideals betrayed. The vision of the Tower returned to ruin culminates in 'desolation' (can memories of that marvellous line 'The swan has leaped into the desolate heaven' be exorcised here?): yet, in the final stanza, triumph is reasserted. Under the auspice of the Primum Mobile, the poet counts his blessings and ends with an assertion designed to defy much that the poem has been hinting, or building up:

And know whatever flourish and decline
These stones remain their monument and mine.

v. 'THE ROAD AT MY DOOR'. This down-to-earth section has been conjectured as the poem's real starting-point: one vivid episode, in itself a reminder of the now daily war and bloodshed come, literally, home. The bitterness in 'cracking jokes', 'finest play' is as new to Yeats, seemingly, as it is unwelcome. Yet the British had already experienced far grimmer realities (jokes in the trenches, women with white feathers, a generation ground into the mud for nothing); for once, sympathy may fail at 'I complain', as if Yeats is scarcely more serious about war than Harold Skimpole was about money. In the final stanza, why 'envy'? Though the object of 'envy' isn't clear, we might suspect some technique of evasion: is 'guilt' the word really meant? The poet turns back to his chamber, 'caught / In the cold snows of a dream'; and, if this were a piece of music to be conducted, we should surely pass straight into part VI without a break – since it follows that line as if in extended comment, and silences any momentary doubt about Yeats's seriousness and mood.

VI. 'THE STARE'S NEST BY MY WINDOW'. The quotations from Yeats given in Jeffares's *Commentary* are helpful. He records the experience of being caught in the middle of civil war, without news or reliable papers, merely with the occasional explosion, or sight of a mansion burning, or passing coffins, to bring home the realities. The comment 'Men must have lived so through many centuries' is made almost in passing. He records this as a mood poem, starting with the spectacle of a stare (the West of Ireland name for a starling) living in a nest built in a hole near his window, and including 'a strange thing' that happened: 'I began to smell honey in places where honey could not be, at the end of a stone passage or at some windy turn of the road, and it came always with certain thoughts. When I got back to Dublin I was with angry people who argued over everything or were eager to know the exact facts: in the midst of the mood that makes realistic drama.'

This material is subtly rearranged, as if the honey-bees existed and had definite meaning and, indeed, were being invoked, to bring sweetness to the horror of war. For once, Yeats confesses his loss of direction and perspective quite vulnerably: the powerful image in ll. 1–2 of the second stanza is archetypal, recalling maybe an image independently spun by Eliot, at about this time, in *The Waste Land*:

> I have heard the key
> Turn in the door once and turn once only
> We think of the key, each in his prison
> Thinking of the key, each confirms a prison
> Only at nightfall, aethereal rumours
> Revive for a moment a broken Coriolanus

(in Eliot, it will be remembered, this is attached to 'Dayadhvam' – 'Sympathise' – in the Buddhist or, maybe more exactly, Hindu section of 'What the Thunder Said'). The concluding stanza reverts to the insight that was new in 'Nineteen Hundred and Nineteen' and now seems familiar – almost frightening in bitterness:

> We had fed the heart on fantasies,
> The heart's grown brutal from the fare;
> More substance in our enmities
> Than in our love. . . .

No doubt, because of the personal force and the concreteness, this remains more powerful for me even than the famous generalities of 'The Second Coming'. It has sent me back at times to *The Celtic Twilight*, to much early poetry not discussed in this volume; and to a sense of the shock for a man so rooted in Ireland, in beauty, in the desire to heal and build, that these words must have been. When looking later at the Crazy Jane poems (and those roughly belonging with them), as well as at the final flowering of major poems in *Last Poems*, we should not forget the psychic turning-point *here*. 'O honey-bees' ('I began to smell honey in places where honey could not be . . .'): well, Yeats is still the magician, the conjurer, the prophet of vision. But, as old age saps strength, the challenge deepens, the invocation grows more urgent and difficult: 'Come build in the empty house of the stare.'

VII. 'I SEE PHANTOMS OF HATRED AND OF THE HEART'S FULLNESS AND OF THE COMING EMPTINESS'. An imposing last title; and, to revert to my analogy, if this were music, I should again join the movements, running the last three together as a complex finale, despite all changes of mood.

Once more, we find Yeats on the Tower roof in a stormy season. The effect is hallucinated: mist 'like blown snow', 'sweeping over all' – and the moon itself unfamiliar. At last, the strands of this strange poem start to come together, or at least to justify their conjunction, as the theme of 'My Table' becomes brilliantly transposed:

> Valley, river, and elms, under the light of a moon
> That seems unlike itself, that seems unchangeable,
> A glittering sword out of the east.

East and West, art and life, time and eternity, beauty and murder meet, in this new perception of Sato's gift:

> Frenzies bewilder, reveries perturb the mind;
> Monstrous familiar images swim to the mind's eye.

Back to Ireland in the second stanza, and a mingling of past and present that again may remind us of *The Waste Land*. Jacques de

Molay was arrested in 1307, burned for witchcraft in March 1314. Yeats, in his note on the General Title of the poem, says,

> In the second stanza of the seventh poem occur the words 'Vengeance on the murderers of Jacques Molay'. A cry for vengeance because of the murder of the Grand Master of the Templars seems to me fit symbol for those who labour from hatred, and so for sterility in various kinds. It is said to have been incorporated in the ritual of certain Masonic societies of the eighteenth century, and to have fed class-hatred.

Here, the poet shows himself almost caught in the general infection of hatred, almost, his own 'wits astray', succumbing to madness, 'senseless tumult', 'the embrace of nothing'.

As if in extreme contrast, the opening two lines of the next stanza describe, according to T. R. Henn, Gustave Moreau's painting *Ladies and Unicorns*, which Yeats knew from illustrations, and possessed (it seems) in 1936. A reader will undoubtedly recall the 'lords and ladies of Byzantium' chosen by Yeats as audience in his putative, non-natural incarnation as golden artefact. The final two lines of the stanza may carry our minds back, also, to the penultimate stanza of 'A Prayer for My Daughter'. In the third stanza, the words 'rage' and 'lean' infuse intimations of life and so of change and destruction, into this image of beauty; as a prelude to the stark return, again, to present realities:

> Give place to an indifferent multitude, give place
> To brazen hawks.

On the surface, we seem to have a contrast between the beauty of art or fantasy, and the reality of war: yet things are far less simple than this. 'Ancestral Houses' has destroyed such an antithesis, as the poem's introduction: the possibility of some escapism existing in the very idea of Byzantium is never absent in Yeats. No doubt a 'golden bird' and 'brazen hawks' are different, yet 'brazen' is surely meant to have literal, as well as metaphorical, connotations. The hawks could still be artefacts (if in a cheaper metal than gold), but they give no comfort to Byzantine fancies, whichever view we take. In the *Commentary* Jeffares, following Yeats's note, and assuming the superiority of the intuitive, remote from present reality as it has now become, accepts the contrast between intuition (symbolised by the ladies and unicorns) and 'logic' (symbolised by the 'brazen hawks'). But Yeats's actual note (again on the General Title of the poem) is itself a little ambiguous; he merely speculates on where his image originated and what it might mean: 'I suppose that I must have put hawks into the fourth stanza because I have a ring with a hawk and a butterfly upon it, to symbolise the straight road of logic, and so of mechanism, and the crooked road of intuition: "For wisdom is a butterfly, and not a gloomy bird of prey".'

The final lines of stanza iv seem to support the obvious meaning, with 'grip of claw and the eye's complacency' both making the hawk symbol of a 'preying multitude', and the moon's extinction. This leads to the heavy-hearted and unexpected conclusion. The poet appears to be doubting his art, as a mere minority interest, separating him from others; or maybe he wonders if he could have made it more accessible, more effective against the chaos to come? The lines

> had such a proof drawn forth
> A company of friends, a conscience set at ease,
> It had but made us pine the more

are doubly difficult, since the 'company of friends' was indeed assembled (and often celebrated, in other poems), while 'a conscience set at ease' is something no poet (including *Il Penseroso*'s Platonist) could readily expect. He finishes with what must be a reference to *A Vision*, and the thread of occult interest that has run through his life, all other changes apart, from youth to age. Yet the word 'Suffice' seems deliberately weak, both in its placing and in its force. It is a word with some ambiguity built into its very structure: the meaning is 'sufficient', yet the suggestion seems closer to 'as much as I could expect' (some hint of the stoic, or resigned, I think always implied). This would reinforce the negative charge of 'abstract' and 'half-read' leading up to it, leaving 'daemonic images' curiously isolated and unattached. The 'images for poetry' brought by Mrs Yeats's visitants were ever welcome yet 'daemonic' and 'demonic' come perilously close, in the context here.

'Meditations in Time of Civil War' is a curious poem, even by Yeats's standards, particularly in the shifting and unresolved role of Sato's sword, the moon and the honey-bees. At one level Yeats is celebrating Thoor Ballylee (the 'My' in the titles of parts ii–vi is important); he is also acknowledging the bloodshed, the un-fulfilments, the doubts brought finally home. The allied ambiguities of the aristocratic tradition, and of the status of art – both weaving in and out, half personalised and half abstract, and in no sense fully consistent – suggest a stream of consciousness striving for the clarity of form, but against monumental odds. My own feeling (a tentative one) is that the syntactical difficulties, though inseparable from the poem, are sometimes out of control; that the apparent assurance of statement is, more than usually, divorced from shifting images too complex for full artistic control. Just possibly, 'Among School Children' invites the same comment, though its scope is briefer, and benefit of all the doubts can more readily be given. 'Meditations in Time of Civil War' is clearly a major statement from Yeats's middle period. Whether it is among his greatest successes is a question I leave open. I am certain that it belongs among poems near the heart of his life and work.

The first four poems in *The Tower* are closely linked and together make a unity of kinds. Yeats has no single poem of the length of *The Waste Land* for critics to work on, yet, if he had chosen to join these four, maybe thematic links would have been more fully explored. It is interesting that each is dated and that they are presented in reverse chronological order. Though the themes criss-cross, I do not doubt that Yeats was right to publish them separately and not to risk dubious juxtapositions.

The four taken together could be seen, however, as a very substantial achievement, and as the watershed between 'early' and 'late'. This is not to deny that their dialectic with many other poems – certainly, with most noted in this chapter – is equally important, and that at times one is tempted to think of Yeats's entire work as being interdependent and complexly linked.

'Two Songs from a Play'

The play was *Resurrection*, a play about Christ's first risen appearance; a view emerges that Christianity terminated a 2000-year cycle of history and introduced a fresh cycle of violence.

On the face of it, this might sound either a view in antithesis to 'The Second Coming', or some confirmation of the interpretation that, during the Christian years, the sphinx's nightmares were both mirroring the dark side of life, and preparing for a further apotheosis of bloodshed.

Jeffares's notes in the *Commentary* should be read, since, as usual, he provides copious and useful references from *A Vision* and from Yeats's other prose. But I admit to finding my own perplexities about Yeats's mathematics – which any reading of *A Vision* can be guaranteed to exacerbate – not really answered. Whether Bethlehem was at the beginning or in the middle of a cycle, and whether cycles last 2000 years or 36,000 years (allowing for 360 incarnations of 100 years each, including, presumably, the shiftings, unwindings, new attempts at incarnations that have gone wrong, and so forth), are puzzles scarcely easier to unravel, from Yeats's remarkable statements, than the still more important problem of what Yeats 'meant' (understood?) by Christ.

The main thrust of this poem appears to stress unity, not disunity, between pagan and Christian notions of resurrection. As we know from *The Bacchae* of Euripides, Bacchus was ready to go to all lengths to prove his divinity, against impious attempts by prudes to deny it. Yeats was aware of Frazer's exposition, in *The Golden Bough*, of the further myth which told that, when Dionysus had been torn to pieces by the Titans, Athene herself, in a trance, snatched the heart from the body, brought it to Zeus, who then swallowed the heart, destroyed the Titans, and begot Dionysus again, upon a second mortal mother, Semele. It seems likely, therefore, that the 'staring virgin' is Athene, but that the Virgin Mary, who is more likely first to present herself, is deliberately fused. The lines

Of Magnus Annus at the spring,
As though God's death were but a play

were originally tacked on, as a second short part, to what is now the second part of 'Fragments' (the poem following) – an 'unexpected' poem, resolving (Yeats is on record as saying) several years of speculation 'that a man always tried to become his opposite, to become what he would abhor if he did not desire it' (this idea had also, we infer, led him astray).

The second stanza takes a hint from Virgil's *Eclogue* iv, ll. 31–6, which hints at some future, exact repetition of the Trojan theme, and from William Morris's *Life and Death of Jason*, book iv, where it is revealed that the prow of the ship was itself prophetic, though this was a secret known only to its builder and to Jason.

In these deep waters, one recognises that death and resurrection is the linking theme – or, if not exactly that, cyclical repetitions, in which great destined events may in time come round again, the same in pattern, though maybe different in portent and consequence. This first half (or song) ends with Athene transformed into the Virgin, Dionysus into Christ. I am forced to agree with Jeffares that Yeats clearly intends us to take Gibbon's view, which was that Christianity came into the Roman Empire as an essentially irrational force, and destroyed it. 'The fabulous darkness' is taken from a description of Christianity left by Proclus, a fourth-century Neo-Platonist, who also saw Christianity as a demonic upsurge of darkness and violence, destroying 'every beautiful thing'.

The second song carries on this thought and, of the two, sticks most vividly in the mind. Here we have no 'pale Galilean' conquering energy with lethargy (the Swinburnian version): rather, a Christ whose 'turbulence' is linked with the extended repetition of a key phrase ('brought / A fabulous, formless darkness in'). The stanza perhaps leaves it open, however, for Christ to symbolise some 'pity' (albeit ineffectually) for 'man's darkening thought'; and for 'Odour of blood when Christ was slain' to move the violence from Christ himself to his destroyers. I suspect, however, that we are intended to see Christ's resurrection as parallel to the rebirth of Dionysus, and the lines

> Made all Platonic tolerance vain
> And vain all Doric discipline

an assertion that pagan rationality was unable to resist the more normal reign of anarchy and irrationality, equally incarnate in Dionysus and Christ.

The final stanza is maybe our first intimation of a thought which will later find its full and complex expression in 'Lapis Lazuli':

> All things fall and are built again,
> And those that build them again are gay.

Here, the full exploration of art's 'gaiety' is still to come, and the emphasis is thrown on the inexorable rule that men's desires and creations exhaust themselves in the moment of completion. Emblems of love, art and war are united (as they will be later in 'Long-legged Fly') and, though it is not declared, the underlying image is phallic, uniting spiritual and physical in thoughts of waning, as well as self-consumed, energy:

> Love's pleasure drives his love away,
> The painter's brush consumes his dreams. . . .

The final two lines undoubtedly take colour from 'Exhaust his glory and his might', although the flash of power in 'Whatever flames upon the night' counters the gravitation towards final depression.

Yeats speaks often of the heart, in varied aspects, but 'resinous' is one of his oddest and most teasing adjectives. The dictionary that comes to hand gives two definitions of 'resin': 'An amorphous substance that exudes from plants, supposed to be the product of oxidation of volatile oils secreted by the plant. Electrically, it is a non-conducting substance, and in the form of amber led to the discovery of electricity.' The word 'resinous' is then defined as 'of the nature of resins', or 'obtained from resin, as resinous electricity'. Possibly the word was chosen for its double reference: to natural growth (and decline), and to electricity (picking up 'flames'). The more general meaning may be that, in the cycles of reincarnation, energy and creation come from man's 'heart' alone, as the temporary seat of dionysiac powers. But in 'Sailing to Byzantium' the powerful plea

'Consume my heart away' suggested different reflections, and one would like to know how the 'Babylonian starlight' in the second song relates to the 'star-lit golden bough' in 'Byzantium'.

As a whole, the poem throws up memorable and even simple ideas and statements, and the measured tread of syntax suggests logical coherence. But both tend to be illusory when some unity is sought, either in mood or meaning. Maybe this is an example of Yeats using his rhetorical powers, magnificently but self-indulgently, in that the discipline which makes his finest poems (among which those we are examining could be included) is deliberately absent. Even so, 'Two Songs from a Play' sticks in the mind, and more than usually interconnects with other, major poems. Our next port of call is an obvious instance.

'Leda and the Swan'

As various critics have noticed, this is a counterpart to the foregoing poem, the rape of a mortal by a divinity. Though it apparently originated in the request for a political poem for the *Irish Statesman*, it mutated by way of a typically Yeatsian reflection that 'the individualist, demagogic movement, founded by Hobbes and populised by the Encyclopaedists and the French Revolution' had exhausted 'the soil', leaving nothing 'now possible but some movement or birth from above, preceded by some violent annunciation'. In the outcome, 'as I wrote', Yeats records, 'bird and lady took such possession of the scene that all politics went out of it'. The editor of the *Irish Statesman* apparently decided that 'his conservative readers would misunderstand the poem', so, though written on 18 September 1923, it appeared first in *The Dial*, in June 1924.

'A sudden blow': from the opening, it is a dramatic, physical poem, much tauter in construction than 'Two Songs from a Play'. Though various images have been traced to Gogarty and to Spenser, this is very much a poem of the Yeats canon. Given the outcome, in the myth of Helen and the slaying of Agamemnon, it could be regarded as the simple antithesis of one aspect of 'Sailing to Byzantium'. Instead of 'intellect' gravitating away from 'youth', 'heart', 'nature' towards artefact, we have violence erupting into life, and producing art. If so, the word 'caught' in l. 3 could once more be suspected of ambivalence. The meaning 'trapped' is clearly paramount, but 'caught up in' (and speculation as to the nature of the experience, which might or might not confer divinity) clearly lurks.

Throughout, suggestions of the light and the dark merge. Rape by a god is no ordinary rape, terrifying though it may also be. The

words 'blow' and 'staggering' balance with 'still' and 'caressed':
'dark webs' and 'helpless' culminate in the unknowable experience,
'breast upon his breast'. The pushing of 'terrified vague fingers'
culminates in 'loosening thighs' (wholly forced, this, or more than
half desired?); while 'feathered glory', 'strange heart' suggest true
divinity at work.

The physicality continues: the 'shudder' which is orgasm, fear,
and maybe supreme fulfilment. 'So mastered by the brute blood of
the air' is judged perfectly. The god/brute antithesis recalls the
temptation of Eve by an angel/serpent as well as Mary's
'overshadowing' – except that the swan is always symbol also of
poetry, beauty, Celtic myths, romantic love (for Yeats, of Coole Park
above all).

The final lines call attention to the double focus, which has been
sustained throughout. The far consequences are there – 'the burning
roof and tower / And Agamemnon dead' – and we recall that Helen
and Clytemnestra, the daughters of the swan, are not to be divided
individually, as symbols of love and destruction. Both, rather, are
among the supreme symbols of love and destruction, indissolubly
fused. Whether foreknowledge of the end caused the rape, or merely
ensued from it, is not explored; the word 'indifferent' suggests that
Zeus acted on impulse (the Father of the Olympians paying tribute, as
often, to one of his own great sons, Bacchus: for this strikes me as a
poem where Bacchus rather than Aphrodite is the presiding force,
though, notoriously, the power of the two is apt to merge). The
notion of 'indifferent' is wholly Greek, and much closer to Yeats
than the Christian annunciation could ever be. There is nothing here
of a woman's consent ('Be it unto me according to thy will'); nothing
of a long intention, foretold by prophets and foreknown even before
the fall of Eve; nothing of huge consequence for salvation (though
maybe the account of Christ in the former poem comes nearer to
this, in its ultimate effect, than any orthodoxy would); nothing of
the sexlessness of the Christian version of the annunciation (a glos-
sed-over episode, characteristic of that gnostic streak that so
strongly prevents Christianity from ever being a religion of the full
self).

'Indifferent' may strike the modern reader as eminently attuned,
also, to those probings of near-epiphanies, near-annunciation, in so
much modern art. The question remains calculatedly suspended: *is* a
mortal half-divinised by the god's descent, however strange and
terrifying; or are men pawns in a greater, and perhaps not even well-
thought-out game, a mere moment's sport?

The question 'Did she put on his knowledge with his power?' will
recur in later poems; and Jack-the-journeyman has his claims to
divinity, too.

'Among School Children'

If I may write for a moment as a teacher, I can say that I tend to pair this poem, in my mind, with 'Byzantium'. The second is the finer artefact, but the two present difficulties of a notorious and not dissimilar kind. They are both extremely difficult, because the syntax absolutely refuses to assist, at certain key points, any assault on the 'meaning'. This would be less worthy of remark in a more openly Symbolist poet; but Yeats in his later poetry usually preferred words such as 'images', 'emblems' and so on to the word 'symbol' and, possibly more relevantly, he maintained the firmest and most delicate control over syntax, with its offer of the *kind* of clarity we usually expect of such poetry, even when the play of opposing archetypes is most teasing. The difficulties I am now remarking upon seem to me less evident in all the poems we have so far considered, up to and including 'Sailing to Byzantium'; and, with certain reservations, to be less evident, again, in the greater of the poems in *Last Poems*. We have encountered it, in less baffling forms, in 'Nineteen Hundred and Nineteen' and in 'Meditations in Time of Civil War', and perhaps it belongs to one or two of the major poems written between these two and 'Byzantium' itself. One piece of evidence (if I can be entirely pragmatic and personal for a moment) that the problem is real comes to me in seminar experience. It is one of the handful of poems where I continually feel that either I or some member of the class is on the brink of a final, definitive discovery of the right terms in which to conduct the discussion; but usually this dissolves again, either immediately or when one embarks on the next rereading. Also, I find that, with the poem now before us, a few students seem very certain of the meaning of the ending, and surprised by my own incomprehension. Several of them have attempted to enlighten me, without success, though their own assurance of knowing what they are talking about is unassailable. Before I embark on it, two further generalities. This poem and 'Byzantium' strike me as being, more than usually, 'stream of consciousness' poems. They are directed by those processes of self-generating thought, memory, association which Joyce and Virginia Woolf were exploring in the novel; and are more concerned to initiate us into a complex experience than to elucidate it. When this is said, the notable difference between the two cannot be unremarked. In composition, at least, 'Among School Children' is firmly guided, I believe, despite everything, by Yeats's conscious mind, reflecting on the more scattered processes of consciousness. 'Byzantium', which he himself recognised as maybe his key poem, seems by contrast hallucinated, transcendent, almost mystical. There, the elusive syntax is entirely at one with the total experience.

One cannot suspect – as I admit I do once or twice here – some flaw in the craftsmanship.

'Among School Children' starts from a simple occasion. Yeats is inspecting a primary school in his official capacity as a political visitor. The occasion was a visit in February 1926 to St Otteran's School, Waterford, which was run on Montessori principles; Yeats was conducted round by the Revd Mother Philomena, the Mistress of Schools. Later Yeats mentioned and praised the work of the school in the Irish Senate, and we may be sure that his report bore little resemblance to this poem. On 14 March 1926 Yeats made a note, 'Topic for poem: School children and the thought that life will waste them perhaps that no possible life can fulfil our dreams or even their teacher's hope. Bring in the old thought that life prepares for what never happens.' As Jeffares (on whose *Commentary* I rely for these facts) speculates, Yeats had asked himself, in an unpublished diary entry of 6 September 1909; why life is 'a perpetual preparation for something that never happens'; and this might have been running in his mind.

In stanza i, which is descriptive, 'the best modern way' has no irony, and is the core, no doubt, of the later more official report. Almost at once, the poet becomes aware of the children's eyes, watching him. 'In momentary wonder' is excellent – exactly right, and reaching back to very personal childhood memories of such inspections. No doubt the children have had impressed upon them the need to be on their best behaviour for this distinguished visitor, and their usual impishness has a touch of awe. For a moment Yeats sees himself, with equal exactness, through their eyes: 'A sixty-year-old smiling public man.' The self-irony and rage would have hovered, but are kept in check; only later, do they come (inevitably) into place.

Stanza ii takes off; and from now on we are only fitfully in the schoolroom. The children and the nun flit in and out, providing now, like his wife's visitants, 'metaphors for poetry'. Doubtless, the great chestnut tree was visible from the school windows, and does not appear from thin air. Yeats's mention of the 'kind old nun' is casual, and one imagines that he attended to her in much the spirit of Wordsworth confronting the leech-gatherer, or Alice's White Knight his 'Aged-aged man'. Had she read the poem and discovered that according to Yeats she 'worshipped images', she might have torn her hair; but niceties of Catholic theology were not high among the poet's concerns.

The first effect takes him back to a moment in his youth of intimate friendship with Maud Gonne, the 'Ledaean body'. Maybe we should not connect this too closely with 'Leda and the Swan', yet the thoughts that Yeats was no Zeus, MacBride no divinity, and the unknown revolutionary father of Maud Gonne's one daughter (to whom the poet had proposed unsuccessfully) no known quantity could not have been absent. Here, he settles for a moment òf recalled harmony, experienced in youth. The 'trigger' is a story she had then confided, of a spoiled day from her own childhood. The actual event (ll. 2–4) is too universal to need comment, but, because of Yeats's love, he recalls the total empathy which it aroused in him.

From here, his mind now passes rapidly back, between childhood, youth and the present, and the miracle happens (miracle, bird or golden handiwork?). This time Yeats is not deliberately conjuring for memories and images; they overtake him, in the processes compressed into stanzas iii and iv. Looking back at the schoolroom, he wonders if Maud Gonne could have looked so, at that age; and the lines qualifying this,

> For even daughters of the swan can share
> Something of every paddler's heritage

allow to each child some possibility of glory, while still preserving the rare supremacy, the once-in-a-lifetime revelation. Almost immediately, a chance similarity of 'colour upon cheek or hair', catches him:

> And thereupon my heart is driven wild:
> She stands before me as a living child.

This leap of the heart creates, indeed, a Maud Gonne Yeats has never seen, never been in love with – except that the memory of her own tale of childhood merges love, creation, image into one. And now we hear a poet whose heart has neither been 'consumed away', nor wishes to be; a poet thinking of a child as unlike his own daughter – should the prayer for her be granted – as imagination could shape. Later Yeats was to define his encompassing social vision, in one of the many kaleidoscopic accounts we have of it, as 'Dream of the noble and the beggar-man'. Here, 'paddler', Helen and Leda are alike swept together, into the perfect and (with no transition) present image of Maud Gonne: 'Her present image floats into the mind'. And still, this new stanza assures us, there is magic. Despite the passage of years, despite the rebuffs and rejections, the politics and anger, despite everything complained of in 'A Prayer for My Daughter' and identified as enemy to happiness, she is still for him, now, as she always was:

> Did Quattrocento finger fashion it
> Hollow of cheek as though it drank the wind
> And took a mess of shadows for its meat?

For a moment, a Leonardo da Vinci beauty confronts him: and, intoxicated, he allows himself an answering reflection from within:

> And I though never of Ledaean kind
> Had pretty plumage once – enough of that. . . .

This, I fancy, is an important turning-point. Doubtless he realises that the magic accidentally performed by one of these children has tricked him; that it is not Maud Gonne's 'present' image, any more than his own, which he has seen ('And Helen has all human hearts betrayed'). Or maybe there is the more bitter suggestion, floating, that those ravages imaged in past poems as aging Maud Gonne have aged him instead; that she remains unruffled, unaffected, while he pines still, his own 'pretty plumage' not only lost but wasted ('Juno's peacock screamed'). The sensible advice, 'enough of that, / Better to smile on all that smile' reverts for a moment to the schoolroom, and the last line of the first stanza; but now the creative energy which, in this same year, produced 'The Tower' cannot be suppressed: 'and show / There is a comfortable kind of old scarecrow'.

The sixth stanza is, in a sense, an expansion of this line, but first we move to the fifth; and it is here that the difficulties already alluded to set in.

Or do they? The difficulties are entirely restricted to ll. 2–4, which are hard to read aloud with any exactness, though the syntax will indeed carry one along. If you skip these lines and opt for the main sense, which emerges if the first line is followed immediately by the second half of the stanza, and the parenthesis is ignored, then everything is clear. It is also extremely despondent. The poet appears to be saying that, if any mother, in her birth-pangs, could see her son at the age of 'sixty or more', she would be bound to think her labour (and this word 'labour', with its multiple meanings, emerges later as very important) wasted. But we then notice that the whole stanza is not a statement, but a rhetorical question – though in the course of reading it the lines we have, for this present purpose, neglected make it hard to remain conscious of this. Obviously, it expresses a mood, and a bizarre one; or it is a deliberate perspective, inserted to jolt the reader, as he moves from the poem's easy opening towards its baffling close? Taken literally, it would mean that no achievements, however impressive, are of the slightest power to balance aging and death (and the next, simpler stanza really does seem to confirm this). It would mean further that the whole of childhood, youth, creativity, love, are cancelled out, as so much wasted labour, when old age takes the stage. (This thought is, as we have seen, one that Yeats had entertained before, and planned to insert into the poem). It would mean that the memories of Maud Gonne already evoked are

ultimately worthless and – unless something intervenes? – that even
the dance and the dancer are ultimately illusion.

On the other hand, we will undeniably wonder *what* mother,
giving birth, would be likely to think in such terms; and recall that
Yeats frequently sets up drastic and simplistic polarities to help his
poems to work. Maybe, also, the deliberate riddles set in ll. 2–4 are
meant to preoccupy us, so that the starkness of the apparent
statement is slightly relieved.

I find here, when reading the poems, two difficulties related but
not entirely merged. First, who is doomed to 'sleep, shriek, struggle
to escape / As recollection or the drug decide' – mother or child?
The phrase 'a shape upon her lap' seems to me calculatedly vague, as
if to prevent us knowing whether the child is in the process of birth,
or already born. We might decide that we are witnessing the pain of
childbirth, without any normal compensations for the mother –
since this deplorable vision of a 'sixty-year-old smiling public man'
has .almost leapt ready-made out of her womb before her. Or we
might (and the syntax does, if I am not mistaken, allow both
possibilities) decide that we are witnessing the baby leaping from the
womb, rather in the manner of Blake's demonic infant:

> My mother groaned, my father wept;
> Into the dangerous world I leapt,
> Helpless, naked, piping loud,
> Like a fiend hid in a cloud. . . .

Line 2 is, in any event, mysterious, but it remains consistent with
either view. We might assume that 'Honey of generation' is sexual
sweetness or compulsion and that the mother has been betrayed, by
this, into giving life. Or we might decide that, in an interim life, some
immortal creature has been betrayed again into birth by the lure of
generation ('Whatever is begotten, born and dies'), risking the final
bitterness of a voyage to Byzantium as old age approaches, for the
sake of that brief 'all summer long' between ('Those dying
generations – at their song'). To take this view is, of course, to import
one reading of 'Sailing to Byzantium' into this poem, without all its
delicate balances and polarities; it is also (no less seriously), to throw a
ruinous spanner into the works of *A Vision*. There, the cycles of
reincarnation are presented as not .only natural but also
exhilarating: an accumulation of differing experiences, through
many lifetimes of contrast, by some ultimately coherent entity or
daemon who will, beyond time, finally reassemble and celebrate all.
Such a view of reincarnation may seem as optimistic as it is unusual –
but it can scarcely survive 'Among School Children', stanza v. If

everything between birth and sixty is to be disregarded, and old age alone to be valid, then any doctrine of reincarnation will sound remarkably like a version of hell.

At this point, a word on the elaborate notes in Jeffares's *Commentary* may be needed, since, though exhaustive, they deflect attention from the poem itself. The passage quoted from Gentile by Torchiana, concerning the psychology of young motherhood, seems to me frankly irrelevant, 'while the long disquisition on Porphyry, though more to the point, may be misleading here. The note on 'Honey of generation', for instance, starts as follows: 'this image comes from Porphyry, *On the Cave of the Nymphs*. . . . Yeats wrote that he found no warrant in Porphyry for considering it "the drug" that destroys the "recollection" of prenatal freedom. He blamed the cup of oblivion given in the zodiacal sign of Cancer. . . .' The following passages, with their references to the Platonic tradition of the soul's journeyings, the 'conversion to intellectual life at the Holy City of Phaeacia', and the complex doctrine of a subsequent 'return via the cave, where the honey is the pleasure arising from generation and the Nymphs and honey-bees are symbols for two types of souls born into the world' are bound to set our minds wandering through other symbols already touched on in this commentary, but I am not sure that stanza v will bear commentary of such weight. If I am right, the deliberate ambivalence I have mentioned is intended (if less clear than it might be), and is then amplified by stanza vi. Here, Yeats compares and contrasts three famous ancient philosophers with somewhat impish freedom, but the clear message is that in the end they all came to the same fate: 'Old clothes upon old sticks to scare a bird'. We cannot escape the importance of this third, and most bitter, repetition of a major motif, once again forcibly placed in the last line of a stanza. It links back with the 'tattered coat upon a stick' from 'Sailing to Byzantium', as well as to the still more forceful images in part I of 'The Tower'. Here, surely, the notion has been driven either to impasse, or to the challenge for some radical change of direction, back towards hope. We expect the last two stanzas to be complex and difficult; equally, we expect that they will prove as elusive as, indeed, they are. The problem confronting us is to decide not their success as rhetoric (which is magnificent), but their success, or failure, in the almost impossible work they are given to do. Has Yeats managed to turn this strange poem from stream-of-consciousness into finished artefact; or is he content to allow further powerful impulses to gather, and break, like a wave:

> Both nuns and mothers worship images,
> But those the candles light are not as those
> That animate a mother's reveries,

But keep a marble or a bronze repose.
And yet they too break hearts. . . .

Fitfully, nun and schoolroom return, but now entirely turned into symbols (emblems?). In fact, his own important word 'images' now appears (it has been used once before in this poem, 'Her present image floats into the mind', where the obvious meaning ʻvisual image' blends, also, with Yeats's long 'worship'). The annoying inaccuracy about the nuns can be allowed, if we accept that their marble or bronze statues must be taken for what they symbolise (the Byzantine amalgam of art and religion), and not confused with the actual object of devotion. This somewhat disturbs the parallelism, unless we also accept that mothers worship their babies for their potential, and not for their immediate reality. If so, then we can now assume that the hypotheses of stanzas v and vi are seen to be unreal ('hope springs eternal'), and that the mothers are 'worshipping' the sacred, given through 'generation', whether with a degree of betrayal inhering in the birth or not. We might conjecture that Yeats also intends us to see both forms of worship as instinctual: yet, if so, there is now not a polarity, but a kinship, between 'nature' and all that makes and belongs to Byzantium.

The phrase 'not as those' introduces, none the less, a distinction between the two forms of worship, even though the word 'images' yokes them; and the fifth line is also concerned with similarity, not difference. The phrase 'That animate a mother's reveries' is bound to remind us that fathers too may be affected – and to bring 'Prayer for My Daughter' back, as a concrete instance ('Imagining in excited reverie . . .'). The next line, however, conjures up the Yeats of 'Sailing to Byzantium'; so that 'And yet they too break hearts' can not be less than complex in effect. Mothers 'break hearts' (whether they have a moral right to do so or not) either through the sufferings of their children or, more probably (given this context), because the children in some way disappoint them. The same might well be true of an artist confronting his artefacts; and, if so, are we to conjecture similar, or dissimilar, reasons? The strong note of mortality has been sounded in the fifth stanza, yet 'Sailing to Byzantium' has sought to confer on art the permanence denied to mortal flesh. (A still more memorable statement of this comes in the third stanza of 'Byzantium', where there is added bitterness, but, of course, greater surrounding ambivalence.) We are thrown back on multiple reflections. Babies can break hearts simply by growing up; or by eluding parental prayers and plans for their future; or by turning into sixty-year-old scarecrows; or by growing apart from and outliving their parents; or in any number of other ways. Likewise, works of art may break even their creator's heart – to such a degree that he pleads for his heart to be 'consumed away', so that he might become a lifeless artefact himself. Maybe there *are* similarities: the art eludes the artist's intentions even in fulfilling them, taking on its own identity, which, by its separate life and its longevity ('Monuments of unchanging intellect'), may seem even to mock him. The artist may say (like the mother?) that he has been called on for a sacrifice which, in some lights, appals him (the sacrifice of life to art recurs yet again).

Even so, these reflections hardly penetrate the mystery of Yeats's lines, where the tone of elation is overriding. The key phrases speak of life ('worship', 'light', 'animate', 'keep . . . repose'), and even the phrase 'And yet they too break hearts' seems to stress triumph rather than sorrow, as if this price, however relentlessly exacted, cannot cancel out the joy of creation, of celebration, itself. The poem is already at the point of take-off; and now lifts, like a great rocket after countdown, into the conclusion, which can scarcely be considered except as a whole:

> O Presences
> That passion, piety or affection knows,
> And that all heavenly glory symbolise –
> O self-born mockers of man's enterprise;
>
> Labour is blossoming or dancing where
> The body is not bruised to pleasure soul,
> Nor beauty born out of its own despair,
> Nor blear-eyed wisdom out of midnight oil.
> O chestnut-tree, great-rooted blossomer,
> Are you the leaf, the blossom or the bole?
> O body swayed to music, O brightening glance,
> How can we know the dancer from the dance?

'O Presences' – here is the language and power of celebration and, whatever the reservations, whatever the difficulties, I think we must trust the rhetoric – trust it all the more for the poet's refusal to simplify. This is not an instance of rhetoric deceitfully triumphing over 'meaning' (the Swinburnian experience), nor of rhetoric madly defying meaning, as one can be tempted to think: in fact, I am inclined to throw myself, and the reader, back on 'real life' in search of the touchstone to bring to this and to bear in mind as one tries to wend one's way through. One must imagine Yeats's love of Maud Gonne; the rapture of religion; the fulfilment of motherhood; and let these realities ride above whatever, in thought or experience, may later cast them in doubt. The final four lines of the poem do this ineffaceably; meanwhile, the poem dances towards them, collecting and transforming its potential for gloom as it goes.

The 'Presences' must (in context) be both Byzantine artefacts and living babies – both dignified and joined, in an invocation fit for a god. Lines 6–7 of stanza vii are triumphant, asserting one of the major truths Yeats has to tell about art, and about life. 'Passion, piety or affection' are words without irony: the assertion that the Presences also 'all heavenly glory symbolise' is no Platonic abstraction, but the dance without which there would be no poems, no Yeats. If the last line seems a counter-truth, then it has been foreshadowed already and, we may feel, can ride, now, mysteriously robbed of its sting. Immediately the poet plunges into the vision of a life which on the surface is antithetical to 'real' experience as the poem has so far presented it, yet which rings out more like a sudden trumpet of faith. The word 'Labour' catches up all pain : the 'labour' of childbearing, the 'labour' of art, the 'labour' of religion ; the pain of love unrequited and, no less, the pain of life as a preparation for something never to happen ; 'Old clothes upon old sticks to scare a bird'. But 'Labour' is not cast down, it is 'blossoming or dancing' (the word 'blossoming' splendidly preparing for ll. 5–6). Admittedly, the vision following seems more wished-for than possible ; yet here a clash of values is most succinctly compressed. For Keats (whom ll. 2–4 call to ?), such reflections would signal a return from the realm of faerie to inevitable knowledge of suffering and death ('Forlorn'; 'Desolate'). Yet Platonists and Neo-Platonists will read them otherwise, seeing in these shadows of reality a promise to be appropriated by trust. The word 'mockery' *is* invoked, but we need not bend to it, however foul the winds, however oppressive the sceptic within ('Mock mockers after that / That would not lift a hand maybe / To help good, wise or great' – 'Nineteen Hundred and Nineteen').

From this point, the poem is released into the two images, cast in the form of unanswerable rhetorical questions, that conclude it. 'O chestnut-tree': the poet's exhilaration is alive with wonder. As we know, 'rooted' was always for him a charmed word ('And here's John Synge himself, that rooted man / "Forgetting human words", a grave deep face'). The very words 'great-rooted blossomer' speak of the twin mysteries of wholeness which we have already encountered in varied explorations. The mystery of *being* is as real and splendid as this incarnate glory, however elusive its logic. And, in the final couplet, the image of static perfection is completed by (fused with ?) a human glory to crown it (as if the polarities which are absolute in 'A Prayer for My Daughter' were also suddenly magically fused). 'O body swayed by music, O brightening glance. . . .' As when reading certain passages in *Four Quartets*, four or five moments of personal vividness return to me, and I scarcely know whether it is these, or Yeats's words, to which I respond.

'How can we know the dancer from the dance?' So obvious, in a sense! The enchanted moment, when two dancers swirl past, their eyes lit with love, in a moment destined to stay with the onlooker long after the dancers have changed, or forgotten, or died. Yet there, in the moment, is reality; and Yeats's triumph, after all, is to unify this poem, which started from scattered reflections, set up in the most mundane of situations; pursued its way through memories of Maud Gonne (youthful; a child; present image); then plunged through metaphysical pessimism, linked with personal suffering and aging, to emerge in a timeless moment when the dance's insoluble mysteries are caught up in the dance.

When teaching, as I have confessed, the 'right' way of discussing 'Among School Children' baffles me; I can neither explain the ending, nor entirely follow those who apparently can. I have to repeat that I do not think this poem as perfect an artefact as 'Byzantium' (is it ultimately too ambitious?); yet, when this is said, one must marvel that Yeats should juggle with material so intensely intractable, and lift a poem which for six stanzas is remarkable, if scattered, into a finally unified and triumphant whole.

'A Man Young and Old'

Yeats was always a master of the lyric and ballad, and as he got older his work in these modes flourished. Though sequences such as this require less commentary than poems of more teasing complexion, there are moments when they seem the jewel in the crown. When browsing, I turn to them first for sheer pleasure; then realise that here, too, are innumerable keys to that infinitely engaging mystery 'Yeats'. A few words, then, on the 'obvious', if only to dispel the notion that my main choice of poems, for discussion, is intended as anything more than a discipline painfully imposed by space.

'First Love' starts the sequence with heartless woman, blighting love. If the genre is that of 'la belle dame sans merci', the treatment is distinctively Yeatsian. I doubt whether any other poet would have hit on 'beauty's murderous brood', or used the symbols of 'moon' and 'heart' in quite this way. Note the line 'She smiled and that transfigured me' – on the face of it romantic, yet the lover has no illusion, even, of being made godlike: 'left me but a lout' is pure, pared-down bitterness.

I have not tracked every use of 'transfigure' in Yeats, but have the impression that he usually uses it in this, the reverse of its Christian, sense. As early as 1893, in 'The Lamentation of the Old Pensioner' (from *The Rose*), it is a key word in a poem about the havoc wrought by time. Like so many of the youthful poems, 'Lamentation'

foreshadows something of the style, as well as the content, of mature
Yeats. The final stanza is worth quoting:

> There's not a woman turns her face
> Upon a broken tree,
> And yet the beauties that I loved
> Are my memory;
> I spit into the face of Time
> That has transfigured me.

Transfigured as disfigured: in 'First Love', this gloss not only links
with the emptying of thought, but also makes a connection between
this state and the 'heavenly circuit of its stars / When the moon sails
out'. This links the poem's conclusion with the beginning, thereby
giving 'Though' almost the force of 'Because'.

Jeffares, who offers little critical comment, sees in this and the
second poem of the sequence and some others a reference to Yeats's
own love for Maud Gonne, and in other poems references to Iseult
Gonne (the fourth) and to Diana Vernon (a pseudonym for a lady
with whom he had a brief relationship in 1896). Whether the
autobiographical references are required for this poem I doubt. It is a
linked sequence intended more, I should imagine, for universal
browsing – a reminder that the personal and autobiographical
elements which loom large in some poems are not a universal
technique.

'Human Dignity' is another lyric of rejected love, linking the
moon with absence of thought (and, in a human, 'no
comprehension'). The last four lines are unobtrusive paradox: would
the shriek be art, or mere therapy? The word 'dumb' is consistent
with writing *this* poem – dignity without power to heal? 'The
Mermaid' links love with death, again through the heartlessness of a
'cruel happiness'. This archetype is the ancient one, of love between
beings destined to destroy each other (or one the other) by natural
laws. The mermaid's laughter is cruel not in intent, but in its
forgotten effect.

The sequence starts, then, with three poems concerning the
destructiveness of love, ascribed each time to feminine cruelty, which
is, however, associated more with thoughtless unconcern (the
moon's indifference) than with intent. After this it proceeds, through
more Imagist poems, with the focus increasingly on women in age –
demented, yet half demonic too (perhaps the first hint of Crazy Jane
is here). The sequence ends with a switch to 'Oedipus at Colonus',
interpreted in un-Sophoclean manner (Yeats apparently said that the
last line was 'very bad Grecian, but very good Elizabethan, and so it
must stay'.). The 'Young Man Old' is identified now with Oedipus,

that most potent of tragic heroes – whose fate is, on any realistic
showing, profoundly untypical, yet who, in archetype, has been
given universal sexual significance by Freud, and maybe universal
religious significance through Christ (as well as Frazer) in the pattern
of death and resurrection. The first stanza offers endurance, stoic
acceptance, as the only 'wisdom' for old age, yet is not without the
bitterness we have come to expect: 'Delight becomes death-longing
if all longing else be vain'. The second and third stanzas offer vivid,
complementary images, and the poem ends with a resonant stanza,
the first two lines of which sound more like Job than the Greeks, and
the third like no one but Yeats, in his tragic mask:

> Never to have lived is best, ancient writers say;
> Never to have drawn the breath of life, never to have looked into
> the eye of day;
> The second best's a gay goodnight and quickly turn away.

It is as if Yeats is preparing us for two of his most enchanting, if less
taxing, volumes or sequences *Words for Music Perhaps* and *A Woman
Yound and Old*. But first there is one more of the 'difficult' poems to
come, concluding *The Tower*; and then the further landmark of
transitional middle to late Yeats, *The Winding Stair and Other Poems*.

'All Souls' Night'

I propose only a note on this poem, for three reasons. The first is that
it belongs to a genre we have met twice already – Yeats's conjuring
up the dead for a special purpose – and which we shall encounter
again, in interesting variation, in my own favourite among all
Yeats's poems, 'The Municipal Gallery Revisited'. I think that, with
the aid of Jeffares's interesting notes on the various persons who are
this time invoked, most readers familiar with the three allied works
will find their way around without difficulty. The second reason is
that, though sonorous, it does not strike me as having the weight, in
Yeats's total canon, of most of the other poems I am choosing. The
third is that most of the difficulties which Jeffares does not pause over
in the *Commentary* elude me also, so that I am aware that I have only
peripheral things to say.

Though placed last, this is almost certainly the fifth of the poems in
this volume to have been written. The earlier four are 'The New
Faces' (1912), 'Owen Aherne and His Dancers' (1917), 'Nineteen
Hundred and Nineteen' (1919) and 'On a Picture of a Black Centaur
by Edward Dulac' (September 1920). In addition, there are two slight
pieces whose date is uncertain. 'All Souls' Night' was written in

November 1920, in Oxford, when Yeats was living in Broad Street, and must have had its inception on 2 November. It first appeared in *The New Republic* on 9 March 1921, but by an odd quirk it appears also as Epilogue to *A Vision*, the first private edition of which was printed in 1925. As we know *A Vision* was later extensively altered, through further occult visitations. Yeats was also led to confess, in his Introduction to the first authorised Macmillan version, of 1937, that the first version came to fill him with shame.

> I had misinterpreted the geometry, and in my ignorance of philosophy failed to understand distinctions upon which the coherence of the whole depends, and as my wife was unwilling that her share should be known, and I to seem sole author, I had invented an unnatural story of an Arabian traveller which I must amend and find a place for some day because I was fool enough to write half a dozen poems that are unintelligible without it.

In addition to such problems, Yeats had also to contend with the fact that the unknown spirit authors were partly taking their cue from Yeats's own *Per Amica Silentia Lunae* (1917); that certain alarming manifestations, also described in the Preface, tended to erupt into his normal life; and that the actual work of transcription was subject to capricious malice of a subtle kind, which only came fully to light when the spirits, who had urgently asked Yeats 'not to read philosophy until their exposition was complete' had to admit 'We are starved':

> Because they must, as they explained, soon finish, others whom they named Frustrators attempted to confuse us or waste time. Who these Frustrators were or why they acted so was never adequately explained ... but they were always ingenious and sometimes cruel. The automatic script would deteriorate, grow sentimental or confused, and when I pointed this out the communicator would say, 'From such and such an hour, on such and such a day, all is frustration.' I would spread out the script and he would cross all out back to the answer that began it, but had I not · divined frustration he would have said nothing. Was he constrained by a drama which was part of conditions that made communication possible, was that drama itself part of the communication, had my question to be asked before his mind cleared? Only once did he break the rule and without waiting for a question declare some three or four days' work frustration. A predecessor of his had described the geometrical symbolism as created for my assistance and had seemed to dislike it, another had complained that I used it to make their thought mechanical, and a

Frustrator doubtless played upon my weakness when he described a geometrical model of the soul's state after death which could be turned upon a lathe. The sudden indignant interruption suggested a mind under a dream constraint which it could throw off if desire were strong enough, as we can sometimes throw off a nightmare. It was part of their purpose to affirm that all the gains of man come from conflict with the opposite of his true being. Was communication itself such a conflict? One said, as though it rested with me to decide what part I should play in their dream, 'Remember we will deceive you if we can.' (*A Vision*, pp. 12–13)

I quote at this length partly to remind readers of the complex status of *A Vision*, and of Yeats's own doubts concerning this; and partly because the poem before us was, all else notwithstanding, allowed also to appear as the 'Epilogue' to the finished work in its 1937 form. 'All Souls' Night' was written only a year or two after the first version of *A Vision* had started to appear. In no sense, then, can it be taken as summing up, or fully depending on, that work; nor is there any suggestion that it was itself a product of supernatural solicitings: rather, it has every hallmark of a normal Yeats poem, and its close connection with *A Vision* must be due to some feature in it which he perceived clearly himself, and which the passage of time did nothing to alter.

I wonder if this has something to do with the central mystery (as it seems to me) confronting us? All Souls' Night is basically a Christian feast, as the 'great Christ Church Bell' reminds us, though it is a point where (non-Protestant) Christianity links and interacts with many other religions in believing that at certain times the dead draw near. Usually Yeats conjures for a purpose. 'In Memory of Major Robert Gregory' was to be a house-warming party of the dead; in 'The Tower', the dead were summoned to hear a question (which is duly asked). Later, in 'The Municipal Gallery Revisited', the process is reversed, since the dead choose to visit Yeats, unexpectedly, and overwhelmingly. Here, however, his stated purpose is even more portentous (stanza ii):

> I need some mind that, if the cannon sound
> From every quarter of the world, can stay
> Wound in mind's pondering
> As mummies in the mummy-cloth are wound;
> Because I have a marvellous thing to say,
> A certain marvellous thing
> None but the living mock,
> Though not for sober ear;
> It may be all that hear
> Should laugh and weep an hour upon the clock.

The three people conjured up this time have in common their interest during life in the occult – indeed, their common membership with Yeats, Horton apart, of the 'Golden Dawn'. Their fitness is not in question; but it is far from clear to me what 'marvellous thing' *is* said in the poem. The portentous claim, again described with a favourite word ('mummy-truths') appears in the penultimate stanza. The final stanza, however, appears to describe, very elusively, the effect the truth has on Yeats himself, rather than to state it; and his audience is presumably not to be instructed (they are themselves, in a sense, the truth stated, rather than its recipients: the final two lines suggest as much). Can it be that the whole of *A Vision* is the offered truth, so that this poem is, after all, in place only as 'Epilogue' to that work?

The strength of the poem seems to me to lie in the three portraits, all of which are vivid, in the light they throw both on their originals and on Yeats. But a few further puzzles. Yeats said in *A Vision*, 'I have moments of exaltation like that in which I wrote "All Souls' Night".' But is the poem consistent with this? My own response is always as if to a dark, oppressed mood (more so than in 'A Prayer for My Daughter' even, where he spoke of 'the great gloom that is in my mind'). The phrase 'platonic love' is used in its popular sense to mean non-sexual love (rather a novelty to Horton, who had been given to sexual adventures until his fiftieth year, when he fell in love with 'a very good, charming, young fellow student' soon after receiving the thought, 'I do not need women but God'). It is interesting that Yeats should describe this new experience as a 'sweet extremity of pride', even though the bereavement which followed made Horton desire his own death. Possibly such love struck the poet as hubris ('I could not tell / Whether of her or God he thought the most'), but this reflection is not typical of Yeats, nor of his own complex reactions to personal love.

The phrase 'mummy-wheat' had been running in Yeats's head, obsessively, and in connection with *A Vision*. He was aware of the dead coming back, with unique wisdom to offer. The word gains in importance (and obscurity) in 'Byzantium'; here, 'Wound in mind's pondering' and 'Wound in mind's wandering' describe the quality most 'needed' by the poet, though 'As mummies in the mummy-cloth are wound' may sound grim?

I do not fully see how the poet moves from the thought in the first stanza that 'our gross palates drink from the whole wine' (where 'our' clearly distinguishes living people from ghosts) to the thought in the penultimate stanza 'No living man can drink from the whole wine'. On the other hand, this problem may be closer to optical illusion than to real contradiction. 'A ghost may come' indicates the privilege of the dead on this night of the year. The statement

> His element is so fine
> Being sharpened by his death,
> To drink from the wine-breath
> While our gross palates drink from the whole wine

presumably suggests that a spirit is 'purified' simply by escape from its body, and not necessarily by moral improvement, as Platonists and members of many religions would think. This is strengthened, as an interpretation, by the low opinion of MacGregor which Yeats confesses to (cf. MacBride in 'Easter 1916', where an heroic death also demolishes the distinctions obtaining 'where motley is worn'); and it is the stanzas on MacGregor, impregnated as they are with a very distinctive mixture of mockery and self-mockery, which leads on to

> But names are nothing. What matter who it be,
> So that his elements have grown so fine
> The fume of muscatel
> Can give his sharpened palate ecstasy
> No living man can drink from the whole wine.

So MacGregor, even if the poet 'thought him half a lunatic, half knave / And told him so' – and even if, further, he may have 'grown more arrogant being a ghost', is still included in the company whose 'elements' have grown finer than anything known to the living. This would allow us to interpret 'No living man can drink from the whole wine' not as a contradiction to the last line of the first stanza, but as a clarification. The phrase 'our gross palates' seems to qualify the first statement: we can drink from the 'real' wine as a ghost cannot, but do our palates filter the 'real' through? In contrast, the ghost can take only of the 'wine-breath' (later, the 'fume'); but this alone can give 'his sharpened palate ecstasy'. The 'sharpened palate' is metaphor, and the 'ecstasy' is presumably spiritual, proceeding from the divine essence of the wine, again in contrast to the intoxication possible to a 'grosser palate' here.

Whether this does reach the main meaning, I am not entirely certain, since the 'whole wine' would in some aspects elude both living and dead. The image is an integral part of Yeats's conjuring and his preparation to entertain his visitants as they come.

Finally, though I am not proposing to examine it, the sixth stanza underlines Yeats's long interest in the philosophy of the East. The 'learned Indian' does not appear to be too indebted to *A Vision* (unless in extremely potted form). But the images of 'whirled', 'moon ... sun', 'free ... fast', 'Chance ... Choice' powerfully suggest the Yin and Yang polarity from the Chinese *Book of Changes* (and other Eastern sources), which is surely central to Yeats's own dialectic and (dare I say it) more readily comprehensible, to this critic at least, than the gyres. But it is the last line I want to point to before passing on : 'And sink into its own delight at last'.

Here, the phrase unequivocably applies to 'the soul'. If we look back to the penultimate stanza of 'A Prayer for My Daughter', a similar recovered harmony is proposed as possible even in *this* life – *if* the uncharacteristic way set out there by Yeats is followed, so that 'The soul recovers radical innocence'. In 'Sailing to Byzantium', it is still 'soul' which sets out on the Byzantine pilgrimage, forsaking the world of body – though there, we have seen, with more complex omens attending. Soon, however, we shall be looking at 'A Dialogue of Self and Soul', where these references will be especially pertinent; and there it is not soul but self which asserts a formula for recovered blessedness – apparently in defiance of 'soul', and by a very different path, though a path by no means strange to the reader of Yeats.

'In Memory of Eva Gore-Booth and Con Markiewicz'

This is the first poem in *The Winding Stair and Other Poems*. One oddity is that there is no poem called 'The Winding Stair', though the image dominates two important poems, 'A Dialogue of Self and Soul' and 'Blood and the Moon', and appears in others. It is the single steep stair which winds up, in a spiral, round the inside of Thoor Ballylee, with the large room which makes each floor opening from it; if you start at the bottom and proceed to the top of the stair, you emerge on the roof of Yeats's Tower. This stair became mingled with the gyres (or Yin and Yang, if you want to avoid the mathematics), and is a symbol of the soul's upward but spiral progress.

The poem before us is one of Yeats's most noble, as several critics have remarked; it must also be among the most liquidly beautiful poems in the language. It is dated October 1927, though Mrs Yeats recorded a memory of the poet still working on it in November, in Saville. Lissadell, the home of the two sisters, still exists, its 'Great windows open to the south'. The Gore-Booth family continue to live there and it is open to tourists as are most of the buildings and places that so colour Yeats's work. (Only Coole Park is destroyed. One may visit the park, and the lake which, Yeats once said, was the most familiar place to him on this earth. Ruins show where the house once stood, among trees – a sight almost uncannily prefigured in 'Coole Park 1929'.)

Lissadell belonged mainly to Yeats's youthful memories, but, though it never had for him the significance of Lady Gregory's home, the mingling of clarity and distance is a peculiar ingredient of this poem's charm. The older sister, Constance, left Lissadell in 1898 to study painting in Paris; when she married Count Casimir Markievicz they settled in Dublin. She became deeply involved in Irish politics, especially through the influence of James Connolly, and was deputy leader of the group that held St Stephen's Green in the 1916 uprising. When reprieved from death she was imprisoned, and on release she continued to be deeply involved in revolutionary Irish politics, supporting the 1922 Treaty which inaugurated the Irish Free State, and fighting in the Civil War. She is, or course, the unnamed woman referred to in 'Easter 1916', along with four named Republicans who died. Her sister Eva was a poet, a suffragette, a student of Indian mysticism and Neo-platonism, and a woman strongly committed to social work. Eva died in 1926, and Constance the year after. As so often, it was the coming back in memory, of the 'Dear shadows', after their passing, which called out one of Yeats's finest poems.

The texture is wonderfully smooth and lyrical. These qualities, which lurk everywhere in Yeats, often appearing momentarily in unexpected contexts, here set the tone. It is like the finest damask, or an ancient tapestry ('And now their breathless faces seem to look / Out of some old picture-book'). There is anger too, of course – the anger of women's beauty wasted in fruitless polemics, which we already know. But it seems transmuted by other qualities, removing any hint of sourness, adding instead something of the serenity of an old man's memory revisiting. 'Nostalgia' would be too weak a word for it (I see nothing wrong with occasional nostalgia, but it is not a quality which, I think, will ever be found, in its pure form, in any poet of the first rank). The prevailing impression is of a tremendous clarity, illuminating and uniting and simplifying grand moods and themes, very much as Mahler does in the final movements of his Third and Ninth symphonies. One notes now in the first four lines a rich sense of the present is created – a present that acquires a kind of timelessness, which ll. 14–20 confirm. Even in the stormier section in between, the tense is present ('The older is', 'drags out', / 'and she seems'). In this ambiance, the awareness of waste seems less like bitter protest than acceptance. The powerful image 'withered old and skeleton-gaunt' suggest events mythic or legendary; though the image itself, which belongs to time, as well as to politics prepares for the poem's heart:

Dear shadows, now you know it all,
All the folly of a fight
With a common wrong or right.
The innocent and the beautiful
Have no enemy but time. . . .

I have delved into these glowing lines for my own title, since they are so final, and so removed from the fray. They are not, of course, in an absolute sense, final – how could such a thing be expected? Even as we stand looking in Drumcliffe churchyard at Yeats's tomb, and the three lines 'by his command' inscribed there, it is hard not to imagine in some quite other region a second tomb, ornately Byzantine and inscribed with other verses, to remind, indeed, of those powerful antinomies which defy unity. But here we have words that I think might be as appropriate for Eliot as for Yeats, though not for R. S. Thomas: 'no enemy but time'. They transcend the 'folly' attached to them, and become the dilemma of transience; inside which all the exploring has to be set.

No doubt Yeats wished that Maud Gonne had married him (to return to a real simplicity); but neither for himself, nor for any elite soul, would he have chosen Lao Tzu's detachment; the fight, the struggle, *is* his life – and his art.

Maybe I can let two other quotations float back, each seemingly final, as far better comment than any my words could make. First,

> How but in custom and in ceremony
> Are innocence and beauty born?

> ('A Prayer for My Daughter')

and second,

> Man is in love and loves what vanishes,
> What more is there to say?

> ('Nineteen Hundred and Nineteen')

We might take 'In Memory of Eva Gore-Booth and Con Markiewicz' as an interim reverie, profoundly inward, yet rather to one side of Yeats's body of work. Undoubtedly, its central lines resonate in one way or another against most of the poems concerning us, but, as if in paradox, they are curiously timeless and apart.

The poem's ending is more routine. The end of the world through fire is a commonplace in Christian as in many other traditions, and for a moment the poet appears to want to play God. Despite the heavy going some critics have made of 'We the great gazebo built', I assume that Yeats is essentially remembering the building of a summer house (in Anglo-Irish, apparently, to 'make a gazebo of yourself' can be to look ridiculous; 'gazebo' can also mean simply 'a place to look from'). 'They convicted us of guilt' is imprecise, but I assume that by now the poet has left behind his strictures on the dead sisters and is finally uniting himself with them in memory, both of the deepest aspirations of their lives and of the valley of death.

But who is addressed, we may wonder, in these concluding lines? Who is asked to 'Arise and bid me' at the start, and to 'Bid me' at the end? Is it the 'Dear shadows', now fully present in memory; or is it some new insight generated in the poem itself? The general 'conflagration' will merely kill them again and the poet with them. Time will remain untouched – along, maybe, with the saints and sages in Byzantium, themselves holding, in stillness, the living fire, waiting to be invoked.

'Death'

This is said to have been written about the assassination of Kevin O'Higgins, Vice-President and Minister of Justice in the Irish Free State. Yeats sufficiently admired O'Higgins to add him to a list, which also included Berkeley, Swift, Burke, Grattan, Parnell, Augusta Gregory and Synge, in a passage which declares 'that a hundred men, their creative power wrought to the highest pitch, their will trained but not broken, can do more for the welfare of a people, whether in war or peace, than a million of any lesser sort' (though see also the short, vivid three-line portrait in 'The Municipal Gallery Revisited', stanza i). The poem was written in September 1927, the year of the assassination, but I see no more reason for connecting 'Death' directly with O'Higgins, than I do for associating 'An Irish Airman Foresees His Death' with Robert Gregory.

This is a short, fragmented poem, by no means, I should have thought, one of Yeats's best, though it is often quoted. The distinction between animal and man at the start is incorrect, as anyone who has the slightest knowledge of animals will know. It is mainly held, in my experience, by dogmatic Catholics, and I am amazed that the author of 'The Cat and the Moon' should have perpetuated so insensitive a lie, even for the purpose of a poetic structure.

Lines 3–4 are, of course, revealing; their very simplicity proclaims the ultimate agnosticism within which all our tentative guesses about Yeats have to be set. The contrast in ll. 5–10 between cowardice and bravery ought to be commonplace, though one suspects complications related to *A Vision*. The ending is by any standards opaque, and perhaps simply has to reach its way, in our memory, towards all those bones upon a beach, and elsewhere, which the entire corpus can provide. My own mind goes back especially, to a passage from 'The Tower' which I find difficult also:

> I mock Plotinus' thought
> And cry in Plato's teeth,

Death and life were not
Till man made up the whole,
Made lock, stock and barrel
Out of his bitter soul. . . .

If the poem were intended to celebrate the death of one admired and brave man, then it surely fails, both in its reticence about naming him, and in its mingling of disparate themes. As a poem on the theme of death, it is strikingly unworthy of Yeats.

'A Dialogue of Self and Soul'

This remarkable poem was written between July and December 1927, a year after 'Sailing to Byzantium', and three years before ·'Byzantium'. Yeats wrote to Olivia Shakespear in October 1927 to say that he was composing a 'new tower poem "Sword and Tower"', which is a choice of rebirth rather than deliverance from birth. I make my Japanese sword and its silk covering my symbol of life.' In many contexts, as I recently remarked, it is 'soul' which is either chosen or seen as the source of ultimate delight. Here, 'My Soul' pursues somewhat gloomier reflections, but 'My Self' undoubtedly steals the poem (in the second part, takes it over unopposed). In this poem, 'Self' symbolises the joy of incarnate life, variety, the world of transience and, at the end, far from reaching forebodings of the kind expressed in 'Among School Children', stanzas v and vi – or, indeed, a choice of life such as had been invoked for the poet's daughter – we encounter, almost for the first time, a full-blooded defence of 'The fury and the mire of human veins'.

The poem is called 'A Dialogue', and Jeffares conjectures that it might have been influenced by Marvell's 'A Dialogue between the Soul and the Body', which Yeats had read in Grierson's Metaphysical anthology. If so, it could scarcely be more unlike its original. 'The Self' cannot, by any juggling, be reduced to 'the body': it is rather the whole consciousness of a man as he exists, incarnate. It takes as its emblem Sato's sword, which, as we have already seen from 'Meditations in Time of Civil War', had come to signify for Yeats the kind of conditional immortality (or defiance of change) associated with works of art. The contrast is therefore not an easy one to assess, particularly as 'My Self', far from entering into dialogue, appears to ignore 'My Soul' – or at least to answer in ways calculated to evade all its challenges.

The first stanza in Part I is 'My Soul's', and we cannot overlook the voice, which is immensely Yeatsian. 'I summon to the winding ancient stair' reminds of all the other poems of invocation we have

looked at (for instance 'I pace upon the battlements and stare / . . . .
And send imagination forth / . . . . and call / Images and memories'
– 'The Tower'). The call of sheer willpower is familiar; so is 'the
breathless starlit air', which surely belongs halfway to Byzantium.
The command 'Fix every wandering thought' has again a familiar
ring; and the last line will no doubt remind of the last line in stanza i
of 'Coole Park and Ballylee, 1931': 'What's water but the generated
soul?'.

In contrast, 'My Self' also sounds like Yeats, if in different mood.
The opening words, 'The consecrated blade', remind that Self, like
Soul, may belong with the occult and mysterious. The defiant claim
that Sato's sword has indeed withstood the onslaught of centuries
may, or may not, lend weight to the final choice for rebirth. Self is
determined to press the case, arriving at some kind of détente with
change, even for the protecting embroidery which 'Can, tattered,
still protect, faded adorn'. The word 'tattered' is bound to echo
against

> An aged man is but a paltry thing,
> A tattered coat upon a stick, unless
> Soul clap its hands and sing, and louder sing
> For every tatter in its mortal dress. . . .
> > 'Sailing to Byzantium'

As if taking a cue from this, 'My Soul' now goes on to the offensive,
in a manner most likely to hurt or influence the poet, as we have
reason to know:

> Why should the imagination of a man
> Long past his prime remember things that are
> Emblematical of love and war?

This is followed by the reiterated association of soul with 'night'
(echoing 'darkness'), and the essentially Eastern (or Platonic) wisdom
of disengaging 'imagination' and 'intellect' from mortal things (the
realm of desire), in search for the ultimate prize, Nirvana:
deliverance 'from the crime of birth and death'.

In the fourth stanza, 'My Self' continues its meditation on the
sword, almost as if Soul had not spoken, except that it does move
round to an answer at the end. The sword is now set in opposition to
the Tower, which is conceded to belong with the 'night' realm
claimed by Soul:

> > and all these I set
> For emblems of the day against the tower

> Emblematical of the night,
> And claim as by a soldier's right
> A charter to commit the crime once more.

A 'soldier's right', not an artist's: the Self comes out fighting: and, if rebirth is 'crime', then the Self will defy whatever alternative charter makes it so. (One cannot help recalling that in *A Vision* Yeats seems to regard the adventure of the incarnations – offering, as they do in that system, the eventual chance to enjoy most types of life, morality and experience – as valuable, and by no means to yearn for the more orthodox escape from this cycle, which 'Soul' speaks of here.)

The fourth stanza is undoubtedly difficult. 'My Soul' appears to be overwhelmed by what it has heard, though the first lines, describing presumably the richness of earthly living just opted for, oddly recall the first stanza, ll. 3–4, of 'Ancestral Houses' from 'Meditations in Time of Civil War', where the apparent riches of the old aristocratic culture are described attractively, in images very like these, before being rounded upon, for very different reasons, as 'Mere dreams, mere dreams!' 'My Soul' goes on, however, to say – as any good Platonist or Eastern mystic might – that, either when offering such thoughts, or possibly as a consequence of offering them, 'man is stricken deaf and dumb and blind'. Soul continues,

> For intellect no longer knows
> *Is* from the *Ought*, or *Knower* from the *Known*

– a statement, it seems, of both moral and spiritual confusion; but this leads to the very elusive conclusion

> That is to say, ascends to Heaven;
> Only the dead can be forgiven;
> But when I think of that my tongue's a stone.

I find that I can do nothing but doodle mentally around this. Is Soul suggesting that the way of Self, which leads to a darkening of the senses (though darkness has been associated with Soul), leads also, by a paradox, to enlightenment? Maybe in Heaven, as in sensuous and sensual unawareness of spirit, the distinctions between 'Is' and 'Ought', 'Knower' and 'Known' cancel out. Different though this is in mood, the rhythms undoubtedly bring back in a ghostly way, that far more joyous and positive conclusion of 'Among School Children':

> O body swayed to music, O brightening glance,
> How can we know the dancer from the dance?

The following thought (connected?) – 'Only the dead can be forgiven' – is not Christian, and not notably like the general current of *A Vision*. If it is a summary of Eastern wisdom, then the use of the word 'dead' is bound to be equivocal (is death-in-life, or actual bodily death, the only path to 'forgiveness'?). At this point one recalls that 'sin' and 'forgiveness' are not high among Yeats's usual preoccupations; and that even the supremely visionary experience of 'Byzantium' (still to be written) follows not the forgiveness, or even the purgation, of life, but merely a temporary withdrawal to another sphere of being ('The *unpurged* images of day *recede*' – my italics).

The Soul in this manner reduces itself to speechlessness, leaving the second part of the 'Dialogue' entirely to Self.

The interesting feature about this poem (perhaps I should say, one especially interesting feature – but it is indeed remarkable) is that Yeats said he was writing a poem about 'rebirth' rather than about 'reincarnation'. 'What matter if I live it all once more?' It is possible, of course, that he is thinking of reincarnation in a different body, yet I somehow doubt it. This view would be far more consonant with *A Vision*, but in that system the very essence is that future incarnations will each be radically different (unless one has to relive one of the phases, through mistakes during one's first attempt). The same impression is given by 'Mohini Chatterjee', a poem following in this volume and dated 1928 (though Jeffares says it was in fact written early in 1929). The material from the poem originated in a lecture which Yeats had heard in the mid 1880s in the Hermetic Society in Dublin, delivered by a Bengali Brahmin. The Brahmin's philosophy had run to a doctrine of total detachment, not unlike 'My Soul's' in the first part of our present poem, but his description of past lives had suggested no continuity between them:

> I asked if I should pray,
> But the Brahmin said,
> 'Pray for nothing, say
> Every night in bed,
> "I have been a king,
> I have been a slave,
> Nor is there anything
> Fool, rascal, knave,
> That I have not been,
> And yet upon my breast
> A myriad heads have lain".'

As will be seen, Yeats adds his own commentary, in direct opposition to the Brahmin's intention, making this thought an encouragement to 'Old lovers' to realise that, despite their present decrepitude, 'Birth is heaped on birth' and they can look forward to almost unlimited new frolics ahead.

But, if we return to 'A Dialogue between Self and Soul', the impression is that the rebirth will be into a life extremely similar to the present, if not an exact repetition of it: there will be the same sex, the same general circumstances and responses to them, the same predicament created by Maud Gonne. It is as if this were a defiant answer to all the doubts expressed in 'Among School Children': doubts which are resolved this time not through beautiful, if obscure, images, but through a triumphant and even ecstatic 'yes' to life as it is.

The first two stanzas of part II do indeed list the degradations of earthly life, piling up words connected with this: 'blind', 'impure', 'toil', 'ignominy', 'distress', 'unfinished', 'pain', 'enemies', 'defiling and disfiguring', 'malicious eyes' and, finally 'wintry blast'. But this time all the doubts are cast in the form of extended rhetorical questions, starting 'What matter if?' and, in the buoyant rhythm, cutting through all doubts and tangles with devil-may-care panache. The final two stanzas demand to be quoted:

> I am content to live it all again
> And yet again, if it be life to pitch
> Into the frog-spawn of a blind man's ditch,
> A blind man battering blind men;
> Or into that most fecund ditch of all,
> The folly that man does
> Or must suffer, if he woos
> A proud woman not kindred of his soul.

> I am content to follow to its source
> Every event in action or in thought;
> Measure the lot; forgive myself the lot!
> When such as I cast out remorse
> So great a sweetness flows into the breast
> We must laugh and we must sing,
> We are blest by everything,
> Everything we look upon is blest.

The Soul's preoccupation with 'forgiveness', whether in Heaven or anywhere else, is swept away in this exuberant self-absolution: a formula which leads straight to a 'song' unlike that of either young or old in 'Sailing to Byzantium', and achieving 'sweetness' greater than, and far differently based from, that of 'A Prayer for My Daughter'.

It is very heady verse: almost (as Yeats so often persuades us) the last word, but of course not really that. There will be much more metaphysics to examine before we come anywhere near such a concept: and, of course, even at an obvious level, the tremendous sonorities of the poem 'Are You Content?' (coming in the *Last Poems*) will have to stay somewhere in mind, along with Plato's unexorcised ghost, waiting to have *its* say.

None the less, I think this one of the valid points of rest in Yeats's unending pilgrimage, and warm to the 'Non, je ne regrette rien' mood. It is also a very distinct pointer to the really splendid celebrations of 'lust and rage' which have their apotheosis (not entirely unchallenged, of course) in the last period. No doubt I should admit, at this point, that, though the late Dr F. R. Leavis, Harold Bloom and other critics have regretted this side of Yeats, I agree entirely with those who, like Nicholas Brooke, find in it the finishing touch of his greatness. The early poems are indeed fine, and it would take someone wholly insensitive to poetry to deny this. I am fairly certain that, had Yeats died just before writing 'The Wild Swans at Coole', my own starting place, I should still consider him one of the twenty greatest modern poets; but not the greatest of them all, as I in fact do. The poems we have looked at up to now are the glory of the middle period, even though old age has so often been their theme. I tend to regard *The Winding Stair and Other Poems*, and perhaps this poem especially, as pivotal; and to feel that the territory we have still to visit, all to sketchily, contains the greatest consistent display of major writing in the *Collected Poems*.

'Coole Park, 1929'

This and its companion poem following must be among everyone's favourites, together with 'In Memory of Eva Gore-Booth and Con Markiewicz'. When Yeats writes about friends, one of his most deeply passionate instincts controls the poems. All symbolic and thematic aspects take colour from love; and I am certain that it is this intensely human quality, for which he had a rare genius, that sets one final seal of greatness on his work. In pure technique, Eliot and R. S. Thomas may be his equals, though Thomas has seldom attempted long flights. With the possible exception of Wallace Stevens, no other modern (not even Graves and Auden) can touch him in craftsmanship. All three – and Wallace Stevens could again be included – have linked their art, to which the discipline of a whole life has been chiefly dedicated, with a continuing exploration of meaning or meaninglessness in ultimate religious terms. Yeats alone, however, has added to this rare and strenuous devotion a warm humanity, an earthiness, along with exhilirating power to celebrate friendship and eroticism equally, which lifts him to a level previously attained by the Greek tragic poets, by Shakespeare, and by very few others who readily spring to mind. In the English tradition, Donne, Marvell and Keats suggest themselves; but the first two, great though they are, have in my personal experience over a period of thirty years been less consistently haunting, enriching and deepening influences; while Keats, the Mozart of our poetry, who seems at times a portent outside any covenant (if I may borrow Bernard Levin's praise of Mozart), died in his mid twenties, at an age when Yeats himself had produced *Crossways*, but not yet *The Rose*.

These two poems require little exposition, particularly for those who have been following the earlier development. It is as if Yeats emerged in them into a rare clarity, even though his imagery and syntax are wrought to beauty and many familiar themes are once more rearranged. In appearance they are as dense in thought and texture as many far more as difficult poems, yet their chief note is of contemplation, ease, even serenity.

'Coole Park, 1929' was completed at Coole Park on 7 September 1929, though not published until 1931. A prose draft reads,

> Describe house in first stanza. Here Synge came, Hugh Lane, Shawe-Taylor, many names. I too in my timid youth. Coming and going like migratory birds. Then address the swallows fluttering in their dream like circles. Speak of the rarity of the circumstances that bring together such concords of men. Each man more than himself through whom an unknown life speaks. A circle ever returning into itself.

The first stanza begins with the swallow's flight, then moves to the house, where Lady Gregory was then still living after the death of son and husband, the last classic private patron of the arts. 'Great works constructed there in nature's spite' refers more, I imagine, to the immense difficulty of concentration experienced by an artist (swallows were symbols of indolence and transience for Pythagoras, who wrote 'receive not a swallow into your house') than to anything unpropitious in the setting. 'For scholars and for poets after us' are a reminder that Yeats, like Eliot, believed in a great tradition and intended his own works to be worthy of a place in Byzantium, whatever the ironies surrounding this concept. The final two lines,

> Thoughts long knitted into a single thought,
> A dance-like glory that those walls begot

express the mystery of unity and diversity, stillness and dancing with great ease. They can be kept in mind at the end of 'Among School Children', and through the whole of 'Byzantium', very much like a landmark that can guide through denser terrain.

The second stanza names the people. Jeffares's *Commentary* provides sufficient notes on these, if any are unfamiliar: we know that it was Synge, and Lady Gregory herself, with whom the poet identified most closely ('The Municipal Gallery Revisited', stanza vi). The phrase 'pride established in humility' is also echoed in this later poem, in the splendid fourth stanza, which concerns Lady Gregory. With every appearance of ease, it unites opposites, as they touch both people and the enterprise of art itself. For a moment, some of those strangely interwoven complexities in 'Meditations in Time of Civil War' might seem resolved, at least if they are applied to this last instance, out of due season, of aristocratic privilege interacting with the status of art.

Stanza iii is a recollection, in tranquillity, of many years. The fifth line glancingly remembers Aquinas's angels dancing on a pinpoint, and the last three lines appear to repose on those qualities least familiar to the poet ('certainty', 'intellectual sweetness'), whilst drifting in the needful balances ('dreaming', 'withershins') with a lightness that does nothing to break the spell. The 'swallow' image now becomes the highest example of creative tact, the power to preserve total freedom, yet to control destiny ('first intent'); and, centrally placed in the poem's economy, symbolises 'a woman's powerful character'. Yeats wrote many things of Lady Gregory during his long association with her in the founding and building of the Abbey Theatre. Perhaps one quotation will suffice: 'When in later years her literary style became in my ears the best written by a woman, she had made the people a part of her soul; a phrase of Aristotle's had become her motto: "To think like a wise man, but to express oneself like the common people".'

Finally, the magnificent last stanza (and compare this especially with the conclusion of 'A Municipal Gallery Revisited'):

Here, traveller, scholar, poet, take your stand
When all these rooms and passages are gone,
When nettles wave upon a shapeless mound
And saplings root among the broken stone,
And dedicate – eyes bent upon the ground,
Back turned upon the brightness of the sun
And all the sensuality of the shade –
A moment's memory to that laurelled head.

The effect is almost indescribable, though the meaning simple. Note how 'traveller, scholar, poet' delicately recalls the 'Soldier, scholar, horseman, he' which had been central to 'In Memory of Major Robert Gregory'. Now 'horseman' becomes 'traveller' – phasing out the special heroism of Lady Gregory's dead son, but allowing the reader, as pilgrim, room in the poem. The word 'scholar' remains (not with 'The Scholars' in mind, but the real creature, of whom many alleged scholars are, maybe, so many Casaubon-like parodies.) 'Poet' replaces 'Soldier' – but, of course, Robert Gregory had been a painter, supposedly of great promise, so might have fitted the company assembled here had he lived. As usual, men of action and men of contemplation or art are not divided by Yeats, but joined, in a common pattern of will and distinction ('Long-legged Fly' is the definitive text.)

The picture of the ruined house is strangely prophetic. After Lady Gregory's death, Coole Park passed to the Forestry Commission, who bought it in her life-time and rented it to her while she lived. After her death, the Commission sold it, and the buyer pulled it down. Today it is possible to see the ruin precisely as the poet foreshadows here, and, if one chooses, possible to offer the homage he asks.

In the end, when we have wrestled with complexities and delighted in the poetry, I have no doubt that this is the moment Yeats would bring us to. Beyond and transcending all is love, and its concomitant, celebration. Is it possible to love a person, appreciate a poem, without giving thanks – in formal prayer, if that is one's habit, or in spontaneous song to the unknown gods? 'A moment's memory': in the end, if Yeats could have been sure that his readers would reach out from his art – out from their own disciplines of literary criticism, literary study too – in this direction, no doubt he would have known one of the two or three 'contents' possible for such a man. Celebration redeems even ruin (possibly that crucial late poem, 'Lapis Lazuli', is already forming somewhere). As the poem ends 'brightness of the sun' and 'sensuality of the shade' are reconciled; but reconciliation is *in* the power to turn from both, for one moment, and give thanks, with the poet himself, for Augusta Gregory.

This incidentally, is why a tour of Yeats and Eliot country is so much more rewarding, in my experience, than any other 'literary tour'. It has to be done alone, even if a crowd surrounds one. It has to turn to pilgrimage as 'words, after speech, reach into the silence'. At Coole Park, one will remember Lady Gregory, as Yeats asks here. In Drumcliffe churchyard, thanks can be given under the shadow of Ben Bulben, and in the enigma of the words carved, for the poet himself.

'Coole Park and Ballylee, 1931'

The first verse is another description of Coole Park, concentrating this time on the underground origin and ramifications of the famous lake. Raftery is the blind Gaelic poet mentioned in 'The Tower'.

Because of the complex underground tributaries, the lake doubles or trebles its size in winter. The last line of the first stanza is one of Yeats's characteristic rhetorical gestures, and strikes me as the one possible flaw in the poem. Jeffares quotes Yeats as saying 'Did not the wise Porphyry think that all souls come to be born because of water, and that "even the generation of images in the mind is from water"?' The idea is also a commonplace in some of the Eastern texts with which Yeats would have been familiar.

The next two stanzas become increasingly evocative, and offer pointers to this poem's mood. 'Nature's pulled her tragic buskin on' sets the scene, and 'dry sticks under a wintry sun' will recall images of old age, as well as of trees in winter. But, against depression, Nature also has 'rant' to offer, which is 'a mirror of my mood'. 'At sudden thunder of the mounting swan' returns to the image which was so powerful in 'Wild Swans at Coole', written fifteen years earlier; the close identification of poet and bird will again recall that powerful line from 'Nineteen Hundred and Nineteen': 'The swan has leaped into the desolate heaven'. Stanza iii uses the word 'emblem', which increasingly has the force of 'symbol' or 'image' in later Yeats. Various critics have spent time drawing destinctions between his usages of these terms, not uninterestingly, but I am inclined to remain agnostic. It is evident that the subtle interactions of consciousness and sense perceptions intrigued Yeats as greatly as it did the early nineteenth-century romantics; but that he is far less concerned than Wordsworth and Coleridge were to theorise about the interplay philosophically, or to separate the creative faculty from the mystery of image-making. As we have seen, for him this is a mingling of invocation and creation, usually with memory attentive, and some occult reference always possible even when it is not explicit. Yet Yeats's own preference for a dialectic on these issues, often pursued by implied juxtaposition between the poems, rather than more directly, is very apparent. Obviously, he is concerned with the primary meaning of 'emblem', as most dictionaries give it (for instance, 'a figurative representation; symbol'), rather than the secondary, and more precise meaning (for example, a family or group 'emblem', with one definite meaning prescribed). 'But seems' is interesting: an arresting phrase, which has both a strong and a weak potential: it could mean 'merely seems', introducing the idea of rootless fancy, or could (as I think is the case) come close to meaning 'becomes, or *is*, in the poetic consciousness'. Lines 3–4 sweep upwards, like the mounting swan, 'sails' infusing them with great force, so that 'no man knows why' has more in it of triumph than of doubt, despite its plain meaning. Once more, we are assured that soul, like swan, flies somewhere, not nowhere, even if beyond the poet's ken. The fifth and sixth lines, where swan, soul and the 'stormy white' appear almost conjoined as subject, continues the elation aroused by healing intuition as a reality superior to 'knowledge' –

> And is so lovely that it sets to right
> What knowledge or its lack had set awry

– yet the stanza concludes on another off-beat note:

> So arrogantly pure, a child might think
> It can be murdered with a spot of ink.

The use of 'arrogantly' is a brilliant reminder of the ambiguity in moments of elation; and, though 'a child might think' gives the impression that the child is wrong (as no doubt he is, in terms of the emblem), Jeffares reminds us that Yeats had written, in 'The Irish Dramatic Movement', words of more sombre import: 'Did not M. Tribulat Bonhomet discover that one spot of ink would kill a swan?'.

Stanzas iv–v rise once more to nobility. Stanza v begins with an image of old age which must be one of the most universal, and sad, that even Yeats has given. We then realise that we are hearing (not seeing) Lady Gregory, as though she were already half a ghost, moving around in the house that has been built over so long a period, in a tradition of untainted honour and genius, and is shortly, like its owner, to take flight into the unknown. Words such as 'Beloved', 'famous', 'Old' (used twice, with reverence now), 'Great', 'Content or joy' celebrate qualities which have been generated, and regenerated, through the great period (personally, the great period of Yeats's own life in its most productive years; emblematically, the great period of the aristocratic tradition at its best, throughout history). 'Those images that yet / Fresh images beget . . .' In balance, the second line remains a haunting presence; while the last line reminds us that we are dealing now not with the poet who dreams equally 'of the noble and the beggar-man' and himself prays for 'folly' in old age, but with the poet who honours all genius; who weighs a multitude of millions against a hundred select souls, and finds the millions wanting; and who returns several times to the thought that few greater crimes can be committed than that of marrying, or begetting children on, an inferior, and so degenerating the human stock.

The sixth stanza, with its strongly placed 'Seemed' at the start of l. 2 turns reality to myth – or starts this transformation – almost unnoticed. Lines 4–5 already belong to a world not wholly anchored in Coole Park, or any earthly reality; though this is then made the touchstone of the sufficiently bitter conclusion, where Lady Gregory

and Yeats himself are now already exiles (or is the'We' reserved for
the rest of us?) 'all that great glory spent'.

The final stanza starts with a further, yet more resounding, 'We',
which tends to convince me that it is intended as a contrast, rather
than a continuation, of the 'We' just commented upon. The famous
phrase 'the last romantics' will naturally link, in our hearing of
them, with stanza vi of 'The Municipal Gallery Revisited'. Happily,
Yeats goes on to offer a comment on the phrase which is, also, one of
the major statements upon his own work and intentions:

> We were the last romantics – chose for theme
> Traditional sanctity and loveliness;
> Whatever's written in what poets name
> The book of the people; whatever most can bless
> The mind of man or elevate a rhyme. . . .

Yeats places himself with Milton, Pope, Wordsworth, Tennyson and
others – a tradition deeply rooted in European culture – among
writers who held the high view of art. Though he has in common
with the English romantic poets a desire to celebrate beauty, to keep
alive wonder, to search after every evidence of divinity at once in the
created world as we perceive it and in the creations which humanity
then offers back and adds, he is nothing like the nineteenth-century
romantics in their rejection of tradition. No doubt it can be argued
(as I have attempted elsewhere) that the English romantics were
rejecting not true classical culture, but the aridly intellectual neo-
classicism spawned in the seventeenth century by scientific
empiricism (a very different thing); in which event, Yeats might be
closer to them than at first appears. But he was far too pessimistic to
share their central vision; his consciousness is too distinctively
complex, too modern, for any real kinship. 'Traditional sanctity and
loveliness' remain his ideal, fated though he is, like the vast majority
of moderns, to reject the original foundations and to be singularly
elusive in his own attempts to construct new ones. The instinct for
blessing outsoars ideology, allowing the actual experience of art to
validate itself, to the degree necessary, even while the exploration for
other forms of validation has no ending.

The mood changes back to the tragic and, some would think, to
the 'arrogantly pure' in another guise. It is as if Yeats is writing
already the elegy of himself, Lady Gregory and her circle; and, with
this, the epitaph of poetry – 'Après moi, le deluge'. Even here, the
choice of images preserves ambiguity. Clearly, 'that high horse'
stands for poetry of Homeric vigour; but can we forget the high
horse, smuggled into Troy, which was Homer's theme? The final
line returns, once more, to the swan imagery, used now in a manner

reminiscent of the beautiful passage, already commented upon, in part III of 'The Tower'.

'The Choice'

The poem, probably written in February 1931, was originally the penultimate stanza of 'Coole Park and Ballylee, 1931'. Yeats was no doubt right to move it from the context where it would have jarred, and to allow it to stand as a statement on its own:

> The intellect of man is forced to choose
> Perfection of the life, or of the work. . . .

Here we have in its most epigrammatic form a thought which always haunted Yeats, one of his unresolved antinomies. But note that the second choice, which is Yeats's own, refuses a 'heavenly mansion' and is doomed to 'raging in the dark'.

Here, I think, we have another pointer to the great dialogue of all the later poems. In 'Dialogue of the Self and Soul' it was the way of Soul which was identified with 'darkness' (and moon): Self, which won its battle with Soul there (and cf. 'Vacillation', part VII), opted for light and joy. Maybe, if the sacrifice included Maud Gonne (and we might think back to the last stanza of part II of 'The Tower'), there is a touch of wishful thinking: as if Yeats is again toying with the possibility that he rejected her, rather than the other way round. Possibly he always felt that, had he been not a poet but a man of action, she would have responded differently.

However, 'A heavenly mansion' could mean the more extreme choice of lust, as well as of love. In 'Crazy Jane Talks with the Bishop', this same phrase is used by the Bishop in his exhortation to the crazed old hag to abandon lust:

> Live in a heavenly mansion,
> Not in some foul sty

but Crazy Jane rounds on the Bishop with the powerful phrase

> 'Fair and foul are near of kin,
> And fair needs foul', I cried.

The echo from *Macbeth* establishes the equivocal note which characterises the seven Crazy Jane poems; but we should recall that Yeats had invented Crazy Jane already, before both this poem and 'Byzantium', and that her poems seized on his imagination with a sense of personal release, caused, as he said himself, by prolonged sexual abstinence due to illness, even though a little later he is also on the record as trying to 'exorcise' them. I shall return to this crux, and to Nicholas Brooke's brilliant article on it, when looking at *Words for Music Perhaps*. But here it is important to notice the ambiguity written into this short, pregnant poem. In 'The Spur', 'lust and rage' will be yoked together, in another short poem which can no more be omitted from any serious consideration of Yeats's 'life' and 'work' than can 'Byzantium' itself.

The second half of 'The Choice' is depressed. Perhaps it is unfair to attribute the 'mark' left by toil, the 'old perplexity' unsolved, purely to this 'choice', since, as the poet well knew, they belonged to man's common lot. Even so, he is approaching the mood more fully explored in 'Vacillation', where radical doubts about the ultimate good of art, and of life itself, moved centre stage: 'the day's vanity, the night's remorse'.

'For Anne Gregory'

This is a ballad in lighter mood, written in September 1930 for Lady Gregory's granddaughter. The rhetorical display has a touch of self-mockery – Yeats still on *his* high horse, even though Homer's creature of the same name is now riderless. The tone is affectionate and teasing, not portentous, but, of course, a serious theme lurks. Is it possible to love a beautiful woman purely for her 'self' alone, or does physical beauty ultimately control 'love'? In Metaphysical poems such as Lord Herbert Of Cherbury's 'An Ode upon a Question Moved, Whether Love Should Continue for Ever?', and Donne's 'The Exstasie', the crucial problem concerning the origin and ultimate destiny of love was debated, at the time when the new science first brought it into prominence. Our own century has heard Freud asserting the total supremacy of sex, not only in love but in most spheres of behaviour – though Jung, to whom Yeats is more akin, always testified to a real, and supreme, spiritual dimension.

This short poem remains, inside the terms of its own playfulness, a graceful compliment with a touch of blarney. But the ice is thin. Anne Gregory has more beauty, it seems, than Yeats has prayed for his daughter; will she, like Helen and all women Helen symbolises,

Consider beauty a sufficient end,
Lose natural kindness and maybe
The heart-revealing intimacy
That chooses right, and never find a friend

('A Prayer for My Daughter')

'Byzantium'

On 16 April, T. Sturge Moore wrote to Yeats that 'Sailing to
Byzantium' had let him down in the fourth stanza, 'as such a
goldsmith's bird is as much nature as a man's body, especially if it
only sings like Homer and Shakespeare of what is past or passing or
to come to Lords and Ladies'. Yeats later wrote to him saying that
'Byzantium' originated in his criticism of 'Sailing to Byzantium',
which had shown 'that the original idea needed exposition'.

This, I think, can be safely ignored. Sturge Moore's somewhat
naïve comment is no more likely to have swayed Yeats than Bulwer
Lytton's remark on the end of *Great Expectations* is likely to have
influenced Dickens. 'Byzantium' uses certain symbols in common
with the earlier poem and their general import continues to be
influenced by *A Vision*. But, that said, the poems are utterly different.
The first poem is a self-contained artefact, beautifully calculated
and achieving its reasonably complex effects with satisfying
completeness. 'Byzantium' is paradoxical, open, opaque to interpretation – one of the great riddles or optical illusions of art. As
Nicholas Brooke has pointed out, it is far better read with the Crazy
Jane poems and 'Vacillation' in mind (and with the later poems to
hand) than in other contexts; 'Sailing to Byzantium' is less akin to it
in almost every aspect.

The prose draft for this poem, in Yeats's 1930 diary, ran,

> Subject for a poem. Death of a friend. . . . Describe Byzantium as it
> is in the system towards the end of the first Christian millennium.
> A walking mummy. Flames at the street corners where the soul is
> purified, birds of hammered gold singing in the *golden* trees [my
> italics], in the harbour [dolphins] offering their backs to the
> wailing dead that they may carry them to paradise.
>
> These subjects have been in my head for some time, especially
> the last.

Yeats also said that, when he was ill again with Malta fever at Rapallo
in the autumn of 1929. 'I warmed myself back to life with
"Byzantium" and "Veronica's Napkin"', looking for a theme that
might befit my years.' This can be linked with his attempt to exorcise
the sexual excitement of the Crazy Jane poems, though, as we know,
the exorcism was far from successful.

We have to remember that a number of other notions were
running in Yeats's mind (along with the whole of *A Vision*) when he
wrote this, his most ambitious attempt to reconcile the great
polarities of body and soul, life and art, time and eternity. In *Anima
Mundi* (1917) he had written,

All souls have a vehicle or body, and when one has said that with More and the Platonists one has escaped from the abstract schools which seek always the power of some Church or institution, and found oneself with great poetry, and superstition which is but popular poetry, in a pleasant, dangerous world. Beauty is indeed but bodily life in some ideal condition. . . .   (*Mythologies*, pp. 348–9)

This passage continues with an account of ways in which souls can manifest themselves to the living, notably through the assistance of a medium is séances. In a note on *The Dreaming of the Bones*, published in *Four Plays for Dancers* (1931), Yeats was to write

the world-wide belief that the dead dream back for a certain time, through the more personal thoughts and deeds of life. . . . The Shade is said to fade out at last, but the Spiritual Being does not fade, passing on to other states of existence after it had attained a spiritual state, of which the surroundings and aptitudes of early life are a correspondence.

For literary echoes, we should not forget that Jon Stallworthy has suggested Blake's 'London' as a presence lurking in the first stanza, and the famous lines from Coleridge's 'Ancient Mariner'

The Nightmare Life-in-Death was she,
Who thicks man's blood with cold

as the actual nucleus of the second. Nor should it be forgotten that one of the key dicta in Blake's *Marriage of Heaven and Hell* had been commented upon by Yeats in 1893, and that in his own copy of Saurat's *Blake and Modern Thought* he had pencilled the comment, 'I think there is no such thought known in England in Blake's day. It is fundamental in Blake'. This was noted against the passage concerning contraries, 'Without contraries there is no progression. Attraction and Repulsion, Reason and Energy, Love and Hate, are necessary to human existence. From these contraries spring what the religious call Good and Evil. Good is the passive that obeys Reason. Evil is the active springing from energy. Good is Heaven – Evil is Hell.'

Finally, before approaching this poem directly, we should bear in mind that in 1935 Yeats was to start work as co-translator of the *Ten Principal Upanishads*, and that, like Hermann Hesse, whose thought and creative writing bear continual resemblance to Yeats's, he could be counted among the 'Journeyers to the East'. Whether he was closely familiar with Lao Tzu's *Tao Te Ching* I do not know; but the thought in a section such as its fourteenth, whether known from this or from some other Eastern context, could have influenced some of the more obscure images (I am quoting from the recent Penguin translation by D. C. Lau, but many English versions have appeared in this century):

> Its upper part is not dazzling;
> Its lower part is not obscure.
> Dimly visible, it cannot be named
> And returns to that which is without substance.
> This is called the shape that has no shape,
> The image that is without substance.
> This is called indistinct and shadowy.
> Go up to it and you will not see its head;
> Follow behind and you will not see its rear.
> Hold fast to the way of antiquity
> In order to keep in control the realm of today.
> The ability to know the beginning of antiquity
> Is called the thread running through the way.

As in 'Among School Children', I have the feeling of a stream of consciousness, but a stream far less closely associated now with the poem's persona (for once, I think this word is needed), or with any tangible external events, than in the earlier poem. In fact, there is a very strong sensation of dream or hallucination, and from the start I always feel, as reader, that the poem's consciousness is at least as much mine as the poet's. If so, then this must be the first of what I have called its optical illusions, since in imagery, theme and progression the poem is pure Yeats. The effect is paralleled by the extraordinary tightness of imagery – calling for concrete, if usually slightly bewildered attention – which co-exists with an experience of free-floating impressionism. When discussing this poem with students, I often find that it is worth taking an hour to doodle around the first stanza, checking where each reader thinks he or she is, and what is happening. The great diversity of response is always illuminating. I shall be offering, of necessity, chiefly my own responses; which I find correspond to about a third of other readers' impressions fairly exactly, though different domes and sensations may of course be mentioned, but which appear to baffle (or annoy as irrelevant) about another third. The remainder usually steer clear of such speculations, but, in the course of spending up to three or more hours on this poem, with various groups, I have found that nearly everyone has something to say on specific aesthetic or religious aspects (most usually both). A very common experience, for me, and I think for others, is to end an intensive session with the feeling that, at last, one is on the verge of penetrating to the ultimate secret of 'Byzantium'. For my part, this has always been transitory, and each session with it (now over a period of twenty-five years) has reinforced my own certainty of the poem's greatness, and of its final elusiveness. Moreover, when reading a critical account with which I have strong sympathy (and I am thinking especially of Nicholas Brooke's), it becomes apparent to me that, even so, he and I are *hearing* two very different poems. I agree with him that in the end the tensions are not balanced. I agree with him in thinking this intentional (though I am not sure if he would admit that word). I agree with him that the celebration – however we take it – has to be balanced against the almost equally complex Crazy Jane poems, and that 'A single imagination must encompass both, but "whoever tries to reconcile them", as Blake said, "seeks to destroy existence". The world *must* be torn to pieces by the energy of the great creators' 'Crazy Jane and "Byzantium",' in *Essays and Studies*, 1974). Even so, when Brooke discusses the stresses of 'Byzantium', they do not correspond at key points to my own reading stresses; which no doubt opens yet another layer of subtle oddity about this poem.

> The unpurged images of day recede;
> The Emperor's drunken soldiery are abed;
> Night resonance recedes, night-walkers' song
> After great cathedral gong;
> A starlit or a moonlit dome disdains
> All that man is,
> All mere complexities,
> The fury and the mire of human veins.

Reading this, I always have a most vivid sense of floating, disembodied, above St Mark's Square in Venice. The dome is one of those riding the cathedral, with a full moon turning it to eeriness. Though the great dome, riding in moon and starlight, 'disdains' me, my feeling is far more of elated empathy with its own mysterious life than with any realisation of being diminished. I have often wondered whether the word 'floats', from stanza ii, at some early stage influenced this response, yet I find that the out-of-body experience, and usually the free-floating elation, is shared by about one in three readers. When pressed, most readers find that they have drafted in a dome of their own – usually either from childhood, or from some moment of serene spiritual contemplation in their own lives. For my part, I can wonder why the single dome of Santa Maria della Salute does not replace the multiple domes of San Marco – also, I am aware that certain far more homely domes, on banks and small buildings in the Paddington I was born in (now mostly 'redeveloped'), lurk somewhere, as if there is an insistent call back to childhood. There is again, a very early dream – so early, that I cannot recall a time when I did not remember it vividly, always from long ago – in which I was in a desert where a bazaar of an Eastern kind was in progress and I saw most clearly a great dome, halfway between brown and pink in colouring, with golden eagles circling above it, which, alighting on various pinnacles, created an impression akin, as I now know, to the carved gryphons of Venice. This dréam was associated with pure joy (something very rare in my personal dream life), and haunted my childhood long before I had any theory of dreams, or any knowledge of Yeats and Eliot. When I first read Eliot's 'Triumphal March' and, still more, this stanza from Yeats, the whole dream flooded back, as it still does, becoming inextricably associated with my response. I mention this since it is precisely the kind of effect Symbolist poets often seek, knowing, as Eliot does, that an element of the private will necessarily colour each individual reader's response, even though the discipline of exact craftsmanship, and not mere vagueness, alone can evoke it ('My words echo / Thus, in your mind. / But to what purpose / Disturbing the dust on a bowl of rose-leaves / I do not know' – 'Burnt Norton').

The impression generated by this stanza usually remains, through each entire reading of the poem, even though each stanza takes one on a magic trip to a different vantage point. The effect is visionary: which may be why, though surges of elation and touches of possible nightmare lurk, I feel nothing of the violent contrasts that Nicholas Brooke reports; and in the end the poem seems to me to have dream logic, which only a Jungian could talk of, even though I am bound to bring the more normal waking, recreative faculties into action as well.

All I can now do is to make a few notes, which may clarify certain effects in the poem, though in a totally 'open' way.

The first line is of particular importance, in setting the mood. Yeats speaks of 'images of day' (and the word 'image', always important to him, is to prove central). These 'images' are 'unpurged' – which means, I take it, that they are suspended, as they may be in rare moments of calm, or vision, or hallucination just before sleeping or waking. They 'recede' and cease to be operative, releasing the soul into a visionary experience of night ('Who can distinguish darkness from the soul?'); but they are not 'refined by fire' – nor can I think that the 'flames' in stanza iv belong either to Purgatory or to Hell, though the case for the former is understandable, and has sometimes been made. 'The Emperor's drunken soldiery' belong with day's images, and cease to trouble. We may reflect that the poem might have in mind, before they leave the stage, not only the soldiers of the Byzantine Emperor – an earthy touch in the spiritual city itself; where the original dome is no doubt that of St Sophia – but also the waking Ireland where

>   a drunken soldiery
> Can leave the mother, murdered at her door
> To crawl in her own blood, and go scot-free;
> The night can sweat with terror as before
> We pieced our thoughts into philosophy. . . .

('Nineteen Hundred and Nineteen')

Lines 3–4 add to the purity of effect – a great cleansing of soul, in the immense spaces between or away from the day. I assume that 'night-walkers' song' need not refer only to prostitutes, but may also refer to the sound of young people singing, not necessarily drunkenly, as they walk home unseen in neighbouring streets or alleys. The powerful phrase 'Night resonance recedes' now moves night, like day, out of consciousness. Though it is 'midnight' in stanza iv, this always feels more like the midnight of fairy-tale and myth than of any normal time-scale. 'After great cathedral gong' allows all to drain away that might spoil the enchantment to come.

For the final four lines are, I find, enchantment, though Nicholas Brooke reports otherwise; I find not explosive shock, but a confirmation that, all day and night images now distanced, soul is freed for exploration in other scenes and worlds. As I have already said, although 'A starlit or a moonlit dome disdains' appears to diminish humanity, 'soul' seems able now to partake in this rare victory, associated with its own great monuments, and with their secret, timeless communing with visionary light (cf. 'The Cat and the Moon'). It is as if, in this moment of pure serenity and peace, the dome belongs with the moon or star light, which silvers it. The final four lines are wrapt into the calm; so that one can survey the life of body (often chosen by Yeats, as we know; and only temporarily transcended) as if from a great height. 'The fury and the mire of human veins' is a god's-eye view of the normal human scene – possibly looking forward to the vision of the old Chinamen towards the end of 'Lapis Lazuli', and, as in that passage, offering itself not for judgement (we are not to wonder whether such Olympian calm is, or is not, propitious for mankind in the end) but rather as initiation into one of the rarer modes of possible consciousness. 'All that man is' is a strong phrase, yet parodoxical in context, since, though this may be the detached view, the poem's consciousness is still human, though temporarily above the reach of 'All'. It is permissible to think that Yeats mildly amused himself when inserting 'mere complexities' into *this* poem; yet the words precisely mirror the degree of detachment achieved.

The second stanza is (with the fifth) the most difficult. If we place conscious artefacts (works of art) and religious visions or revelations (the transcendental) at centre, then we home in directly upon Yeats's Byzantium. But to these must be added memories (from the past); hopes, wishes, fears and plans (for the future); fictions and fantasies (to one side of time); dreams, visions, hallucinations, delusions, delirium, drugged or dislocated consciousness (all experienced as 'real' inwardly, but judged by other people and maybe by the self later as not 'true' to waking consciousness); as well as symbols, images, emblems (those favourite Yeats concepts, rooted in time, but signifying things beyond, with varying claims to 'truth' status); and, of course, ghosts, shades, the dead between incarnations, and the entire realm of real or fancied beings conjured up or 'experienced' through the occult. Even this list is far from exhaustive, but it indicates, for practical purposes, the range of inner awareness that (say) any group of students in a seminar might have available, should the appropriate centres of individual consciousnesses be activated. The one thing they have in common, as a rough and ready distinction between this order of events and waking consciousness, is that, however vivid they may seem, they have none of the consequences that would attend them in the present moment. The final line of the fourth stanza, 'An agony of flame that cannot singe a sleeve', encapsulates this thought to perfection. In great works of art, in dreams, delirium and other such states, we might have mighty fires – all hell let loose; yet, in the prosaic surrounding of the present time – the time of 'The fury and the mire of human veins' – no sleeve would be singed. Only an immediate conflagration could produce *that* result. On the other hand, much of our 'reality' must be bound up with whatever of this immense other order of events we find valid – *unless* we are to assume that 'our' reality dwindles, always, to the present moment. This would mean not only that our entire potential, from the past and from imagination, is downgraded (as it scarcely can be, when a poem such as this is actually playing on it), but that the totality of human history and tradition, along with whatever we may designate by names such as 'Anima Mundi', 'the Collective Unconscious' and so forth, can be said to exist only in the focal second of any individual experience.

Perhaps this perspective helps to give some status to the 'image' in the second stanza. This 'image' cannot be exactly the dome, from stanza i, nor can it be identified with the bird of stanza iii, though in the poem's economy it is set between the two. The swift interplay ('man or ·shade, / Shade more than man, / more image than a shade') defies exegesis, yet leaves a distinct impression. 'Shade' necessarily suggests an actual ghost, as well as the shade cast by something not seen (I am always reminded of the more precise yet haunting ambivalences of Hardy's 'The Shadow on the Stone'). Nonetheless, 'Shade more than man' rapidly replaces 'man or shade', to be in turn superseded by 'more image than a shade'. If this is puzzling, we should recall that Yeats said of the spirit authors of *A Vision*, and with their own authority, that they came to give him 'metaphors for poetry': Yeats has his own version of the egotistical sublime.

The third and fourth lines tend, like the gyres, to paralyse my imagination, though various students have been kind enough to demonstrate the mechanism of sewing-machines, while Jeffares usefully directs us to the myth of Er in book x of Plato's *Republic*, where a similarly daunting mechanism, with 'the distaff of Necessity' fastened at the extremities, and the three Fates (or daughters of Necessity), Lachesis, Clotho and Atropos, in attendance, is said to hold 'together the whole revolving universe'. There is a clear reference to the 'shiftings' and unwindings and dreaming-back between incarnations, which is central to *A Vision*, but the main effect appears to be, as Nicholas Brooke says, one of a cluster of images which assert goings and comings between the spirit world and our own.

Lines 5–6 present one of the syntactical problems I have already alluded to, and I think it finely judged. Whether the mouth in l. 5, or the mouths in l. 6, function as subject is not clear; though, either way, the mystery seems somewhat akin. 'A mouth that has no moisture and no breath' is decisively dead and belongs, no doubt, to a ghost. 'Breathless mouths' may also be dead or very much alive, according to the meaning you give 'Breathless'. If taken literally, it also means dead; if figuratively, then it can mean panting with eagerness, or fatigue, or passion. Perhaps the lines tell us that we may be called by the dead; perhaps that the dead may be summoned by ourselves. (This second interpretation strikes me as more consonant with Yeats's normal thinking, but I do not imagine that either view is meant to exclude the other.) Finally, the 'me' who has entered only with the second stanza now becomes a scarcely less shadowy 'I': yet here we may at least sense that the Yeats who is so familiar to us makes his appearance, to preside over the remaining stanzas. 'I hail' has all the panache of the old magician; but the exact force of the concluding lines is far from clear. If this *is* the spectral figure which so appals Coleridge's 'Ancient Mariner', yet which prefigures his return to life and destiny (though not, be it noticed, his final purgation from sin), then 'superhuman' is no doubt earned. It should not be forgotten, however, that, despite the vivid if uncanny effect of the stanza, the word the poet has settled for is still 'image'. In 'The Circus Animals' Desertion', all his work will be described as 'masterful images' – a phrase not without irony, but undeniably transcending all its ironies as well.

The third stanza introduces the golden bird, in a formula echoing that which opens the second stanza, and presumably depending upon it, so that 'miracle' here becomes what 'image' was before. This bird cannot be the same as the bird in 'Sailing to Byzantium', despite its origin in similar mythology. It is immensely more impersonal and mysterious – linked not with Yeats's anger at old age, and still less with Yeats's apparent wish to *become* an artefact (neither of these themes seems remotely appropriate to this poem), but more directly with the 'dome' in stanza i, and the Byzantine permanence. The choice of 'miracle' gives it status even higher than 'golden handiwork', and 'glory of changeless metal' deflects attention away from the paradoxes which diminished the 'golden bird' in 'Sailing to Byzantium'. The word 'Planted' has no irony, I think. True, the bough is also an artefact, not a growing thing, so 'Planted' could have ironic overtones (this matter is one where each reader will have to judge for himself). The phrase 'star-lit golden bough' is bound to link the bird both with the 'starlit . . . dome' and with the whole territory of Frazer's exploration of mythology. When the artefact is said to 'scorn aloud . . . Common bird or petal', it appears exactly to echo the pattern of the 'dome' which 'Disdains / All that man is' in the first stanza, and this is underlined by the last line ('And all complexities of mire or blood') which also refers back. Nicholas Brooke has conjectured that the 'golden bird' is implicitly criticised through (among other things) the comparison 'Can like the cocks of Hades crow' – which admittedly downgrades it to a 'cock', and offers 'crow' as an odd description of the song of this 'miracle'. But Jeffares reminds us, for a further comparison, of 'The Adoration of the Magi', one of Yeats's three occult fictions dated 1897 and published in *Mythologies* (though, as usual, I wish it were clearer in the present Macmillan editions how much later rewriting appears in the text). Perhaps rather than attempt comment I can quote the passage at some length. Three Magi, mourning the reported death of Michael Robartes, are sent off by a strange voice speaking through the second oldest, who has fallen asleep, to Paris, 'where a dying woman would give them secret names and thereby so transform the world that another Leda would open her knees to the swan, another Achilles beleaguer Troy'. Coming to the place, these latter-day Magi find a beautiful woman lying asleep, and another beside her; they are led in by 'an old over-dressed woman, who said, 'O, you are her three kinsmen from Ireland. She has been expecting you all day.' The passage continues,

> 'We have been deceived by devils', said one of the old men, 'for the Immortals would not speak through a woman like this.'
>   'Yes', said another, 'we have been deceived by devils, and we must go away quickly.'

'Yes', said the third, 'we have been deceived by devils, but let us kneel down for a little, for we are by the death-bed of one that has been beautiful.' They knelt down, and the woman sitting by the bed whispered, and as though overcome with fear, and with lowered head, 'At the moment when you knocked she was suddenly convulsed and cried out as I have heard a woman in childbirth and fell backwards as though in a swoon.' Then they watched for a little the face upon the pillow and wondered at its look, as of unquenchable desire, and at the porcelain-like refinement of the vessel in which so malevolent a flame had burned.

Suddenly the second oldest of them crowed like a cock, till the room seemed to shake with the crowing. The woman in the bed still slept on in her death-like sleep, but the woman who sat by her head crossed herself and grew pale, and the youngest of the old men cried out, 'A devil has gone into him, and we must begone or it will go into us also.' Before they could rise from their knees, a resonant chanting voice came from the lips that had crowed and said: –

'I am not a devil, but I am Hermes the Shepherd of the Dead. I run upon the errands of the gods, and you have heard my sign. The woman who lies there has given birth, and that which she bore has the likeness of a unicorn and is most unlike man of all living things, being cold, hard and virginal. It seemed to be born dancing; and was gone from the room wellnigh upon the instant, for it is of the nature of the unicorn to understand the shortness of life. She does not know it has gone, for she fell into a stupor while it danced, but bend down your ears that you may learn the names that it must obey.' Neither of the other two old men spoke, but doubtless looked at the speaker with perplexity, for the voice began again: 'When the Immortals would overthrow the things that are to-day and bring the things that were yesterday, they have no-one to help them, but one whom the things that are to-day have cast out. Bow down and very low, for they have chosen this woman in whose heart all follies have gathered, and in whose bodies all desires have awakened; this woman who has been driven out of Time and has lain upon the bosom of Eternity.' (*Mythologies*, pp. 311–12)

In *The Golden Bough*, cocks are frequently associated with sacrifice, and with death and resurrection patterns. There are no 'cocks of Hades' specifically, though, in the chapter on Dionysus in *Spirits of the Corn and of the Wild*, vol. I, Frazer records, from sources in Pausanias and Apollodorus, a myth that Dionysus descended into Hades to bring his mother Semele from the dead. The local Argive tradition was that he went down through the Alcyonian lake, and that his return from the lower world, or resurrection, was celebrated on this spot annually by the Argives, 'who summoned him from the water by trumpet blasts, while they threw a lamb into the water as an offering to the warder of the dead'. Frazer says that among the Lydians this was associated with the advent of spring, and the god was supposed to bring this season with him.

When we have a final look at the third stanza of 'Byzantium', we notice that the golden birds appear to have two alternatives. One, we have just considered at length; the other, introduced by 'Or', in l. 5, is the major parallel with the dome from which I started. If the birds make the first choice, do they themselves shuttle back to the world of the living, of death and resurrection, and forfeit, for good or ill, the right invested in 'changeless metal'? The complicating phrase, in this option, is 'by the moon embittered'. The moon is, we know, associated both with inspiration and with night (the sphere of soul), yet also with change, which alone can produce art (cf. not only 'Sailing to Byzantium', but also 'My Table' from 'Meditations in Time of Civil War': 'Yet if no change appears / No moon; only an aching heart/Conceives a changeless work of art'). The choice of 'embittered' is especially interesting, since all three of its normal meanings belong to life and shade into each other (impart a bitter taste to; make sour, morose or unhappy; intensify in anger). There is no other possibility in the word to balance these, so maybe the second option invested in the bird, which *appears* to fit in with the poem's dreamlike serenity, does, rather, move sharply against it at, or from, this point. If so, 'scorn' would have something now of real derision for common man, as well as 'Common bird or petal', and would potentially reflect this reality back into 'disdain' in the first stanza, even though the plain meaning there always seems to me, as I have said, neutralised.

The next stanza has undoubtedly attracted differing interpretations. Jeffares assumes that the fire purges the 'blood-begotten spirits', who are ghosts, and offers this as his note on 'all complexities of fury leave'. I very much doubt this – partly, as I have said, because I think the whole poem visionary, and controlled by the 'unpurged' in its first line. A more hopeful clue can be found, I think, in notes which Yeats made for *A Vision* two years before writing this poem, and which Richard Ellmann quoted in *The Identity of Yeats* (1954):

At first we are subject to Destiny . . . but the point in the Zodiac where the whirl becomes a sphere once reached, we may escape from the constraint of our nature and from that of external things, entering upon a state where all fuel has become flame,

where there is nothing but the state itself, nothing to constrain it
or end it. We attain it always in the creation or enjoyment of a
work of art, but that moment though eternal in the Daimon
passes from us because it is not an attainment of our whole
being. . . .

The 'Emperor's pavement' is no doubt the marble floor of the
Forum in Byzantium, called 'The Pavement'. At midnight (chosen as
the 'witching hour') the moonlight sets the depiction of flames
dancing, so that art takes on the appearance of life, and one has an
effect which can be compared either with Yeats's invocation to the
mosaics in stanza iii of 'Sailing to Byzantium', or with the creative or
recreative process itself. I assume, in fact, that this passage from the
living world to the Byzantine is effected by imagination or by sheer
intensity of being. Far from purgation, it is the raising of life in
'blood-begotten spirits' to a pitch where 'The fury and the mire of
human veins' finds temporary release, and, while the moment lasts,
mortal men can again say,

> O body swayed to music, O brightening glance,
> How can we know the dancer from the dance?
> ('Among School Children')

But the world of art *is* removed from primary reality, as if self-
generated ('Flames that no faggot feeds, nor steel has lit, / Nor storm
disturbs, flames begotten of flame'), so that, though in this stanza the
living flesh, in vision, appears to have outsoared even the 'miracle' of
one Byzantine artefact, it too has a price to pay,

> Dying into a dance
> An agony of trance,
> An agony of flame that cannot singe a sleeve.

For a moment, a simple reference back to 'The Choice' might
suffice, to get the main bearing, though in my own reading
experience the enchantment set up in the opening line still
continues, at least while the poem lasts; the undercurrents working
against it are also assimilated, at least in the art itself.

So to the final stanza, which I find an exultant climax, notably in
the last line (thereby once more radically differing from Nicholas
Brooke's report). The opening suggests a great wave of spirits,
carried over here to the dance by dolphins (one of the creatures
named by Mrs Strong in *Apotheosis and the After Life* as bearing the souls
of the dead into the next world). But the dolphins too are living
creatures of 'mire and blood', so that they surely belong as much

with the living vision of art as with 'life after death'.

The major puzzle, I always find, is the word 'break', twice repeated. Unlike 'embittered', this is indeed a word of many meanings, including virtual opposites, and no doubt Yeats chose it carefully with this in mind. In balance with meanings such as 'destroy', 'deprive', 'fragment', it can also mean 'to force an entrance into' (as in 'breaking and entering'), or to control (as with a horse), and various other things. We have to decide, I think, whether the degree of triumph achieved in the fourth stanza is confirmed and thrown back again from eternity to the world of the living; or whether it is decisively checked, in the end, by 'The golden smithies of the Emperor!' Opting, as I do, for a triumphant rhetoric, and for the assertion that enchantment is ultimately supported, rather than undermined, by the all-important question of tone as the poem progresses, I prefer the former view. Essentially in this poem, the tide of dolphin-born spirits is 'controlled' by the smithies, and 'bitter furies of complexity' are destroyed, or dissolved, in the experience of 'Marbles of the dancing floor'. In this reading, we can arrive at the crucial lines

> Those images that yet
> Fresh images beget

with some certainty that Yeats is once more celebrating the power of art and vision to break through the 'fury and the mire of human veins' and transcend them, even though they remain the stuff from which art is most usually made. The dance of images prefigures, I think, one of his last, and most interesting, explorations of art, 'Lapis Lazuli'. The final line, 'That dolphin-torn, that gong-tormented sea', requires, I think, stresses on every word, leaping exultantly; and, though 'torn' and 'tormented' are undoubtedly there in balance, the rhythms have surely achieved, by way of the contemplative opening and the withdrawal from 'unpurged images', a détente between imagination and life.

If this is agreed (and I admit again that an entirely different reading, turning on the word 'break', and on the tone chosen, is equally possible), it still needs to be said that this is no more 'final' than any other poem we have encountered. That the triumph is won at considerable cost is attested by the images and the ambivalences; also by the difficulty endemic to the poem itself. Again, the apparent reconciliation of human veins and the dance is momentary – as Yeats himself said in the passage from his prose most recently quoted here. The condition prescribed in line one is 'given', and rare; more than any other Yeats poem, this seems to me to border on the visionary. Sooner or later – very soon – the 'unpurged images' will return, and this poem in its turn recede; at best, it must live with that chain of dialectic set up throughout the poet's total work. What I am certain of, is that no one but Yeats could have written 'Byzantium'; and that it could not have been conceived, except by way of the development I am trying to sketch.

'Vacillation'

This poem was written in 1931 and 1932, immediately after completion of the Crazy Jane sequence, which spans the period from March 1929 to November 1931, and slightly more than a year after 'Byzantium'. Nicholas Brooke conjectures that the order in which they finally appeared in *Collected Poems* is calculated by Yeats to reverse the order in which they were apparently conceived (Crazy Jane an embodiment of 'original sin', 'Byzantium' 'very obviously to do with "soul" as distinct from "heart"', and 'Vacillation' a poem 'where Heart triumphs in a dialogue with Soul and announces original sin as its chosen theme') and adds, 'But the search for a theme [i.e. 'a theme that might befit my years', as Yeats had said of 'Byzantium'] is not necessarily the finding of it, and reversing the order of these poems gives to that crytic note the ironic twist that the theme found appears to be the opposite of the one searched for'. Since I substantially agree with this – whilst again wishing to assert that Yeats is too elusive for any formula to do justice to the complexity of dialectic between poems – I am this time considering the poems strictly in the final order he chose for them.

'Vacillation', which in form has something of the appearance of 'Meditations in Time of Civil War', though it is far less substantial, juxtaposes opposites in its final arrangement. A considerable amount of work has been done on the dating of the parts (see Jeffares's *Commentary*), and at first they each had titles: I, 'What is Joy?'; II, 'The Burning Tree' (which became split into II and III subsequently); IV, 'Happiness'; V, 'Conscience'; VI, 'Conquerors' (inserted here later); VII, 'A Dialogue'; and VIII, 'Von Hügel'. Part I was written in December 1931 (a month after the final Crazy Jane poems ('Crazy Jane and Jack the Journeyman' and 'Crazy Jane Talks with the Bishop'), and in a letter written to Olivia Shakespear on 15 December Yeats speaks, with a classic touch of part-exuberant, part-despairing wildness, about having begun 'a longish poem called "Wisdom" in the attempt to shake off "Crazy Jane", and I begin to think I shall take to religion unless you save me from it'. The mutation of the title from 'Wisdom' to 'Vacillation' is clearly a piece of wry realism, and indeed 'Wisdom', for which Yeats spent a lifetime searching, is no fit title for any single poem. The 'attempt to

shake off' Crazy Jane suggests that 'Byzantium', which was
surrounded by her, has not done the trick; while the remark about
religion hovers between flippancy and continual openness. To my
mind, the title eventually chosen very precisely pinpoints one of the
central Yeats preoccupations, which maybe 'Byzantium' and 'Crazy
Jane' had equally, if in different ways, cut through. 'Vacillation' is
again about the predicament of old age: the desire to come to terms
with it, purging 'rage'; the desire to place it in various perspectives
that could point forward; the desire somehow to defy it still, if any
way can be found. The first of these hopes remains impossible, the
second tentative, the third a battle of will against irony. All of this
Yeats knows full well, yet he never repeats himself. In the late poems,
we have, no doubt, to put 'The Circus Animals' Desertion' and
'Lapis Lazuli' side by side, if we want a deeper and final exploration
of the poet's unending vacillation. None the less, Yeats went on
writing, and writing splendidly, by the sheer determination of
unbeaten craftsmanship and indomitable will-power, even though
the irreversible betrayal of self, heart and soul by body went
relentlessly forward. If I can risk the sacrilege of returning to 'Sailing
to Byzantium', and slightly altering the words towards what I take to
be the truth of the matter, Yeats clapped his hands and sang, and
louder sang, for every tatter in his mortal dress. Purists will be aghast
at this violation for every sort of good reason, but I am willing to risk
'Yeats' as the word I want at this moment, rather than his own 'soul'
– or indeed 'heart' or 'self', though these come nearer the mark.

The first section of 'Vacillation' was enclosed in a letter to Olivia
Shakespear, postmarked 23 November and dated 'last Sunday', that
also included this paragraph:

> I went for a walk after dark and there among some great trees I
> became absorbed in the most lofty philosophical conception I
> have found while writing *A Vision*. I suddenly seemed to
> understand at last and then I smelt roses. I now realised the nature
> of the timeless spirit. Then I began to walk and with my
> excitement came – how shall I say? – that old glow so beautiful
> with its autumnal tint. The longing to touch it was almost
> unendurable. The next night I was walking in the same path and
> now the two excitements came together. The autumnal image,
> remote, incredibly spiritual, erect, delicately featured, and mixed
> with it a violent physical image, the black mass of Eden. Yesterday
> I put my thoughts into a poem which I enclose, but it seems to me
> a poor shadow of the intensity of the experience.

> Between extremities
> Man runs his course.

A brand, or flaming breath,
Comes to destroy
All those antinomies
Of day and night;
The body calls it death,
The heart remorse.
But if these be right,
What is joy?

The affinity with Blake is clear, different though the two poets
ultimately are. The marriage of opposites is powerfully expressed,
with ll. 1–2 a motto for the entire poem. What is the 'brand, or
flaming breath'? In 'Byzantium' I ventured the guess that the
'flames' are not purgatorial, but connected rather with inspiration,
with images. Here, the matter is left open. Body has one name for it,
heart another. The body is the materialist: 'heart', as often in Yeats,
is a more shifting concept, and here I should rather have expected
'soul'. However, 'heart' is Yeats's word (and is to be the key word
mutating through 'The Circus Animals' Desertion'). Both body and
heart leave out 'joy'; and the letter I have quoted is useful as a
reminder that the poem originated in precisely this emotion.

Part II (as it later became, being no doubt correctly separated from
the present III) combines his personal experience of walking among
great trees with a tree described in *The Mabinogion* and mentioned in
'The Celtic Element in Literature' (dated 1902):

> When Matthew Arnold wrote, it was not easy to know as much as
> we know now of folk-song and folk-belief, and I do not think he
> understood that our 'natural magic' is but the ancient religion of
> the world, the ancient worship of Nature and that troubled ecstasy
> before her, that certainty of all beautiful places being haunted,
> which it brought into men's minds. The ancient religion is in that
> passage in the *Mabinogion* about the making of 'Flower Aspect'.
> Gwydion and Math made her 'by charms and illusions' 'out of
> flowers' . . . and one finds it in the not less beautiful passage about
> the burning tree, that has half its beauty from calling up a fancy of
> leaves so living and beautiful, they can be of no less living and
> beautiful a thing than flame: 'They saw a tall tree by the side of
> the river, one half of which was in flames from the root to the top,
> and the other half was green and in full leaf.' (*Essays and
> Introductions*, pp. 175–6)

In context, Yeats goes on to agree with Arnold that there is a 'Celtic
influence' in English poetry, notably in Keats and Shakespeare, and
to mingle the pagan instinct for nature worship with the distinctively

shadowy eroticism that underlies a lot of his own early work: 'If men had never dreamed that fair women could be made out of flowers, or rise up out of meadow fountains and paved fountains', he goes on, certain passages of famous verse from the past could never have been written.

No one will fail to notice the typical fusion of opposites in 'troubled ecstasy', or the many delicate withdrawals from reality-status ('haunted', 'brought into men's minds', ;charms and illusions', 'a fancy of leaves') which surround the vigorous assertion of 'beauty' as supreme experience.

This short section conjures up other archetypes. According to Acts 7:35, 'This Moses . . . the same did God send to be a ruler and a deliverer by the hand of the angel which appeared to him in the [burning] bush'. But Yeats is still more preoccupied with pagan sources, and drafts in Attis, the vegetation of god, who castrated himself because, Ellmann has suggested in *The Identity of Yeats*, he conceived of the artist as forced to sacrifice his life for the sake of his art. Attis's worshippers, hanging the image of Attis in March festivals between the body and soul of the tree, castrate themselves also, rejecting normal experiences for 'the ecstatic state of non-grief which may be called joy'. The final two lines suggest both peril in this image (destructive fire) yet also partial initiation, into the god's consciousness. This would seem to be negatively defined in the curious phrase 'May know not what he knows, but knows not grief'. Yet we recall that Epicurus himself defined pleasure chiefly as the absence of pain; and the fusion of Yeats's personal experience of positive joy (as transitory as the episode occupying part IV, which, with part V balancing it, forms the comparatively simple centre of this complex poem) with this more negative notion picks up the question with which the Part I had ended.

Part III appears also to tackle the question 'What is joy?', but with more earthy and familar enigmas. The first three lines are a rhetorical exhortation to satisfy desire (wealth, ambition, pleasure in trivial days), followed by the warning 'And yet upon these maxims meditate' – which leads on, however, not to its antithesis (which comes in the second stanza), but to two typically exaggerated statements encompassing all women and all men:

All women dote upon an idle man
Although their children need a rich estate;
No man has ever lived that had enough
Of children's gratitude or woman's love.

The 'All women' maxim is a return to a sore spot (Maud Gonne and MacBride notably), as well as to the growing obsession with genetic as well as other forms of deterioration. The 'No man' maxim is perhaps more authentic, at least on one side of Yeats's personality. Though never promiscuous himself, and fastidious about any debauchery, he had admitted to half envying Lionel Johnson and his like, even while condemning them; also, one suspects that 'woman's love' might again call to Maud Gonne, rather than to sexual *laissez-faire*. It is noticeable that the images in part II sprang from spiritual vision, but encompassed, through pertinent cross-references, a half-innocent mythological eroticism from the Celtic twilight.

The second stanza balances the first, partly as a contrast between youth and old age. I have been told that the Eastern Orthodox Church has a tradition which phases out middle-age, recognising only the young and the old, with the age of forty as dividing line. Even Yeats's eclecticism might not have come across (or welcomed) this piece of lore: and, as Jeffares says, he could have been thinking of his own fortieth year (1905), when the style of his mature work started to come into its own, and when Maud Gonne, although she had separated from MacBride, refused a divorce, since she had become a Roman Catholic. More generally, the thought would link with the second stanza of 'Sailing to Byzantium', part III of 'The Tower', and the wry aside in 'Among School Children' ('And I though never of Ledaean kind / Had pretty plumage once – enough of that'). In total, the part III embodies Vacillation in itself, without resolution; and parts IV–V, in their final arrangement, span the poem's centre with two further contrasts, simpler to grasp. Part IV takes us on to the Yeats we have chiefly been considering, his fiftieth year gone, and a sense of being 'solitary', but describes one of those occasional 'given' moments of happiness – caused by nothing that can be traced, and fading away to its own laws, but leaving a memory likely, for its result, to be particularly precious:

And twenty minutes more or less
It seemed, so great my happiness,
That I was blessèd and could bless.

Part V, in contrast, is more normal and prolonged consciousness not readily purged: 'Responsibility so weighs me down'. The occasional fear that haunted Yeats, at least from 1919 onwards, that his own poetry might have had violent political effects of a kind far from the intention, receives one of its clearest and bleakest expressions. We are pointed to an unrest, rooted now in time past and in personal history, which is inescapable and unredeemable. This is the seed of one of the major dilemmas stated by Eliot in 'Burnt Norton', and only fully solved (on Eliot's terms) in 'Little Gidding' (the present poem may be one of the many in Yeats which influenced Eliot's similarly disillusioned view of old age).

Part VI invokes the great lord of Chou, who has been tracked by critics through Yeats's reading of Richard Wilhelm's translation of *The Secret of the Golden Flower* to Chou-Kung, a twelfth-century member of the Chou dynasty; but no doubt a general sense of famous and distant Eastern potentates is enough. The refrain 'Let all things pass away' may remind us of two similar refrains, and the poems attached to them ('Mad as the mist and snow'; 'What then sang Plato's ghost, what then?'). The inclusion of Nineveh will bring to mind also Kipling's 'Recessional'. Here, 'branches of the night and day' are alike attributed, now, to 'man's blood-sodden heart' (not, after all, 'consumed away' as a prelude); and the inclusion of 'What's the meaning of all song?' would, if taken alone, come close to the notion, familiar in Wallace Stevens, that all structures are man-made, whether of war or art, and wholly transient. In its own fashion, this section could be regarded as equalising and even exorcising both happiness and responsibility (the two previous sections); and it leads immediately to the very pared down dialogue of Heart and Soul.

This, though short, is not easy. Nicholas Brooke says that 'Heart triumphs in a dialogue with Soul and announces original sin as its chosen theme'. On the face of it, this seems right, with Heart, 'blood-sodden' or otherwise, roughly standing in for Self in 'Dialogue of Self and Soul'. But Yeats, sending it in a slightly different version to Olivia Shakespear on 3 January 1932, surrounded it with somewhat baffling comments. He said that this poem 'puts clearly an argument that has gone on in my head for years', and announced that the theme would be taken up again in greater fullness. Then, after quoting the poem, he went on,

> I feel that this is the choice of the saint (St. Theresa's ecstasy, Gandhi's smiling face): comedy; and the heroic choice; Tragedy (Dante, Don Quixote) live tragically but be not deceived (not the Fool's Tragedy). Yet I accept all the miracles. Why should not the old embalmers come back as ghosts and bestow upon the saint all the care once bestowed upon Rameses? Why should I doubt the tale that when St. Theresa's tomb was opened in the middle of the nineteenth century the still undecayed body dripped with fragrant oil? I shall be a sinful man to the end, and think upon my death-bed of all the nights I wasted in my youth.

These heady reflections appear to outsoar the poem, but are a useful reminder that even Yeats at his simplest may have undeclared thoughts. Jeffares, in the *Commentary*, tells us that, a few weeks before her death, Lady Gregory had told Yeats that she admired certain poems translated from Irish because they came out of original sin. We have to note that in its closing sections, this poem homes in on Christianity, though as usual not accepting it. Whether 'original sin' has any clear meaning, apart from the one it has acquired in Christian theology, is doubtful, but, by referring it back to Homer, Yeats appears to unbaptise it. If he means the split nature of human desires, this is a fairly universal theme; likewise, if he is simply referring to the fact of mortality.

What seems clear is that Soul is co-opting 'reality' as its own realm, and beckoning in a Byzantine direction, by way of Isaiah's famous vision (Isaiah 6:1–9). This includes the prophet's conviction of sin, as a result of angelic revelation; the ritual cleansing through the coal of fire placed on his tongue; and the confirmation of his election, which he accepts, for the prophetic role. Heart, which has insisted that its own singing theme will not come from Soul's 'reality' (a rejection of 'Sailing to Byzantium' in the direction of 'The Spur'), is predictably unimpressed by Isaiah. The phrase 'the simplicity of fire' is difficult: it strikes dumb and is therefore not after all, according to Heart, a source of prophecy (or art). This has little connection, I should think, with the 'flames' in 'Byzantium'. In fact, Isaiah's flames purged acknowledged guilt, to release into God's service, as Soul elucidates in its next and final comment: 'Look on that fire, salvation walks within.' This would seem to prefigure the New Testament doctrine of atonement (extremely foreign to Yeats), and Heart clearly does win (or at least announce unabashed defiance) in its final comment – which is couched in Christian language perhaps out of simple courtesy to Soul.

Part VIII brings Von Hügel, with a degree of violence, into the picture, along with the enigmas set out in the letter to Olivia Shakespear. Yeats had been reading Von Hügel's *The Mystical Element of Religion*, where Homer's view of immortality is described as 'miserable shrunken consciousness', itself dependent on the faithful ministration of the living to the grave of the dead. This, and other defects, are contrasted with a far nobler Christian view. The final part of 'Vacillation' answers with the rhetorical 'Must we part?' addressed to the Christian writer and is followed by a passage foreshadowed in the letter already quoted, where Yeats claims to find the more miraculous and bizarre elements of Christianity credible, but not its central theology. The ending has to be quoted:

> I – though heart might find relief
> Did I become a Christian man and choose for my belief
> What seems most welcome in the tomb – play a predestined part.

Homer is my example and his unchristened heart.
The lion and the honeycomb, what has Scripture said?
So get you gone, Von Hügel, though with blessings on your head.

Scripture (needless to say) is at its own most enigmatic on the subject, since the phrase 'What is sweeter than honey? and what is stronger than a lion?' (Judges 14:5–18) is the tentative answer to a riddle with which Samson teases everyone: 'Out of the eater came forth meat, and out of the strong came forth sweetness.' The context is a highly curious vision from the Lord, including a young lion which roars against Samson, but which a little later is found dead, with a swarm of bees and honey in its carcase. In between, Samson has taken a woman either for a wife or for a mistress (a wife seems most likely, though the translators of the Authorised Version seem to think otherwise). When his riddle is not answered, the spirit of the Lord inspires Samson to go down to Ashkelon and slay thirty men, again in pursuit of an answer to his riddle. Upon his return he finds that his wife has been given to a friend, since his father has concluded that Samson hates her; and the father suggests that her younger sister is fairer, and would surely make a better wife. This precipitates Samson into further acts of violence against the Philistines (he sends 300 burning foxes into their standing corn, which is consumed in the conflagration, together with their vineyards and olives). In return the Philistines, morally outraged both by this action and by Samson's private affairs, burn Samson's father and his wife to death; which precipitates Samson into further revenge, involving great slaughter and havoc.

Conceivably, this is not one of the portions of Scripture most attuned to conversions; yet Yeats's actual attitude to it is not made clear. Perhaps it is another instance of baffling antinomies, more in tune with Homer's accounts, however untidy they seem to Von Hügel, than with whatever Yeats conceives Christian theology to be. I find it interesting that for once he says that the Christian view of the afterlife might be 'more welcome' (does this mean more welcome than *A Vision* as well, I wonder?); also, that he says his 'heart' might find relief in Christianity, even though Heart has so robustly declared itself otherwise in the preceding section. Yeats dismisses Von Hügel with blessings, in a manner more generous than many sceptics would conceive appropriate; but why does he say he must 'play a predestined part'? His entire search for truth, of which 'Vacillation' is a piece in the jig-saw, presupposes a robust belief in free-will: the note of resignation to destiny is a rogue touch. I take it that by 'predestination' he means, in fact, the entire course of his life, including all its choices and perplexities; and the decisive rejection of a Christian writer is in keeping with some ultimate personal freedom perceived, however dimly, amid all complexities.

'Vacillation' clearly exorcises neither 'Byzantium' nor Crazy Jane, but it does register many of Yeats's current tensions in unresolved juxtaposition. In closing, I wonder if I should question my own assertion that 'Wisdom' would have been an impossible title? Maybe vacillation of this sort is kindred to wisdom. We know that Yeats toyed with the alternative title. If he did not use it, then I suspect, still, that this was because he would regard it only – with great luck – as a word to be applied to his entire life's work, and, even then, not by himself. He might, more mundanely, have concluded that, though fascinating, this is not among his very best poems.

'Stream and Sun at Glendalough'

Though Iseult Gonne and her husband lived near Glendalough at the time of this poem (23 June 1932), I see for once little personal reference. In the preceding poem, 'Remorse for Intemperate Speech', Yeats has confessed to having 'A fanatic heart', which he has tried to cure, but accepts now as a heritage from Ireland ('Great hatred, little room, / Maimed us at the start') and from his 'mother's womb'. Here, his heart features in a different role. The poem is slighter than most we are examining, but says more than appears on the surface. The phrase 'all my heart seemed gay' introduces one of Yeats's good words (and the word on which 'Lapis Lazuli' will turn). 'Gay' includes merriment, creative energy and resilience. The next stanza, with the defiant opening 'Repentance keeps my heart impure' is mockingly non-Christian, but in an off-beat way; and leads to the thought that, since the poet is after all mortal, why should he expect of himself the exemplary? For once, 'common man' becomes a phrase he identifies with – but in this rather enchanted moment at one of Ireland's many places where natural beauty and religious tradition unite. The last stanza banishes remorse, to allow another moment of happiness: 'Self-born, born anew', qualified by only the most unobtrusive 'seem'. Like the end of 'Vacillation', and of 'A Dialogue of Self and Soul', the poet accepts himself, in one of his rare moments of serene detachment.

Words for Music Perhaps: the Crazy Jane Poems

Yeats wrote that in the spring of 1929 (a year and a half before 'Byzantium'), 'life returned to me as an impression of the uncontrollable energy and daring of the great creators; it seemed to me that but for journalism and criticism, all that evasion and explanation, the world would be torn in pieces. I wrote "Mad as the Mist and Snow", a mechanical little song, and after that almost all that group of poems, called in memory of those exultant weeks *Words for Music Perhaps*'. On 2 March he confided to Mrs Shakespear that he was writing twelve poems for music, not so much that they should be sung, as that they should define to Yeats himself their 'kind of emotion'. 'I want them to be all emotion and all impersonal.'

I do not propose to comment closely on all of these, though the famous seven Crazy Jane poems spanned the years from this beginning (when 'Crazy Jane and the Bishop', 'Crazy Jane Reproved' and 'Crazy Jane Grown Old looks at the Dancers' were written) through 1930, when 'Crazy Jane on the Day of Judgment' was added in October, to 1931. 'Crazy Jane on God' is dated 18 July 1931, and the last two poems, 'Crazy Jane and Jack the Journeyman' and 'Crazy Jane Talks with the Bishop', completed the cycle in November. No doubt it is important for readers to bear in mind this original order, the length of time covered, and the other poems contained within it (at which we have already looked). On the other hand, the other songs which were added to the volume were all written in 1929 (from 'Girl's Song' to 'I am of Ireland') except for the final four poems (three on Tom, and 'The Delphic Oracle upon Plotinus', which come from 1931).

I do not think that the collection *Words for Music Perhaps* can, even on the most stretched formula, be considered a unity, except in the choice of what Nicholas Brooke has called 'the light ballad tone and the witty ironic refrains', remote 'indeed from the monumental splendours of the holy city'. There is, however, a unity in the Crazy Jane sequence, reflected perhaps in the final ordering, and independent of those occasional revulsions from the sequence recorded by Yeats after the enchanted weeks during which the first three were written. My own reading is so indebted to Professor Brooke's article that I shall merely sketch a few notions, with acknowledgments to him taken, I hope, for granted. In particular, he pointed out that, though the difference between these poems and 'Byzantium' seems, and in poetic terms is, extreme, there are more similarities than one would at first think. These include a shuttling between two worlds – that of living men and that of ghosts – in addition to certain shared images, and, inevitably, a strong awareness of antinomies.

In the first poem, Crazy Jane recalls her dead lover, and the bishop who sneered at him as 'coxcomb'. She is a profoundly interesting invention: crazed, and so maybe a fool, and having something of the advanced status which this figure occupies in *A Vision*. It will be recalled that, after a cycle of twenty-eight lives, the first and fifteenth of which have no descriptions except 'Complete plasticity' and

'Complete beauty', the final three phases, before the soul is due to withdraw from the cycle into its own Daimon, are the Hunchback, the Saint and the Fool. The Fool is the twenty-eighth and last. A brief quotation runs,

> The natural man, the Fool desiring his *Mask*, grows malignant, not as the Hunchback, who is jealous of those who can still feel, but through terror and out of jealousy of all that can act with intelligence and effect.... At his worst his hands and feet and eyes, his will and his feelings, obey obscure subconscious fantasies, while at his best he should know all wisdom if he could know anything. The physical world suggests to his mind pictures and events that have no relation to his needs or even to his desires; his thoughts are an aimless reverie; his acts are aimless like his thoughts; and it is in this aimlessness that he finds his joy.... (*A Vision*, p. 182)

I think that Crazy Jane – of whom Yeats wrote to his wife in the winter of 1931–2, 'I want to exorcise that slut, Crazy Jane, whose language has become unendurable' – is not precisely a fool in this sense, though some of the notions can be kept in mind. In the first place, her name was to be 'Cracked Mary', the nickname given to an old woman who lived near Lady Gregory, and was 'the local satirist and a really terrible one', as Yeats also wrote. She is sour, and malignant, yet her resounding defence of compulsive eroticism is undeniably compelling (I find it so myself, as clearly Yeats did). It has a type of dignity – not unlike that of Shakespeare's Cleopatra, if I can risk this comparison without too much eccentricity: what Crazy Jane lacks in beauty, subtlety, majesty and so on, she perhaps gains in straightforward loyalty. She has, to my mind, dignity: the type which slut, scold and whore *can* have if a choice of life is accepted wholeheartedly, without any whining in pain, and with resolute defiance of prudes and judgmental moralists. Further, we can discern in her qualities of love as well as of loyalty, both of which are consistent (and I think this is why I risked Cleopatra) with the most unillusioned knowledge both of self and of dead lover, and which flourish not in spite of, but because of, the primal presence also of 'lust and rage'.

Finally she has the good fortune, again like Cleopatra, of having one of the world's greatest and most memorable poets in charge of her language (however 'unendurable' he found it, in some moods); and, moreover, a poet who was undoubtedly aroused to explore his own idiosyncratic promptings through her *persona*, at a most sensitive transitional point in his own life.

The first poem finds her at 'midnight upon the stroke', ready to curse. This is the same hour, as it happens, as that of the spiritual dance in 'Byzantium' (at the witching hour, many opposites may coexist). Maybe the hour, the mention of the 'blasted oak', and the imagery in the second stanza of the sixth poem, also remind us of the witches in *Macbeth* (a more immediately plausible suggestion than Cleopatra). Jane is not here, however, for capricious malice, or for equivocation: on the contrary, she is straightforwardly repaying the Bishop in kind. In her 'dear Jack's' lifetime, the Bishop denounced him as 'coxcomb' and worse, himself using the 'old book in his fist' as a model for cursing.

As Nicholas Brooke has said, the refrains, with great wit, switch to and fro in application. 'All find safety in the tomb' applies first to Jack, finding safety from a cursing Church (yet in the end he 'Wanders out into the night' as a restless ghost). Then, it applies to the Bishop, unable in age to 'hide in holy black / The heron's hunch upon his back' (a sign, maybe, of something demonic), and in turn denounced by Jane, a willing pupil in cursing. No doubt the time will come when *he* will ask mountains to fall upon him (if his religion is right), and the tomb will have no automatic safety for canting self-righteousness. In a similar manner, the first stanza makes the Bishop a 'solid man' (in his own eyes and society's), denouncing the 'coxcomb' outsider. But in the second stanza we may wonder if a change is starting – since the one who bans must be as open to judgement (and Crazy Jane's is apparent) as the fellow-human upon whom his ban falls. In the third stanza, 'coxcomb' seems more appropriate to the Bishop, especially since 'solid man' has now taken on (especially from 'birch-tree') phallic suggestions, and 'cock' (hidden in coxcomb), for all its disrepute, may be more truly an agent of love than the man of hate who claims apostolic affinity with Christ.

The final stanza is a powerful celebration of lost virginity. Crazy Jane has no regret for *this* – only for the loss of her lover to death. Unlike the ghosts of Byzantium (and, of course, of 'the system'), Jack becomes more like Catherine Linton, as she appears in Lockwood's nightmare in chapter 3 of *Wuthering Heights* – a night wanderer, exiled from any world and not finding his Jane. But she is there – ready to shelter him if he should come; and ready to spit at the Bishop. In this anger, life, love and resilience meet; both as a human quality and as spiritual discernment, it is immensely superior to the anger of the man who 'Cried that we lived like beast and beast'.

The second poem shows Crazy Jane defying Heaven – both in its superstitious and in its Olympian form – yet in the second stanza she appears to regret her love after all.

Yeats would be less than himself if his sequence did not proceed by contraries, but, as always, there are lurking complexities. Jeffares, in the *Commentary*, takes the title literally, and feels that Crazy Jane is being reproved (but by herself, or by the poet?). He points out Yeats's partiality for delicate shells (which could be proved by several quotations), and reminds us that Zeus's escapade with Agenor, in the disguise of a bull, was less dignified than (say) his rape of Leda, and less spectacular in its offspring (Minos, Sarpedon and Rhadamanthus).

Even so, a god *is* a god, and maybe if Crazy Jane is not to know the divinity that produces 'daughters of the swan' (however ambiguously), she is to experience the dark gods (vested again in Zeus) in direct form. In this poem, the little refrain '*Fol de rol, fol de rol*' is the kind in which a fool can include himself in mockery without cancelling out either pathos or, sometimes, a tragic undercurrent. The second stanza is ambiguous, but it seems likely that Jane is saying that, just as Heaven has a price for creating the beauty of the shell, so a woman pays a price for the beauty of love. Her advice,

> So never hang your heart upon
> A roaring, ranting journeyman

is undeniably good: the author of 'A Prayer for My Daughter' endorses it. Yet the swinging rhythms, verbal energy and phrases of defiance ('I care not', 'Can but show', 'played the fool', 'crack', 'roaring, ranting') are light-years from contrition. Maybe Crazy Jane is simply in her cups here, enjoying yet other delights than those known to 'custom' and 'ceremony'.

The third poem is beautifully judged. I agree entirely with Nicholas Brooke in his judgement that 'unsatisfied' in l. 2 is uninhibitedly sexual, and think that this and the sixth poem are among Yeats's subtlest shorter constructions. The pun on 'whole' is unmistakable (and is taken up, more complexly, in the sixth poem). The middle two stanzas are wholly without illusion, yet totally authentic. Jane offers herself nakedly, first in spirit, then in body. Both revelations have all the stuff of shame – everything the Bishop could wish for – yet one senses, too, that they belong with a more whole relationship (with or without pun) than many which would appear more reputable – or glamorous. The fact is that Jack has taken her; so that, though she confesses what she seems to herself ('sour'), and what she seems to the world (a sinner in darkness), the link which transcends death and remains true to itself is woven. The last stanza rises from this with great power:

> 'What can be shown?
> What true love be?
> All could be known or shown

If Time were but gone.'
'That's certainly the case', said he.

The beauty of this is that it could be transferred to any love poem, no matter how exalted, and its essential truth and enigma would remain. The two questions haunt every love story in the world. Expanded, they would be fitting motto to much of the world's tragic literature, or fitting celebration of all happy love. They have the seeds alike of all religion, all philosophy, all psychology, if these disciplines go, with whatever sophistication, in search of 'love'. As to the third and fourth lines, they speak not of judgement but of hope (if there is hope); or of the man's universal mortality, if that should turn out to be the only truth. Jack's final comment works either way; and from this very different starting-point, we are back at the general motto I have taken for this chapter on Yeats: 'no enemy but Time'.

The fourth poem is the most ghostly in tone, and the oddest in its reminders of the bobbin imagery of 'Byzantium'. It has the additional strangeness of coming very close to being an exposition of ideas of death, shiftings, rebirth from *A Vision*, while in fact it is the poem of Jane's inner vulnerability – loneliness and despair. For all that, it again has universality, this time in the realm of love's transience, whether through inconstancy or death; and of love's endurance, in the mind and heart of a sour, aging woman. In the first stanza, the social furtiveness of their love is stressed – the door unlatched and lover no sooner come (it seems) than gone. Hence that desolate 'but' –

Love is but a skein unwound
Between the dark and dawn

– where sadness at the end of all sexual encounter co-exists with the other, last 'dark', without a return. (Yeats once remarked that 'the tragedy of sexual intercourse is the perpetual virginity of the souls'.) The second stanza is about the loneliness of the ghost who cannot now unlatch doors, yet who has the power to pull Crazy Jane towards the tomb, and maybe to new life. For once, the doctrine of reincarnation sounds as desolate as it surely is: no reunion with the lost ghost, but at best the equivocal leap into 'light lost' (what light?), which is also in 'my' mother's womb (whose 'my': Crazy Jane's now dead mother; or whatever mother will bear the unremembering baby?). The third stanza turns to her own loneliness – the empty bed – and ends with an assertion as passionate, yet as troubled, as Heathcliffe's long search for the lost Cathy.

What makes this so affecting, I think, is partly the last line, which, jumping over everything sour and sordid, embodies love in its most bitterly authentic form of enduring grief; and, even more than this, Jane's absolute refusal to contrast her present fruitless fidelity with Jack's random and dubious fidelity in life. Whatever hurt may have underlain the rhetorical flourishes of the second poem is now buried, beneath grief and loneliness that the most sensitive soul on earth could perhaps not surpass ('We three alone in modern times had brought / Everything down to that sole test again, / Dream of the noble and the beggar-man').

The fifth poem counterbalances the fourth, as we have learned to expect, rewriting it when day, and day's courage, have returned. The refrain is far nobler than anything possible to the Bishop, even though (or perhaps because) it is not quite 'simple faith'. On Jane's part, of course, it may be: Yeats often wrote of the easy affinity between Celtic peasants and the occult, and made much of it, as we have seen, in his prose. How far his own sceptical intellect ever rested, he frequently questioned: in the poetry never, I think; in any total sense, maybe never at all. Be that as it may, 'Men come, men go' is now taken philosophically; war and love are, as so often, compared. The third stanza has the unexpectedness of suddenly revivified memory; the last stanza celebrates love as it was. Crazy Jane, in her old age, 'sings on', in the accents of faith, certainly – yet not taught by the 'singing masters' invoked by the aging Yeats.

The sixth poem returns to the Bishop, who once more gets better than he gives. November 1931 now – the period when Yeats in his letters was calling Crazy Jane a 'slut'; shall we trust the teller, or the tale?

The first stanza is the Bishop's – consecrated as such, by now, but further than ever from God. His . . . the taunt is contemptible; the offer of 'a heavenly mansion' blasphemy on his lips. Jane's reply takes off with dazzling magnificence; the voice is hers, but the hands are those of Yeats:

> 'Fair and foul are near of kin,
> And fair needs foul', I cried.
> 'My friends are gone, but that's a truth
> Nor grave nor bed denied,
> Learned in bodily lowliness
> And in the heart's pride.
>
> 'A woman can be proud and stiff
> When on love intent;
> But love has pitched his mansion in
> The place of excrement;
> For nothing can be sole or whole
> That has not been rent.'

The first two lines encapsulate a wisdom so central to Yeats, that the many possible comments are maybe best left alone. But notice how 'bodily lowliness' is redeemed, as 'grave' and 'bed' are boldly accepted; and recall the two legacies bequeathed in Yeats's literary will ('The Tower', part III).

Jeffares draws our attention to a line in Blake's *Jerusalem*: 'For I will make their places of love and joy excrementitious': the thought is not new, but I know of no more splendid or definitive expression of it than this. Arguably, a reader's response to this formula is one of the major human touchstones. There are those who find the conjunction of sex, love and excrement painful, and even semi-pornographic when mentioned; there are those who exalt in it with a mixuture of humour and joy. For the non-religious, it can be accepted perhaps as one of nature's stranger economies; for the religious, it is a seal of laughter, reverence and unity in creation itself. But those who remain embarrassed, whether religious or not, are usually puritan; and doubtless incapable of reading Yeats, or any major writer, without some anger or fear.

The final lines virtually spell this out – deliberately repeating and intensifying the sexual punning in the third poem, while making a statement of profound religious and psychological, import. Looked at one way, it could be a Christian insight: either the doctrine of the 'fortunate fall', with its notion that by falling man opened the way for a redemption that makes him greater than he ever could have been in perpetual innocence; or the doctrine of life through death, wholeness through brokenness, divinity through degradation that is at the heart of the New Testament (and, of course, of many mystery religions as well). Totally apart from this, it would be endorsed by many modern psychotherapists, literary critics, artists and others who believe that the only way to wholeness must lie not through repression, but through total openness to the whole of life – dark and light gods, or powers, alike – and the harmonising of these through some mutual integration. When one has allowed the sound of 'sole' and 'soul', 'whole' and 'hole' to play in one's head, and the final word 'rent' to unite those sexual and spiritual rendings that alone can prelude fulfilment, then ' "Fair and foul are near of kin / And fair needs foul", I cried' can return as final comment. At this point, I am by no means certain that this poem is as far away from 'Byzantium' as it looks.

The final poem (one of the first to be written) originated in a dream. Yeats saw ragged people dancing in a ring, the most visible of whom were a man and a woman. The man was swinging round his head a weight, they had their eyes fixed on each other, and the dreamer did not know if he would strike her dead. Yeats added, 'I suppose it was Blake's old thought "sexual love is founded on spiritual hate" – I will probably find I have written a poem on it in a few days – though my remembering the dream may prevent that – by making my criticism work upon it.' In the event, he gives the poem to 'Crazy Jane grown old', looking at dancers, and alters the images, while allowing both man and woman to be on the verge of destroying each other. Crazy Jane describes this (Blake's insight) as dancing 'heart's truth', and adds,

> I could but leave him to his fate;
> For no matter what is said
> They had all that had their hate. . . .

The last stanza opens with the mystery

> Did he die or did she die?
> Seemed to die or died they both?

The sexual meaning of 'die' itself adds to the dream image, and to the assertion of the closeness of love and hate – mutated, as it is, to an opposition between body and soul. The refrain '*Love is like the lion's tooth*' underlies the ancient Jane's choice of life: uncaring participation in the dance when she was young, all risks notwithstanding; and a blessing on the times past when she 'had the limbs to try / Such a dance as there was danced'.

Though this is dated 6 March 1929, and is therefore the second of the poems to be written (in the exuberant dawn), Yeats doubtless removed it to the end for reasons of sequence, and perhaps because it rounds off the poems with a flourish. As a poem of dancing, it belongs with the end of 'Among School Children' and 'Byzantium', illustrating once more the widely different routes leading to that momentary out-of-time ecstasy of the dance.

Words for Music Perhaps: the Remaining Poems

Yeats wrote to Olivia Shakespear on 29 March 1929 ' "Lullaby" . . . I like . . . I have done two or three others that seem to me lucky and that does not often happen. Yet I am full of doubt. I am writing more easily than I ever wrote and am happy, whereas I have always been unhappy when I wrote and worked with great difficulty. . . .'

The remaining poems need little individual commentary, though they seem to me among Yeats's most sheerly delightful in a lighthearted way, and are full of phrases that stay in the mind and sing in the heart. Basically, they amount to a set of variations on the theme of love, with the viewpoint shuttling between the usual extremes, yet a new quality of acceptance running through all. 'Mad as the Mist and Snow' is included and has fine rhetoric, even though Yeats chose to call it 'mechanical'; it is the earliest, by a short head (12 February). 29 March was a vintage day, since no less than five of these songs bear that date; 'Lullaby' was a few days earlier. As I have already said, the last five songs stand apart, like the final 'Crazy Jane' ones, belonging to 1931, and bearing dates between 27 July and October. (For exact details, see Jeffares's *Commentary*.)

'Girl's Song' is a contrast of youth and age in a man, as seen by a girl in love. Turning from her lover, she notices another man coming in sight 'That on a stick relied'. Her response is to weep: this could be general compassion, or could be a brief prefiguring of the end of all love. The power is in the ending. The poet would have identified himself with this second figure, and his question touches lightly on the far more painful dialectic we find elsewhere:

> When everything is told,
> Saw I an old man young
> Or young man old?

The 'Young Man's Song', in balance, shows a young man contemplating time's ravages:

> 'She will change', I cried,
> 'Into a withered crone.'

The answer this time is given by his heart, speaking from 'noble rage'. Here, the heart offers a massive rebuke, which the young man accepts, kneeling before it for pardon:

> 'Uplift those eyes and throw
> Those glances unafraid:
> She would as bravely show
> Did all the fabric fade;
> No withered crone I saw
> Before the world was made.'

This could be a Platonic statement, and link with the poem 'Before the World was Made', which starts the next sequence but had been written earlier, in February 1928. More probably, it is a reflection of the dignity and unbroken spirit of Crazy Jane in age, counterpointed with consciously suspended knowledge. The young man comments that 'the heart cannot lie', and, though 'O who could have foretold / That the heart grows old?' does not belong here, it hangs in memory, either to mock the young man, or to be mocked itself – most probably both.

'Her Anxiety' and 'His Confidence' are, in fact, the antimonies, waiting to answer doubt. The girl expresses fear not only that love will fade, but that it will also degenerate: who can tell which thought brings the sharper pang?

> All true love must die,
> Alter at the best
> Into some lesser thing.
> *Prove that I lie.*

No proof possible; but the young man defends 'undying love' with greater seriousness. He acknowledges its riches:

> What payment were enough
> For undying love?

and asserts, in a passage suggesting a more tested wisdom than playful Platonism (the images of Moses striking water from the rock lurks?):

> I broke my heart in two
> So hard I struck.
> What matter? For I know
> That out of rock,
> Out of a desolate source,
> Love leaps upon its course.

'Love's Loneliness' and 'Her Dream' again pair off, approaching the threat of 'lover's loneliness' differently. In the first, 'Old fathers, great grand-fathers' are invoked for reassurance, but the best on offer is: 'Dread has followed longing / And our hearts are torn'. The second summons, instead, 'All night's fathomless wisdom' (though in a dream), and the apotheosis of Berenice's hair is the emerging image. According to Yeats, if we look at 'Anima Mundi', one real-life incident behind this poem might have been a somewhat farcical incident in his own past: 'A couple of years ago, while in meditation, my head seemed surrounded by a conventional sun's rays, and when I went to bed I had a long dream of a woman with her head on fire. I awoke and lit a candle and discovered presently from the odour that in doing so I had set my own hair on fire.' A better (and irresistible) association is the glorious passage in Pope's *Rape of the Lock* when Belinda's ravished lock undergoes the same transformation:

But trust the Muse – she saw it upward rise,
Tho' mark'd by none but quick Poetic Eyes . . .
A sudden Star, it shot thro' liquid Air,
And drew behind a radiant *Trail of Hair.*
Not *Berenice's* Locks first rose so bright,
The Heav'ns bespangling with dishevel'd Light.
The *Sylphs* behold it kindling as it flies,
And pleas'd pursue its Progress thro' the Skies.

(*Rape of the Lock*, Canto v, ll. 123–4, 127–32)

'His Bargain' functions maybe as a comment, insisting on
Platonism, and on apparatus culled from *A Vision* (inappropriate
enough to make this the weakest of the sequence). But 'Three Things'
is vintage: a ballad starting 'O cruel Death, give three things back',
and then offering motherhood, erotic love, and the final satisfaction
of meeting and sleeping with 'my rightful man' as the impossible
demands. The refrain underlines transience, but the poem is mainly
celebration of fulfilments achieved and remembered.

'Lullaby' moves off on to other territory: a song for mother to
child, but on themes the child cannot understand. Once more, the
sleep following sexual ecstasy is invoked, as life's sweetest
experience. This time, Paris's 'first dawn in Helen's arms',
Tristram's erotic frenzy after the potion, and the post-coital sleep of
Zeus himself ('the holy bird'), who, when he had

Accomplished his predestined will,
From the limbs of Leda sank
But not from her protecting care.

The tone is tender, as befits a lullaby, and for once all ambivalences,
both in the experiences and in their consequences, are phased out, so
that sexuality can be celebrated in climax, and linked in the mother's
song with innocence.

'After Long Silence' once more restores balance. The shift to
lovers 'estranged or dead', 'Unfriendly lamplight', 'unfriendly night'
moves us from the mother's lullaby to 'Speech after long silence' in
age. The theme announced as 'the supreme theme of Art and Song'
is austere disillusionment, pared down to two lines:

Bodily decrepitude is wisdom; young
We loved each other and were ignorant.

Immediately following, 'Mad as the Mist and Snow' and 'Those
Dancing Days are Gone' provide yet further contrasts. Both concern
old age; both are elated, in rhetoric and refrain. But the first is
ominous:

> Bolt and bar the shutter,
> For the foul winds blow

introduces three stanzas in which the poet and an old friend are compared with the mighty dead, and all are found, in the light of time, reduced to a common plight '*Mad as the mist and snow*' (cf. 'Among School Children', stanza vi). In the following poem, an old woman is reminded of the 'foul body' which age has left her, along with the dead 'knave / That the most could pleasure you, / The children that he gave', but the tone remains elated. The refrain,

> *I carry the sun in a golden cup,*
> *The moon in a silver bag*

cuts across the meaning; and in the last stanza the old man himself makes a virtue of the famous Yeats predicament, albeit in the mood of Crazy Jane:

> I thought it out this very day,
> Noon upon the clock,
> A man may put pretence away
> Who leans upon a stick,
> May sing, and sing until he drop,
> Whether to maid or hag:
> *I carry the sun in a golden cup,*
> *The moon in a silver bag.*

At first sight, 'I am of Ireland', slipped into the sequence from August 1929, seems odd man out, maybe because, alone of the poems, it introduces a political note. If it belongs, then it does so again because of a refrain, which a girl continues to sing, against all discouragement:

> '*I am of Ireland,*
> *And the Holy Land of Ireland,*
> *And time runs on*', cried she.
> '*Come out of charity,*
> *Come dance with me in Ireland.*'

This functions as first, middle and last stanza, and is unvaried. Interspersed, in two eight-line stanzas, 'one man' counterpoints comments which take up her phrase 'time runs on', attempting to infuse malice, through reminders of the unpropitious times and the discord of the music. But the girl is undeterred – as if, as Ellmann has said in *The Identity of Yeats*, 'indifferent to his prudential explanations, like the cry of all idealism and heroism'.

The next poem continues the theme of celebration, probably through the persona of an obscure saint; 'Tom the Lunatic' – who has three short poems, and is a fool – also celebrates life, once more in the manner of Crazy Jane, yet with a distinctive note that might be lunacy, tiredness, drunkenness or vision. The possibilities are all open; but, interestingly, Yeats inserts the reference to 'Huddon and Duddon and Daniel O'Leary', three characters who had 'delighted him as a child', as he reveals in *A Vision*.

The other two Tom poems are brief, but pregnant. One song,

> 'The stallion Eternity
> Mounted the mare of Time,
> 'Gat the foal of the world'

perhaps puns on 'foal' and 'fool'. In deliberately bawdy images, it verges on Blake's famous 'Eternity is in love with the productions of Time' (one of the 'Proverbs from Hell' in *The Marriage of Heaven and Hell*). 'Old Tom Again' would also be consistent with Neo-Platonism, notably the doctrine that we emerge into time from eternity, to exist here briefly as a wave that has formed on the sea, and then return to the divinity which endlessly manifests itself in such phenomena of transience, before dancing back to unity. This would prepare for the happy ending, 'The Delphic Oracle upon Plotinus'. Since Jeffares's *Commentary* offers extensive quotation, I shall not spend time on the sources. Enough to offer a few marginalia. Plotinus, rescued now from the taint of 'abstraction' somewhat unjustly foisted upon him in 'The Tower', is 'great' again, and a symbol of the return of a pure soul to the place where 'blessed spirits have their birth-home and live in days made happy by the Gods'. The setting is pagan (and not unlike the ending of 'Byzantium'). Perhaps for personal reasons, I am glad to see this last and greatest of pagan writers given by Yeats the reverence he deserves. Living in the third century, and surrounded by growingly ascetic and half-crazed Christian 'Fathers', he left us, in his posthumously published *Enneads*, one of the great spiritual classics of the world. It is reassuring, too, to find Minos and Rhadamanthus, two of Zeus's offspring by Agenor, rescued from the stern gloss placed upon them by Jeffares in his *Commentary* upon 'Crazy Jane Reproved', and returned to their rightful divinity and blessedness.

'A Woman Young and Old': a Note

This sequence was written between 1926 and 1929. It is therefore early (though placed last) and overlaps with 'A Man Young and Old' in *The Tower*.

Since the themes would take us over now familiar ground, I will be content here to recommend it as a sequence rewarding to read, and again full of phrases that resonate against other major poems. The outstanding poem, I should say, is 'A Last Confession', which I should want in any anthology. The delighted eroticism transcends deceit, ambiguity, danger, making the poem's title splendidly ambiguous: not a 'last confession' in the sense of being broken down on the death-bed to regret life; but a last confession to the validity of ecstasy, whether we can hold it or not.

'A Prayer for Old Age'

On the whole, I doubt whether *A Full Moon in March* is more than a pause for breath on the threshold of the great final phase. But this small poem cannot be omitted from these notes. It is that rather rare thing in Yeats, a prayer – this time for himself. The syntax is ambiguous and the wish 'That I may seem, though I die old, / A foolish, passionate man' does smuggle in that 'seem'. It is there, also, in the preceding stanza, equally pertinent to the whole canon:

O what am I that I should not seem
For the song's sake a fool?

'Last Poems': a General Note

The volume called *Last Poems* is dated 1936–9, though, as usual, one or two earlier poems got into it. The first reviews were mixed, and critics have continued to give widely different accounts. Jon Stallworthy's *Yeats's Last Poems* in the Macmillan Casebook series collects much of the material and a diversity of response.

Like the Crazy Jane sequence before them, these *Last Poems* have attracted naïve and oversimplified views about Yeats's 'development', concerning which my own reflections will, I trust, be clear. But perhaps I can be forgiven for pausing, at this point, to quote three further passages from Jung's *Modern Man in Search of a Soul*. These extracts, though made in differing contexts, have a peculiar appropriateness here. They throw light both on Yeats himself, in this disputed area of his greatness, and on the more pervasive concern with 'the modern' in this book. They strike me as being at least as relevant today, when 'the modern' is coming under many new challenges from resurgent religious and political dogmatists, as they were when Jung first published them in 1933. I judge it a happy coincidence that, in the ferment of the 1930s, half a century ago now, minds of this calibre were independently pioneering the psychic, and creative, potentials of post-Christian man.

It is painful – there is no denying it – to interpret radiant things from the shadow-side, and thus in a measure reduce them to their origins in dreary filth. But it seems to me to be an imperfèction in things of beauty, and a weakness in man, if an explanation from the shadow-side has a destructive effect. The horror which we feel for Freudian interpretations is entirely due to our own barbaric or childish naïveté, which believes that there can be heights without corresponding depths, and which blinds us to the really 'final' truth that, when carried to extremes, opposites meet. Our mistake would lie in supposing that what is radiant no longer exists because it has been explained from the shadow-side. (p. 47)

. . . the work of the poet comes to meet the spiritual need of the society in which he lives, and for this reason his work means more to him than his personal fate, whether he is aware of this or not. Being essentially the instrument for his work, he is subordinate to it, and we have no reason for expecting him to interpret it for us. He has done the best that in him lies in giving it form, and he must leave the interpretation to others and to the future. A great work of art is like a dream; for all its apparent obviousness it does not explain itself and is never unequivocal. A dream never says: 'You ought', or: 'This is the truth'. It presents an image in much the same way as nature allows a plant to grow, and we must draw our own conclusions. (p. 198)

The man whom we can with justice call 'modern' is solitary. He is so of necessity and at all times, for every step towards a fuller consciousness of the present removes him further from his original '*participation mystique*' with the mass of men – from submersion in a common unconsciousness. Every step forward means an act of tearing himself loose from the all-embracing, pristine unconsciousness which claims the bulk of mankind almost entirely. . . . Indeed, he is completely modern only when he has come to the very edge of the world, leaving behind him all that has been discarded and outgrown, and acknowledging that he stands before a void out of which all things may grow. (pp. 227–8)

In content, the final volume is full of contrasts, and I shall have to miss a number of poems that I greatly like. There is a group on Irish themes – Parnell, Roger Casement, Cromwell revisited – which stands a little apart, now, from this approach. I propose, also, to depart from Yeats's order – both in the original composition and in the published arrangement – and to conclude this study by grouping together the most relevant themes. 'The Municipal Gallery Revisited' comes first; then, three poems concerning old age; then, five with an erotic base; and then three returning once more to the relationship between 'life' and 'art'. Among major poems left out are 'The Gyres' and 'The Statues', since most of what I should say on these is included elsewhere.

'The Municipal Gallery Revisited'

This was started in August and completed early in September 1937. It was, with 'Lapis Lazuli', among the poet's favourites. He said to Edith Shackleton Heald on 5 September that it was 'one of his best poems' and, writing on the same day to Dorothy Wellesley, commented, 'perhaps the best poem I have written for some years, unless "The Curse of Cromwell" is'.

As I have already mentioned, it is my personal favourite among Yeats's poems, though, for reasons which I hope will be apparent, I would find it impossible to call this, or any other, 'greatest'. The whole opus, at least from 1916 onwards, has a shared authenticity, which makes it hard, at times, to abstract single poems from the whole. The fact that I have myself been forced to select is endemic to Yeats's strategy, since the reader's energy in re-creation is a process he often mentions as complementary to creation. It is equally necessary to the life of the poems, and so to their existence ('Lapis Lazuli' is the poem most relevant to this theme). At times, re-creation may seem almost as difficult as creation – though any notion of equality between writer and reader is, of course, ruled out.

The explorations, the echoes, the unfolding and always changing patterns, no less than the individual uniqueness vested in each single poem (however slight it might seem) are all aspects of which Yeats was unremittingly aware. He would have recognised that for any serious reader of his poems, his own consciousness would loom ever more powerful – becoming interwoven with the reader's aesthetic, spiritual and even personal life. He knew, in short, that he belonged with that very rare company of writers, composers and artists (fewer than a hundred in all?) who become part of the lives of their admirers, in the deepest sense. This does not amount to absorption, or total agreement; but it does amount to a presence that might ultimately influence commitments and actions in 'life'.

Even so, Yeats recognised, no less gladly, that personal relationships take precedence over everything – including art and religion, which begin and end *somewhere* in man's heart, mind or soul. Maybe it is because 'The Municipal Gallery Revisited' does justice to this strand of thinking that I personally return to it again and again. The penultimate line of the poem – if Yeats had chosen to leave it hanging – might have pointed in two or three possible ways. It is entirely because of the final touch that I name it 'favourite', and think that no critic can afford to pass it by.

In transcending his art (seemingly), Yeats gives it an added dimension – a seal on whatever other forms of greatness we find it to have.

By and large, this is not one of the more difficult of his poems. In the past, Yeats has often called to the dead, on his own terms and for special purposes. Now, walking in the gallery where their portraits hang, they rise up unexpectedly, surprising him – insisting on a poem which is definitively their own:

> Heart-smitten with emotion I sink down,
> My heart recovering with covered eyes;
> Wherever I had looked I had looked upon
> My permanent or impermanent images:
> Augusta Gregory's son; her sister's son,
> Hugh Lane, 'onlie begetter' of all these;
> Hazel Lavery living and dying, that tale
> As though some ballad-singer had sung it all. . . .

Before returning to this, stanza iv (one of the most beautiful) must be placed beside it, since here is Lady Gregory herself. The three concluding stanzas pick up the main themes in ordered sequence, leading the poem to its magnificent end.

What, then, are the themes? Obviously, 'images' again, and their validity: 'Around me the images of thirty years'. At first, his eyes roam round the paintings which depict his Irish martyrs and heroes; and the first paradox is remarked:

> 'This is not', I say,
> 'The dead Ireland of my youth, but an Ireland
> The poets have imagined, terrible and gay.'

Other phrases will float gently beside this ('A terrible beauty is born'; 'Gaiety transfiguring all that dread'; and many more) but here the emphasis falls on the inevitable dislocation between life and art. The substitution of 'poets' for painters makes clear how closely Yeats identifies the arts; and how totally he is reminded not only of the dead people depicted, but of their 'images' in his own art as well. 'This is not . . .' – the resounding phrase suggests almost a total discrepancy, as if either the status of art itself, or the shifting interpretations imposed from real life by the artist's personal vision and talent – or more likely both – turn even the truest art into the most feigning.

The sharp stab of mortality is repeated, this time more painfully, as portaits of the people Yeats had loved most come into view. It is here that, overcome, he has to cover his eyes. Maybe art is not after all therapeutic – or, if so, only during the actual work of creation, and then very partially for the artist. The finished artefact is another matter ('O self-born mockers of man's enterprise ...'); and very possibly the artist, even more than his other audience, will be especially tormented as one inevitable limit (no, it cannot in truth immortalise) is brought tragically home.

Note that a number of discrepancies, opening from here, are lightly touched on, as the poem shifts delicately between life and art. First, the strange sense that this is not the 'real' past, for at least two reasons. The past is 'dead' (a stark word, unadorned in context): then, it is 'imagined' by an interpreter who is inevitably defeated, whatever his greatness, by the originals as they were, in their life, to the particular eye of love:

> A great ebullient portrait certainly;
> But where is the brush that could show anything
> Of all that pride and that humility?

Again, just as art fails to live up to its originals in their now lost vitality, so also it may distort, by remoteness or be exaggeration, to laws of its own ('terrible and gay'; 'As though some ballad-singer had sung it all'). Moreover, the final status of images is still unresolved, in a specially sensitive area. In balance with the living dance ('Those images that yet / Fresh images beget' –' Byzantium') stands this appalling other perspective: 'My permanent or impermanent images'. Just as the King of Hearts shuttled between 'important' and 'unimportant', trying to decide which sounded best in Wonderland, so Yeats juggles 'permanent', 'impermanent' in his own crucial impasse. They are 'his' images for the most obvious, and most personal, reason ('A portion of my life and mind, as it were'); they are 'his' also, as the stuff of so much of his art.

So here is the rub: permanent, with such permanence as art has (and 'Lapis Lazuli' is dated June 1936, over a year before); but lost in death, and betrayed by even genius in art:

> And I am in despair that time may bring
> Approved patterns of women or of men
> But not that self-same excellence again.

Even so, the final line, which is the stuff of despair in one aspect, could, in another light, be the ultimate ground for hope. If people are unique, at least the universe is living; we are not carbon copies, to be brought round again in any cycles or gyres. Is it not precisely in the particularity of love – whether known briefly in the dance, or more normally in foreboding or bereavement – that there may the one strong, clear pointer to religious hope? A pointer not a proof (which would be asking the impossible); yet some consolation, maybe, even failing any leap into faith?

That Lady Gregory was, for Yeats, greater than himself in her prime reality confirms the highest value that can be placed on men and their loves.

Before he proceeds to the marvellous last stanza – which picks up these reflections for a very personal epiphany – two other thoughts emerge from the 'images', and fall into place. In stanza v, with its deleted line and consequent appearance of unbalance, there is a final sad retrospect to Coole Park. The 'Honour' which 'lived so long' is departed; the end has come, beyond any envisaged (no doubt in the last stanza of 'Coole Park, 1929' he had thought it much further away):

> Childless I thought, 'My children may find here
> Deep-rooted things,' but never foresaw its end. . . .

This reaches back beyond Yeats's marriage, and beyond my starting place for this chapter; it reaches to those nineteen years already remembered, even then more than half way to elegy, in 'The Wild Swans at Coole'.

In 'A Prayer for My Daughter', the 'deep-rooted' things hoped for had also had the aristocratic tradition behind them: a tradition as inaccessible now as Coole Park itself. (The word 'rooted' does appear again, however, attached to a person – and I think Yeats penetrates as near to 'roots', in this poem, as he ever did.)

Stanza vi, in counterpoint with v, recalls the hope which 'John Synge, I and Augusta Gregory' kept alive during the years of ascendancy. For a moment, Yeats departs from the main drift of the poem (though not from its centre in his own stirred consciousness) to reiterate the ideals touched on in 'Coole Park and Ballylee, 1931':

> All that we did, all that we said or sang
> Must come from contact with the soil, from that
> Contact everything Antaeus-like grew strong.
> We three alone in modern times had brought
> Everything down to that sole test again,
> Dream of the noble and the beggar-man.

If this is not the entire picture, it is part of it; and it leads straight into the allied, but translucent, thoughts of the poem's close:

> And here's John Synge himself, that rooted man,
> 'Forgetting human words', a grave deep face.
> You that would judge me, do not judge alone
> This book or that, come to this hallowed place
> Where my friends' portraits hang and look thereon;
> Ireland's history in their lineaments trace;
> Think where man's glory most begins and ends,
> And say my glory was I had such friends.

'You that would judge me' – ourselves. The purpose of criticism is not alone, it seems, 'the common pursuit of true judgment', but, before that even, initiation into art; and, through art, deeper contact with the very roots of life in ourselves.

So we are invited, before we write books or articles, to take a ticket to Dublin and look on Yeats's 'permanent or impermanent images' through yet other eyes.

Is this a rhetorical flourish? There is a touch of it; but I doubt whether Yeats was ever more serious in his life. It is not that he downgrades the importance of critical reading: this, as we have seen, is our personal, and indispensable, task. But, before we start judging single poems, or indeed single volumes ('This book or that'), we are reminded that literature belongs not to literature alone, but to life. Perhaps this is, after all, one more summons to Byzantium – but Byzantium conceived now, in refashioned terms. The song is still the *raison d'être* of the journey, yet the 'monuments of unageing intellect' are no longer an end in themselves. We are not to exchange 'heart' or 'nature' for 'artifice' (even 'of eternity'); still less are we to become artefacts ourselves. Rather, we are to find first in the Dublin Gallery, and then in Yeats's pages as we return there, one possible, glorious détente between art and life.

'. . . come to this hallowed place': 'Coole Park, 1929' has already said this; but remembrance and thanksgiving are now a source of new life. Though the various discrepancies between life and art remain uncancelled, they are somehow transfigured into a larger, if still circumscribed, hope. Doubtless the portraits are 'not . . . / The dead Ireland of my youth' in many important aspects, yet they are still the repository of human consciousness, wrought to intensity, as it then was. So, despite everything, the poet can now say 'Ireland's history in their lineaments trace'; for where but in art, at its greatest, is the past – its 'reality', especially as known in ideals and potentials – to be found? The Geneva critics spoke of art as a 'history of human consciousness'; and human consciousness is, and remains, the dance itself. So Yeats can proceed in his penultimate line to a supreme human challenge; and, as it registers, pass his own answer – a man bearing gifts – to ourselves.

After warning so continually against abstracting 'last words', I had better not attempt this myself. Perhaps the end of 'The Municipal Gallery Revisited' can be seen as a point of rest, rather; a firm rock, washed by the seas.

Yeats had a tremendous gift for love, and deep human friendship; if we removed this, what of substance would often be left? Some readers find aspects of his personality odd, or even embarrassing; some who ought to know better take the fairies, the ghosts, gyres and so forth less seriously than they should. His fascination with aristocrats, with heroes and lovers and martyrs, is endemic, and a less democratic poet cannot readily be found. Yet, when this is said, Yeats's elite rests upon independence, self-acceptance, totality of commitment, not upon anything that could be called 'class' in the social sense. Crazy Jane earns her right to belong there, as much as Helen.

Beyond this, he was a man of friendship, of love and warmth; and are these not the qualities we finally miss in T. S. Eliot and R. S. Thomas, great though they are? Wherever we find ourselves as we journey with Yeats – floating in pursuit of visionary perfection above Byzantium, or bedded down with sour old hags and drunken scoundrels in the hay – we never miss that commitment to humanity which is inseparable from all the imagery, rhetoric, paradox, verbal magnificence and energy.

I am not saying (to be totally plain) that great humanity results in great art; if it did, great art would be less rare than it is. But the converse may be true. The greatest art is crowned with humanity, however elusively (I think here particularly of Shakespeare). Certainly, a poet who can point away from his poems, away from himself, away from personal suffering and vulnerability, when he points to his 'glory' is one in whom we need not be surprised to find art wrought to its uttermost pitch.

'The Spur', 'The Chambermaid's First Song', 'The Chambermaid's Second Song', 'The Wild Old Wicked Man' and 'News for the Delphic Oracle'

You think it horrible that lust and rage
Should dance attention upon my old age;
They were not such a plague when I was young;
What else have I to spur me into song?

This was written on 7 October 1936. In December, Yeats sent it to Dorothy Wellesley, following a letter a week before in which he had said, 'Forgive all this my dear but I have told you that my poetry all comes from lust and rage'; he also sent it to Ethel Mannin, with the comment 'Certain things drive me mad and I lose control of my tongue.' Conceivably he was thinking also of the critics who had taken exception to the Crazy Jane phase, and who were predictably unrelenting about this and allied poems, even nearer his death.

It has much claim to be considered, with that other rare gem, 'Westron Wind', as one of the two or three unforgettable short poems in English. We may see it as a short, polar opposite to 'Sailing to Byzantium'; or as a sudden mood poem welling up almost from nowhere; or as an exquisite concentration of everything dionysiac in the poet's sensibility and work. Short as it is, I should choose it if I had to take any twenty Yeats poems for an anthology, since its universality soars beyond even Yeats himself. The verdict must surely be, 'not horrible, but splendid', to cut through so great a web of cant with truth's two-edged sword.

Truth, not the whole truth; yet as much truth as the Byzantium poems, or any one single poem can have. The quest for perfection and the compulsions of energy: can there be any truth which does not accept and celebrate both?

The urge to unite opposites, resolve antinomies, is also inescapable, since sanity, as well as genius, depend upon no letting-up. Yet genius always, and any wholesome sanity usually, rest on tormented, good-humoured awareness that unity cannot be achieved (except fleetingly), and certainly cannot be stabilised. In Byzantium, when 'lust and rage' have receded, a 'miracle', or something akin, may seem dimly afloat. But, even there, the images of day and night remain 'unpurged' though suspended: the witching-hour has *its* enemy, in time.

The two 'Songs of the Chambermaid' follow a mood of honest eroticism, but now stir in some of those contradictions that 'dance attention' as well. The first song might look to some like a one-night-stand idealised, yet the waking girl's questions bode little good:

> How came this ranger
> Now sunk in rest,
> Stranger with stranger,
> On my cold breast?

'How came' could lend itself to cheap cynicism, but she is probing far beyond her proclivity for nights such as these:

> What's left to sigh for?
> Strange night has come;

God's love has hidden him
Out of all harm
Pleasure has made him
Weak as a worm.

The two questions in the poem are both rhetorical, with no hopeful
answers lurking beyond. The man's phallus satisfied, he retires to
sleeping, but 'Weak as a worm' is her waking, and ambiguous, view.
Though pleasure was mutual, the aftermath differs; serpent-in-Eden
lurks in the physical image, even if God's love and protection are
briefly vested in her. The man is 'ranger' and will soon have
forgotten; for her, 'stranger with stranger' will be all that remains.
As the language presses relentlessly into loneliness ('sunk', 'rest',
'stranger', 'cold', 'Strange night', 'Weak', 'worm'), will an hour's
remembered pleasure and solace bear her up?

The second song intensifies this sombre aspect, with 'pleasure of
the bed' all too sadly placed. The Chambermaid's intention is no
more towards judgement than it is towards penitence, yet her
expectations are more sunken, maybe, than the man's physical sex.
In the past, 'His rod and its butting head' – but these are now already
a memory, as the whole man turns 'Dull', 'Limp', 'Blind' as a worm.
The phrase 'His spirit' yokes sperm and total humanity together.
Both have 'fled', with no return for her to hope for; and this *is* 'her'
song.

'The Wild Old Wicked Man' was written when Yeats wanted to go
to India with Lady Elizabeth Pelham. It is full of exultant rhetoric,
splendid phrases and rhythms, unrepentant panache, but perhaps
exists a shade nearer the Blarney Stone than the two apparently
slighter poems we have just looked at. The third stanza is the lady's
rejection of the offer of an elderly romp, explicitly (politely?) pinned
to religious convictions. The rest is a splendid rampage through
erotic memories, seductions, 'Bawdy talk' and so on, with most of
the pain of reality drained out. In the last two stanzas, however, Yeats
deepens the poem, characteristically offering the two contrasting
new notes of deeper purport, though without spoiling the tone. The
penultimate stanza accepts universal suffering with stoicism, and has
every hallmark of Yeats writing at his best. The last stanza opts for a
more realistic, if humdrum, tragedy, and ends with self-knowldge of
the *persona* that is without illusions but not without pathos:

But a coarse old man am I,
I choose the second-best
I forget it all awhile
Upon a woman's breast.

No, this is not really Yeats, nor was meant to be: not his choice, not his technique of forgetting. The phrase 'Girls down by the seashore' no doubt recalled a youthful memory, recorded in *Reveries*, as Jeffares says. When Yeats was sailing with his cousin, a boy who was part of the crew talked ecstatically about universal favours supposedly on offer from the local girls. Yeats commented, 'He pleaded with excitement (I imagine that his eyes shone) but hardly hoped to persuade us, and perhaps but played with fabulous images of life and sex.'

This is a good sentence and, if transposed from the young boy to the aging Yeats, comes as near to describing the mood of this poem as any words could.

Finally in this group, 'News for the Delphic Oracle' has a note all its own. In it 'all the golden codgers' are the immortals, seen with delicious irreverence – and it is as if Yeats really wanted to cross Dionysus with Byzantium, partly in jest, but perhaps chiefly in earnest. The pushing together of Greek and Celtic myths makes for a heady brew: Plotinus and Pythagoras once again preside over a heavenly festival of love, but it is as if Crazy Jane had been metamorphosised into the act. The first part combines heavenly and bodily love in a way consonant with paganism at its most optimistic; and it is into *this* setting that the disembodied souls of the dead get pitched by the dolphins as they arrive back from incarnation and enter the 'ecstatic waters' beyond. The mingling of earthy phrases such as 'pitch their burdens off' with images fit for Byzantium has a certain charm, which culminates in the last stanza as Pan raises men to divinity through animality, in a welter of images that no one but Yeats could have concocted:

> Slim adolescence that a nymph has stripped,
> Peleus on Thetis stares.
> Her limbs are delicate as an eyelid,
> Love has blinded him with tears;
> But Thetis' belly listens.
> Down the mountain walls
> From where Pan's cavern is
> Intolerable music falls.
> Foul goat-head, brutal arm appear,
> Belly, shoulder, bum,
> Flash fishlike; nymphs and satyrs
> Copulate in the foam.

If this really could be the 'last word', how pleasant to opt for it; but in truth, Yeats, now a man in his seventies, was already looking death in the face. The date is 1938, almost certainly; who else could have written, with this gaiety and courage, of fantasies past?

We have now to turn to three poems in different mood; and then to four final, major handlings of the great themes of Yeats's life.

'What Then?', 'Are You Content?' and 'An Acre of Grass'

'What Then?' is an ironic ballad, reviving radical doubts such as those in 'Among School Children' (stanzas v–vi), but in a mood of lightness and song. Plato's ghost mocks the world one degree removed from 'reality', where all human achievements are by the ultimate test found transient. The poem envisages early promise fulfilled; hopes of public and private happiness gained and well-nurtured; a world where the obvious moral seems to be 'success'. 'Everything he wrote was read', 'All his happier dreams came true', ' "The work is done", grown old he thought'; how many of us could say as much? And beyond, there is the higher claim, 'Something to perfection brought', which soars past the calculated cosiness to a more exclusive ambition and claim. The poem's persona, though close to Yeats, is subtly diminished, as if to allow any reasonably contented reader to join in. Against this success, mockery recurs unabated, simplified to the single, unanswered challenge, 'What then?'

This is neither Plato nor Yeats in any fullness, so the mockery swings whichever way we will. For Plato, it would be a correct perspective upon worldly standards, but no deflating assertion of cosmic despair or defeat. For a non-Platonist, it might appear all too true at the negative level, though unbalanced by any real hope of transcendence in the world of Ideals. If so, then the ghost of 'Plato' mutates towards ghosts of more gloomy mockers, offering the vanity of human wishes as their sole theme.

'Are You Content?' appears more personal (and is undeniably more resonant), since the poet is now very directly concerned with himself. When read aloud, the panache is splendid, and a very positive delight, in lost ancestors, survives *this* recurring and deflating refrain.

On the surface not dissimilar to the former poem, the poem carries more point and weight. We notice that Yeats calls back to ancestors, themselves greatly varied in talents and reputation, inviting them to return, their authority equal, as *his* judge. The last four lines of the first stanza ask a question, which he can answer only in the partial terms 'not content'. In balance, the opening lines of the last stanza hold a kind of contentment, reposed in the memory of his ancestors and delight in them:

Infirm and aged I might stay
In some good company,
I who have always hated work,
Smiling at the sea. . . .

'I who have always hated work': maybe – but the partial truth in this
will not be missed. The poem returns, by way of Browning (an odd
route?) to its chief assertion, which is a wisdom starting where 'What
Then?' leaves off. For *any* man to say 'I am content' would be
foolish, and in real terms impossible. This poem returns us to the
complexities waiting off-stage.

'An Acre of Grass' moves further, as we return towards the last
major poetic engagements in Yeats's life. Another personal poem, it
describes the new and final home to which Yeats moved in the
summer of 1932, when Thoor Ballylee became too strenuous for his
years. He described it, with a pleasure that does not get into this
poem, in letters to Olivia Shakespear: 'There apple trees, cherry
trees, roses, smooth lawns and no long climb upstairs . . . I shall have
a big old garden all to myself – the study opens into it and it is shut off
from the flower garden and the croquet and tennis lawns and from
the bowling-green. . . .'

The references given in Jeffares's *Commentary* are particularly
helpful and I have no need to repeat them here. He reminds us that
Yeats had been reading Nietzsche's *The Dawn of Day*, and that
Nietzsche's exhortation to avoid easy contentment, which might lead
to posthumous neglect, was now at war with an equal desire to come
to terms with old age in serenity for the final phase. In fact, the
reading of Nietzsche had led Yeats to describe 'What Then?', written
in the same year as this (1936), as 'A melancholy biographical poem'
– a judgement which is misleading, if my own view of that poem is
correct. The influence of *The Dawn of Day* on 'An Acre of Grass' may
be more important, if only because a deeper intensity and
restlessness now prevail:

Picture and book remain,
An acre of green grass
For air and exercise,
Now strength of body goes;
Midnight, an old house
Where nothing stirs but a mouse.

This is deceptive: the mood suggests resignation (or inescapable
acceptance) of life's dwindling, but the verbal energy remains taut
with power. In one perspective, Yeats still has all he has ever truly
needed: picture, book, grass guide us through much of his work.

'Midnight' may signal renewal, as well as ending; both Byzantium and Crazy Jane knew *that* hour. The final line cannot be dissociated from the last stanza of 'Long-legged Fly', where the optical illusions of art are much to the fore.   ˎ

'My temptation is quiet': this line continues the deliberate ambivalence. Yeats had written letters at the time, welcoming quiet and peace as escape from tumult, yet the syntax allows a reverse reading. Is 'quiet' itself the temptation, the last enemy? Yeats's reading of Nietzsche had suggested as much. 'Here at life's end' is a floating phrase, leading to images which belong integrally with 'The Circus Animals' Desertion'. The suggestion is that Crazy Jane and her like have now finally eluded him – yet 'The Spur' was written a month before this, and the two 'Songs of the Chambermaid' at the same time (November 1936). The words 'Can make the truth known' are not, as they almost seem here, a feature of waning power, but the condition of the whole human quest from adolescence to grave.

Scarcely surprising that the second half of the poem soars into immense vigour, with an invocation as memorable as Yeats ever made:

> Grant me an old man's frenzy,
> Myself must I remake
> Till I am Timon and Lear
> Or that William Blake
> Who beat upon the wall
> Till Truth obeyed his call.

Significantly, 'frenzy' is linked now with Blake and Michelangelo, not with mere physical strength, so that Byzantium and 'rag and bone' are made to unite. The ending expresses a major fear, whilst doing much to dispel it: 'An old man's eagle mind' is still at full stretch.

'The Circus Animals' Desertion'

This poem is not dated precisely, but probably belongs to the period between November 1937 and September 1938. The main references are to Yeats's earlier work, notably his drama, though *The Wanderings of Oisin* (1889) features as well. One obvious theme is, again, that of 'The Choice': a sacrifice of life to art through so many years. We notice, however, that Yeats tends to choose examples of his work that were most nearly related to his life: notably *The Countess Cathleen*, which he wrote for Maud Gonne, in the hope that she would notice a personal application. As we know, the play pleased her as much, or as little, as Yeats's other outpoured tributes, and her 'fanaticism and hate' continued, unhealed by the art. In *The Wanderings of Oisin* Yeats had hoped that his symbolism would remain undetected, and that through it he would penetrate to deep truths of the heart. In a letter written to Katharine Tynan on 6 February 1888, he had explained the 'three enchanted islands, allegorical dreams' as representing 'three incompatible things which man is always seeking – infinite feeling, infinite battle, infinite repose'.

During the years between Maud Gonne's marriage to MacBride (1903), and 1910, Yeats was largely preoccupied, together with Lady Gregory, in establishing the Abbey Theatre and exploring drama. As a poet, he mainly lay fallow – and here he appears to suggest that there was an element of escapism in this period, as if the art really had usurped his capacity for love as well as for work. The last two lines of the third stanza, and the whole (virtually) of the third, are relevant – hanging in balance as they do with the earlier awareness, of 1888, that his narrative poem was, in some sense, known at the time as a poor second best:

> But what cared I that set him on to ride.
> I, starved for the bosom of his faery bride?

'The Circus Animals' Desertion' is ostensibly a retrospect and its title suggests that art has finally, in old age, let him down. The brilliant image of the circus turns his whole work into a kind of clowning – a show put on to amuse, yet masking the pain. This ironic perspective is one thread of the structure, and no doubt dictates the choice of the word 'dream' in places where grander words for imagination would normally appear (part II, ll. 3, 15–16, 20). This strand of irony culminates at the end of part II – though, as it does so, we note that the more positive word 'emblems' makes an appearance:

> Players and painted stage took all my love,
> And not those things that they were emblems of.

and this leads immediately into the amazing and powerful reversal that everything has in truth led up to. Here, the major word 'images' enters, accompanied by 'masterful'; and the counter-truth of *this* poem arrives.

At this stage, we can glance back for a second theme, which has been moving unobtrusively alongside the more obvious one. If we look carefully, we notice that while 'life versus art' has been pursuing its course, the word 'heart' has been living a life of its own. It could be described as the dominant word in the whole poem, since it appears in three of the first four stanzas (parts I–II) in a key position, and is then the word on which the poem reaches its climax and rests. (In 'Lapis Lazuli', the word 'gay' has a similar function, and is also the best clue to the poem's fullest life).

First, in part I, we find this:

> Maybe at last, being but a broken man,
> I must be satisfied with my heart, although
> Winter and summer till old age began
> My circus animals were all on show. . . .

What can Yeats mean ? It would take too long to travel back through previous territory, but the ambiguous uses of 'heart' have been a feature throughout. We will not forget the 'Consume my heart away' in 'Sailing to Byzantium' – a sacrifice needed, along with 'nature', if 'soul' is to sing. But we shall recall also that 'heart' has had its triumphs, in dialogue with 'soul', in other places; and that its sacrifice by the Irish martyrs in 'Easter 1916' cast doubts around their actual lives, as well as their deaths ('Too long a sacrifice / Can make a stone of the heart'). The poet who prayed 'That I might seem, though I die old / A foolish, passionate man' was more heart than head (on that occasion, anyway); and many other inplications from the poems, as well as direct statements, will rise into our minds.

Is 'the heart' something to be fallen back on when 'broken'; and was the circus, while it lasted, made up wholly of 'dreams'? Yet, if so, these dreams take us back to 'heart' again, as the first stanza of part II makes suffiiciently clear:

> What can I do but enumerate old themes?
> First that sea-rider Oisin led by the nose
> Through three enchanted islands, allegorical dreams,
> Vain gaiety, vain battle, vain repose,
> Themes of the embittered heart, or so it seems. . . .

The 'embittered heart': the heart broken by unrequited love and other circumstances, long before it is 'broken' by age. One recalls the unexpected and teasing use of 'embittered' in 'Byzantium', as 'all complexities', including heart, are scorned in a passage where the word is inimical to life:

> Or, by the moon embittered, scorn aloud
> In glory of changeless metal
> Common bird or petal
> And all complexities of mire or blood.

In the present stanza, the poet adds that, though the 'themes' of Oisin's journey 'might adorn old songs or courtly shows',

> . . . what cared I that set him on to ride,
> I, starved for the bosom of his faery bride?

This predated the days of Maud Gonne, yet surely refers to the young poet's desire for love. His own heart might then have been in conflict with art, yet 'embittered' could encompass both; and with regret.

The next stanza moves us briefly to 'soul', Maud Gonne's in particular, both in its reality and in its dramatic presentation through Countess Cathleen. In the play, 'masterful Heaven' intervenes; in real life, the terrifying word 'destroy' has to stand. It is of importance that the word 'masterful', used here, is preparing the way for the poem's conclusion, where its authenticity is affirmed in the realm of 'images', whether or not these images had the poet's particular, intended effect (and I would stress the limits of this as a criterion) in real life.

The final stanza of part II hinges on the play *On Baile's Strand* (1903), where Cuchulain dies fighting the sea. Here, the word 'ungovernable' will remind us not only of 'murderous innocence', elemental power unruled by meaning , but also of the failure of art ever fully to embody vision without subtracting, as well as adding, to 'life'. 'Heart-mysteries there', this poem comments;

> and yet when all is said
> It was the dream itself enchanted me:
> Character isolated by a deed
> To engross the present and dominate memory.
> Players and painted stage took all my love
> And not those things that they were emblems of.

The poet has announced that he must be 'satisfied with my heart'; now, in the concluding stanza (part III), he lifts this poem effortlessly to its famous end. The very unexpectedness of this has led some critics to the by now familiar delusion that here, at last, *is* Yeats's 'last word'. A powerful word certainly, and at first sight disenchanting; yet even here the old magician has an ace up his sleeve:

> Those masterful images because complete
> Grew in pure mind, but out of what began?
> A mound of refuse or the sweepings of a street,
> Old kettles, old bottles, and a broken can,
> Old irons, old bones, old rags, that raving slut
> Who keeps the till. Now that my ladder's gone,
> I must lie down where all the ladders start,
> In the foul rag-and-bone shop of the heart.

The 'ladder' is bound to suggest, no doubt rightly, Plato's ladder, and the plain sense is that all that this symbolises was always a dream. In part III of 'The Tower', faith and pride are the poet's legacy: maybe these, along with will, were always the key? While youth lasted, the poet mounted the ladder nightly, keeping the circus going, all the fun of the fair. Now, unable to mount, his ladder is useless: or does it turn out to have been illusion all along?

Yet notice how interesting is the choice of 'sordid' images, which figure (or do they?) as the realities he has transformed. In a curious way, most are familiar, and the transformations have always made for a splendid show. 'Old kettles . . . a broken can': here is the opening of 'The Tower' again, and images the poet has raged against – in public, of course, and to tremendous effect. Again, 'old bones, old rags' have surely been omnipresent, from Byzantium to schoolroom – until the poet has invoked song, or dance to transfigure; and they *have* danced to his tune.

As to 'that raving slut': well, she is no doubt someone glimpsed in a shop, or personally encountered, but is she not also Crazy Jane? If so, the old slut's reply to the Bishop rings in memory, not an inch or an ounce less powerful than it ever was. More astonishingly, could the 'old slut' have been Maud Gonne, Eva Gore-Booth and Con Markiewicz, under the dire spell of polemics – the 'loveliest woman born' burning Troy after Troy?

We know that Yeats's vision had shifted in other poems, and that the transformations were not always (or chiefly) to do with his art. Just as the more bitter visions could arise from real-life disappointments, so the more idealised ones were most often presented as objective truth. The picture of Maud Gonne in stanza iv of 'Among School Children' is 'Her present image' purged of personal bitterness, still and always Ledaean in kind. Eva Gore-Booth and Con Markiewicz may have hastened their ageing; but their enemy was neither politics nor Yeats's art but simply time. As for Lady Gregory, her beauty outsoared Yeats's own art, as much as Mancini's remaining testament to unique and irreplaceable love.

And Yeats's own heart? Well, we know it too by now, from numerous occasions; well enough to protest that this statement does it wrong. That the foul rag-and-bone shop existed is never in question; but what poet was less likely than Yeats to leave it at that? The play of antinomies is his theme from the beginning; it is not likely to be swept away at the end.

The core of this poem is the statement opening the final stanza – which *needs* this context in which, alone, it exists:

Those masterful images because complete
Grew in pure mind, but out of what began?

The irony surrounding 'masterful images' has been established: sufficiently for us to respond, at last, to its inalienable truth. Yeats was destined to rank among the earthly immortals and he knew it – just as Shakespeare did when writing the *Sonnets*, and Pope when he finished *The Rape of the Lock*. 'Those masterful images' describe the works he alludes to; but also the entire opus – and, not least, the poem containing these words.

Questions remain and he goes on asking; this question is deliberately couched in a puzzling form. Are the images 'complete' *because* they 'Grew in pure mind'; or is it because they 'Grew in pure mind' that they are 'complete'? They began – like all art – in real life and *its* images, which are restored now from a golden bird, singing languidly of transience, to the total 'fury and the mire of human veins'. Yet the artistic process remains a mystery. 'Grew in pure mind' is itself a paradox, since 'growth' suggests soil, earth, body – not abstract thought. My tentative conjecture is that Yeats is close, here, to Henry James's thinking, and that the Preface to *Portrait of a Lady* is as good a gloss as any. The 'germs' of art blow into mind; bury themselves below consciousness; and, in the mystery of creation, reappear with form, shape, substance, when their season for birth has come round. At that stage, all is still to be done – the writing, the structuring – yet the seeds have grown and shaped distinctively, while hidden in 'mind'.

I said that Yeats still had an ace up his sleeve: and this is the audacity of the poem's opening. The poem begins by announcing that Yeats can no longer write poetry; this theme is then demonstrated in the way we have seen.

'Long-legged Fly'

In this poem Yeats speaks of the actual moment when creation happens; it exhibits an economy of style remarkable even for him. The imagery in each of the three stanzas is spare, yet extremely precise. The stanzas are linked by close parallels in syntax and theme, and above all by the refrain, which offers a unifying image.

The structure of the stanzas must be particularly noted. Each opens with 'That' – a resounding 'that', rather in the manner of a conjurer: 'in order that' is the force. The first two lines go on to prescribe a condition that must be fulfilled if something of great importance is to occur: the saving of civilisation (stanza i), the destruction of Troy and the making of legend (stanza ii), the awakening of generations of schoolgirls to sexual desire (stanza iii). The third line of each stanza continues with an imperative – 'Quiet', 'Move', 'Shut'; and the action commanded looks, on the face of it, entirely trivial: silence the animals (stanza i), silence yourself (stanza ii), silence the children (stanza iii). The fifth line of each stanza, after these preliminaries, introduces a famous historical or legendary figure, caught at a moment of supremely significant choice. In the first stanza it is Caesar, studying his maps and deciding (we infer) whether or not to cross the Rubicon. In the second stanza it is Helen, more child than woman, alone in a room, deciding (we infer again) whether or not to elope. In the third stanza it is Michelangelo, isolated high in the Sistine Chapel, achieving in 'The Creation of Adam' one of the supreme works of art. Then, in the seventh and eighth lines of each stanza, Yeats underlines the apparent ordinariness of all these scenes. To look at them, you would expect no great outcome. Caesar is like any other man as he gazes vacantly in front of him, his head resting on his hand; Helen, like any other young girl, as her feet move in a 'tinker shuffle'; Michelangelo, like any workman, high on his scaffolding, his hands moving as quietly as the mice.

The main direction of the poem is, then, clear. Yeats presents to us certain moments of great importance, which can be linked in a recurring pattern and unified, despite their apparent dissimilarities, in a refrain. Caesar is soldier, Helen lover, Michelangelo artist; but all, in their own spheres, are creative. In the poem they are seen confronting themselves – and us – in moments of vital creative activity or creative choice. Even Helen is included in these terms, since, though neither her decision to love, nor the resulting violence, is strictly 'creative', the legend which she was to become, her significance in European mythology, haunts us all ('And Helen has all living hearts betrayed'). To see this is to notice the transpositions of roles throughout, very closely meeting Yeats's feeling for paradox. It is the soldier who 'saves' civilisation, through fighting; it is the lover who destroys it, through causing war. As to Michelangelo, he produces a work which is the essence of Byzantium, but which sets the fires of sex at work to unknowable ends.

The factors that Yeats most isolates in his depiction are the need for silence, and the apparent ordinariness of the events. These are moments of lasting significance for the protagonist, as well, indeed, as for the onlookers, if they could know. The choice is to be made, the action completed, by which legend and history will be shaped. Caesar, the saviour of civilisation, Helen the destroyer of civilisation, Michelangelo the creator of civilisation; 'That civilisation may not sink', 'That the topless towers be burnt', 'That girls at puberty may find' – all of these grand consequences stem from this moment. Yet for the onlooker, for the attentive onlooker even, there is nothing to see. No fanfares or public spectacle announce the moment. No onlookers are welcome, and, if onlookers there be, the one role assigned to them is silence. In the stillness, creation occurs. *Then* the consequences stream out, the fanfares and spectacles, for all to marvel at now and forever.

So Yeats links the great man of action, the legendary lover, the greatest of artists, in an image suggesting that somewhere, in their moment of glory, all are alike. The image of the refrain unites them, in its quiet beauty; and suggests that silence and sudden movement alike distinguish the creative mind. The poem reveals itself as one of Yeats's many explorations of Byzantium, in that it concerns the border-country where events in time remove themselves out of time, into the symbolic permanence of recorded history, of legend and art.

The poem is a definition then, of the creative moment; of something which all creators of any importance can be said to share. It is also, in its particular force, an exaltation of a small and heroic elite. The protagonists may *seem* ordinary to the onlookers, but this is because the onlookers see only the external scene. The poem's manner adds a dimension which the images themselves, considered in isolation, would scarcely have. There is, for instance, a strong sense of awe surrounding the protagonists – an awe not unearned, yet offered on equal terms. Whether they save a civilisation, like Caesar, or destroy it, like Helen, they are to this degree exceptional: to this degree also exemplary, as beings who have defied the normal tryanny of time. The onlookers, correspondingly, are cut down to size. The phrase 'Our master Caesar' identifies us, who are not Caesar, with Caesar's slaves; and, indeed, the imperatives throughout the poem – addressed, the reader might legitimately feel, to himself – are coldly deflating. 'Quiet the dog', 'Move most gently *if move you must*' (my italics), 'Shut the door': the abruptness of tone diminishes the onlooker to one who can be minimally helpful to the great man, or minimally unhelpful, according to his success in effacing himself and his kind. Awe, again, is expected of him as a response, even though he fails to see reason for awe. In the second line of stanza ii, the word 'that' is most carefully placed. The tone requires a kind of reverent emphasis – not 'your' face, or 'my' face, but *that* face – an emphasis which we must give, in reading the poem, before we have even discovered to whom the line refers. In the third stanza, 'those children' invokes a tone of active contempt. Depersonalised, like the dog and the pony, they are so many transient irritants to the great man, so many bubbles in the stream of time. This leads again to the placing of the actual name in a line of its own, where both the demand for emphasis, and the additional grandeur achieved by using the split form 'Michael Angelo' rises again towards reverence.

One further matter must be touched on, if only to ensure that it does not nag. The chief links between the stanzas have been mentioned and, along with them, the obtrusive dissimilarities. The apparent man of war is saviour; the apparent woman of love is destroyer; the apparent creator of timeless beauty brings turbulence in time. Such implicit ironies are subtly underlined, more by implications carefully left unstated than by words added to the extreme economy of style. In stanza ii, Helen is 'part woman, three parts a child' till aroused by Paris, to a full womanhood whose results, for Troy, we know. In stanza iii, Michelangelo's work will stir 'girls at puberty' much as Paris stirred Helen; but is every such visitor to the Sistine Chapel then likely to destroy a town?

No doubt Yeats is saying that the Helens and Caesars and Michelangelos are the cream of humanity, and vastly greater than those smaller mortals whom they make or mar. No doubt he further implies that it matters far less whether little people are made or marred than that great people should pass through their moment of choice to lasting fame. But, almost certainly, he is drawing attention to the closeness of creation and destruction – so interdependent that their very inception and celebration must be inseparably linked. If so, then doubts about the Irish martyrs and about Yeats's own possible effect upon them, are resolved (for the moment at least) in this perception that psychological realities override mere moral debate.

Vocabulary and syntax converge on the central image, which establishes itself as a (for once) simple 'truth'. We recognise that there are such times, when a man waits in quietness, to any outward gaze aimless or disengaged; when he is like the neck of an hour-glass, with all the past funnelling down to a point of apparent rest, then opening out again as it passes through. At such moments, choices are made of the highest destiny. A whole civilisation flows through the still point of his choice.

'Lapis Lazuli'

On 6 July 1935, Yeats wrote that Harry Clifton

has sent me a present of a great piece carved by some Chinese sculptor into the semblance of a mountain with temple, trees, paths and an ascetic and pupil about to climb the mountain. Ascetic, pupil, hard stone, eternal theme of the sensual east. The heroic cry in the midst of despair. But no, I am wrong, the east has its solutions always and therefore knows nothing of tragedy. It is we, not the east, that must raise the heroic cry.

This poem, which turns on the lapis-lazuli carving, was written a year later, in July 1936. It falls into five sections, of which the fourth is a precise, pared-down description of the scene depicted. The linked meditations surround this, and, though Yeats's final ordering is extremely subtle, readers new to the poem might look at section iv first, to get their bearings.

If 'Long-Legged Fly' is a poem concentrated upon the moment of creation, 'Lapis Lazuli' considers where art really 'is', and what value it has. The life of the artefact is no longer identified with the actual moment of conception (which is transient), nor with the object itself (since even 'monuments of . . . intellect' are, after all, ageing), nor with its creator (who is mortal), nor with the original inspiration (the real-life Chinamen, if there were such, who once caught an artist's eye). The totality of its life is to be looked for, rather, in the dance of creation and re-creation – at the point, in fact, when, for Yeats looking at the lapis lazuli or for ourselves reading this poem, imagination comes into play. For the first time, he incorporates thoughts of the mortality of art, and its slow erosions by time, as major themes (though they had lurked, uneasily enough, as early as 'Nineteen Hundred and Nineteen': 'Many ingenious lovely things are gone'). When this poem was written, the Italians had invaded Abyssinia, and the Germans had reoccupied the Rhineland. Yeats at the end of his life, as much as Auden at the start of his, knew that war and devastation were now inevitable.

Of what use is art, in a time of crisis? The word 'gay' is at first an abuse, a badge of the irresponsible; but the abuse is hysterical, even if we are, as the women fear, to be destroyed. In the artist's 'gaiety' there is a hope beyond tragedy, a miracle somewhere in the hinterland between art and life: 'Gaiety transfiguring all that dread'. But this gaiety is not escapism: it is a supreme conquest, in the light of which even the death of a civilisation might be faced:

> All things fall and are built again,
> And those that build them again are gay.

The miracle of these lines if their near effrontery. The insupportable burden of the first! – surely the myth of Sisyphus incarnate?: then, the granite-like assurance of the second. It seems that, just as an existing work of art requires the effort of re-creation, to live in a consciousness, so even a destroyed work of art might be recalled from the dead.

The word 'gay' is the word on which this poem turns, moving between its assertion of art's irrelevance to crisis, by the hysterical women, and the entire triumph released in it, by Yeats, at the poem's end.

With this in mind, we can follow through a few points of detail. The opening section has a certain rhetorical panache: the 'women' are unknown, and vaguely reported to Yeats – 'I have heard . . .' has a lordly, even Olympian, ring. But they represent a world near panic, in the fear of bombing, and inclined to write artists off as flimsy irrelevances, so many Neros fiddling while Rome burns.

'Aeroplane and Zeppelin' continues the maybe deliberate vagueness – as if Yeats matches the women's superficiality with some of his own. He would have known that Zeppelin's were obsolete (though recalled from the First World War, vividly); but aeroplanes were still, to him, novel and not wholly real. The concluding lines are, however, sufficiently serious – as if the women's fears, and the reality, start to match. 'King Billy bomb-balls' characteristically quotes an Irish context (a ballad about the Battle of the Boyne), but the German Kaiser would have been chiefly in mind. In fact, bombs had been fairly literally 'pitched' from Zeppelins in the First World War; and Yeats did not live to describe from experience what was to happen next time.

The poem proceeds now to its most difficult section, which generalises the hysterical women (and their male counterparts?) in Shakespearian terms. But, by a sudden transposition, it is the real-life characters who botch the show – weeping, wailing, contributing to formlessness: in art, things are, after all, better arranged. The actors, 'If worthy their prominent part in the play / Do not break up their lines to weep'. In formal tragedy, suffering is turned into celebration – which is, by extension, a 'transfiguring' power in the nature of art itself.

An exact gloss on these lines is difficult, though their main drift seems clear. The imagery includes the play's ending – apocalypse, and maybe the world's ending; and also a reminder that 'Tragedy wrought to its uttermost / . . . cannot grow by an inch or an ounce'. An obvious comment would be that one man's tragedy is, in a sense, every man's; and that, sooner or later, disaster or death come for us all. Allied to this is the universal search for some means of turning ashes to glory: which some find in religion, but Yeats pins on the *true* power of art. One problem of syntax hovers over the lines:

> All men have aimed at, found and lost;
> Black out; Heaven blazing into the head. . . .

Where do these belong exactly? Though 'Tragedy wrought to its uttermost' appears to conclude the section (certainly, it ends with a full-stop) we discover that this line is, none the less, needed as subject for the thought five lines below ('It cannot grow . . .'). Given this, the two lines just quoted might be a floating sequel to everything preceding them, even though 'Gaiety transfiguring all that dread' also ends a sentence and rounds off a thought.

Jeffares, in his *Commentary*, quotes a substantial section from Yeats's 'A General Introduction for My Work' (1937), where much emphasis is placed on 'ecstasy at the approach of death' in Shakespeare's plays. Yeats records that he also recalls Lady Gregory saying 'Tragedy must be a joy to the man who dies'. To this degree, the suggestion is that great tragic writers infuse glory into suffering, and that this feat – though dependent partly on the sheer mastery of language – might justly reflect all greatness and dignity achieved by men in the face of approaching death.

But I find the passage which follows (also from the 'General Introduction') still more illuminating, since it more particularly concerns the nature of art itself:

> Nor is it any different with lyrics, songs, narrative poems; neither scholars nor the populace have sung or read anything generation after generation because of its pain. The maid of honour whose tragedy they sing must be lifted out of history with timeless pattern, she is one of the four Maries, the rhythm is old and familiar, imagination must dance, must be carried beyond feeling into aboriginal ice. Is ice the correct word? I once boasted, copying the phrase from a letter of my father's, that I could write a poem 'cold and passionate as the dawn'. (*Essays and Introductions*, p. 523)

These words remind me (specifically) of the third and concluding section of 'The Tower', as well as of the epitaph Yeats was to write for himself. Even so, I imagine that this passage concerns those transformations which are endemic to art. The prime idea must be that necessary infusion of joy, into the most tragic 'content', which form, structure, beauty, inevitably achieve. Northrop Frye conjectured that when Shakespeare finished writing *King Lear* he would have been elated. This is the experience of the audience also when a great production fully succeeds.

That both creator and audience know pain is inevitable – and the pain is one element without which *Lear* cannot work. But creator and audience alike have survived: pain has led not to suicide, but creation; and in this there is both resilience and the hope inseparable from art.

A parallel experience will be the experience of an actor, as he or she nears the end of a performance that has been worked for, and (for want of an aesthetic equivalent) blessed. Who can doubt that the passions mimed will be deeply felt, at one level – but, in balance, that the joy of achievement will inwardly be rising to laws of its own? As Peggy Ashcroft nears the end of a perfect *Hedda Gabler*, the character's anger and bitterness are *not* broken by tears. Actor, like artist, re-creates human suffering: yet, as the last curtain falls, triumph prevails.

Concert-goers will know the same magic tension, as a performance nears its climax, when from first to last the occasion, or the gods, or good luck, have borne everything up. There is surging joy as the work sweeps, unfaltering, to its last great statement – then unrestrained celebration, in the mounting and insistent applause.

'Gaiety transfiguring all that dread': the word 'transfiguring' has an odd career in Yeats, but here its most powerful suggestions (the Christian ones) are surely at work. 'All perform their tragic play': this phrase begins, half ironically, about the women, then itself moves to its opposite, as the realities of art are explored. The second section of 'Lapis Lazuli' fuses 'transfiguring', therefore gaiety with a more sombre thought awaiting further images: 'All men have aimed at, found and lost'.

Section iii turns directly to the sting in 'lost', with its quick evocation of war, migration, defeat:

> Old civilisations put to the sword.
> Then they and their wisdom went to rack. . . .

But immediately it proceeds to the specific, by way of Callimachus, a passage in which Yeats is at his devious best. We note that, for the purpose, he has slightly exaggerated: one work of Callimachus has indeed survived and come down to us, but Yeats prefers the totality of destruction as an image to face. From now on, the mortality which affects the works of men as much as their creators is central, and the poem's further movement towards hope has, in addition, to encompass the grimness built into this.

Yet in this section Yeats not only asserts his theme but enacts it, as the lost work of Callimachus returns to life in his own lines. The evocations call back to the lost marble and bronze not in arid description, but in new art which brings them, living, into our mind. The 'draperies that seemed to rise / When sea-wind swept the corner' are again before us, along with the miracle of an art that 'handled marble as if it were bronze'. Beside it, 'His long lamp-chimney shaped like the stem / Of a slender plant', which, though lost to time, seems as real here as works of art we have actually seen. To the dance of re-creation which takes place in acting, in close reading, in 'Delight to imagine' (the poet's own role in the poem's climax), is added a demonstration of one art (poetry) recalling another (sculpture in marble) from the dead. The optical illusion, if such it is, is powerfully assisted by syntax, which is near to the heart of the effect. 'No handiwork . . . stands' is the framework of meaning; but, because the verb is delayed to the end, until we have forgotten its subject and been swept up in re-creation, 'stands' has positive force – even triumph – in its place. The following 'stood but a day' is already coloured by this conjuring, as the section culminates in the further affirmative triumph on which I have already remarked.

It is here that Yeats inserts the description of the lapis lazuli he is *looking* at, since this is needed now for the poem's last phase. The interaction between art and life remind us of Keats and of the Grecian Urn especially, but Yeats is saying vitally different things. The 'Ode to a Grecian Urn' unfolds around the unhealed dichotomy of intensity and permanence, with the two fated never to meet. In life the one, in art the other; and poised between the poet, whose recall to 'life' through the word 'desolate' prepares for a final statement whose status can never be known. In Keats's ode, one work of art (the Urn) gives birth to another (Keats's poem), but the original lovers recede from us, and the artists themselves recede in the time-scale of art.

In 'Lapis Lazuli' a work of art dies, but is recalled by another artist – the art depends on the artists as much as the artists upon the art. Moreover, the very erosions of time are assimilated to the lapis-lazuli image, where 'Every discoloration of the stone, / Every accidental crack or dent' becomes part of the beauty to be discerned and transformed. Just as the 'gaiety' may have permanence neither in the living old men nor in the original artist, nor in the lapis-lazuli image considered as unviolable and timeless, none the less these three together attest the continuance of life and creation in a tragic world. The triumph centres now in the human spirit: *there*, in creation and re-creation, is the triumph of life.

This leads into the poem's last, unforgettable image, with its transforming power. The poet, contemplating art, becomes engaged with it: 'I delight to imagine', he says. His delight is touched off by the art and then re-creates it, precisely following our own relation, as readers, to *him*. The old men desire music, and music is played for them. Somewhere between the poem and its audience, the miracle occurs. 'Accomplished fingers begin to play.' Meanwhile Yeats's own fingers reach for an affirmation. On the brink of destined war and possible European destruction, the artist testifies,

> Their eyes mid many wrinkles, their eyes,
> Their ancient, glittering eyes, are gay.

'The Circus Animals' Desertion', 'Long-Legged Fly' and 'Lapis Lazuli' all add further insights to the long dialogue, in which art has been one of many vital doors into 'life'. Is there a final religious or creative doctrine to be extracted? – no more from this achievement,

I think, than from *King Lear* (or from Shakespeare's work as a whole). By attempting to abstract one poem, a few prose sentences, a recurring theme isolated, no doubt the attempt to construct something 'final' could be made. But Yeats's work is a flux, surging round highly complex and finished artefacts; his wisdom is 'masterful images', left in our hands.

Suppose that he had lived a further ten years; would he have written 'Lapis Lazuli', or would certain changes have had to be made? In the early 1940s, Hitler did his best to level London, but Winston Churchill, in a famous speech, said that, standing on any of the city's 'high eminences', one could rejoice that most of the buildings still stood. The year 1945 was to introduce a new dimension, as man's power to destroy himself at length became real. Suppose that a nuclear war destroyed the human race, the globe, every single human thought and achievement? Would 'Lapis Lazuli' remain valid then?

Maybe no artist has risen to the challenge of the nuclear world, and Yeats's long journey ended while it was still a dream. Our gods, or beasts, presiding in Bethlehem, are not his business: instead, we have in 'Under Ben Bulben' one added word. Old themes revisited; new exhortations; untamed energy: and then the last act of panache, embracing himself and the world. He died at Roquebrune on 28 January 1939, and was buried there; in 1948, his body was brought to Ireland, and reinterred in Drumcliffe churchyard in September of that year. There, 'by his command', he lies in death as he decided: his last words carved for human horsemen (if any are left) or their motorised equivalent; or for the Sidhe, in their nightly riding under Ben Bulben's head:

> Cast a cold eye
> On life, on death.
> Horseman, pass by!

2 T. S. Eliot's *Four Quartets*: Disturbing the Dust

Footfalls echo in the memory
Down the passage which we did not take
Towards the door we never opened
Into the rose-garden. My words echo
Thus, in your mind.
                But to what purpose
Disturbing the dust on a bowl of rose-leaves
I do not know.
                      ('Burnt Norton')

'Burnt Norton': There the Dance Is

I

I propose to write on 'Burnt Norton' as the separate, and complete, poem which it was when Eliot wrote it (1935). Later it became part of the famous longer work, closely modelled on it, where it now also forms part of another organic whole. The evolution of *Four Quartets* is itself part of its radically exploratory nature, to which 'Burnt Norton' fitly sets the mood.

Four Quartets is sometimes said to be 'Eliot's great Christian poem', and contrasted with his earlier work as if tentativeness had somehow given place to dogma. In fact, it seems to me neither more nor less Christian than *The Waste Land*, if by 'Christian' one understands some definite commitment or clear credal formula. The difference is mainly tonal, and the challenge for the reader is defined by this. Discernment – shared insights and questions – is the only useful approach; a mutual journey through an essentially psychic maze.

II

'Burnt Norton' is even less close to Christianity than the ensuing Quartets (less close, I should say, than *Ash Wednesday*, which had been written some years before). This is no doubt deliberate. It is drenched in the numinous, which is its own experience, attached to no single faith but assuredly central to all. No other English poet but Wordsworth (perhaps Vaughan once or twice) evokes the numinous so powerfully, and I doubt whether even 'Tintern Abbey', or the 'spots of time' passages in *The Prelude* approach this poem in greatness on its own chosen ground. Otto would surely have recognised it as a major document for his *The Idea of the Holy* (1923) – and I should like the word 'holy' to hang somewhere in the background – though, interestingly, it is not a word that the author presents directly himself.

In essence, I take the poem to be an exploration of human consciousness, at the point where it faces time, and eternity in their elusive dance. Equally, it is an exploration of words – the trade of the poet – but of words bearing *logos* in mind, and maybe lines already quoted from Tennyson as well:

> For words, like Nature, half reveal
> And half conceal the Soul within.
>
> *(In Memoriam*, section v)

These themes link it, of course, with the sequel in *Four Quartets*, and, despite the five year gap between this and 'East Coker', Eliot may have realised that 'Burnt Norton' was unfinished business – complete in the manner intended, but pointing irresistibly to another work, which would crown, and effectively end, his poetic career.

If I can for a moment simplify – in order to mention this link with the later poem, before returning to my declared intention – it might be said that 'time' is explored, in each Quartet, in differing but converging modes. In 'Burnt Norton', we shall be confronted by two enigmas: first, movement 'out' of time and strangely suspended; and, then, the enigma of consciousness itself ('And all is always now'), including consciousness raised, as it sometimes is, to mystical intensity. The poem is haunted by a dangerous, unanswered question, which moves in and out fitfully; if time is illusory, where is there room for change? The spectre of determinism, Calvinism – a spectre that Augustine himself failed to lay successfully – is announced near the start:

If all time is eternally present
All time is unredeemable.

Where will there be room for expiation, salvation, transfiguration
out of the given; where will there be any possible escape from the
heaven, or hell, built into consciousness itself? In contrast, 'East
Coker' will be concerned chiefly with the things that do change –
with living and dying, growing and falling, generation and
mortality, with the pattern of birth and death set against varied
possibilities of renewal and escape. Even so, 'East Coker' will choose
for the lyrical interlude that constitutes its fourth movement Good
Friday – one of those out-of-time moments that bridge the poem's
avowed polarities. 'In my beginning is my end', 'In my end is my
beginning'. 'The Dry Salvages', again chiefly in contrast, turns to the
opposite phenomenon, 'time the destroyer is also time the
preserver', finding, in 'The bitter apple and the bite in the apple' one
familiar human constant – 'such permanence as time has'. Yet this
poem chooses the rhythm of the sea to counterpoint stasis, and, in *its*
fourth movement, links the 'hardly, barely prayable / Prayer' (itself
emerging, in part II, from the 'unprayable / Prayer') with an image
of the Virgin – gazing placidly out to sea, from a promontory, the
repository of so many desperate petitions and last-ditch hopes. Only
in 'Little Gidding' will prayer enter fully, a dynamic breaking at last
through the apparent stasis of 'Burnt Norton', and releasing, for the
fourth movement on this occasion, dramatic eruption – the coming
into time, at last, of 'refining fire'. Arguably, the conclusion of 'Little
Gidding' is, at last, arrival, at the maze's centre – but that is beyond
my present writ to explore. I offer this map merely as a reminder of
the territory: which is, of course, as familiar in Yeats's poetry as in
Eliot's, though in wholly different forms. No doubt, the main crisis of
Four Quartets (if I can call it that) is the crisis that haunts 'Byzantium' as
well. How is one to reconcile 'flame that cannot singe a sleeve' with
'Those images that yet / Fresh images beget'? How, in fact, are those
elusive flames of memory, fiction, hope, fear, dream, prophecy, art,
symbol, archetype – perhaps even purgatory also – to be reconciled
with the indubitably 'real' flames – the flames that singe a sleeve here
and now, in an actual conflagration; the inner flames of hell,
presently real and fearful to many a tormented consciousness,
however elusive purgatory may be?
   In the same area of exploration, Yeats and Eliot were much
preoccupied with the torment of deterioration – mental and
spiritual, as well as physical – that mocked not only their own youth
(though that especially) but all youth, all hope and promise; and
equally all religious promises of gains to balance the losses: wisdom;

sanctity; transfiguration 'from glory to glory', whether towards Christ or towards any other goal.

Can there indeed be any human quest which does not accept shipwreck – sooner or later, in this form or that – as the one certain end?

III

'Burnt Norton' is my theme; and I start with ll. 11–18:

> Footfalls echo in the memory
> Down the passage which we did not take
> Towards the door we never opened
> Into the rose-garden. My words echo
> Thus, in your mind.
> 　　　　　　But to what purpose
> Disturbing the dust on a bowl of rose-leaves
> I do not know.

This is language *being* what it intimates, *doing* what it says; images calling up memories, dreams, reflections (as the eighty-year-old Jung was later to do, is his lovely book of that name). Literary and musical themes will crowd in, for each one of us different – precipitated by the image immediately alluded to: Alice, at the bottom of the well, in the underground room at last, full of doors. All the doors are locked, so her choices prove illusory. And the small door to the rose garden is the wrong size to pass through, even with the aid of magic which is also illusion (when she comes upon the rose garden later, by another route, and wholly unexpectedly, it still turns out to be quite other than she had thought).

Eliot conjures amazingly in the labyrinth of probability. (All those might-have-beens: failed roles, forgone adventures, lost fulfilments or humiliations, forbidden encounters, failed dreams. Our fault? Sometimes, of course; but would we choose differently now?) 'My words echo / Thus, in your mind.' What are we to do with it, this rising excess of regret and memory? Is it a vision of richness: parallel worlds, riches still somewhere existing, somewhere possible, if only in memory; or is it a vision of loss: the valley of dry bones with no prophet to guide, no reviving power to be called? In one of R. S. Thomas's poems 'the god' speaks, and says, 'Write what it is / to be man.' Is Eliot's poetry telling us the answer, in his negatives – 'did not take', 'never opened' – and in his more universal archetype that we all relate to, not merely privately: the rose garden which we lost so far back, or hope for so far in the future, that at least we know the angels, with swords, remain on guard *now*, as always?

We may each provide a different gloss for the rose garden – whether it is in history, or myth, or psychology, or some other place that we search for our frame – but the elusive, lost charm is not to be denied. No way to evade the concreteness, the elusiveness, the resonance, unless we retreat into idiocy; *Four Quartets* is pre-eminently a poem that *works*, that won't let us go.

'But to what purpose': is it possible that the poet himself does not know his power, or pretends not to? Yet he directs us, now, to a calmer, more serene vision of the potent spell. Memories like rose-leaves in a forgotten bowl, the dust disturbed for a moment; a forgotten part of the house, once fragrant, now (perhaps) almost robbed of its power?

A psychiatrist might probe, using his own tools and theories, and with the hope of healing. The poet's purpose is confessedly more obscure. Two young men, singing in some hidden alley, one night in Dubrovnik – their voices fading (for me) from earshot, but not from memory. Two other young men in a boat, near Tower Bridge at sunset; not singing, but radiantly happy: an image of sweetness, seasoned with one sharp pang, of selfish regret. A house in February 1944, gutted and destroyed the previous night by bombs ('Dust in the air suspended / Marks the place where a story ended' – 'Little Gidding'); and, etched ineffaceably in memory, like a snapshot, the picture of a man standing on the step there in brilliant sunlight, holding a cat and waving farewell the morning previously, a few hours before both man and cat were killed.

> We appreciate this better
> In the agony of others, nearly experienced
> Involving ourselves, than in our own.
> For our own past is covered by the currents of action,
> But the torment of others remains an experience
> Unqualified, unworn by subsequent attrition
> People change and smile: but the agony abides.

> ('The Dry Salvages')

Any reader who does not supply his own images will not be reading the poem. But, if we want some of the poet's own special moments, they can be tracked down in various places: for instance, speaking of his friend Verdenal in *The Criterion* for April 1934, he said 'I am willing to admit that my own retrospect is touched by a sentimental sunset, the memory of a friend coming across the Luxembourg Gardens in the late afternoon, waving a branch of lilac, a friend who was later (so far as I could find out) to be mixed with the mud of Gallipoli'.

Yet we are not to linger: almost sharply, there is a change in tempo, calling us back from the merely personal to the archetypal:

> Other echoes
> Inhabit the garden. Shall we follow?
> Quick, said the bird, find them, find them,
> Round the corner. Through the first gate,
> Into our first world, shall be follow
> The deception of the thrush?

Shall we follow? Yes (and, for me, heaven knows how long ago and God knows where, the first gate was a stile, near a dairy, somewhere in the country outside London) – through the first gate, for this 'Burnt Norton' visit (the gate that will not return again, at least in *Four Quartets*, until the closing lines of 'Little Gidding', where its power is, of course, in part a magic of accumulated echoes).

The passage *in* the garden is hard to comment upon, since it is the numinous heart of 'Burnt Norton', perhaps even of *Four Quartets*. When I read, 'for the roses / Had the look of flowers that are looked at', it is not just the multiple literary suggestions, or Wordsworth's 'living' universe that strikes me, but, again, personal moments when the universe has lit up, with this visionary radiance – moments always rare, always given (I know of no technique for achieving them), never deserved, always unexplained or self-explanatory – and so it is with the verse.

'There they were, as our guests, accepted and accepting': and 'they' – who arrive as soon as we pass the gate, to haunt the scene (our dead parents? Adam and Eve? our dead selves even?) – conduct us, with grave ritual, through one part of the lost country.

Note how marvellously poised the poem is, linguistically, between reality and illusion: perhaps one should say, between that illusion of reality when we think things long lost are recovered, and the illusion of dreams, visions, revelations – ultimate teasing, or momentary grace? 'Into our first world': paradise, innocence, inexperience, yet also fullness. Is it possible that our 'first world' is still in some sense accompanying us, though taboo or custom deny it, and with this occasional power to break vividly in, its own claims still valid, so that what we call the 'real world' for a moment wavers, or fades? Yet note the word 'deception'; the elusiveness of 'unheard', 'unseen'; the first impression of 'empty', 'drained', 'dry', 'brown edged'. Then vision again: 'And the pool was filled with water out of sunlight' (Psalm 84 lurking somewhere?); 'The surface glittered out of heart of light' (lovely and radiant: yet in *The Waste Land* the hyacinth girl evoked similar words, perhaps from the dying and betrayed Tristan, 'Looking into the heart of light, the silence' – a passage in which there was no ultimate hope). 'Then a cloud passed, and the pool was empty'. Familiar enough to everyone this, with its recurring and unquenchable sense of let-down – and beautifully caught also by Louis MacNeice, in one of his best poems:

> The sunlight on the garden
> Hardens and grows cold;
> We cannot cage the minute
> Within its nets of gold,
> When all is told
> We cannot beg for pardon.

('The Sunlight on the Garden')

We notice further that right at the heart of the vision, the flower is the lotos: source of opium and delicious deception; Tennyson's Lotos-eaters and their Homeric originals; all the flower-children of the 1960s, a little after Eliot's own death; all the utopians past, present and still to come.

'Go, said the bird' – and is this mocking? Is the bird whose 'deception' enticed us returning us now, bleakly, home? Not unequivocally, surely. In 'East Coker' the poet associates 'risking enchantment' with all and any hope of true vision. 'Go, go go, said the bird: human kind / Cannot bear very much reality' – and 'reality', of course, *is* the problem. What is reality? What is truth?

At the end of the 'Ode to a Nightingale' Keats writes, 'Fled is that vision; do I wake or sleep?' Shakespeare's unfortunate Bottom, in *A Midsummer Night's Dream*, much imposed on, wrestles to keep his vision intact: 'The eye of man hath not heard, the ear of man hath not seen, man's hand is not able to taste, his tongue to conceive, nor his heart to report, what my dream was.' And, before that, Lady Julian of Norwich, on the night of 8 May 1373, received a sequence of fifteen revelations from our Mother Christ, within a five-hour period – and, after twenty years of pondering, produced a glowing book, *Revelations of Divine Love*, along with words that are to be both motto and crescendo in 'Little Gidding' itself: 'And all shall be well and all manner of thing shall be well'.

Eliot is, after all, simply being faithful to life: fled is that vision (perhaps) but, of course, the vision was there. Otherwise, how should verse be here; or our response to it? In 'The Dry Salvages' there is yet another of those marvellous lines which readily detaches itself from its context to haunt the memory; and which surely presents itself, in ghostly form, here: 'We had the experience but missed the meaning'. The story of all our lives, at almost any level – from the extremely mundane at times, to the unnoticed sublime. (And, if the context in 'Dry Salvages' does continue – 'And approach to the meaning restores the experience / In a different form, beyond any meaning / We can assign to happiness' – what does it matter? Eliot is not writing about 'happiness' in any normal sense, but about reality. The poem is a challenge to discernment, in its own musical and autonomous medium; the polarity of 'servitude' and 'freedom' challenges us, from first to last).

Perhaps the 'too much reality' which we cannot bear is, simply, that the pool is empty; perhaps it is that it was (even is) full, for those who can see ('Blessed is the man who, going through this vale of misery, use it as a well: and the pools are filled with water'). Symbolist poetry – the tradition in which this poem ultimately stands – was of course, always divided, about the status of the precise and personal evocations it exists to conjure with. Are they 'merely' individual memories ('A rose is a rose is a rose'); or are they maybe part of Jung's Collective Unconscious (or Plotinus's Anima Mundi); or are they divine revelations lying to hand, but seldom seen, since God chooses to hide them, or possibly special revelations for us, at God's time and choosing, a 'hint' or 'guess' for the soul? Many moderns evoke 'epiphanies' but stay well *this* side of religion; and there is indeed much to be pondered, and discovered, in the mysterious realm of the 'self' as it may be illuminated during such experiences. Others will move towards religion, finding anything less than this dimension intolerable – yet very few will forsake ambivalences for direct assertion – and no one, no artist worthy of respect, will be dogmatic, in this age of Jung.

It is here that we are returned to the main challenge. How do we take the *tone*? I have suggested that the ambivalences in the passages so far looked at are scarcely less than those in *The Waste Land*; but the *feel* of the two poems is surely poles apart. Some sense of excitement, serenity, arrival even, suffuses this passage; it is as far from the feverish depression of mood, the breakdown, of early Eliot as it well could be.

My standard test remains that of reading *Four Quartets* aloud. I find, when attempting this, that the syntax is mainly clear throughout, despite its apparent complexity, and that the occasional elusiveness is never a practical problem for the reading voice. The flow of words suggests unfolding argument (or at least, related insight), and there are frequent stresses on conjunctions – on words such as 'only' – which very subtly guide the reading voice. No doubt, one possible reading brings out some sense of uncertainty and tension (Eliot's own reading has moments of weariness – but maybe his voice was tired, or the recording demands were too great). To read in this way seems to confirm the ambiguities which appear in analysis; yet this is not the reading that rings truest, I would say, to the verse. A 'natural' reading seems redolent of mystery, beauty, incipient happiness: the secret is closer to the Chinese jar than to débris tossed up by the sea. To assert this is not, I think, to read 'Burnt Norton' with hindsight, since, as I have implied already, its own numinous moments and its musical structure, are so clearly model and dynamic alike for much still to come. The visionary moment in the rose-garden is, I would suggest, a test of 'reality' – and of course, it frames the more apparently abstract sections that I have so far ignored.

IV

Back for a moment then to the opening lines – those apparent abstractions which touch off, none the less, the marvellous description, and enactment, of Symbolist verse. We turn to ll. 1–10 (noting that ll. 9–10 return, to conclude the whole section, and can be regarded, at the very least, as an important – perhaps *the* important – musical theme):

> Time present and time past
> Are both perhaps present in time future,
> And time future contained in time past.
> If all time is eternally present
> All time is unredeemable.
> What might have been is an abstraction
> Remaining a perpetual possibility
> Only in a world of speculation.
> What might have been and what has been
> Point to one end, which is always present.

I would point, in passing, to the word 'Only' (l. 8) since this is one of the words that runs, like an elusive thread, through the *Quartets*. If my rapid count is correct, it appears forty times – thirteen in 'Burnt Norton', fifteen in 'East Coker', seven in 'The Dry Salvages' and five in 'Little Gidding'. The multiple 'meanings' shade into each other, often defying exegesis (and what dictionary could hope to do justice to even simple words, when a great poet is working?). A little later, we shall encounter the mysterious phrase 'but that which is only living / Can only die'. In context (where, as it happens, there is a further cluster of three onlies to assist), a few of the possible resonances are, to some degree, limited. But the balance between irony, insight, longing is not to be netted: like so much of this poem, there is the power in such phrases of music to return in snatches, at moments when we might or might not trace the trigger (even if we want to), and when the 'meaning' is manifestly not of a kind that can even tempt towards paraphrase.

This opening of 'Burnt Norton' might *appear* like a 'statement', but, if it does, we are starting on a very false trail. With thoughts of Bradley, Plato, Augustine, we might be tempted to seek some 'familiar compound ghost' for assistance, and even imagine we have a code before us, for reason to crack. But, in truth, is this not already a symphony of echoes? – the abstractions as little amenable to logic as the roses, or the garden itself? The 'perhaps' in l. 2 may suggest extra precision, or even pendantry, but in truth (I think) it signals the end of pure reason's writ, at the very onset of the poem. It confesses the enigma in all such thinking; and the poet's determination to be evasive exactly to the degree forced on him by so complex a theme. 'Time present' (now?) – time past (then?) – time future (what will or may come?): and, yet, not a simple 'this year, next year, some time, never' game. The word 'present' in l. 2 is not exactly a repetition from l. 1; the context forces it to be something else. Perhaps it simply reminds us that we carry the past with us, in present consciousness, and verges on the words of Tennyson's Ulysses, 'I am a part of all that I have met'. But, then, the third line seems much more elusive: *how* is 'time future *contained* in time past?' (my italics). Does this imply that what we are, and will be, is so wholly conditioned, that there is no room for option – no room for real choice, merely for the illusion of choice?

The next two lines would appear to support this, approaching (as I have already suggested) possible determinism – T. S. Eliot's main intellectual worry, I suspect; or should one say, rather, the dreadful paradox that only *Four Quartets* as a whole will in its own terms finally resolve?

> If all time us eternally present
> All time is unredeemable.

I do not wish to comment here at length on these opening lines, if only because the rest of the poem awaits us. But maybe the nub of the matter is that strange, inescapable tension between the 'now' where we always are – at any moment, it is neither five minutes ago, nor five minutes in the future: this *is* the mode of our consciousness – and the experience of transience, which makes 'now' always fleeting, or sequential – but where? (or a 'pattern of timeless moments', if we keep 'Little Gidding' in mind). I suggest – I think as Eliot does also – that our consciousness *is* an experience of 'eternity'; which may therefore prove more familiar in the after-life, if there is one, however strange the idea sounds, than time itself. Time is naturally a mystery, as anyone knows on reflection, with clocks a pragmatic expedient (very effective, admittedly) to make personal and social life possible in the unruly flux. St Augustine conjectured – surely rightly – that, if past and future have any 'real' existence, then the future must flow *through* present, in its measured pace, and disappear into past. The flow is in the direction opposite to our own experience, in fact – not from past to future, but from future to past. And, indeed, if one believes, as Augustine apparently did, that the past exists only in memories and the future exists nowhere, we are indeed precariously located, as apparent entities, in time.

Since Augustine pointed out also that the 'present', in this sense, passes too rapidly to be effectively registered, we have to wonder whether our whole complex reality – as it seems – is more than a sequence of passing harmonies, or discords, in an amazing void. I hope that a quotation from *Confessions,* x, will not seem irrelevant, since, different though the context is, I find it hard to doubt that this passage was not somewhere in Eliot's thoughts.

It is in my own mind, then, that I measure time. I must not allow my mind to insist that time is something objective. I must not let it thwart me because of all the different notions and impressions that are lodged in it. I say that I measure time in my mind. For everything which happens leaves an impression on it, and this impression remains after the thing itself has ceased to be. It is the impression that I measure, since it is still present, not the thing itself, which makes the impression as it passes and then moves into the past. . . .

When we measure silences and say that a given period of silence has lasted as long as a given period of sound, we measure the sound mentally, as though we could actually hear it, and this enables us to estimate the duration of the periods of silence. Even without opening our mouths or speaking at all, we can go over poems and verses and speech of any sort in our minds, and we can do the same with measurable movement of any kind. We can estimate that one poem takes proportionately more, or less, time than another, just as if we were reciting them both aloud. If a man wishes to utter a prolonged sound and decides beforehand how long he wants it to be, he allows this space of time to elapse in silence, commits it to memory, and then begins to utter the sound. It sounds until it reaches the limit set for it, or rather, I should not use the present tense and say that it sounds, but the past and the future, saying that it both has sounded and will sound. For as much of it as has been completed at any given moment has sounded, and the rest will sound. In this way the process continues to the end. All the while the man's attentive mind, which is present, is relegating the future to the past. The past increases in proportion as the future diminishes, until the future is entirely absorbed and becomes wholly past.

But how can the future be diminished or absorbed when it does not yet exist? And how can the past increase when it no longer exists? It can only be that the mind, which regulates this process, performs three functions, those of expectation, attention, and memory. The future, which it expects, passes through the present, to which it attends, into the past, which it remembers. No one would deny that the future does not yet exist or that the past no longer exists. Yet in the mind there is both expectation of the future and remembrance of the past. Again, no one would deny that the present has no duration, since it exists only for the instant of its passage. Yet the mind's attention persists, and through it that which is to be passes towards the state in which it is to be no more. So it is not future time that is long, but a long future is a long expectation of the future; and past time is not long because it does not exist, but a long past is a long remembrance of the past. . . .

You, my Father, are eternal. But I am divided between time gone by and time to come, and its course is a mystery to me. My thoughts, the intimate life of my soul, are torn this way and that in the havoc of change. And so it will be until I am purified and melted by the fire of your love, and fused into one, with you.

Augustine offers the dilemma which might be crystallised in the question, 'Where am I? Where in a flux of future, present and past all so lacking substance can "I" exist?' But, if you assume that 'past' and 'future' do exist somewhere, however inaccessibly, then the further difficulty looms: we cannot alter the past, not by prayer or fasting even (this is bitter experience) – how then can we be sure we can alter the future, or effectively change it at all? One has an image of a vast, predestined film, running inexorably backwards, with an hour's time, and a year's time, rolling towards 'present' (and then 'past'), whatever we do. Note, of course, Eliot's important 'If': he is keeping options open; and this 'If' is in a sense the question on which all other questions will turn.

But the poem goes on, with that exquisite precision which seems half conjuring trick, half immensely delicate, surgical probing, to bring the realm of probability into its equations as well. 'What might have been is an abstraction' – no doubt; but some abstractions of this kind – vivid fantasies, pseudo-memories, inner compulsions long entertained if never given expression – may seem almost as real (quite as real?) as the shadow land of 'memory' itself. Undeniably, the decisive things – love or bereavement, poverty or riches, self-acceptance or self-rejection – *have* happened; undeniably, their

influence is more decisive than what might have happened instead.
Nevertheless, the poem daringly reminds us of the power of might-
have-been 'Remaining a perpetual possibility': yes, but where? – in
memory (again)?; in some kind of healing (why else believe in
religion, or psychotherapy?); even perhaps in forgiveness, salvation,
redemption, transfiguration towards holiness – those things
Christians pretend to take seriously, and conceivably (some of them
anyway) really do? For the latter, one requires of course God – and
God himself, one need scarcely add; not merely 'the idea' of God,
unless one is confessedly ready to opt for delusion and lies. The
notion of 'perpetual possibility' is a tremendous offer: but now, our
first 'only' arrives – with most elegant timing, and strangely
poignant effect. 'Only in a world of speculation'. Worlds of
speculation are the stuff of hope, of fiction, of image making and art,
of redemption (supposing there *is* redemption), so the poet is not
exactly snatching everything back before it has had time to culminate
in a truly heady effect. Yet, speculation is unused to being qualified
by so regal an 'only' – and the impression of something stunningly
conditional prevails over all other response.

Even so, the poet has not finished, and his next two lines (qualified
and enriched as they seem to be by all that follows, since they return,
as we have seen, as this section's last word) push us, for a moment,
into the mystery's very heart:

What might have been and what has been
Point to one end, which is always present.

This comes perilously close to seeming a clarification into pure
nonsense (one of Eliot's hallmarks also at other crucial moments, in
the *Quartets*). When all is said about the psychic hold of fantasy, hope
and even religion, does the sane mind not keep some grip on the
difference between memory itself (what has been), and the might-
have-beens? We know (God knows) our frustrations, pains, failures,
humiliations and limitations; is Eliot really offering to dissolve all
these, in some magic of words? One recalls perhaps Yeats's
conjuring for the dead in 'The Tower' – and the two questions –
surely pertinent – which he wants them to answer (though of course
they do not). First, the question they have all been called to hear, and
maybe to comment on:

Did all old men and women, rich and poor,
Who trod upon these rocks or passed this door,
Whether in public or in secret rage
As I do now against old age?

And, second, the question reserved for Red Hanrahan, when the rest
of the ghosts are dismissed again:

> Does the imagination dwell the most
> Upon a woman won or woman lost?

Yeats, for all his blarney, and vision, had firm hold on realities; these
are questions that will haunt our last years, our death-beds, do what
we will. We shall maybe also ponder then, as C. P. Snow conjectured
in one of his novels, the sexual experiences we have had, or those
that we have not had; and, unless I am much mistaken, we shall give
the same honest answer that he does – yes, it will be the sex we lost,
not the sex we had, that we really regret. To imagine a real confusion
between 'memory' and 'desire' is to toy with insanity; we simply
must believe, in some sense, that the things we think 'really'
happened 'really' did.

But the function of 'Burnt Norton' is precisely to question this
kind of thinking, plunging us into the underlying uncertainties we
might prefer to evade. How far *is* 'our life' a construct of selected and
touched up memories, a somewhat shapeless fantasy; how far does it
have any solid existence, in a world poised against void?

I trust that I have removed any impression of dogmatism in the
poem's opening, and illustrated how, and why, the passage starting
at l. 10 is framed by speculations less overtly resonant, but in fact
merely extending the technique of symbolism to the putative realm
of metaphysical thought. The first movement of this Quartet
concludes theme and variations with main theme restated; then, the
poem plunges into a second movement (not the slow one) with a
certain unexpected, self-mocking vulgarity, of the kind that Mahler
so effectively pioneered in the modern symphony.

V

The opening of this second movement is cast in the form of an
almost-old-fashioned lyric. Lines can just about be scanned, with
four iambics apiece; there are rhymes of a sort. The mood is
exuberant, even euphoric, with the words 'mud', 'Clot' and 'sodden'
absorbed into a generally celebratory élan. In essence, the theme
appears to be an unusual, if uneasy, détente between 'Garlic' and
'sapphires' – despite the 'mud', human opposites coexist in a
workable tension. But the meaning succumbs to deliberate
obfuscation, not of the kind which attends necessary complexity (as
in most of the 'difficult' passages), but, simply, bad writing. Lines
such as

The trilling wire in the blood
Sings below inveterate scars
Appeasing long forgotten wars

appear to bypass a lot of subtle Yeats territory (not to mention most
of human history) with deliberate blandness; while the suggestion of
some link between the 'circulation of the lymph' and the 'drift of
stars' requires explanation or at least some indication of whom he is
thinking of (Yeats and Jung – very serious explorers – or charlatans
such as Madame Sosostris, who will get further sharp treatment in
'The Dry Salvages', part v?). I wonder very much, also, how a poet of
Eliot's stature could write the apparently totally meaningless line
'But reconciled among the stars'.

In 'East Coker', of course, he makes the poetic and logical falsity of
the passage that structurally corresponds to this one deliberate – and
calls attention to it. Was this, I wonder, some kind of amends for
what he had come to see as a major flaw in 'Burnt Norton', a belated
attempt to make virtue out of necessity – or had he perhaps taken for
granted that his readers would register the deliberate quality of
vulgarity as part of the strategy (hence my analogy with Mahler), and
been disconcerted when some did not? In the last two Quartets, this
part of the technique is dropped; and, though the same pattern of a
formal lyric, followed by more normal free verse, is adhered to, the
lyrics there are remarkably fine in their own right (the one in 'The
Dry Salvages' is surely a *tour-de-force*).

The second section of part ii takes us back to the thoughts
generated in part i, and develops, or builds upon, them, now in
formal meditation. To call this and similar passages 'prosaic' might
be marginally helpful (one recalls Eliot's ambition to develop a kind
of verse for his drama which would be able to move backwards and
forwards between ordinary statement and symbolic evocation
without too much strain); but of course it is not prose, and nothing
like it (Eliot had long before reminded people that one should never
write in verse anything that could be better put in prose). However
much this might look like meditation, the statements are still pared
down and resonant. Only once more in this poem (at the beginning
of part v, of course) does he achieve the intensity of his first
movement – yet the flow of interlinked themes, symbols, ideas
continues, and it is in our awareness of this that the growing and felt
power of the poem resides. It must be recorded also, I believe, that
'Burnt Norton' deals with the most difficult and elusive themes that
even Eliot ever had to cope with. For this reason, its writing must
have been especially difficult – and, when we remember that it did
then become the natural beginning, and model, for a larger,
triumphant whole, of which it remains the cornerstone, any notion

that parts II and III were written at comparatively low pressure should
be most carefully reconsidered; this view is not, I am sure, tenable.

What we have is not low pressure but inevitable *carefulness*;
material of this kind cannot be hurried (and this is as true of the
reading as of the writing; of the rereading also, since there are parts
that yield themselves very gradually to each reader, and even then,
not once for all).

'At the still point of the turning world': despite Eliot's immediate
attempt to amplify, and therefore also to limit, this pregnant phrase,
it has a most resolute life of its own. Occasionally I wonder if it has,
among other things, a literal point of reference: is there for instance,
at the earth's core, as it rotates on its axis, some point which in fact
does not move? Perhaps a scientist would know the answer, if I
bothered to seek it (and I realise that such a point would be moving
round the sun, and moving in other complex cosmic relations, even
if not in relation to the rotation of the earth). Is there, at the magnetic
poles, a point where the compass ceases to have meaning, and all
instruments for measuring east or west, up or down, have to yield?

Of more immediate interest, is there, I wonder, a 'still point' in the
psyche? Is there, in the flux of genetic make-up, ideas, instincts,
moods, feelings, fears, hopes, reactions, development and
deterioration, some reliable, unchanging core of a putative 'self'?
The old idea of a soul would suggest this, but as a modern I find it
immensely hard to believe. Yet I remember then the mystery of
individuality, of unique identity; and it may indeed be that God has
set some seal, some name – in no determinist mode, some still point
– on or in us all.

We think that we can predict the reactions on important matters
of people we 'know well'; perhaps we even still think that we can
predict our own. Often this turns out to be true, or seems to be; yet
are we not, at best, beset with the multiple, illusory structures we
build, in vain battle with change? Sudden disaster or loss; sudden
discovery or betrayal; words in a doctor's surgery – what is our 'still
point', at such moments, but a shattered myth? Most of the
literature I teach and admire would reinforce this notion: *Anna
Karenina*, *Death in Venice*, *The Wings of the Dove*, *Riders in the Chariot* – no
point in prolonging a list that might never stop.

The 'still point' might also return us to thoughts of determinism –
and these Eliot wards off, often very violently, himself. There is rage
against old age, of almost Yeatsian intensity, in 'East Coker' and
'Little Gidding'; as we move through the *Quartets*, there are formulae
with a special power to shatter complacency at the pole opposite to
determinism. ('The knowledge imposes a pattern, and falsifies, / For
the pattern is new in every moment / And every moment is a new
and shocking / Valuation of all we have been' – 'East Coker'. 'You

cannot face it steadily, but this thing is sure, / That time is no healer'
– 'The Dry Salvages'; and, of course, the 'gifts reserved for age'
revealed in 'Little Gidding'.)

It seems increasingly apparent to me that the desire to ward off
determinism is a major dynamic, and that the descent of the Dove in
'Little Gidding' is a moment immensely powerful, if for this reason
only. Yet 'Burnt Norton' is also a gravitation towards the inner
meaning of stillness, and the realisation that only through achieving
stillness can one come at all upon 'the dance'.

I find that the phrase 'The still point of the turning world' teases
me not only through some compulsion to *deny* it (generated partly by
the poem, but not confined there) but also through the desire to
discover why it so attracts. The image of the Chinese jar in part v
develops this second aspect beautifully (so, in real life, can something
as simple as a child's spinning-top). There *is* an illusion of stasis
sometimes or a desire for stasis, and notably when life is intense and
satisfying – when one is nearer to Heaven than Hell. Consider John
Donne's striving for a 'still point' in erotic ecstasy:

> What ever dies, was not mixed equally;
> If our two loves be one, or, thou and I
> Love so alike, that none do slacken, none can die.

> ('The Good-morrow')

And again, in the same poet's quest for eternity through religion:

> One short sleep past, we wake eternally,
> And death shall be no more; death, thou shalt die.

> ('Holy Sonnet x')

Two triumphant statements, but with just the right knowledge of
their own precariousness built into them (the deliberate sexual, and
therefore undermining, connotation of 'slacken'; the fact that if
death can die, death after all in some sense lives). No wonder we trust
this remarkable poet, at such moments – little, with good enough
cause, as he often trusted himself. And beyond *that*, we might hear
the voice of Paul, clear across the centuries – 'For me, to live is Christ,
and to die is gain'; and of Lady Julian (who will be especially
important in 'Little Gidding') – 'All shall be well and all manner of
thing shall be well'; or, if we want this granite-like and unqualified
assurance in a version post-dating *Four Quartets*, to be certain of its
continuing status, why not the words of John XXIII, when a
journalist asked him what it felt like to be a dying pope? – 'Any year
is a good year to be born; any year is a good year to die'.

'The still point of the turning world': surely, for such men, there is such a thing; but is its reality 'eternal life', or is it just death? Again, is it the thing itself, or just the wish for it – that desire, built into perfect moments, as so many testify: 'Now more than ever seems it rich to die' (Keats in the 'Ode to a Nightingale'); 'What made us dream that he could comb grey hair?' (Yeats, of the recently dead Major Robert Gregory); 'I go on to say that I see the sexhunt as an art form too. The beautiful abstract choreography, balletic, symphonic. . . . Enter the saboteur with his recurrent motif: "Though sometimes", I hear myself add, "after a night of hustling and dark cruising alleys, I think of suicide" ' (Rechy, *The Sexual Outlaw*).

And, before I finish with this theme, there is that other possibility, already touched on, which I in fact think a certainty, though I cannot prove it, that the 'now' of our consciousness might, after all, be the 'still point'. Perhaps the endless moment we inhabit (except when unconscious), with change washing unceasingly over it, is a nearer experience of eternity than usually we imagine we have. The remainder of this section leads up to Eliot's most striking, single announcement of this theme; but I had better move towards it, as he does, by the devious path.

The first sentence is followed immediately by definitions – and this is one of the famous and characteristic moments when the poem works through negatives. 'Neither' this, 'neither' that, 'neither' the other – five 'neithers', in fact – framing the hardly more positive (though unforgettable) exhortation 'And do not call it fixity / Where past and future are gathered'. And, embedded in the whole, the tremendous declaration, 'there the dance is' – the dance which the passage is, after all, concerned with, as its major theme:

> Except for the point, the still point,
> There would be no dance, and there is only the dance.

Yeats frequently uses the dance image in the same manner, and it is, of course, common European property, at least since Plato. Life: or life at its intense moment – a couple passing, gazing into each others eyes, eyes sparkling and time forgotten – a moment which some other memory might treasure long after the couple themselves have changed, or forgotten, or died:

> O body swayed to music, O brightening glance.
> How can we know the dancer from the dance?
>
> (Yeats, 'Among School Children')

For Yeats too, an unanswerable question; and, in his different way,
Eliot also is concerned to pinpoint the impossibility of answers:

> I can only say, *there* we have been: but I cannot say where.
> And I cannot say, how long, for that is to place it in time.

But he immediately plunges, by way of a transition which I never fail
to find disconcerting, though not entirely inexplicable, into the
obsessive desire for escape, which suggests little but illusion or strain
in the major enterprise:

> The inner freedom from the practical desire,
> The release from action and suffering, release from the inner
> And the outer compulsion, yet surrounded
> By a grace of sense, a white light still and moving,
> *Erhebung* without motion, concentration
> Without elimination, both a new world
> And the old made explicit, understood
> In the completion of its partial ecstasy,
> The resolution of its partial horror.
> Yet the enchainment of past and future
> Woven in the weakness of the changing body,
> Protects mankind from heaven and damnation
> Which flesh cannot endure.

This brings Eastern and Western mysticism together, reminding us
that both systems of religion still have a strong hold on Eliot. He is
reported to have said, when asked about his frame of mind when
writing *The Waste Land*, that 'the man who wrote that poem' might
have become either a Buddhist or a Christian (presumably he might
also have remained neither, if one judges by the poem). And in 'The
Dry Salvages', part III, Eliot turns partly to Hindu scriptures for his
scenario, paying a magnificent poetic farewell perhaps to this other
loved part of him, before turning, finally and fully, into the Western
religion he had embraced. (I had almost said, 'before turning to
Christianity', except that one then recalls that Father, Son and Holy
Spirit are nowhere directly mentioned, at least by these names;
though they are abundantly if often ambivalently present in
incident, image and symbol, and in the ubiquitous lurking presence
of Dante.)

The whole passage I have just quoted is striking. Eliot still finds
some place for 'a grace of sense', despite the powerful effect of
'enchainment', and the general thrust of the notion that past and
future (like 'history' later, in 'Little Gidding') may be servitude, may
be freedom. At times I wonder whether the claim 'made explicit,

understood' is fully justified, but no doubt there has been sufficient of the visionary to make 'ecstasy' and 'horror' understandable (interesting, though, that both are qualified by 'partial', while the one earns 'completion' and the other 'resolution'). I should find it hard to gloss these two lines in any detail, but feel that they reinforce my general claim that the poetry itself belongs now to positive vision – even happiness of a kind – and no longer remotely to the *Waste Land* period, however potently the echoes from that linger.

It is the three lines following which I find most significant – not surprisingly, given the direction implied in these comments. 'Time past and time future / Allow but a little consciousness': In context, this seems almost natural – yet the White Queen's famous pronouncement 'jam yesterday, jam tomorrow, but never jam today' is, I imagine, its antithesis; and much truer to what we think of as a rule as 'normal' experience. Is it not more apparent, in one obvious sense, that time *present* allows but a little consciousness? At any given moment, so little of us – our potential, our extension, our whole being as we might conceive it – is remotely represented; an immense amount is invested in memories of the past, hopes of the future, and plans or fantasies are more in 'those' dimensions than in 'this'. It is the triumph of Eliot's art that he has arrived at the point where this strange statement can seem almost commonplace, and can be followed by the line which I would point to as the spiritual heart of 'Burnt Norton' (if challenged to do so). Interestingly, it is a line which also stands as a sentence – very unusual in late Eliot, and reinforcing its rather special place. When reading the poem, I think it ought to be both emphasised, and lingered upon, since it brings 'the still point' home in the manner which to me, clearly, seems fittest of all. 'To be conscious is not to be in time. . . .' True, of course, that this returns us, in a way, to the determinist dilemma: if so, then, is 'consciousness' not simply trapped? But by now, I think, Eliot has established that we need not think of time as the place of change, and eternity as changeless: rather, eternity may have (and this surely is the seed of the later Quartets) modes of change linked with glory yet *not* with decay.

For, if 'the dance' is at the still point, then all life is there; it is 'time past, time present and time future' where the dance is *not*. In time, we enact our drama of consciousness, fitly protected by past and future, as we have just learned, 'from heaven and damnation / Which flesh cannot endure'. But, in time, we are also voyagers, strangers and pilgrims; we are at best fitfully and transiently placed. 'The dance' is eternal life – life where intensity flourishes; and to reach it one needs a key that all his life Eliot has looked for, and that still he has not found (or not found words fully to convey).

I have heard the key
Turn in the door once and turn once only
We think of the key, each in his prison
Thinking of the key. . . .

That is from *The Waste Land* – and there, with F. H. Bradley's
philosophy still running through his mind – a philosophic solipsism
co-operating with solipsism of temperament – only 'fragments' to
shore 'against my ruins' really emerge. We have encountered in *The
Waste Land* death and resurrection patterns in plenty (not excluding
the Christian one); there have been the words also of *Brihadaranyaka
Upanishad*, v, 1, 'Datta, Dayadhvam, Damyata', to use almost as a
mantra – but there has still not been release. The missing word *will*
appear, at last, as the Quartets continue, and in 'Little Gidding' the
place where the world ends – at least for the poet – will be found. In
'Burnt Norton', it is as if Eliot were still trembling on the brink, but
going no further; no doubt, this difficult exploration had to be
made, and had truly to convince him, before he could honestly
proceed to the seemingly easier stages ahead.

Part II concludes with evocations again. Each Quartet has a passage
using these images, though only 'Little Gidding' can transfigure
them, in its actual close. The numinous moments – in and out of
time – remain crucially important, while one waits for such 'hints
and guesses' to grow clear. 'The moment in the rose-garden' – that
we have encountered; 'The moment in the arbour where the rain
beat' – this has still to come, in 'The Dry Salvages', 'The moment in
the draughty church at smokefall' – this, the moment *of* moments, as
we shall find in 'Little Gidding', is still one among others, and it is for
us, as readers, still to evoke as we can.

The final line, 'Only through time time is conquered', eludes me.
It sounds triumphant; no doubt, it refers to Good Friday, and
incarnation, and to the coming of the Spirit – but I am never sure, in
context, that I hear it aright.

VI

Part III is, I think, easier to understand when one grasps that Eliot is,
in his physical presence at least, mainly on the Piccadilly line in the
London Underground system, and very particularly down in
Gloucester Road station. He roams overground London also – its
magnificent hills, which are maligned here – and, reverting to the
Waste Land mood almost, for the occasion, very nearly slips, with
ourselves and London in tow, back into Hell.

The whole of *Four Quartets* was very nearly called 'South Kensington

Quartets', and Gloucester Road would normally (I should have thought) have been his point of emergence into Heaven, not the other way round. He was not yet churchwarden of the nèarby church of St Stephen; but no doubt he worshipped there, and it is one of the most numinous and lovely places in London (my personal impression of this has been confirmed by others, numerous times). At the same time, of course, he would have emerged even more often – still from the Piccadilly Line – at Russell Square station; and maybe it is a matter of tact that Faber and Faber (the publishing house Eliot worked for) is nowhere allowed to creep in.

For whatever cause, the London images are tinged with damnation, and the famous double perspective of early Eliot re-appears. It is an odd passage to find – given that *Ash Wednesday* has been written already, and *Murder in the Cathedral* belongs to the same period – or so it always seems to me. How far, as yet, *has* Eliot's accepted, and much proclaimed, Anglo-Catholicism rescued him from willed loneliness, shuddering distaste of his fellows ('Wind in and out of unwholesome lungs / . . . Eructation of unhealthy souls', etc.), and from a personal and inner extreme dissociation? – if the famous word he coined, for a certain type of sensibility, may be applied to himself? Just as part II of *The Waste Land* was a considerable injustice to dozens of jolly Cockney ladies in East End pubs at closing time (true as far as it goes, but selective; and – the deceitful part – somehow palming the selective off as the typical), so the same could be said here of all those non-twittering souls who ply the Piccadilly Line daily, perhaps even enjoying it, and themselves, more than Eliot clearly did. In the second half of the section, he reverts yet again to the *via negativa*, this time in images that I find hard to relate to, and more than a little bizarre. The invitation to faith by *this* route is not my own way (but then, I am personally allergic to *The Cloud of Unknowing* and mystical doctrines of that type). I am by no means certain that the phrase 'World not world, but that which is not world' conveys to me anything; and I hope this is not due to basic lack of sympathy (my admiration for *Four Quartets*, only just this side of idolatry, will be clear enough by now, I suppose). The piled-up negatives strike me, disturbingly, as a list, without a great deal of vigour – 'darkness', 'deprivation', 'Desiccation', 'Evacuation', 'Inoperancy' – a little too much? – and, in the general annihilation, 'sense', 'fancy', 'spirit' seem to have got lost as well (what of 'mind?'). And then, when one might hope (I think) for the reversion to something more positive (as one in fact gets in every following context at all like this in kind), the only offer is another 'way' – sounding, if anything, more negative than the last. Abstention from movement: well, in 'East Coker' this becomes clearer, and perhaps Eliot is building; I tend to think of part III of 'Burnt Norton' as foundations – heedful, but bare. Perhaps Eliot is having a bad moment; perhaps he feels that bad moments must be recalled again before we can rest in the rose-garden. It is reassuring to sense at the end that the Piccadilly Line is still running – though once more (a final carp), I cannot see it as the most brilliant of Eliot's images either for 'the world' in its brokenness ('appetency'), nor for 'time past and time future' ('metalled ways').

VII

Part iv is the lyrical interlude which all the Quartets will have in this position. It is the only one of the four that is not Christian (for afterwards Eliot identified this as an occasion for some of the most explicitly Christian pieces) and poetically it seems to me undoubtedly the best. A brilliant mood poem – purging much of the darkness that has just been accumulated, and purging itself also, in a strange way. Looked at abstractly, there is much that might seem gloomy or threatening in the short section ('buried', 'black', 'carried . . . away', 'stray', 'clutch and cling', 'Chill', 'Down on us'), but the general effect is one of light and enchantment. Once more, nature is aware of, and attending to man; there is something of the magic reciprocity of the 'roses' in part i. The final image is keenly beautiful. I recall a somewhat solitary man who once confided to me that the sight of a kingfisher, flashing through the evening sunlight, had constituted one of his two moments of pure happiness in the previous twelve months. The section returns us to 'the still point of the turning world' by this beautifully positive route, and prepares for a final movement of complex suggestiveness. In fact, the final movement evades a climax (rather like much modern mood-music), but starts with an adagio of great serenity, where the major themes come together again, and take new form and grace.

VIII

Words move, music moves
Only in time; but that which is only living
Can only die. Words, after speech, reach
Into the silence. Only by the form, the pattern,
Can words or music reach
The stillness, as a Chinese jar still
Moves perpetually in its stillness.
Not the stillness of the violin, while the note lasts,
Not that only, but the co-existence,

Or say that the end precedes the beginning,
And the end and the beginning were always there
Before the beginning and after the end.
And all is always now.

To systematic minds, this might be classified as one of the passages
(and each Quartet has one) when the process of words, and art,
become the subject, and the poet incorporates insights into his craft
as part of the vision. So it is; but it cannot be limited. Immediately
after the passage just quoted there is almost an explosion, as the poet
shares the anguish of composition – yet the anguish is built into the
experience itself. As usual, 'word' suggests 'the Word' – revelation
and Logos; along with the special temptation of the Word in the
desert (we cannot forget Eliot's long personal trek to this point: the
terrible desert passages in *The Waste Land*).

I have repeatedly urged reading the poem aloud as its best exegesis,
and here the *sound* of old themes, rearranging themselves, is almost
the whole effect. 'All art aspires to the condition of music' ran the
Symbolist motto; we are indeed fortunate that our greatest poets in
English have been rooted in this tradition, with whatever slight
reservations at times, ever since.

What then can the critic do? Point to this and that – not trying to
explain, except maybe in questions. In the first nine lines, the word
'only' (to return to this) appears five times. On each occasion, it
invites verbal emphasis; on each occasion, its function changes and
shifts subtly, bearing the music along. 'Words move, music
moves / Only in time' – true, in the most obvious sense. Words and
music cannot move on the written page, or on the musical score;
books and scores remain dead until there is time, and a
consciousness related to time, to start up the dance. Nor, of course,
can that illusion of architectural existence which we feel in great art
ever be located. A major novel such as *Bleak House*, a work such as
Verdi's *Requiem* or a Mahler symphony, will tease us with an almost
absolute sense of solid, three-dimensional existence, somewhere in
time or space; but nowhere known to us can we track it down. This is
a fairly functional 'only', then? – but note how quickly this opening
is caught up, and changed, in the further thought which it prompts:
'but that which is only living / Can only die'. Out of context, this
phrase prompts reflections of varying *kinds* (most of them ironic) as I
have already indicated. In context, it appears to be a reminder that,
after all, words and music do have some life independent of
'movement' in time – otherwise, how could they belong with our
consciousness? 'Through memory', no doubt one answers, 'and the
strange, often untraceable triggers of memory'. Yet Eliot has already
achieved that line of great import 'To be conscious is not to be in

time', and in approaching the further line I could point to as almost
still more central, given its place in the main development: 'And all
is always now'. It seems to me certain, therefore, that the two onlies
now concerning us pinpoint, with a shade of irony certainly, the
shallowness of any philosophy which fails to account for some
dimension of experience in counterpoint with time, and able,
therefore, to contain 'the dance' in its truest form. 'Words, after
speech, reach / Into the silence': this 'reach', so active in its placing
(and so accentuated by the lift of sudden rhyme) suggests that words,
far from merely fading into nowhere, positively court some far fuller
fulfilment, *pushing* themselves towards the 'silence' where it awaits
them. And immediately we are further reminded that any words
destined to be separated from ephemeral verbiage, for a more
sublime destiny, require some permanent corner of consciousness. It
follows equally that, while individuals will be especially conscious of
whatever corner of their personal consciousness such words may
occupy, we recognise that solipsism is transcended, at last, by
something far wider. The 'silence' occupied by words and music is, at
the very least, shared with many other human memories – each with
slightly different associations, each likely to be triggered in different
ways; yet each united in a 'common' experience – since the words
and music are, after all, of transpersonal resonance. And, if we
follow a little further, each points to, or requires, some still further
and more permanent home.

> Only by the form, the pattern,
> Can words or music reach
> The stillness, as a Chinese jar still
> Moves perpetually in its stillness.

The image of the Chinese jar will need little glossing for anyone who
has ever been captivated (even hypnotised) by some perfect specimen,
and been amazed by a stillness which seems far more like perpetual
motion disguised as stasis than 'stillness' itself.

The next image reveals Eliot pushing still further towards that
mysterious place where Beethoven's Ninth Symphony really is the
majestic and perfect structure we know it to be, and not simply the
experience of it which time and space fleetingly allows. His further
leap, to an intuition that all beauty which exists must, in some sense,
have existed always, may seem unheralded, yet is surely fulfils the
logic of suggestion that has pervaded the whole. In fact, in one sense
it merely returns us to the thinking of Plato – where all particular
beauty partakes of an ideal beauty; and, still more, to the *Enneads* of
Plotinus, where particular beauty is also, in some sense, permanently
unique. 'Eternity is in love with the productions of time' (that was

Blake, offering a 'Proverb from Hell' in *The Marriage of Heaven and Hell*, and so arriving from a very different direction; but, if I may anticipate the final Quartet, adapting words there for my own purpose, 'If you came this way, / Taking any route, starting from anywhere, / At any time or at any season, / It would always be the same').

I invariably wonder, at this point, whether the strong affinity with Neo-Platonism in my own consciousness is as eccentric as most modern culture would have me believe; or whether it is far more universal than most of us are allowed to know? 'And all is always now'. This rare thing – the single sentence, arising from an anguished battle yet looking almost like axiom – is as good an instance of the triumph of 'Burnt Norton' (and the Quartets collectively) as any other single line that could be pointed to. For me, it is one of those sentences also that gives some insight into the culturally, and personally unfamiliar, territory of the mantra. It is a sentence I can repeat – and often find repeating itself, under its own volition – always with a sense of deep initiation, coupled with insoluble mystery. There is no further to go; yet it is only a beginning: no wonder, perhaps, that at this point Eliot plunges, almost with anguish, into the process that has led him here. 'Words' link, in his mind, with Logos, and the sufferings of the Logos – he speaks of the terrible battle for the purity of language, against increasing barbarism and rapine: 'The Word in the desert' links this further with satanic temptation, and with the endless, unending battle, in time, between evil and good.

Even so, the final two lines depart from the New Testament reference, settling for a conclusion that is bizarre rather than clear. The final line, 'The loud lament of the disconsolate chimera' strikes me as one of the few genuinely metaphysical (and amusing) images in Eliot (his debt to the metaphysicals, except in pastiche, was surely much exaggerated in earlier days). In his own reading, the voice takes on a profound, almost portentous desolation – as if the improbable creature were really lurking, howling its protest back at scepticism, from some inaccessible thicket.

The 'ten stairs' returns us to the territory of *Ash Wednesday* (as well as to St John of the Cross), and the poem ends with a further amalgam of mystical insights, from East and West. The next few lines constitute one of the few passages from *Four Quartets* of which I can make very little. Maybe this is because I make very little also of Aquinas, and of scholastic speculation on the Unmoved Mover; and find the introduction of the word 'Love', heart-warming as it is in the work of the poet of *The Waste Land* and 'Prufrock', somewhat frigid in the context of a philosophy that could never be mine. 'Love that is itself unmoving / Only the cause and end of movement' is not, for me, identifiable – though mercifully, the word 'Love' becomes caught up later, in the dance of the Christian Trinity – and in the still more delightful pagan dance (unless I misread) of Plotinus's Trinity. Even the 'Only' here does not seem to signal much of significance (I realise that it might, if I could respond as the poet evidently did himself.)

Fortunately, the poem's end is preceded by a return of evocation: 'Sudden, in a shaft of sunlight' – and the perfect image of the 'dust', stirred very thoroughly now from the forgotten bowl of rose-leaves, 'moves' in tune with 'the hidden laughter / Of children in the foliage'. No need to mention that here, once more, we find a seed that will be splendidly fruitful throughout the *Quartets*, and notably at its climax.

I wonder continually about the closing two lines. How does one read them? They are the two most difficult lines in *Four Quartets* to read aloud. Eliot's own reading sounds slightly depressed, but is this an accident? Or is it an interpretation that we might choose to challenge as somewhat perverse? The last two lines *might* be made to merge with the 'laughter' – ridiculous that the Waste Land *still* has to exist for some, in so living a world. Indeed, perhaps Eliot's own intonation was due to the merely personal reflection that he had had so hard and long a trek through it himself.

But I suspect also that the poet does not want this to be thought of as a 'Christian' poem, or in any manner to forgo its ambivalence at the end. Perhaps we should do best to let the last two lines rest as a riddle, a challenge to discernment.

What *is* the 'reality' which human kind finds so hard to bear? – if we believe the thrush (whose 'deception' has, however, led us that far). Where is the elusive dance, and how are we to reach it?

'East Coker': Only the Fight

I

T. S. Eliot's English roots were in East Coker and, like many Americans, he returned to them. Later, he chose to be buried in the church at East Coker, rather than in St Stephen's, Gloucester Road, where he had been for twenty-five years church warden, or in the grander places available to an OM and those whom most of us 'cannot hope to emulate'. 'In my beginning is my end' has one very personal meaning.

Professor W. Moynihan and others have written of the persona in *Four Quartets*, reminding us not to identify the poet with the narrator too naïvely. Of course they are right. Yet I suspect that this now

familiar, and important, understanding of the distance between the
artist and his art needs occasional scrutiny; the artist's intention and
consciousness remain key factors as well. It was Hugh Kenner who
pointed out, in his aptly named book *The Invisible Poet*, that the
speaker of 'The Love Song of Alfred J. Prufrock' is nowhere named
in the poem itself; and that possibly one reason for Eliot's choice of
the delightfully ridiculous title was to divert attention from any
question of 'The Love Song of Thomas S. Eliot'. We are less likely to
suggest such possible identification in 'Portrait of a Lady'; but *The
Waste Land* again raises vexed dilemmas. The psychic breakdown, the
social pessimism and the religious quest were all Eliot's; and I am by
no means certain that, if it were not for the Notes, the notion of
Tiresias being in any sense the poem's presiding consciousness would
enter most readers' heads. Given the 'many voices' which
undeniably exist in the poem, and its dramatic as well as
fragmentary quality, we are unlikely to identify any special episode
with the poet, or with his personal life. But certain phrases – for
example, 'By the waters of Leman I sat down and wept', 'On
Margate sands / I can connect / Nothing with nothing' – are now
known to have a highly personal reference.

Let me be clear. I am not questioning one of Eliot's own famous
obiter dicta, that there is always a distinction between the man who
suffers and the artist who creates; indeed, if there are such animals as
literary truisms, this is surely one of them. Nor am I ignoring the
necessary and important dislocations between art and life, which I
have discussed sufficiently elsewhere, and would like to be taken as
read among my assumptions. It remains true, however, that works of
art are not natural objects like trees; nor are they revelations from
any supernatural oracle, however Delphic. They are made by a man
speaking to men in the language of men and, certain though we are
to agree with R. S. Thomas's reminder that, even in the hands of a
master, words often have a habit of getting their own way, the
'intolerable wrestle with words and meanings' conducted in 'East
Coker', and in all the Quartets, is very much Eliot's own.

Reading *Four Quartets* aloud, and (very particularly now) hearing the
poet's own recorded reading, are I think indispensable to anything a
critic can write. The elusive, many-sided quality is present, as we
should expect; Eliot is the equal of Yeats himself in this realm. But
there is also at times, unless I am wholly wrong, a deliberate
dropping of defences; a less obsessive desire, than in former days, to
'disappear'. While the famous circling rhythms in *Prufrock* and the
earlier work are in large measure ritualistic, even liturgical (I think
here of *Ash Wednesday*), they become, in *Four Quartets*, the signal mark
of a personal voyage. Perhaps, too, I can quote again Eliot's words on
In Memoriam, on which comment was made in the Introduction: 'It

happens now and then that a poet by some strange accident expresses the mood of his generation, at the same time that he is expressing a mood of his own which is quite remote from that of his generation.'

One final clarification, before I start to comment: just as I am implying no direct autobiographical intentions here (only one or two more than usually explicit autobiographical allusions), so I am certainly not implying a 'romantic' intention of Wordsworth's kind. In no sense was Eliot concerned to chart 'the growth of a poet's mind', as in *The Prelude*; the 'self' in 'East Coker' is inextricable from ambiguities as much part of our present century, and of each individual reader, as of the poet. Here, and in the other most personal of the Quartets, 'The Dry Salvages', he continues to set up echoes and resonances from each reader's personal store. The wider allusions, to Dante, various mystics, and other literary and religious sources, are a further link with tradition, thereby keeping the balance between individual, and tradition, which was always an ideal of his art.

In 'East Coker' we are reading a poet who is still classicist as well as Symbolist, but who is more overtly than before concerned with 'experience' direct. If the poem works, it does so by evoking, in us, a common experience, which is also a common experience of *strangeness* – the very precision of imagery underlines this particular aspect of the work.

'Burnt Norton' originated in one of those mystical moments which might visit us anywhere; the second and third Quartets concern, respectively, Eliot's ancestral and his childhood home. 'In my beginning is my end'. The 'my' cannot be merely personal, if only because each reader will respond differently to the vast, if familiar, probing set up by such words. I want to insist also that the more apparently difficult insights achieved in the first Quartet should be remembered, and held in tension with all that now follows. The phrase 'To be conscious is not to be in time' is one such; so is the surprising corollary 'And all is always now'. We see at once, of course, that the musical structure pioneered in the first Quartet is to be used again, with little basic variation – as it will be (with variations more important in the first part of each second movement than elsewhere) for the sequence as a whole. The two central Quartets are, I fancy, simpler than 'Burnt Norton' – which is of necessity the most difficult – and their more elusive passages usually refer back, by implication, to wrestlings in this earlier source. Yet 'East Coker' and 'The Dry Salvages' are no less grand than 'Burnt Norton' in concept and in the general quality of their artistry; and in tone and theme they continue the exploration which culminates (either decisively or elusively, I shall suggest, according to the way one decides to read it)

in 'Little Gidding'. Eliot calls the poems 'Quartets', and late
Beethoven is doubtless the nearest analogy, though I am reminded at
times also of a Mahler symphony. How shocking this would have
seemed to Eliot, I have no way of knowing; but the progress and
method of Mahler's Second and Third symphonies float in my mind
– and, speaking personally, I can conceive of few greater
compliments. 'Little Gidding' turns out to be the finale, where
themes return, to receive their final apotheosis. How far Eliot could
have anticipated such a culmination in 1935, when he wrestled with
'Burnt Norton', who can say? Towards the end of 'Little Gidding',
he offers us words that are profoundly useful as hindsight:

> What we call the beginning is often the end
> And to make an end is to make a beginning.
> The end is where we start from.

I frequently feel that 'Burnt Norton' is the most satisfying end, as
well as the undeniable beginning, of *Four Quartets*, but that it is an
'end', in this sense, only because what it began was carried fully
through.

Part I of 'East Coker' requires little exegesis. It shares something of
the numinous quality of part I of 'Burnt Norton', notably in the lines
running from 'Now the light fails' to 'Wait for the early owl'
(ll. 15–24), though also, a shade more diffusely, in the whole section
following. The opening reflections combine that vision of transience
that is basic to Old Testament Wisdom literature (especially
Ecclesiastes) with images of 'an open field, or a factory, or a by-pass'
that merge the ancient wisdom (still alive for some, admittedly,
through religious worship) with purely twentieth-century
experience. In the ensuing theme, the poet approaches the place
of his ancestral origins, on foot, on a hot afternoon. Beautifully exact
observations of the quality of light and silence are caught up in more
mysterious suggestions of hypnosis. This is not the willed removal of
consciousness from harsh reality to enchantment 'on the viewless
wings of poesy' such as Keats makes in his 'Ode to a Nightingale'. It
is more akin to visionary or 'given' moments – more akin to the
moment in the rose-garden in 'Burnt Norton', though less vivid – yet
there is an important difference: the 'Burnt Norton' experience is
entirely unheralded, and this is its nature; but 'East Coker' is sought
out by the poet with expectations of intensity, and the charm is half-
expected, though wholly open to fate.

Part I of 'East Coker' is unlike Keats (again) in that it does not culminate in
the unwinding of a spell ('Forlorn'), or resort to the deliberately weak
word 'fancy' to define its magic. The status of Eliot's hypnotised (or
half-hypnotised) images is harder to plumb; and this is surely

deliberate. The moment could be vision, but it is not claimed as such. The sudden transition from 'warm haze' of afternoon to 'summer midnight' once more recalls the 'Ode to a Nightingale' ('Already with thee; tender is the night') and doubtless this is more than half intended. But the calling up of these long-dead peasants – the stock from which Eliot came – from their rest through the centuries is more immediately suggestive of Yeats's invocations to the realm of shades. Like Yeats indeed, Eliot half drifts into the spell, with a simple yet potent warning to do nothing to break it:

> If you do not come too close, if you do not come too close,
> On a summer midnight, you can hear the music. . . .

The images combine what many children know, from fairy lore or intuition, with one of the conditions of religious vision at deep levels of 'truth'. 'Do not all charms fly / At the mere touch of cold philosophy?', the young Keats had written in *Lamia* (but more than half feeling, as Matthew Arnold and many Victorians were to do with deeper gravity later, that the 'charms' were illusion, and the 'cold philosophy' truth, like it or not). An early poem by Yeats, 'The Song of the Happy Shepherd' mutates this feeling slightly – away from lost faith (though that element is not lacking) towards nostalgia that might be able to exist now only in words ('words alone are certain good'), yet might also point, through Symbolist resonance, to other kinds of reality, still safe somewhere, when the Christian dogmas were gone, in Celtic mythology:

> The woods of Arcady are dead
> And over is their antique joy;
> Of old, the world on dreaming fed;
> Grey Truth is now her painted toy. . . .

Yeats soon abandoned this mood (even if he ever did much more than toy with it); Eliot was its conscious enemy for much of his life. In the famous essay on Arnold (1930) he implied that religion is not the offspring, but the father, of culture; and he always asserted that the 'modes' of poetry, philosophy and religion remain distinct. You can accept, or reject, any or all of them; what you cannot do, without succumbing to confusion, is to imagine that any one might become the substitute for another. There can be no question then of poetry in any sense 'replacing' religion, or compensating for its loss: since upon the truth or otherwise of the religious view of man rests the very basis of our culture and our ultimate view of the significance of poetry and philosophy – which, in turn, becomes inseparable from our 'humanism', our understanding of the nature of man himself.

As we return to the passage in question in 'East Coker', I think it possible that we might almost detect a conscious exercise of fancy, as Eliot allows his mind, half spellbound, to conjure with stylised and utopian images of a long vanished past – the past from which he himself mysteriously emerged. Or perhaps he *is* experiencing vision, though I doubt it; the claim is not made, as it is in both 'Burnt Norton' and 'Little Gidding', in their differing ways. The fairy-tale signals seem to point to fancy; and the strand of primitivism is too alien to Eliot, as a waking person, for its undoubted charm to be anything but entertained myth. We have to notice also that this passage does not take its place with those three or four moments of vision which recur, throughout the poem, at numinous moments. It remains as a single, if memorable, moment, 'in and out of time', for which hypnosis might after all be the most accurate description.

Hypnosis, or self-hypnosis: conceivably the poet is using his image-making faculty in order deliberately to balance the utopian music of rural peace and ritual against the more sombre weight of Old Testament Wisdom rhythms from which he starts. 'Vanity of vanities, says the Preacher, vanity of vanities; all is vanity' (Ecclesiastes 1:2). But when the Preacher's mood takes over again with the phrase 'Keeping Time, / Keeping the rhythm', it is softened by the intervening music. The sombre severity of Ecclesiastes, so congenial on other occasions to Eliot, is transmuted into something akin to a dance.

The final images are, after all, happy – and this passage often strikes me as a once-for-all healing for the poet, of many old wounds (by no means all, as we are shortly to see). The quotation from Sir Thomas Elyot sanctions marriage as dignified sacrament (Eliot uses the archaic words in his text, but modernises them entirely in his own recorded reading of the work). And, as if by magic, that long quarrel with sexuality which has marked Eliot's work – the many squalid and sterile encounters in *The Waste Land*, the implications of 'birth, copulation and death' in *Sweeney Agonistes* – gives way at last to

A dignified and commodious sacrament,
Two and two, necessarye coniunction,
Holding eche other by the hand or arm
Whiche betokeneth concorde.

Perhaps, at long last, the poet is putting himself *in* 'the scheme of generation', at least imaginatively; 'coupling' is redeemed, the rustic is touched with divinity. Even 'Dung and death' bears no hint of unpleasantness, as surely it would have done in early Eliot. The final 'dawn' is not disillusion – not here anyway (though 'The Dry

Salvages' is still to come) – and not a time of anxiety. It is a curious
release into newness of life, unprecedented freedom:

> Dawn points, and another day
> Prepares for heat and silence. Out at sea the dawn wind
> Wrinkles and slides. I am here
> Or there, or elsewhere. In my beginning.

This is the moment too in his verse when Eliot first roots himself into
his personal past and into human history. At the start, there was the
complex uprootedness of urban loneliness, psychic breakdown,
isolated personal quests, unhappy marriage, symbolised at best by
the Fisher King, seated alone, the arid plain behind him. Then, when
Eliot looked for roots, it was in traditional forms and structures with
no personal connotation; 'in art classicist, in politics royalist, in
religion Anglo-Catholic'. Also, we might add, in philosophy
Bradleyan, in nationhood English, in culture European. These
fragments – augmented by much literature, and only marginally
more coherent even up to *Ash Wednesday* – he had shored against his
ruins. Only now do we find some provisional hint of *arrival*: not yet,
to be sure, of the kind to which the poem is insistently pointing, the
end of the long, supernatural quest, but arrival, and of a curiously
American kind, in the place of family origin – 'East Coker', the very
soil of which takes on enchantment and generates happiness. About
now, or shortly afterwards, there was also that other rooting, outside
the poetry but not, except for the most high-and-dry formalists,
irrelevant to it, in happy marriage. Later again, there was the
inevitable rooting back into the same soil itself, chosen from all
places on earth for the purpose – 'In my beginning'.

II

Part II of 'East Coker' opens with a lyric modelled on 'Burnt Norton',
which poses in traditional rhetoric the old question of cyclical decay.
Phrases such as 'the disturbance of the spring' return us to *Waste Land*
contexts ('April is the cruellest month'), while 'aim too high',
'tumble down' and so forth suggest hubris, even though the rhythms
of the seasonal round are purely natural. There seems a reversion to
the characteristic sickness of response which the first movement had,
for a moment, so beautifully banished. The fusion of mortality with
guilt could be arguably Christian, but, if so, this is a morbid version,
at best, of the doctrine of 'the Fall'.

As in the corresponding section of 'Burnt Norton', the rhetoric
has a deliberate touch of extravagance, almost vulgarity, including

the obscure suggestion of apocalypse by fire at the end. The syntax is loose. I am never certain whether 'late roses' is a separate image, as seems natural, or whether it is an odd transformation of 'hollyhocks', as the lack of punctuation disconcertingly suggests. The transition, when it comes, is not only from 'poetic' to 'prosaic' (with the inverted commas signalled), but from exhilaration, or simulated exhilaration, to downright depression. In Eliot's own recording, the weariness which enters his voice at this point seems more than a calculated effect; it is almost as if for a moment we hear the man himself:

> That was a way of putting it – not very satisfactory:
> A periphrastic study in a worn-out poetical fashion. . . .

Has any poet (except possibly Tennyson, in section v of *In Memoriam*) written into his own poetry so ruthless a dismissal? Yet, clearly, both poets knew their craft. Both were talking not of their own limits (not those only) but of the limits of language; both are moderns, feeling the personal oppression when language fails, and their own mission with it – the tone of Atlas at moments of unbearable strain. If Eliot had wished he could have deleted the passage and started again in sober reality; its inclusion *and* dismissal are alike the wished-for effect. The following powerful two lines would lose much of their point if the process they describe were not being enacted before our eyes:

> Leaving one still with the intolerable wrestle
> With words and meanings.

'Intolerable' must include its root meaning, 'unbearable', along with the connotation of sin and failure which everyone familiar with the 1662 General Confession in Cranmer's Holy Communion service would have picked up at once. Yet Eliot is speaking of the special burden of art, the cost of perfection; and, perhaps even more, the particular burden when art is left with so much to attempt. We have noted that, though he did not believe art could 'replace' religion, he accepted for it very special difficulties and responsibilities towards culture at a time when religion burned low. Almost, he might have assented to the role implied in the opening of Yeats's 'Long-Legged Fly': 'That civilisation may not sink, / It's great battle lost. . . .' All the other passages about words in *Four Quartets* take account of the pain of linguistic failure as a whole society loses subtlety, refinement, discernment, along with its critical sharpness.

'The poetry does not matter': one sentence; and here, we *must* tread with care, unless we are to risk a crass mistake. What the poem

is warning against is false rhetoric, of the type used in the first section
– tired rhythms, frameworks no longer appropriate, 'last year's
language' – and, also, the wrong claim for poetry: the notion that
poetry can inherently save us, or failing that, help us in some way to
'escape'. Perhaps he had specially in mind the indictment he had
made of Swinburne, along with some two-edged praise, in
'Swinburne as Poet' (1920): 'It is, in fact, the word that gives him the
thrill, not the object. When you take to pieces any verse of
Swinburne, you find always that the object was not there – only the
word.' But, when this is allowed, the poetry, of course, does matter: it
matters supremely, since it is the effort peculiar to artists in words
'To purify the dialect of the tribe'.

So, 'to start again' follows – in parenthesis, but as a reminder of
much that Eliot had said elsewhere. We must no doubt balance his
belief that a thing should never be said in poetry if it could be better
said in prose (an inheritance from Imagist days) against the search
which he was now making, in the early 1940s, and in his role as a
dramatist, for the kind of speech that is suitable at times for
statement but can be lifted, at any moment, to pure symbolism with
no noticeable sense of transition or strain. There are moments in the
Quartets when the same kind of verse is used, and this is one of them.
To my mind, it succeeds better here than it usually does in the plays.
The passage following the 'new start' is both relaxed and, in
intention, almost a statement, but the subtlety of tone, the discreetly
archaic vocabulary, and the unobtrusive internal rhymes and
assonances, accompanied by images whose serious intensity most
delicately counterpoints anger and disillusion, add a dimension
wholly distinct from normal 'statement' or prose. Then, with the
line beginning 'In the middle', a phrase which both takes us back to
the opening of the *Divine Comedy* and prepares us for the more
personal note to come at the start of the fifth movement, the mood
changes. There is quick rhythmic excitement and virtuosity,
mounting evocation, leading to a climax where the main *statement*
sounds with fresh urgency, and then dies away into a lyrical
conclusion of serene detachment and quietly distancing beauty.

The main theme is old age, treated here in a manner
foreshadowing the second movement of 'Little Gidding', though the
moods wholly differ. In 'Little Gidding', old age is associated with the
universality of human failure, and the imperative of redemption; it
is caught up in the supernatural, by way of that still pending
dilemma from 'Burnt Norton' that is never forgotten, even when it
lies quiescent: 'If all time is eternally present / All time is
unredeemable.' But here, in 'East Coker', the context is human and
personal. It relates more to his own ancestors, as befits the setting,
than to the entire human race. We become aware that those remoter

and rustic ancestors summoned up in the first movement, idealised,
and then laid to rest again, are replaced now by far more
sophisticated 'elders' recalled by the poet from his early years in New
England. In my personal reading of these lines, English grandparents
and their generation come readily to mind – not the same culture, to
be sure, but near enough for no great imaginative gulf to intervene. I
recall the Victorian snubbing of children ('seen but not heard'),
backed up with crushingly unanswerable 'logic': 'you'll understand
when you're older'; 'you'll be sorry when I'm gone'; 'after all the
sacrifices I've made for you'; and the rest. It was a successful and
maybe wicked bluff, while it lasted; and the revenge of youth since is
understandable, if scarcely less cruel. One must make allowances also
for altered worldly circumstances; no doubt prudence, money-
making, status, political ascendancy conferred a certain safety in that
long-lost world, which is nowhere available now.

Eliot's soft and delicate words evoke here his New England variant
of the tradition, more puritan and gracious, yet touched also maybe
by the harder rock, harder climate, harder natural conditions
prescribed for the fight for civilisation in north-east America. From
this challenging setting has emerged the subdued charm of white
steeples, spacious houses, human graciousness, unobtrusive
affluence, the memory-stirring smell of burning pine-logs, where the
'quiet voiced elders' once kept up their empty pretence. Some special
beauty lingers now in New England, where the juxtaposition of this
serener world, still existing between networks of motorways and the
dramatic urban contrast of Boston and New York City, makes Eliot's
words easier to savour for readers lucky enough to have been
welcomed in that country. There, 'autumnal serenity' lingers, along
with those other last enchantments – 'wisdom of age', 'serenity',
'deliberate habetude', 'the darkness into which they peered / Or
from which they turned their eyes'. None of these concepts entirely
corresponds to my own English memories, where childhood
(admittedly thirty years later than Eliot's, and a cultural universe
away) was coloured by cruder imperialism, the smell of poverty,
more purely *shameless* conservative cant. We cannot miss the charm,
as well as the dismissal, in Eliot's depiction; a charm that the next
Quartet will do much to explain. Compassion as well as censure
touch the picture: 'Had they deceived us, / Or deceived themselves?'
is delicately and wisely said. Somehow, 'the dark cold and empty
desolation' must be held at bay by some mythology: if our myths are
not theirs, we have our myths, too. This phrase, fusing the sea's
darker rhythms alike with early memories and general mortality,
foreshadows the transitional passage to 'The Dry Salvages' at the end
of 'East Coker'. The gist of Eliot's indictment, abstracted from this
larger canvas, is that the elders spoke of wisdom but evaded reality;

they failed to acknowledge the uncertainty surrounding all life. Their choice was still of dogmatism and evasion, not of terror and tension; they denied 'the boredom, the horror and the glory' alike.

False ease, lying wisdom, useless knowledge, framed by underlying fear of the dark. Is Eliot merely suggesting that puritanism sustains less faith in the supernatural, less empathy with suffering, than his new-found Catholicism? Perhaps marginally he is; but the vision reaches deeper, as the sequel shows:

> There is, it seems to us,
> At best, only a limited value
> In the knowledge derived from experience.

This is the only moment in *Four Quartets* when I detect a perhaps unintended ambiguity. Eliot is obviously referring not to the empirical tradition, and to 'knowledge derived from experience' as Locke would have used the term, but simply to pragmatism – the personal experience, and conceivably understanding, that comes with age. The lines immediately following call to mind 'Burnt Norton' territory – the fluidity of human consciousness, the difficulty of locating a 'self', even of the most fleeting reality, in any time-scale thought of as accumulation. Three pregnant, linked statements are compressed into five lines, which contrast with the falsity already explored as a mark of the previous generation, and the sharp modern challenge to draw a borderline between principles and complacency. Like so many sections of *Four Quartets*, these lines have, in my experience, the power of arriving unheralded in the mind in varied contexts – touched off, no doubt, by some latent recognition or part recognition of their truth, whether in some minor matter that can scarcely be identified as the trigger, or in one of the more lacerating recognitions among the 'gifts reserved for age':

> The knowledge imposes a pattern, and falsifies,
> For the pattern is new in every moment
> And every moment is a new and shocking
> Valuation of all we have been. We are only undeceived
> Of what which, deceiving, could no longer harm. . . .

The first of these statements has also of course a wider implication, reaching out, at least potentially, to the whole realm of hypotheses in the sciences and arts. But the poet attaches it immediately to the more specific wound of self-knowledge, which is the main concern of this section, producing, it almost seems, its own dogma – since 'the pattern is new in every moment' implies a degree of continuing self-assessment that exaggerates, and 'a new and shocking / Valuation of all we have been' is, perhaps fortunately for sanity, slightly rarer than a literal reading suggests. (Is this where we fail, however? Do we really harden to stone, or equivocate like the 'elders', when discernment should remain alert to every lie in the heart?). Usually, weeks, months, even years pass, without the sharpest of challenges homing in – yet at any moment such challenges may, and perhaps more frequently should, come. Eliot's clarity is as disconcerting, in its way, as R. S. Thomas's in 'Judgment Day', and may remind us of the puritanism always lurking in both poets. Charles Wesley's plea 'Show me, as my heart can bear / The depth of inbred sin' is altogether less harrowing, though no less incisive; I have heard a distinguished psychotherapist quote the Wesley lines, with special emphasis on 'as my heart can bear', as a key to the tact, as well as the confrontation, required in his daily work. But Eliot's final turn of the screw shows him far from relenting. Yet again, we are brought to the verge of a penitence useless to help and helpless to redeem.

It might be argued, of course, that I take the sternest reading, and that the poet is basically warning us against complacency, at the expense of the 'quiet-voiced elders'. The faults detected in them remain constant, he assures us, and, for reasons rooted in some fault or maybe even defence, built into the 'self'.

Very possibly, less puritan readers might opt at this point for hedonism, deciding that, if all consequences prove evil, why bother about them at all? But I think it likely that, in the deeper plan of the poem, Eliot may be building a bridge between the gloomier possibilities already explored but unresolved in 'Burnt Norton' and a further insight, of crucial importance, still waiting release – 'for history is a pattern / Of timeless moments' ('Little Gidding', part v).

If I am right, we are left with the thought 'If all time is eternally present / All time is unredeemable' offered now not in the seduction of detached reflection, but sharply and practically attached to failed 'elders and betters', and failed selves. Surely this is why the poem now plunges once more into enchantment – lines that are rhythmically and mentally among the most satisfying in *Four Quartets* (or so I repeatedly find them) and which, turning suddenly away from depression, call us rather to recklessness, and continued hope:

> In the middle, not only in the middle of the way
> But all the way, in a dark wood, in a bramble,
> On the edge of a grimpen, where is no secure foothold,
> And menaced by monsters, fancy lights,
> Risking enchantment.

The turn in the verse is marvellously satisfying, and not least because it introduces experiences, not arguments, to dispel the apparent

impasse always blocking our way. For a moment, we are with
Tolkien's hobbits, lured by elf-lights, yet still voyaging bravely; and
Eliot plunges again, into an anger that would now have pleased
Yeats:

> Do not let me hear
> Of the wisdom of old men, but rather of their folly,
> Their fear or fear and frenzy, their fear of possession,
> Of belonging to another, or to others, or to God.

The last line would of course have been different if Yeats had written
it; but some of the great moments of the *Last Poems* ('Grant me an old
man's frenzy: / Myself I must remake') must have gone home to Eliot
and in a healing way.

After this climax, the passage sinks to a dying fall. 'Humility': not
a popular lesson; not one that most moderns speak of frequently;
not this present critic's favourite virtue – and therefore, a word
needing special scrutiny. I have a feeling that 'humility', like
'gratitude', is a 'real' virtue which has become so tainted by the cant
of accepted social injustices that the twentieth century is generally
wary of both. In Dickens, to go back a little in cultural context,
'humility' veers between the sheer cant of Uriah Heep, using it in his
armoury of malice and self-seeking, and the far more real virtue of
heroines such as Esther Summerson and Amy Dorrit, in both of
whom, however, it is coloured by deep psychic wounds, as well as by
love. Though the Church has at times excessively stressed 'humility'
as a New Testament virtue, I sense that most religious leaders prefer
to rethink it, nowadays, in a more positive light. Christ himself
treated all humans, however sinful or unfortunate, with respect and
dignity – qualities pre-eminently apparent in his own ministry and
life. True Christian 'humility' is a recognition of creaturely status
and the ultimate mystery of transcendence in our mysterious
universe, and became greatly debased (this is the connection also
with 'gratitude') when linked with merely human standards of status
and class. No doubt, a recognition of superiority where such
superiority is unmistakable, is right and wholesome; but, in normal
living, self-love (in its scriptural sense) extended to all men ('love thy
neighbour as thyself') seems a far better way.

The beauty and profound rightness of Eliot's lines depends, to my
mind, on his recognition of these distinctions, which has already
been established by relegating to fear or cant the claims of the
'elders' for 'humility' from their children:

> The only wisdom we can hope to acquire
> Is the wisdom of humility: humility is endless.

The houses are all gone under the sea.

The dancers are all gone under the hill.

Here 'humility' is restored to a usage closer to Christ's, and powerfully cleansing; it suggests the need for endurance and empathy in a transient world. The 'dying fall' is as memorable as Yeats's at the end of 'The Tower'; and perhaps the older poet's legacy of his 'pride' and 'faith' are not, after all, so different from this. The final two lines return us to the long-dead rustics of the poem's first movement – to those earlier, if consciously idealised, Eliots – and to the melancholy preacher of Ecclesiastes, preaching his sad, unanswerable wisdom long before the Incarnation of the Logos and the Descent of the Dove.

III

The third movement is one which as a young man I resented, from some obscure sense that Milton's Samson required a nobler echo. It seemed to me less artistically tactful than either the ubiquitous echo-chambers of *The Waste Land*, where shock is essential, or the liturgical echoes that haunt *Ash Wednesday* like a Surrealist dream.

If I no longer feel this, the change is rooted more in reading the passage aloud on numerous occasions and succumbing to its own magnificence than in a formal resolution of earlier doubts. I still fail to see the relevance of Samson's lament from his blindness, or the ironic appropriateness of the heroic tale. What has the grandeur and savagery of Milton's Old Testament story to do with our own century; or Samson's final destruction of the enemy temple to offer, except as horror, today? These words were written, like Yeats's 'Lapis Lazuli', a few years before Hiroshima; but in the event, bitter hindsight is less damaging to Yeats than to Eliot. If Eliot is picking up 'darkness' from the second movement, then he is far too dramatic: something akin to Gray's 'Elegy' would have been more in keeping with that. And Samson is scarcely relevant to 'fame is the spur' when OMs are in question; a lesser irony would better have served the personal mood.

The passage works for me when I simply forget Samson, as far as possible, and allow the deliberately rotund and overdone rhetoric to exist on its own. Then, the unlikely images do take on something of the grandeur of a funeral cortège, observed with mingled awe and derision and surrounded by darkness; the wisdom of Ecclesiastes surrounded now with comic and tragic irony alike. And this tone is justified by the effectiveness of the ensuing transition – from *fortissimo* to *pianissimo*, pomp to eerieness:

And we all go with them into the silent funeral,
Nobody's funeral, for there is no one to bury.

So, with the drastic reduction of 'everybody', as the world judges
fame, to 'nobody', the poet can return to his solitary soul and
personal destiny, where *Four Quartets* centres in its journey towards
faith:

I said to my soul, be still, and let the dark come upon you
Which shall be the darkness of God.

The *via negativa* recalls us again to 'Burnt Norton' – through the word
'still', of course – and to the plunge from vision into dereliction in
the third movement of the first Quartet especially.

But I have to admit again to personal difficulties in these parts of
the poem: how, precisely, do they relate to the moments of vision?
The answer is doubtless that Eliot pursues faith by both the way of
light and the way of darkness, and that I find the second way harder
to grasp – at least in its mystical form – than I do the former.
Numinous moments come upon us unheralded, with their own kind
of stillness, which is 'given', and therefore requires no words to
explain. But there is the other 'stillness', cultivated through
discipline and reaching towards darkness, of the kind spoken of by
the author of *The Cloud of Unknowing* (an English mystic roughly
contemporary with Lady Julian of Norwich, but far removed from
her in temperament; I cannot disguise that I find its unknown
author far more elusive than Lady Julian, at almost every key point).
In the *Cloud* we read, for instance,

Lift up your heart to God with humble love; and mean God . . .
hate to think of anything but God himself so that nothing
occupies your mind or will but only God. Try to forget all created
things. . . . Let them go and pay no attention to them. . . . Do not
give up but work away. . . . When you first begin to find only
darkness and a cloud of unknowing . . . Reconcile yourself to wait
in this darkness as long as is necessary, but go on longing after
him you love . . . strike that thick cloud of unknowing with the
sharp dart of longing love and on no account think of giving
up. . . .

In a strange way, this is counsel more frequently arrived at (I should
judge) through near despair than through mysticism – though maybe
to sever the two oversimplifies, in a specially modern mood of
shallowness. Impossible to forget Tennyson writing in section LV of
In Memoriam

I falter where I firmly trod,
  And falling with my weight of cares
  Upon the world's great altar-stairs
That slope thro' darkness up to God. . . .

and later, in section cxxiv,

And what I am beheld again
  What is, and no man understands;
  And out of darkness came the hands
That reach thro' nature, moulding men.

Impossible, too, to forget the dark sonnets of the anguished believer Hopkins ('I wake and feel the fell of dark, not day') or to overlook the contrast with passages from those profoundly moving poems written by the unbeliever Hardy on the death of his estranged and doubly lost wife, Emma:

  Yet I wanted to look and see
  That nobody stood at the back of me;
But I thought once more: 'Nay, I'll not unvision
  A shape which, somehow, there may be.'
So I went on softly from the glade ·
  And left her behind me, throwing her shade,
As she were indeed an apparition –
  My head unturned lest my dream should fade.

('The Shadow on the Stone')

Throughout history, feeling men (all?) have known the darkness; throughout history, some have come through it to God, or even found it the main road to God. Eliot, before taking us more fully back to this territory, chooses to offer three distinctively modern images, all converging on emptiness, but easier for pragmatism to grasp. The first refers to the 'picture-frame' stage of the theatre – already discredited among some *avant-garde* dramatists as Eliot wrote this, and maybe bringing back for him, as it does for me, childish and delightful memories of the music hall: the magic of the darkened theatre, the rumbling of scenery; the knowledge that one illusion is being replaced by another which is, at once, familiar and satisfying, since it threatens little and promises much. Then, the image of the Underground train stopped too long between stations – very familiar to travellers on London's Northern Line, where it is a familiar feature of northbound trains entering Camden Town, but maybe indicating the longer, unexpected stops on any line, when a shade of fear and claustrophobia may enter. Eliot glosses it as we should expect of the *Waste Land* poet; but I am not sure that the compound of emptiness, fear, accentuated loneliness is more than a minority response. I still suspect that this is a personal sensibility, masquerading as universal: the viewpoint of the poet who had been unable to appreciate the good humour of *some* Cockney women, at least, in London pubs at closing time; and who was ever over-inclined to generalise from particular to universal responses in his social critique. The third of these images is far more compact and concentrated, and admirably describes sensations that anyone who has experienced surgery will know. All three images converge on a repetition of the command, 'I said to my soul, be still', and the six lines starting from here, whose quiet beauty is appealing to listen to but impossible to gloss.

A critic such as myself to whom the *via negativa* means little may feel exonerated from further comment; yet there are undercurrents which always trouble me as I read. Is Eliot not in some degree challenging St Paul at a point where even Paul's enemies often forgive him – and reversing (or rearranging) the 'theological virtues' in a non-Christian way? 'And now abide faith, hope, love, these three', says Paul; 'but the greatest of these is love' (1 Corinthians 13:13).

I find it hard to conceive of the Christian religion at all without these emphases, which seem precisely faithful to the recorded teaching of Christ. But Eliot rejects – or seems to reject – the two greater virtues, leaving only the first: which becomes particularly frail on its own. What *is* 'faith', except mere superstition and credulity, if it is faith in *anything*? I cannot see how 'faith' can be separable from credulity, or mere rubbish, if it is not grounded in love and sustained by some experience of hope. The lines 'wait without hope / For hope would be hope of the wrong thing; wait without love / For love would be love of the wrong thing' strike me as not only a needlessly gloomy deduction from disillusion with the 'elders', but even as reversal and rejection of Christian faith. The entire New Testament starts from witness ('and we beheld his glory'), and proceeds to that account of Love walking the earth which crystallised in the doctrine of Incarnation. Love is authenticated by Christ, and then identified with him: from this proceeds rational hope, based on grounds more solid than wishful thinking. Finally, faith gathers love and hope into personal commitment – a 'leap', it is true, but a leap into all the light there is, not into all the dark.

'. . . there is yet the faith': what does this mean? It eludes me; nor do I find the line 'But the faith and the love and the hope are all in the waiting' in the least degree helpful. It has rhythmic *élan*, but small support in the meaning (St Paul's three virtues are again rearranged, if now in a different way).

I tend to feel, therefore, that the three concrete images which precede the passage, though in themselves excellent, are not an adequate preparation for such startling ideas. The conclusion of the section is, admittedly, memorable; but even the phrase 'So the darkness shall be the light, and the stillness the dancing' requires Yeats (I find) and Plotinus, not *this*, to make the words dance. The line 'Wait without thought, for you are not ready for thought' echoes *The Cloud of Unknowing*, and produces in me precisely the same irritation: the fault is no doubt mine, but this appears to be nonsense claiming the mantle of sense. Only the positive parts of 'Burnt Norton', taken in conjunction with its mysteries, reconcile me to this, as part of the poem: for the link between vision and darkness has still, perhaps, to be made.

Fortunately, some link (whether the missing one or another, I remain unable to decide) immediately appears through the return of evocation. The passage starting 'Whisper of running streams' sets off all the magic required – with 'Burnt Norton' to support it. But still Eliot has not finished with abstractions. The ending of the third movement, starting with 'You say I am repeating' could be justified, in musical terms, as a deliberately discordant scherzo; but, that apart, I justify it in what must be a peripheral mode. The images have a certain Surrealist charm (passages that lead unexpectedly backwards; dream transitions, as in Lewis Carroll's Alice books, and in the images allied to these in Eliot's *The Family Reunion*). At the same time, certain prosaic pieces of common-sense lurk in the basically mystical assertions, to be clutched at, as straws, if the poem threatens to float away. The first statement,

> In order to arrive there,
> To arrive where you are, to get from where you are not,
> You must go by a way wherein there is no ecstasy

half defeats me (though I can read it aloud with pleasure and every appearance of conviction, which the unusually systematic and even emphatic syntax does much to assist). But the idea, or image, remains tantalising: unless indeed the poet is merely saying, obscurely, something that he has said much more clearly before. If this simply means, in order to arrive at where one 'really' is rather than at where one falsely conjectures oneself to be (i.e. at accurate self-knowledge), then 'no ecstasy' is shorthand for things that *have* been splendidly 'said'. But, if the concept is more metaphysical – that is to say, our actual *arrival* at the 'real' rather than 'less real' concept of *homo sapiens* – then 'ecstasy' would still seem to me, for many, the more normal path.

Maybe we are, in Wordsworth's memorable phrase, 'greater than we know'. But, for readers of *Four Quartets*, as of *The Prelude*, this discovery can come more liberatingly through 'spots of time', 'rememberable things', call them what one will, than through this deliberate courting of aridity. These two poems, in many aspects so dissimilar, as has already been acknowledged, remain pre-eminent among verbal evocations of numinous 'reality'. Wordsworth's skating among the mountains, his crossing of the Alps, along with many equally precious moments of heightened consciousness, almost merge with 'the moment in the rose-garden', 'the evening circle in the winter gaslight', 'the whisper of running thyme' in *Four Quartets*. Only Vaughan, among other mystical English poets, has the occasional power to move us in this way. It is sudden illumination, opening insight, unexpected memory and ecstasy that lead towards 'Little Gidding' – in this reader's experience, certainly.

Why, then, these very different notes in 'East Coker'? I suppose because emptiness, hollowness, 'the whimper' have still to be purged somehow, and the *via negativa* is still, for Eliot, an essential part of the route. One recalls the deliberate ambiguities built into the first movement of 'Burnt Norton' (little though they lessen its numinous power, its realised achievement); also, the fact that similar or apparently similar epiphanies did not lead Virginia Woolf, or Wallace Stevens, or many others, to God. So, perhaps, impatience should be curbed if we feel it, and the poet trusted in his very deliberate and laboured wrestling, once more, with old ghosts.

> In order to arrive at what you do not know
> You must go by a way which is the way of ignorance.

My slight quarrel with this is not that I find it equally difficult, but rather that a further signpost or so might have helped. 'The fool for Christ's sake' is ancient Christian paradox; so is St Paul's famous insight 'For after that the world in the wisdom of God by wisdom knew not God, it pleased God by the foolishness of preaching to save them that believe. . . . Because the foolishness of God is wiser than men; and the weakness of God is stronger than men' (1 Corinthians 1:21, 25). These specifics apart, one appreciates that purging false knowledge, false theory, false supposition is a prelude to vision; that self-esteem must perish before grace can be given; that the doors of perception open to intuition only, if the mystics are to be trusted, when certain supposedly 'rational' truths have been set aside, or even radically expelled.

It could be contended, of course, that multiplicity of meaning is precisely the essence here, and that these lines *are* reverberant with symbolic suggestion, though apparently dry. Am I quibbling if I urge that, whereas most of Eliot's symbolism by its nature calls to deep personal responses, these lines throw us back rather on personal conjecture, too purely intellectual in kind?

The next lines, in contrast, make psychological sense which anyone will appreciate without difficulty who has grasped that possessiveness is always and everywhere an enemy of love. This flies in the face of the worldly belief that you acquire objects only by amassing them, that you earn riches only by industry – but it requires only experience of ordinary living, not abstruse philosophy, for its truth to be grasped:

> In order to possess what you do not possess
> You must go by the way of dispossession.

Here I find again one mark of Eliot's particular mastery, which is to bypass intellect even when seeming to work by its rules. But he plunges us back into baffling territory, with the teasing lines

> In order to arrive at what you are not
> You must go through the way in which you are not.

When reading this, I often feel tempted to omit the 'not' at the end of the first line, on the conviction that this would make more readily accessible, if intuitive, sense. But, then, I suspect that I am unconsciously translating 'what' into 'where', and trying to make this a restatement of the 'Where am I?' explorations that have gone before. Eliot does write 'what', in .fact – with its more ultimate suggestions – and doubtless the conception, though elusive, is delicately planned. If we are indeed journeying to 'what' we are not (and the insistent fear of determinism must be dispersed is this is to happen?), then some completely new track through reality must be sought. The allusion is now I think again to lost perfection (our ideal image? – the divine gift once given and universally lost?). The final three lines may further clarify thoughts of lost paradise; or they may repeat, with yet more austerity, the general theme:

> And what you do not know is the only thing you know
> And what you own is what you do not own
> And where you are is where you are not.

Eliot's own reading, as we have it on record, draws from this conclusion a certain beauty – portentous perhaps, but lyrical and insidious also, in its deeper effect. In my own reading, 'the more portentous the better' was once a rule of thumb guidance, but I think that this was the culmination of doubts I have here admitted to and should now wish to recant. I find that I once noted in the margin of a copy of the poem 'These floating paradoxes can be referred to human love – possessiveness kills, renunciation may nurture – but they do not wholly belong here and are perhaps warped, if pushed too hard in this direction, as I tend to do?'. This records not only previous defeats, but the fact that the passage *has* always convinced me – though I have always hoped, too, for a reading that I can get away with before a seminar group or audience, without being pressed too hard to explain. Certainly, the final line, with its 'where', refers us to temporal reality, and so to ground more powerfully and completely covered, I had supposed, in 'Burnt Norton'. But the truth must be that Eliot wants to translate such insights into the more personal soil of his homecoming. To read the passage as, in some manner, personal witness, may be to add the apparently missing quality of warmth.

I should also record that certain students have always claimed to find no difficulty with this passage, and have been clearly surprised that I should myself. One or two have explained it, and I have remained baffled. The opposite processes have also occurred. So it seems that for me, though not for everyone, this is the 'difficult' part of 'East Coker' – which otherwise appears to be comparatively simple, as I have already said.

IV

The fourth movement has been called by some critics the finest part of the poem. This frankly amazes me, since I regard it as the weakest section in *Four Quartets* as a whole.

The reason is that it imitates metaphysical imagery and falls into allegory; and both modes seem inappropriate and badly executed. The 'metaphysical' component is virtually pastiche Donne, but I cannot imagine Donne ever being clumsy.

As to the 'allegory', I recognise that some critics have questioned whether it *is* allegorical, and have offered readings, assuming the usual multiplicity of meaning and effect. Certainly it is odd if Eliot does resort to allegory. I should have expected him rather to agree with Tolkien, who wrote in the Foreword to *Lord of the Rings*,

I cordially dislike allegory in all its manifestations and always have done so since I grew old or wary enough to detect its presence. I much prefer history, true or feigned, with its varied applicability to the thought and experience of readers. I think that many confuse 'applicability' with 'allegory', but the one resides in the freedom of the reader, and the other in the purposed domination of the author.

This is the first moment in the poem when Christian references appear that are (to me, anyway) totally explicit; and it is sad that Eliot's habitual subtlety should falter at such a point. It is precisely here that I should have hoped for his more floating or dreamlike effects; a use of imagery associating the Christian pattern with other mysteries of death and resurrection, other patterns of regeneration for the wounded mind or the derelict soul.

But, despite the denial of some critics that we do confront allegory, I find the matter very little open to doubt (and this understates). 'The wounded surgeon' must be Christ – though in the first stanza, taken alone, wider references to many religions and rituals could, of course, be found. The wounds of God – some necessary, some foreseen, some perhaps a surprise to the Divinity – is also a theme of Sophocles and Jung, Aeschylus and R. S. Thomas (a great spectrum of writers, ancient and modern). But 'bleeding hands', with its transference of wounds from healed to healer, is very specific; and 'sharp compassion' is undoubtedly a Christian frame. The word 'resolving' also suggests success (a Christian dogma?) while the fever chart' surely tracks the ravages of original sin (though seems curiously flat as an image, given the work it has to do). As we proceed, the 'dying nurse' seems to me to be the Christian Church – in its theory, at least – almost beyond question: if only because 'our and Adam's curse' roots the painful cure so totally into Jewish and Christian myths. I take the view that 'the ruined millionaire' must be Adam (or Adam and Eve together), and that the deliberate archaism of 'prevents' (extremely familiar to Anglicans in the 1940s through one of Cranmer's most famous Collects) establishes the context as the Christian Eucharist, well before the movement's ending clinches this. The phrase 'absolute paternal care' conjures up that authoritarian view of the Christian religion which Eliot came to accept with apparent ease. The fourth stanza strikes me as better: here, the imagery is more generalised, and the paradox of Purgatory (along with its crucial possibility in this poem) is introduced in a manner foreshadowing the much fuller territory of 'Little Gidding'. The final stanza, linking Good Friday with the Eucharist, is extremely explicit; it challenges the mind, but lacks the mystery which is surely required.

The three poets we are considering here are all different, and cross-references can be only of a superficial nature. None the less, I am haunted by a conviction that this particular section required the technique – or at least the sensitivity – of the poet of *H'm* and *Laboratories of the Spirit*, who might have written it superbly. It is fortunate that the corresponding sections of the last two Quartets found Eliot on form again (though I shall argue that the fourth movement of 'Little Gidding' really *is* open-ended, in a way seldom allowed). Perhaps Eliot later recognised that he had here violated the spirit of the *Quartets*, and was on guard against repeating the mistake.

V

The opening of the last movement touches, once more, a very personal note, lifting it at once, however, towards the universal. The echo of Dante ('the middle way') was a trifle optimistic if one takes it literally. Eliot was not the scriptural thirty-five years old of the *Divine Comedy*, but a man over fifty, well past two-thirds of the way. Maybe 'the middle way' refers not only to the whole period between youth and old age, when spiritual renewal is continually necessary, but to the fact that he had not arrived at 'faith' as completely as the fourth movement declares. 'Twenty years largely wasted' is curiously depressing: an assessment of his own early verse (life?) that few would share, but which obviously disturbed him; and an assessment of those uneasy years between the end of the First World War (the war to end wars) and the very generally foreseen start of the next.

I imagine that readers of my own generation (born 1928; at school in London during the 1939–45 period) find the mood of the 1930s especially hard to assess. For us, it was childhood, largely the time of freedom; the period beautifully described by Jung in *Modern Man in Search of a Soul* as 'governed by impulse', when 'few or no problems are met with. Even when external limitations oppose the subjective impulses, these restraints do not put the individual at variance with himself. He submits to them or circumvents them, remaining quite one with himself. He does not yet know the state of inner tension which a problem brings about' (p. 114). I can recall war and rumours of war from the 1930s as a meaningless story. The 'eruption of sexual life', the 'psychic revolution' which Jung says is 'sometimes called "The unbearable age" ', had yet to happen to me. Before that, there was a world as far from the one I now read of in Auden and Eliot, in Yeats, as could very well be.

Obviously, for those born after 1945 the problem is different again. How can anyone who has lived only in our atomic world, with destruction as a perpetual possibility and human 'reason' no abstraction but a life-or-death gamble even imagine the myth of stability on which so much that passed for 'civilisation' has been built? To have lived always in a world that might be destroyed by man himself at a moment's notice must be to disbelieve in the future in a wholly new way. In 1945 I was myself seventeen, and had formed opinions; if there is a 'generation gap', the coming of the bomb seems to me to pinpoint its date. In 'Lapis Lazuli', Yeats talks of impending apocalypse – but he could not have believed that man might really destroy the whole earth, as we believe now.

As for the poets of the 1930s – 'exploding like bombs' (Auden, 'Spain'), personally menaced – how is one to think back to their crisis, so strangely far off? Our very closeness to apocalypse keeps uneasy peace – it has for thirty-three years now – and we still hope that reason will prevail over unreason, self-preservation over idealism or madness, on however slender a base. In the 1930s, it was not universal destruction that threatened in quite this manner, but particular evils, already hard to sort out. There was the certainty of war; the danger of a total change (collapse or renewal) for a failing social order; social injustice, not least in England, that could not be allowed to continue; the possibility (for poets younger than Eliot, especially poignant) of foreshortened life, unfulfilled love, to be followed by violence and death in lands where the 'Mind of Europe' had once slowly matured, and produced so much beauty, and lulled so many fears. There were also other aspects of 'the Mind of Europe' which Eliot, by and large, would not look at, but which aroused in some the desire to eradicate and destroy.

Yeats, knowing that his own death was approaching along with the holocaust, held despair at bay by the very power of his art. As Yeats died, Eliot was at work on this second Quartet. 'Little Gidding' was to be finished the year before the atom bomb came into history. Perhaps because the bomb was, however, peripheral to its particular hope (or its particular ambivalence) nothing affecting the final Quartet was changed in 1945 – and no more was written (no more major verse, which is all that concerns us here).

In 'East Coker' we are confronted with the poem where time looms largest; the theme is age, decay – the realm where personal and social cohere, if they do at all.

In these lines, Eliot records the sense of failure – necessary failure – to master words perfectly; the phrase

> And so each venture
> Is a new beginning, a raid on the inarticulate
> With shabby equipment always deteriorating
> In the general mess of imprecision of feeling,
> Undisciplined squads of emotion

links a personal 'failure' with a theory of cultural decline. This, at least, is my assumption: the lines could be read as confessional in a more personal sense. But I suspect that Eliot is indicting his age, as well as his personal weaknesses and the depredations of personal aging. Perhaps fortunately, he does not do so in a manner inviting general commentary, or depending upon a shared cultural pessimism for the fullest effect. Enough that he is recording personal experience; and that the battle, at least, is known to all who try to use words. But, still more reassuringly, he now moves backwards as well as forwards – indicating (as he does also in *The Waste Land*) that the past is as tainted and difficult as the present, for those who desire to rise above time.

> And what there is to conquer
> By strength and submission, has already been discovered
> Once or twice, or several times, by men whom one cannot hope
> To emulate – but there is no competition –
> There is only the fight to recover what has been lost
> And found and lost again and again: and now, under conditions
> That seem unpropitious.

Like Yeats, in fact – though less triumphantly – Eliot is recognising the unique authority of great men: not 'heroes' in the Nietzschean or Wagnerian sense, but an elite all the same, in which creators, lovers, warriors have their place, as they do in Yeats. Though his most ardent admirers would not claim for Eliot very great fame as a love poet, there is no doubt that Dante's Beatrice makes a feature in Eliot's 'Dante', and in the final 'rose'.

But in essence Eliot would seem to value most highly saints, martyrs, artists, fighters for causes (perhaps in that order). It seems profoundly important that the Roundheads are eventually admitted to glory, along with the 'broken king' on whose side Eliot himself would surely have fought. Yet this very perception arouses new basic questions: surely it *must* matter what your ideals are, as well as that you are willing to live or die for them? This issue I defer until considering the third movement of 'Little Gidding', where it more completely belongs.

In Eliot's own reading of 'East Coker', certain cadences of weariness seem to carry over from the opening lines into those which I have reproduced above. This always strikes me as sad, if understandable; I think a clear transition from weariness to vigour would do more justice to the inner resonance at this point.

For this is, in more than one way, a bridge in the poem – and a bridge demanding homage, celebration, joy, a release from strain: 'there is no competition'. These figures whom 'one cannot hope to emulate' are not to be a burden, a reproach, an occasion of bitterness and breakdown; they are rather to be encouragements on the path we all tread. Perhaps there is no greater choice a man makes than his attitudes to the heroes: does he envy them, hate them even and seek to deny them; or does he salute them as possible ideals, the very glory of life? Our own inferiority may yet turn out to be the long-sought gateway to wisdom; but only so long as we are willing to celebrate and to fight with the heroes, rather than resent and despair.

This glances back, for a last time, to an earlier theme, but now more positively: the wrong path taken by the 'elders', and the search for a way to do better ourselves. Do we seek and, so far as possible, accept accurate self-knowledge, whatever the pain of it; or do we settle for some pretended arrival, and wisdom, attuned to deceive others, and still more ourselves?

Eliot had learned the lesson himself by a costly route, as his approach to 'Little Gidding' by way of *The Waste Land* makes clear. Reading his early prose, I suspect that he had often to wrestle with feelings of superiority verging on snobbery, at least when he pondered the masses – balanced by corresponding depression when he gazed upwards instead to Goethe, Dante and others of the handful of men like gods. But by now he had arrived (in his poetry, at least) at the immensely more hopeful (and Christian?) insight, that just as the true gods do not wish to judge *us*, so even the humblest may find hope, not condemnation, in *them*.

Whether we shall ever be as celebrated as Cromwell, as talented as Dante, as holy as Nicholas Ferrar, is unlikely; but, far more to the point, it is seen now to be unimportant, as long as we continue to fight. It cannot be accidental that the words 'but there is no competition' are not left floating, but later receive substance from the frailty, as well as the triumph, of the models themselves. Nicholas Ferrar has his place in *Four Quartets* not as the initiator of an historical triumph, but as the initiator of an historical experiment that appeared to have failed. Charles I is not the divinely appointed monarch at the height of his glory, but the 'broken king at nightfall' seeking refuge, just before the end. Even Milton is not the polemical thunderer of *Tenure of Kings and of Magistrates* (1649) or the epic master of *Paradise Lost* (1666), but 'one who died blind and quiet'. The 'familiar compound ghost' in the second movement of 'Little Gidding' captures many masters, transforming their wisdom from earthly fame to universal purgation, in one final waste land. Fame is not the spur, Eliot is surely saying: the spur should be that quest for wholeness where all have their part, all fail, all have the one hope. 'For us, there is only the trying' should, to my mind, ring out in the reading, as a moment of triumph – not unalloyed triumph indeed, but triumph still, though heard through pain. 'The rest is not our business' will depress only those whose faith is still in themselves – who have never sung, with Mary, that very different message, 'He has put down the mighty from their seats, and has exalted the humble and meek' (Luke 1:52; Prayer Book version).

So the poem is freed to move to its lovely conclusion, a transition both in mood and tone to 'The Dry Salvages' in the closing cadences, yet also rising first to a climax, where the weariness, so frankly faced, seems truly resolved. 'Home is where we start from' is one of those phrases in Eliot which seem hand-made for parody, yet which links with the near approach now of the poem's chief mutation ('In my beginning is my end'; 'In my end is my beginning'), and also with the more complex echo, half depending upon it, in 'Little Gidding', 'The end is where we start from.' The next sentence in 'East Coker', 'As we grow older ...', used to strike me again as fairly simple – an assertion that, in any vital life, what accumulates is not static 'wisdom' but shifting experience – but I see it too, now, in a more literal sense. People die, receding into history and into memory, and 'the pattern' 'of dead and living' does in fact become more complicated, in the minds of those who knew them, as well as in public record and myth. In place of the false 'wisdom' of the 'quiet voiced elders', we have something both more modest and more plausible – a reminder that each phase of life brings its own experiences, which are known only when they are reached (or maybe only when they have been reached, and then lost again); and that whatever we learn may be too late for pragmatic use, or for personal pride. In turn, this opens out from the individual to the general, surrounding our brief flicker of consciousness with those darker reminders into which we 'peer', or from which we too turn our eyes:

> Not the intense moment
> Isolated, with no before and after,
> But a lifetime burning in every moment
> And not the lifetime of one man only
> But of old stones that cannot be deciphered.

Here, Eliot is treading the same path as Jung in his great work on archetypes, linking archaeological mystery with rhythms of consciousness inaccessible to logical theory and structuring. Fittingly, the numinous echoes return for three lines; and the introduction of 'Love' –

> Love is most nearly itself
> When here and now cease to matter'

– seems far more acceptable than the appearance of the word, in the same general position, towards the end of 'Burnt Norton' – even though there is maybe *still* a lack of the full warmth one could ideally wish for. There is no evading the fact that Eliot's voyage remains a lonely one, and that the communion of saints looms less large in *Four Quartets*, as he approaches release, than the communion of the damned had done in earlier days.

The conclusion brings the explicit themes of old age, of roots, of

Eliot's own end and beginning, into harmony with the larger theme
of time as an unfolding process in the course of any one life, and of
the life of the earth. 'Burnt Norton' has concerned one kind of
moment that evades time – the moment in the rose-garden – and
explored the mystery of consciousness in its aspects when time ceases
to be. 'Little Gidding' will revolve around another such moment
prefigured in 'Burnt Norton', in 'the draughty church at smokefall',
when a man falls to his knees to pray (the previously missing
dimension) and comes to one of those many places – but the healing
one – where the world ends.

Between these two Quartets, Eliot offers us 'East Coker', which is
about beginnings, middles and ends, and the search for wisdom *in*
time; and 'The Dry Salvages', which deals with another type of
constant – a grim one – in time itself.

Fittingly, 'East Coker' anticipates the change of tone towards the
minor key of the third Quartet – its exquisite slow movement – but
only after spelling out the hard-won hope for those of us still battling
through time:

> Old men ought to be explorers
> Here and there does not matter
> We must be still and still moving
> Into another intensity
> For a further union, a deeper communion
> Through the dark cold and the empty desolation,
> The wave cry, the wind cry, the vast waters
> Of the petrel and the porpoise. In my end is my beginning.

'The Dry Salvages': Such Permanence as Time Has

I

'I do not know much about gods': Eliot's lifelong religious quest
points a wry irony at the start. 'The Dry Salvages' is to range through
many religions, open to most and condemning only shallow modern
imitations, as the poet declares them to be. From the pagan
suggestion which immediately follows, 'but I think that the river / Is
a strong brown god', we move through various Christian references,
deliberately fragmented and scattered; through a section mainly
indebted to Hindu sources; and, before concluding, encounter
miscellaneous modern 'gods' (where genuine science is oddly
mingled with the charlatan). In this Quartet, no approach is made to
Christian commitment. Even the strong *'Figlia del tuo figlio'* from
Dante scarcely reclaims the Virgin from superstitious and pagan

colourings. Part IV, as in all the Quartets after the first, is close to Christianity, but retains the mood of a prevailing melancholy. The Virgin is poised between 'annunciation' in part II, and 'Incarnation' – announced near the poem's end; but doctrinal tentativeness is caught up in thematic flux. This is a poem of 'hints and guesses / Hints followed by guesses', leading finally only from sea to 'significant soil'.

The whole Quartet resounds to the sea's rhythms. If we think of the entire work as music, this is surely the slow movement, in a minor key. Its peculiar beauty mimes the changing moods of great waters, neither unduly stressing symbolism nor ever wholly deserting it. In part I, there is a curious mingling of childhood associations, reaching far back and deep inwards, with all the technical sophistication we have learned to expect. 'The river is within us, the sea is all about us' includes particular memories of the north-east coast of Cape Ann, Massachusetts, as well as Eliot's near-engulfing personal floods of 1922. This music of the sea, anxious, restless and unceasing, beautifully matches the poem's main theme. This, I take to be defined in the phrase used for my title – 'such permanence as time has' – and the clustered images which further define this: for example,

> Time the destroyer is time the preserver,
> Like the river with its cargo of dead negros, cows and chicken coops,
> The bitter apple and the bite in the apple

The untamed elements seem as impervious to man's prayers, and as restless reminders of his mortality, as the Madonna herself. Serenely, she gazes over the waves which wash about her, absorbing the prayers which rise day and night from 'anxious worried women', beseeching the safety of those who will never return, whose end will never be known. Throughout 'The Dry Salvages' we seem far closer to death by water than to notions of baptismal regeneration. The 'trial and judgment of the sea' is endemic in Eliot, as strong in early poems and in *The Waste Land* as it is in all the Quartets. Even in 'Little Gidding', the 'sea's jaws' will be among those many places that are 'the world's end' – though there the finality is less and the hope greater, as the closing assertion of 'East Coker', 'In my end is my beginning', meets at last with some semblance, however ambiguous, of Christian faith.

Despite the beauty which we find in all the Quartets, and the particular sonorities of 'Little Gidding', 'The Dry Salvages' is, in my view, the most consistently beautiful. Even the 'prosaic' passages, coming where we have learned to expect them, have (with one exception) very haunting resonances. The recurring yet ever-deepening music of death has much to do with this – along, if I judge correctly, with another judgement that I have formed over the years. 'Burnt Norton' and 'Little Gidding' both evoke numinous moments more powerfully, but, of all the Quartets, this one has the most continual ring of truth. In many ways, it picks up and resolves themes from the earlier poems, while still leaving open the final resolution to be found in the experience of prayer. While 'Little Gidding' develops its own ambivalences, perhaps where we least expect them, 'The Dry Salvages' alone, on its own terms, is nearly all of a piece. The one flaw – a serious one – is in part v, but I reserve my comments on that to the appropriate place.

I hope that this introduction will exonerate me from directly confronting Donald Davie's essay on 'The Dry Salvages', which has attained a certain fame. Starting from the notion that 'The Dry Salvages' stands out from the other Quartets as a comparative failure, Davie proceeds to cope with the 'problem' arising from this. Other critics have followed him, embroidering the 'problem' – which for me, very clearly, does not exist. I can only assume that they fail to hear the music that I hear, and read a different poem; no dialogue is possible or needed when such a gulf yawns. We all have critical blind spots somewhere or another, and either Davie or myself is having one here.

II

Like that of 'East Coker', the opening of 'The Dry Salvages' requires little comment. It has a similar theme: the dehumanising effect of urbanisation on human perception. When the river is exploited and bridged, men fail to notice it, becoming detached from creation: note 'almost forgotten', followed by 'choose to forget'. The refusal to honour might be seen as an escape from paganism; here it is presented as imprisonment, in a darkness far worse. The 'worshippers of the machine' forget the Creator, along with his original creation: 'Unhonoured, unpropitiated' is a disease of the modern world.

In balance, the poetry asserts that the river bides its time, unchanged, if neglected; 'His rhythm' reaches backwards to childhood, forward to 'rages' in store. Note the use of 'His', underlying godhead: the river divinity will not be denied. Throughout, the river is presented as conscious, and powerful: 'Keeping his seasons and rages, destroyer'. By a fine sleight of hand, there is also enchantment, since 'nursery' memories hold a still earlier charm. No doubt the river's menace 'waited, watched' for the child, also unnoticed: yet the child responded, with pleasure, to its rhythms, as city-dwellers do not.

Lines 10–14 function a little like ll. 9–13 in 'East Coker'; their incantation calls back to primitive powers. Here, it is childhood nostalgia, clinched in 'the evening circle in the winter gaslight' (I wonder if 'gaslight' has the same power, for those who never experienced it, as for those who did?). The effect is of a 'Proustian' moment, or epiphany: memory vividly stirred, mainly through association. Childhood and pagan responses to the river elide.

As the opening continues, 'The river is within us, the sea is all about us', we might fear that there is to be a descent into allegory (with part IV of 'East Coker' in mind). Instead, there follows a passage of exceptional beauty, where 'hints of earlier and other creation' (hints earlier, and later, associated with terror) are softened by innocence carried over from childhood. Or maybe one should speak of this effect as transitional, since a picture of a child browsing on the sea's edge (created, I think, by subterranean connections in the mind spanning 'nursery', 'earlier and other', 'our curiosity') fades back into more adult awareness. Perhaps scientific discoveries are transformed into an artist's imagination, and then into trains of personal memory; 'our losses' strikes me as bringing personal losses (childhood and earlier life) back into focus with more general losses of the human race (specifically, pagan reverence). By implication, evolutionary doctrines of progress are rejected (as they will be explicitly, later), while the poetry opens out, again, to encompass personal and adult moments of dereliction (the 'anxious worried women', in their inner time, the waste regions of tension or pain).

Any attempt to analyse the verbal music would be both protracted and tedious; better to let the words 'echo, thus, in your mind'. The sea's softer music merges with the long procession of relics moving from an unknown past into a measureless future, offering fruit more for brooding than certainty, yet vividly realised. The phrase 'offers to our curiosity' combines, with the half-ironic memory of childish wonder, intimations of a divine, or at least untraceable, teasing. Though some hint of 'O brave new world' survives, the images are all of mystery, when forms of sea life are listed; and of breakage, when the human enters ('torn', 'shattered', 'broken', 'foreign dead'). Note that the more obvious rhymes, so alluring to the reading voice ('reaches ... beaches', 'tosses ... losses', and so on) are counterpointed by soft assonances ('algae', 'anemone'), and lead up, through a reassertion of pagan mystery ('The sea has many voices, / Many gods and many voices') to one of Eliot's many numinous phrases: 'The salt is on the briar rose, / The fog is in the fir trees.' Meanwhile, certain more menacing echoes (the play of 'foreign' against 'torn seine', for instance) lead the way into one of the finest examples of onomatopoeia (if such a label does not trivialise) known to me. Between 'The sea howl' and 'heaving groaner', the reading voice enacts at least seven distinct, yet merging sea voices, all instantly recognisable, all menacing, all still touched both by childhood nostalgia and by adult awareness. In this elemental play of forces there can be enchantment (for the man walking and musing, responding to otherness), yet reminders too of strangeness, menace and transience – nature's inescapable symbolism, its own pre-human art, 'riding the echo'. The pattern here draws towards fear. 'The tolling bell' links with 'oppression', 'silent' (now a dangerous word), then 'time not our time'; this Quartet's major theme becomes more ominously pre-human, prehistoric, as 'unhurried / Ground swell' sets off the godlike indifference of centuries against answering, but fearful, immensities within human minds. 'Trying to unweave, unwind, unravel' is purely human, as is the insight (or fancy) of impending disaster:

> Between midnight and dawn, when the past is all deception,
> The future futureless, before the morning watch
> When time stops and time is never ending. . . .

The brief echo from Psalm 130 reminds, obliquely, of those prayers 'out of the deep' which, still more universal, reassert the 'Ground swell' of life itself. Here we are experiencing one more of the Quartet's 'timeless moments': not vision now (as in 'Burnt Norton', nor roots that will also be graves (as is 'East Coker'); but, more simply, human life confronting what cannot be altered, cannot be tamed. *Still*, there is no redemption, no purgation, no escape into meaning; it is merely that our defences – personal, cultural or merely technical and commercial – yield to the music of time. This is not unlike the 'Descend lower . . .' passage from part III of 'Burnt Norton' – but far more compelling and powerful. Why? Possibly because we can no longer associate the descent with city violations or even with personal breakdown; the sea's impersonal message is the bell that tolls for us all.

III

Eliot now proceeds to one of the triumphs of his art, the first section of the second movement. Here he sweeps away the technique of the first two Quartets – a deliberately 'poetic' passage, which is then to be dismissed and approached more soberly – and instead writes a lyric as sustained as any in his work. Instead of offering a contrast with the mood brilliantly created in part i, he continues it: the effect is of an adagio, moving still deeper into the music, and implication, of the sea.

Technically, this is the masterly handling of what could have been disaster: a rhymed pattern requiring the utmost skill. There are six stanzas, each of six lines, where the rhymes are spaced out so that the last word in each line is a full, or near, rhyme with its counterpart in each other stanza. Only 'annunciation', in the last lines, appears three times (stanzas i, iii and vi), mutating from 'calamitous', through 'last', to 'one', where, finally, it acquires a capital 'A'. Even so, it is still held in check by the qualifying phrase 'the hardly, barely prayable / Prayer', so that the phrase immediately before, 'Death its God', carries far more weight.

The experience of reading this is remarkable, since rhymes which on the page look, at best, mere ingenuity mingle perfectly with the gentler but still destructive sea swell (for instance, 'wailing', 'withering', 'drifting' repeated as a litany, played off against the prevailing theme of an unsteered voyage, in an unseaworthy boat, between nowhere and nowhere). It will also be noticed that, while most of the rhymes contribute to dereliction and melancholy, there are more positive if unstressed signals from internal rhyme. Thus, while the sequence 'motionless', 'emotionless', 'devotionless', 'oceanless', 'erosionless' and – again – 'motionless' is all negation and stasis, we encounter 'emotion', 'devotion', 'ocean' *within* the lines.

If Eliot had allowed himself to drift towards allegory, the effect would again have been greatly harmed. This might even have seemed simply a more serious version of Edward Lear's 'The Jumblies' (an avowedly comic poem, which reaches its own seriousness, however, through that apparently opposite route). Instead, we are carried along by incantation arising from the end of the Quartet's first section, and weaving a spell that is deepened, not broken, in the second. No doubt the imagery of perpetual autumn, perpetual drifting, perpetual wreckage is not the whole of life: yet the images are not, in themselves, to be denied. Sea, mortality, bewilderment are human constants, not subject to 'answer', since they are experience itself.

The general effect is also slightly hypnotic, as if to keep analysis, for a time, at bay. Yet it must be said that, though on its own terms the symbolism is faultless, not all men will assent to the assertions that are smuggled in. Look, for instance, at the end of the second stanza. Is it puritan, stoic, bitter? Do we endorse it ourselves?

Years of living among the breakage
Of what was believed in as the most reliable –
And therefore as the fittest for renunciation.

Likewise, the image of human life as 'a drifting boat with a slow leakage', while undeniably effective, entirely negates the alternative possibility of growth in wisdom, or even in eternal life, as a countervailing aspect of human experience. Rather, it picks up the pessimism concerning old age yet again – 'the failing / Pride or resentment at failing powers' preparing the way for that curious trick in stanza iv, where the apparent development of an imagery not to be logically controverted turns also into an (equally apparent?) assertion of unanswerable cosmic pessimism:

> We cannot think of a time that is oceanless
> Or of an ocean not littered with wastage
> Or of a future that is not liable
> Like the past, to have no destination.

The last stanza, with its doubly repeated 'no end', moves, through a strange paradox ('To the movement of pain that is painless and motionless'), and 'the drift of the sea and the drifting wreckage', to an ending that can be said to contain hope only from the greatest possible way off. There are the seeds here also of part III, which moves to the East for its images – though immediately, part II now plunges into its second half which, more obviously than the opening, links with the general pattern of the *Four Quartets*. Even so, the deliberately prosaic quality evident in the corresponding sections in the earlier two poems is far less in evidence, except in the first five lines and other occasional touches: indeed, the mood of intense if sombre lyricism which has been established prevails, almost unabated, until the abrupt change at the start of part v.

The opening statement, as I have already indicated, is one which has seemed true to me in different ways, at different moments of life. Undeniably, it harks back to part v of 'East Coker': 'As we grow older / The world becomes stranger, the pattern more complicated / Of dead and living' – just as it possibly hints at a moment of seminal insight still hidden, and awaiting 'Little Gidding' for articulation: 'A people without history / Is not redeemed from time, for history is a pattern / Of timeless moments.' Here, the poem is concerned to counter the idea of history as 'pattern' and 'mere sequence / Or even development' (that 'Or even' seems to me to have a splendidly wide-eyed innocence), by attacking – not evolution itself, of course, for Eliot is not a crank; but a 'partial fallacy': superficial notions of evolution, 'Which becomes, in the popular mind, a means of disowning the past'. No doubt Eliot has in mind the over-easy optimism of some late-nineteenth-century evolutionary optimism (including the type that Yeats confessed to in 'Nineteen Hundred and Nineteen'); but 'the popular mind' (a touch of elitism that has crept in from the prose?) hints at more widespread Micawberism, while 'a means of disowning the past' ensures that the indictment is both bitter and strong.

Its challenge must have come home to Eliot with very special violence – if not for 'populist' reasons, or indeed for superficial ones, at least for the reason that has haunted his exploration from the opening words of 'Burnt Norton' and is still very far from resolved. If 'All time is unredeemable', why brood on time? If 'What might have been and what have been / Point to one end, which is always present', why brood on guilt or expect forgiveness? If all 'pattern' shifts, and deceives, why labour to pattern? How is this, or any poem, to bypass such insights; how can art be even justified, let alone resolved?

Very possibly, this is a pivotal moment in the *Quartets* – a pause on the path not followed here. From the 'popular mind' hoping to the saint praying requires a transition dimly prepared for but not yet attained. So here, the poem chooses for a moment a more obvious direction, though one which will produce complexities enough of its own. 'The moments of happiness' (not very normal Eliot territory): what do we make of these? In the first place, a strong contrast between 'the sense of well-being' which occasionally breaks through, for natural reasons, and the 'sudden illumination': numinous moments, where the key long sought will be found. But notice the extraordinary syntax: one prolonged parenthesis, separating the subject from its more profound sequel, in a manner perhaps deliberately designed to tease. Are we in the presence of an obscure (or of a deliberately elitist) irony – or do we have a sudden, unexpected glimpse of Eliot off guard? I insist on 'Eliot', rather than 'the poet' or 'the persona', at this juncture, since the note struck is personal to an unusual degree. Look again at the things which get written-off under the general umbrella of 'sense of well-being': are they not a very odd lot? 'Fruition': the word belongs to natural processes, nurtured and perfected; is this such a small thing to hope for, after all? 'Fulfilment': well, the word has been battered and debased, with other words, amidst our modern complexities; but does it not span whatever high, as well as shallow, ideals a man may conceive? 'Security': at a very heroic level, this may seem trivial; but what is the *summum bonum* if not security – lifted, again, to its highest plane? That we live with pain, doubt and tension is the warp and woof of this poem; is it so shallow to seek even a humble point of rest? A 'very good dinner': if this includes friendship, it is worth far more than an 'even'; worth far more indeed, than the throwaway anticlimax of a casual aside. No wonder, then, that 'affection' also slips into the list, with equal casualness – one more 'sense of well-being' cancelled, and diminished, by 'not'. At this point, the present reader at least is affronted – either as the poet intends, or by an accident the poet fails even to see. 'Affection' may be lower than love (on some absolute scale), but neither of these blessings has loomed large, as yet, in Eliot's world. Is it not worth recalling that God gives all good things (if there is a God: and that is certainly in question); and, again, that for Christians, and others, affection, love, is his highest gift – indeed, his nature itself? 'Little children, love one another', says St John (1 John 4:7–8), 'for love is of God, Every man who loves is God's son and has some knowledge of him. But the man who does not love cannot know him at all; for God is love.'

I have laboured this point partly because of its intrinsic importance, and partly because of the context in which it occurs. When we reach Lady Julian, the Descent of the Dove, 'the drawing of this Love and the voice of this Calling' in 'Little Gidding', are we to assume that human experience has been assumed into love, or that we still depend on 'moments of illumination' utterly different (and higher?) in kind? With this large question in mind (and what we make of *Four Quartets* can scarcely bypass it), the immediate context can be examined again. The 'moments of happiness' are snatched away as suddenly as they are presented – admittedly, in one of those marvellous lines that no reader will ever forget:

> We had the experience but missed the meaning,
> And approach to the meaning restores the experience
> In a different form, beyond any meaning
> We can assign to happiness.

I have already said that the first of these lines seems to me sufficiently floating to escape its context, applying itself to events of the most varying kind. That 'happiness' is known as happiness only when it is gone may be a cliché (true often, though surely not always), but the line probes deeper than this. One encounters people who claim never to have loved, never to have experienced wonder, never to have *known* 'happiness' – all such 'nevers' could be encompassed by Eliot's extraordinary line. 'We had the experience but missed the meaning': the story of all our lives, looked at one way; the failure of all our striving, if you give it a twist. It is a rare line – true in so many ways, true so harrowingly often, that it seems to transcend 'meaning' in any simple sense.

Yet 'meaning' is precisely what it continues to gnaw at: the word is twice repeated in the lines following, while 'happiness' is the quality conjured away. Here, further references backwards and forwards may be essential, if this is to have its integrated effect in the poem as whole. We look back to part II of 'East Coker', with its lacerating insight

> And every moment is a new and shocking
> Valuation of all we have been. We are only undeceived
> Of that which, deceiving, could no longer harm

and we look forward to the scarcely less bleak description of the 'gifts reserved for age' in part II of 'Little Gidding'.

Here I return to the ambiguity of syntax. If we can assume that the 'sense of well-being' and its attendant parenthesis has been removed, for better or worse, from the equation, then this passage we are now considering applies only to 'the sudden illumination' itself. If so, then we must assume, I think, that the numinous moments are particularly in question when they are shown as 'happiness' neither fully grasped at the time nor fully recovered, later, in their original terms. It seems that the ultimate quest can never *rest* in happiness, though it may briefly pass through it: whatever is finally in store for us – oblivion or abundance – will be 'happiness' in a more absolute sense than anything experienced on earth.

The poem now passes back to an evolutionary framework and to the time-scale of the sea's rhythms – the immensities both within and without. It appears that 'the past experience revived in the meaning' must not be given purely personal connotations, but must be related to 'the ineffable', 'the primitive terror', the things not ourselves. For a moment, 'many generations' briefly meet in a kind of collective unconscious – an experience linking men, alone though we know them to be.

At this point we move from 'moments of happiness' to 'moments of agony' with almost dreamlike transition, as much that has been said of the one proves true of the other in this spiritual realm. If I am right, the marvellous lines following are the explicit heart of the poem – though, of course, the poem is 'explicit' in images, suggestions, evocations, not in mere abstractions or thoughts:

> Now, we come to discover that the moments of agony
> (Whether, or not, due to misunderstanding,
> Having hoped for the wrong things or dreaded the wrong things,
> Is not in question) are likewise permanent
> With such permanence as time has.

The 'likewise' fuses happiness and agony with the poem's special magic: those rhythms of the sea which, in theme and variation, carry this through to its end.

Eliot is still not ready for his fuller revelation; but much that is timeless can now be caught up once again. The moments of vision and the moments of anguish together: not purged yet; but 'permanent', whether time or not-time is their home. I mentioned my own sense of the deep truth of this when writing of 'Burnt Norton' – notably 'the agony of others, nearly experienced', culminating in that perfect line 'People change, and smile: but the agony abides.' For one moment Eliot allows himself a reference to Eve and Adam, and the lost Paradise, but he is not ready yet to leap beyond this. Instead, the sea rhythm returns – 'halcyon day' briefly deluding: then, 'in the sombre season / Or the sudden fury, is what it always was'.

IV

To an unusual degree, the movements of this Quartet merge into each other, as if theme and music are supremely at one. The opening image of the third movement has a weird perfection that both clarifies and depends upon the second. In a cyclical world, future and past produce the same experiences. Who but Eliot could have hit on phrases so inherently mysterious (and lovely) as 'faded song', 'wistful regret', 'Pressed between yellow leaves of a book that has never been opened', and applied these to 'the future' with such elegant ease? Almost breathtakingly, he leaves this passage standing, as if in casual homage to Krishna, and plunges to a brisk restatement of one of the two original mottos of 'Burnt Norton' (from Heraclitus). In turn, this leads into an apparent direct challenge to us, the readers: 'You cannot face it steadily, but this thing is sure, / That time is no healer'. From this point onwards, the entire passage is characterised by a calculated paradox, brought very directly home. The recurring 'You' is apparently a direct address to us the readers, which culminates in the inclusive vocative towards the close 'O voyagers, O seamen . . .', and in the final imperative, 'Not fare well, / But fare forward, voyagers', where an element of irony is inescapable, though its direction is obscure. In balance, the very idea of identity dissolves in the major images, leaving us stranded almost as no one, existing nowhere. In place of the 'still point' of 'Burnt Norton' – intensely vivid, if isolated – there is something closer to the vacuum envisaged in the *via negativa*, but now secular and trivialised.

'. . . the patient is no longer here.' The choice of 'patient' as image reverts deliberately to part IV of 'East Coker', a notion strengthened by the later emphasis on 'the time of death'. But the major, and simpler, images are now of voyaging – though the poet continues to impale us on unbearable spikes. In 'Burnt Norton', time was also no healer; and there we were again taunted, by the bird: 'human kind / Cannot bear very much reality'. 'East Coker' and 'The Dry Salvages' have also encompassed inescapable anguish,

inescapable mortality, the one emphasising all that life takes
(including rustic moments of happiness), the other, all that life spares
('The bitter apple, and the bite in the apple'). And still there has been
no purgation, no escape. 'You cannot face it steadily': this bleak
assertion receives further force from 'but this thing is sure' –
anything 'sure' is sufficiently rare in Eliot.

The images immediately following may however, remind us of
F. H. Bradley (or, still more, of Hume) and of a solipsism where the
very concept of 'You', of a self or identity, becomes shadowy – even
as a focus of pain. The two brilliant images of the rails narrowing
behind the train, and the furrow widening behind the ship, merge
together the dubious realities of a past that disappears, leaving no
trace, and a present that will 'fare forward' towards a future likewise
inaccessible and withdrawn. To 'fare well' requires no doubt, more
substance than this world offers, where we 'shall not think' without
thinking illusion:

> You are not the same people who left that station
> Or who will arrive at any terminus. . . .

The curious paradox appears to be that, if our existence is an
illusion, so too is our temporary illusion of escape from it. In an
obvious sense, we do exist in St Augustine's isolated present, as
'Burnt Norton' established: a corollary is that there is no continuity,
no 'self' securely to relate the reader of this page to the reader of the
pages before.

How then account for the pain, the strong sense of reality; how
account for the pattern in the poem, the response to art, artist, self,
life, or anything at all? The whole passage revolves, it seems, round
optical illusions, played off against earlier intimations, almost
equally dismaying:

> We cannot think of a time that is oceanless
> Or of an ocean not littered with wastage
> Or of a future that is not liable
> Like the past, to have no destination.

With this in mind, the lines

> You shall not think 'the past is finished'
> Or 'the future is before us'

would seem to offer a perspective where 'fare forward' is at least as
useless an exhortation as 'fare well'; and it is here that the main
difficulty exists. At the end of part III, we begin to move towards the

transition to 'Little Gidding' (if still from a very long way off); but
how, precisely, is the gap between two concepts spanned?

> Here between the hither and the farther shore
> While time is withdrawn, consider the future
> And the past with an equal mind.
> At the moment which is not of action or inaction
> You can receive this. . . .

In these lines we encounter what on the surface are flat
contradictions, even literal nonsense. If 'time is withdrawn', then
how are 'future' and 'past' to be considered with 'an equal mind' or
with any mind at all? Again, if 'action' and 'inaction' are alike
banished, how (or where) is a consciousness to 'receive' any concepts
at all?

I am aware of being on difficult territory. Parallel statements could
be found (or statements apparently as problematic) among Eastern
and Western mystics; and, as I hope this commentary has made
clear, the attempt to push language beyond its roots, towards
meanings only subject to hints – meanings literally beyond human
intellect – is at the heart of *Four Quartets*. One will take the poem
seriously only if such an attempt is regarded as the legitimate and
ultimately the most challenging task facing human art: an attempt
on the borderline where art and religion meet in their quest, and
where the unknowable is regarded as more real, more valid, than the
'simply' knowable, *if* religion is 'true'. The perennial problem is to
distinguish vision from nonsense, experience from delusion,
profound wisdom from charlatanism; and in a poem the only test to
apply is witnessed success. No doubt the great hold which this poem
has had upon me, and upon many other readers, for an adult
lifetime, is some kind of evidence: perhaps readers accepting it must
accept, also, some residual bafflement as a price to be paid. I shall
have to admit that the few lines now in question, and their sequence
in part v, worry me; but I am prepared to accept that I miss what to
others will present few problems, or no problem at all.

The Cloud of Unknowing may be an accessible text to refer to, since it
describes contemplative prayer and is widely read. The unknown
author speaks of the need to withdraw from all sensuous images, as a
prelude: this can be achieved to some degree, by those not suffering
physical pain, by withdrawing into a totally darkened and silenced
room or environment, where tastes and smells are also banished
(though some purists believe one should float on water, the more
totally to exclude sensations of touch). The author then speaks of
banishing from the *mind* all sensuous images and memories: and this
I have certainly never achieved, or conceived of as possible for

myself. Even so, his summons is not to dreamless sleep, or unconsciousness, but to alert awareness pared down to one exercise of the will. One must say God and mean God, sending persistent arrows into the darkness: from which the reward of such discipline will eventually come (cf. again part III of 'East Coker', notably 'So the darkness shall be the light, and the stillness the dancing').

Conceivably, the phrases of Eliot which I have called 'flat contradictions' take on meaning if this mystical state is achieved. Even so, I should have thought that 'action' rather than 'not of action or inaction' would be the appropriate description; I still find this phrase not consonant with consciousness at all.

Anyway, the poet proceeds to another thought, which was once, and perhaps still is, a commonplace among both Catholic and Protestant Christians, though in differing forms. This is the belief that the moment of physical death has particular importance, related to the final destiny of the soul. Catholics would stress the importance of 'grace', together with a 'good confession' and the last sacrament – though the doctrine of purgatory mercifully allows for progress after death. Certain Protestants would throw their emphasis on 'justification' – which depends upon the willed acceptance of Christ's atoning sacrifice (a conversion experience), and not upon human works, which inevitably earn damnation – and this would suggest that the moment of death is the moment of final judgement also (hence the Protestant hostility to prayer for the dead).

Both views accept the concepts of judgement and of salvation: in *Four Quartets*, 'salvation', whether by purgation or any other method, is still in the scales. Is this, I wonder, why the poet twists the idea back on itself, making it a mere metaphor for the different (but interesting) notion that 'the time of death is every moment', so that we live under judgement constantly, whether in or out of 'time'? It seems to me likely that this notion is much closer to the original teaching of Christ, than are its later Protestant and Catholic variants, since the exhortation to 'take no care of the morrow', to live each moment as if directly in God's presence, is central to 'the kingdom of Heaven', and so to Christ's moral ideas.

'Little Gidding' is the poem where such thoughts can blossom and flourish, since there the long impasse blocking 'salvation' is resolved. And here it is possible that the poem is saying something basically simple, even though its right to this has not yet been earned. What we now do, we are told in effect, can '*fructify*' (my italics) – and this word, as strong and hopeful as it is unexpected, does suggest some escape from stasis, from moral neutrality, into life and growth. The rider 'fructify in the lives of others' is especially encouraging, in view of F. H. Bradley's notion, very influential upon Eliot, that each consciousness is entirely isolated in itself. ('My eternal sensations',

Bradley had written in 1893 in *Appearance and Reality*, 'are no less private to myself than are my thoughts or feelings. In either case my experience falls within my own circle, a circle closed on the outside; and, with all its elements alike, every sphere is opaque to the others which surround it.') There can be little doubt that Eliot's poetry presupposed from the first a denial of this – fascinating though it was to him – since Symbolist poetry not only depends upon, but also demonstrates the transference of 'images', through art, beyond a closed soul ('My words echo thus, in your mind'). Also, the poet does not necessarily take the offer of 'fructify' away again with his further rider 'And do not think of the fruit of action'. This, rather, is another very central teaching of Christ: that he is the vine, we are the branches; and 'fruits' are not to be calculated by intellect, but to be achieved through grace.

So this movement can proceed, through one of its many reminders of voyagers who will die at sea, to talk of a 'real destination': returning to Krishna, but depending for the breakthrough upon the development we have been examining.

Even so, the twist at the end still baffles me: 'Not fare well, / But fare forward, voyagers.' Does not 'fructify' precisely suggest faring 'well'; and is it possible for 'fare forward' and 'fare well' to be anything other than complementary commands? At the risk, once more, of labouring the point slightly, I want to spell out my doubt. The answer to it may be that Eliot is using the words in a limited sense, which one has to be careful to sort out. 'Fare well' is a traditional valediction, warm and human if meant sincerely, and the stuff of blessing. It is also the final blessing given by priests to the dying (the superb musical setting in Elgar's *Dream of Gerontius* comes to mind). Why, then, should we be warned against it? Perhaps Eliot is thinking not of this high usage, but of modern debasements – 'fare well' as the inferior concept of 'getting on', 'making good', earning worldly approval (a 'very good dinner' even, on expense account). This might be in tune with the more trivial images, already established, of relaxed and unaware 'voyaging', but, if Eliot does mean 'fare well' in its blinkered or complacent sense, I feel he should have spelled this out. We have also to recall that 'farewell' can also be the word of final human parting – the sad, or maybe casual, casting off of commitment, which is virtually the opposite of its use as a word of blessing. If the ending means in fact that we are not after all to say 'farewell' in this sense to the past, then it would balance the fact that, with 'fare forward', we can also greet the future with confidence.

As I have said, the ground for this new confidence has not, to my mind, been established, though already the sternness of 'Time is no healer' appears to be slipping away.

V

The lyrical fourth movement shares honours, I think, with that in 'Burnt Norton' for poetic success. It picks up the mood of the fine lyric opening to the second movement, and in its final stanza gives further memorable expression to a recurring theme:

> those who were in ships, and
> Ended their voyage on the sand, in the sea's lips
> Or in the dark throat which will not reject them. . . .

The second section, combining as it does its powerful Catholic tribute to the Virgin with a simple recognition of the ineffectiveness of her prayers to prevent suffering, is oddly effective. The 'Women' for whom she is asked to pray will themselves have prayed, from the anguish captured in the first movement, for their men's safe return. All have prayed vainly; and the Virgin, to whom (through whom?) many such petitions will have been directed, is now asked to pray for their consolation, and for the souls of their dead. The tone returns us to the Quartet's minor key, and to its sombre main theme, as if to remind that the third movement has not yet declared its ground for hope. The one flaw (and it is an unfortunate one) is the use of the prissy and wholly inappropriate word 'lawful' in the fourth line. Through centuries of Catholic piety, Mary has been 'friend of sinners' – traditionally, a saint hand-picked by those least 'lawful' since, however dubious the theology, it has been assumed that her wholly human, and maternal, love would be unable to reject even the most outcast and degraded fellow humans. Here we are dealing not with the Mary of the theologians, but with the Mary who belongs to seamen, their wives and lovers. With the one word 'lawful', Eliot slips into the 'Establishment' mood which makes his religious prose unreadable (by me, certainly), yet which he manages to exclude on the whole, from this wonderfully honest and open exploration in verse.

VI

The opening lines of the final movement are briskly prosaic, and possibly do deserve that stricture which Davie oddly applied to whole *Quartet*. They stand out like a sore thumb both as indifferent verse and as sloppy thinking. In intention, they take us back to the Madame Sosostris passage in *The Waste Land*, which, though surely marred by the poet's failure to take the Tarot pack seriously, none the less has dramatic relevance and point. Eliot clearly believes that the instinct for worship is irresistible, but that, in the absence of a subtle theology or a long and tested tradition, it will apply itself to shoddy and dangerous second-bests. The first fifteen lines are a listing and dismissal of modern 'gods', all thought of as inferior to ancient deities, pagan, Christian and Eastern alike.

As a list it seems deplorable, mingling science, medicine and superstition indiscriminately. The mood of irritation overrides discernment in a manner hard to reconcile with so cultured a source. A complete survey would be superfluous, but there are two points that cry aloud to be made. The first is that the scientific things listed ('to communicate with Mars', 'barbituric acids', and, notably, to 'dissect / The recurrent image' and 'To explore the womb ... or dreams' have good as well as bad uses, and some (notably, the study of archetypal images, of dreams, of the therapeutic use of drugs and hidden memories) are among the greatest contributions to knowledge and happiness, made in our century. Leaving these aside, I fancy that most people would regard the Loch Ness Monster (for instance) more as harmless fun than as a menace to civilisation; and also discriminate more clearly among the remaining items than Eliot does. The observation of 'disease in signatures' may be in the realm of possibility; I know little about it, but it is now a sphere of serious research. Conversing with spirits is a form of religion as ancient as any and, though again I have no personal experience of it, there are many, among those who have, whom I greatly respect (Yeats, for one). This leads directly to the second point, which is that Eliot fails to recognise the possible reality and the possible evil in 'pentagrams' and the like. I shall return to this, briefly, in a moment; but a mention, at least, is needed here. In *The Waste Land*, Eliot treated the Tarot as though it were a form of superior fortune-telling, and allowed himself to invent cards and interpretations to his personal scheme. Had he wished, he could have seen the pack as reconstructed by, for instance, members of Yeats's Golden Dawn Society, and realised that the occult is not precisely an extension of seaside credulity or party games.

The misfortune is that this leads into one of the most important moments in the whole poem – the positive to which these unfortunately chosen negatives lead:

Men's curiosity searches past and future
And clings to that dimension. But to apprehend
The point of intersection of the timeless
With time, is an occupation for the saint –
No occupation either, but something given
And taken, in a lifetime's death in love,
Ardour and selflessness and self-surrender.

This in turn leads into a beautiful recapitulation of many of the numinous moments encompassed in the *Quartets*, linking them at last with the possibility of revelation, and then with a more definite (though still inconclusive) introduction of Incarnation itself.

This part of 'The Dry Salvages' is so important (intrinsically, and as transition to 'Little Gidding') that it deserves a far subtler and finer introduction than it gets. The image of music, linking with passages of great beauty in 'Burnt Norton' and 'Little Gidding', is one of the finest things in the poem: an evocation of the experience of being caught up in ecstasy – now positively – which adds a much-needed artistic dimension to the more mystical out-of-time experiences themselves. The words 'These are only hints and guesses, / Hints followed by guesses' are marvellously precise, and right: the repetition of the main phrase, with 'and' mutating to 'followed by', both suggests revelation and yet checks too easy a leap in that direction. We are reminded of the importance of moments of epiphany among Eliot's peers – Proust, Virginia Woolf, Joyce and others – and of the many interpretations, religious, psychological and physiological, to which these may lend themselves. It is characteristic, if for some chilling, that the poet should now interpose an extremely careful progression of activities depending upon choice, will, intellect, before he allows himself a deliberate, if not dogmatic, statement:

> and the rest
> Is prayer, observance, discipline, thought and action.
> The hint half guessed, the gift half understood, is Incarnation.

Before continuing to probe this slightly and then trace its link with the extremely difficult conclusion of the poem, perhaps I can return, for a moment, to the opening. I have already expressed my reasons for dissatisfaction with it, but one has to wonder why, none the less, it is there. If we look for a link between the disparate activities condemned, could it be divination? Is it that *this* activity, whether religious or scientific or obviously charlatan, was the one Eliot found most distasteful, or misleading, given his particular understanding of time? In fact, 'Little Gidding' is to move towards a resolution in which all moments in history are in some sense timeless, so that divinisation would be impossible, as well as foolish, by any route.

The vision in 'Little Gidding' is compelling and heady, but two dangers ought, at the risk of repetition, to be stressed. The first is that Eliot (of all poets!) might be overlooking evil by too easily putting different forms of divination together, for reasons of his own. On the one occasion when I saw the Tarot used, evil was present, and a brief mention of the incident might be in place. It occurred at a party, and

took place as an apparent aside. The host unexpectedly produced a
Tarot pack, and forced a demonstration of divination on one of his
guests. She was a young woman, clearly troubled about something,
and the demonstration was very much against her expressed will.
However, the host proceeded, despite the violation of hospitality,
foretelling for her unhappiness in love and death within a year. This
incident left a decidedly unpleasant impression, which was not
lessened when the 'prediction' came true. The Tarot user appeared
neither surprised nor distressed at the prediction, nor especially
interested in the sequel, and this again left an impression of acute
unease. Very possibly, the cards fell out as he said they did; when
examining the pack, as a prelude to writing on Yeats, I discovered
that the archetypes are immensely more dangerous, if turned to
divination, than Eliot knew (cf. 'I am not familiar with the exact
constitution of the Tarot pack of cards, from which I have obviously
departed to suit my own convenience' – Notes on *The Waste Land*). I
should imagine that the powerful combination of the Page of Cups
reversed, the Two of Wands and the Tower could produce no
hopeful reading at any time. Such a combination, interpreted by
someone strongly intuitive and with considerable personal
knowledge of his unwilling subject, no doubt guided a 'prophecy'
which was unsoftened by any suggestion of pretence. Possibly the
incident preyed on a disturbed mind, prompting towards suicide,
through psychic fears of a kind easy to guess. The insistence with
which the divination was made, its odd impressiveness, and the lack
of any regret at its apparent fulfilment were all sinister, because
humanly off-key. While forces of evil could not, with any exactness,
be located, I am convinced that this is one of several occasions when I
have experienced evil at work.

  If this is one side of the picture – Eliot's apparent unwillingness to
examine each of his listed phenomena on individual merits – the
other is his complementary unconcern about the possibly good. Most
of us have experienced personal healing or the healing of those
known to us through wholesome psychotherapy, where 'divination'
is merely a probing of the unconscious (and the probable?) with
intention to help. Any ambition to 'change the future' can no more
be ascribed, in this case, to undesirable agencies than can the
exercise of surgery or curative medicine, or humane social reform.
Eliot's lumping together of very disparate phenomena as
'usual / Pastimes and drugs, and features of the press' has possible
seeds of quietism, withdrawal from human engagement, uninterest
in everything unconnected with his own personal quest for the
supernatural – and even an underestimate of religion itself, on its
darker side.

  'Men's curiosity searches past and future / And clings to that dimension': very possibly; but our existence appears to be *in* time, despite the paradoxes, and a total contrast with 'an occupation for the saint' is a little extreme. One cannot fail to note that 'Men's', an inclusive word, is very widely dismissive, leaving saints or would-be saints much on their own. Eliot's own progress towards salvation had been admittedly complex, but I seem to detect a touch of that elitism which *Four Quartets* cannot afford to admit into itself, on pain of extreme self-violation.

Maybe this is why the transition to that key word 'Incarnation' is both more unexpected and less universal in appeal than we might expect. There have been mentions of 'prayer' before in the *Quartets*, but prayer without healing; yet that apparently innocent, if beautiful, line in 'Burnt Norton', 'The moment in the draughty church at smokefall' is to be discovered in 'Little Gidding' as the vital key to our prison house in unredeemed time.

How have we reached 'Incarnation'? If I am right, abruptly, without preparation; for surely 'Incarnation', the Word, is fulfilment of *all* paths, positive and negative, that the poet has trod? I have the strongest feeling that what is now needed is 'Little Gidding', and that the actual conclusion would have been better reduced to its final ten lines (starting with 'And right action . . .'), with the rest omitted. Had Eliot done this, he would have retained the tentativeness of the first three Quartets, and allowed them to be read, as if as a whole, by those who are unable or unwilling to accept the resolution in the fourth. (This is a matter I propose to return to.)

The lines starting 'Here the impossible union' and extending to 'Driven by daemonic, chthonic / Powers' defeat me. If they are merely a statement of incarnational theology, shorn of paradox and assimilated to Aquinas, then they are too bald, too simple altogether, at this point. Presumably, 'that which is only moved / And has in it no source of movement' refers to life untouched by the Unmoved Mover, and ascribes this to inferior powers. The word 'Driven' suggests compulsion (though what is the Logos, if not also a compelling force, a hound of heaven?). 'Daemonic' is not precisely 'demonic' (could Eliot be thinking of Yeats's *A Vision*?); 'chthonic' has two major meanings: the first, 'pertaining to or sprung from the earth, native'; the second, 'of or pertaining to the nether world, underground, subterranean', with special reference to the Greeks. There are also 'chthonic' deities, who were usually deified heroes, credited with protective and retributive powers and appealed to in sickness. If we refer back to the opening of 'The Dry Salvages', then 'daemonic, chthonic / Powers' ought to be at least marginally reputable, as the pagan gods ignored by modern 'worshippers of the machine'. No doubt, for those who follow Eliot into Catholic Christendom, they will have to bow, in turn, to more powerful deities, but for other readers they may be sufficient redemption in themselves.

I have known *Four Quartets* for many years now, appreciating its mysteries; but this is the one passage where I always feel simply baffled. The next sentence, 'And right action is freedom / From past and future also' is resonant and, taken alone, multivalent. It conjures up the major dilemma of Eliot's St Thomas in *Murder in the Cathedral* ('This then is the greatest treason / To do the right deed for the wrong reason'); it sums up much that Christ said when speaking of the Kingdom ('Take no thought of the morrow'; 'sufficient unto the day is the evil thereof', and so on). But how have we arrived here? 'Burnt Norton' has spoken of 'The inner freedom from the practical desire', and other freedoms in 'the dance', but has added,

> Yet the enchainment of past and future
> Woven in the weakness of the changing body
> Protects mankind from heaven and damnation
> Which flesh cannot endure.

And, though the counterbalancing theme 'To be conscious is not to be in time' has been developing alongside, we have for the most part been experiencing tension, rather than resolution, between the two.

'Little Gidding' will produce resolution; but here the sudden introduction of 'Incarnation' and the appearance out of thin air of words as definite as 'actual', 'conquered' and 'reconciled', does not seem in keeping with this Quartet's first four movements. We have approached 'Incarnation' by a powerful assertion of positives, only one of which ('the unattended / Moment, the moment in and out of time') is as yet fully familiar. The saint, with his 'lifetime's death in love / Ardour and selflessness and self-surrender', is a new start, and, indeed, is explicitly dissociated, for good or ill, from 'most of us'. The third strand, 'prayer, observance, discipline, thought and action', is presented as more normative, but seems to belong to the kind of ordered, church-going life far removed from the enigmas and agonies of *Four Quartets*, or the spiritual progression charted earlier by the poet himself. I can therefore neither gloss the four lines starting 'Here the impossible union' with conviction, nor meaningfully link them with the contrast ('Where action were otherwise . . .') that follows.

This is the only part of the whole poem where I feel dissatisfied, and may signal little more than obtuseness: on reflection, I suppose that 'impossible union' and 'spheres of existence' are my real stumbling-block. Readers who are less perplexed might see the crucial link, if there is one. Meanwhile, I think that the last movement of 'The Dry Salvages' has one fine passage (the last eight lines), and one moment of vintage greatness (ll. 16–30): if these had been otherwise approached and assimilated to the tentative beauty of the prevailing sea-rhythms, then the third Quartet would have been the most perfect and satisfying of the four, as a whole.

A final comment, then, on the conclusion. The lines

> For most of us, this is the aim
> Never here to be realised;
> Who are only undefeated
> Because we have gone on trying . . .

revert to, and reinforce, the same grave yet satisfying notion in part v of 'East Coker': 'For us, there is only the trying. The rest is not our business.' This leads fittingly into the final four-line coda, on a note chiefly sombre, but not without limited hope. Irresistibly, the mind goes back to the lost peasants in the second movement of 'East Coker'; and here 'content at the last' introduces a consolation stopping short of religion, but curiously satisfying as an ending to *this* poem:

> We, content at the last
> If our temporal reversion nourish
> (Not too far from the yew-tree)
> The life of significant soil.

Death is accepted as 'temporal reversion', but linked with 'nourish': the 'life of significant soil' links all men in a chain of continuity, where suffering, pursued from East Coker, by way of Cape Anne, back to East Coker, is not without dignity, matching the endless, elemental rhythms of earth and sea. It would have been sufficient for 'yew-tree' to have stayed in parenthesis, still waiting the grander possibilities to be activated in 'Little Gidding' ('The moment of the rose and the moment of the yew-tree / Are of equal duration').

The fifth part of 'The Dry Salvages' had to be transitional (this is now established, and links the Quartets organically); but for once, *if* I am right, Eliot's touch faltered.

'Little Gidding': Not in the Scheme of Generation

I

This Quartet presents certain critical problems akin to those encountered in 'Burnt Norton'. The first Quartet started life as an autonomous poem, and can clearly be read as such, though it contained seeds of the major new poem in which it now chiefly belongs. The two central Quartets complement each other in the larger poem, and to read them in isolation, though possible, would seem somewhat perverse.

But how are we to take 'Little Gidding'? Should we regard it simply as the final movement, the consummation, of one organic whole (some would say, its final resolution); or might it also be able to live a life of its own? Philip Larkin included it in *The Oxford Book of Twentieth Century Verse* isolated from its context; and, while one can readily imagine that this was a compromise dictated by permission fees and other technicalities, it is of interest that he did not use 'Burnt Norton' instead, as the more obvious choice. A reader of 'Little Gidding' who does not know the *Quartets* would miss many vital echoes, along perhaps with some of the major significance; yet it must be able, in Larkin's opinion, to stand on its own.

Perhaps I can start with three or four random reflections in this peripheral territory, which have none the less nagged at my mind over the years. The first is that, had Eliot stopped with 'The Dry Salvages', leaving three Quartets only, a union comprised by these – though of a different order – might have been critically perceived. The second is that 'Little Gidding' has often been called, by some of Eliot's admirers, a 'Christian poem', or has even been said to 'make' a 'Christian poem' of the Quartets as a whole. The poet was, by 1944, churchwarden of a famous Anglo-Catholic church in London; he was writing, in prose, works approximating to Christian polemics and, at times, to Christian dogma; and the temptation to trivialise 'Little Gidding' on the strength of this knowledge is perhaps one which ought to be countered, even at the risk of seeming a little perverse. Whatever else it may be, 'Little Gidding' remains exploratory ('Old men ought to be explorers'), and 'We shall not cease from exploration' is one of its themes. Undeniably, 'the end of all our exploring' is also hinted at; but 'Will be' leaves open an element of conjecture, and the mode remains one of highly resonant symbolism, 'riding the echo'. The poet presents himself, indeed, not as a formal Establishment figure, pleasant or unpleasant to meet (and his continuing self-irony has not deserted him), but as a somewhat hallucinated fire-watcher, or air-raid warden in the London blitz. The Holy Spirit, as Dove, makes its first appearance (unless I am greatly mistaken) as a doodle-bug; while the 'familiar compound ghost' has proved dogma-proof almost to a fault.

This brings me to my third, and most important, preamble: the poem itself contains a new and unusual constructional feature, not encountered elsewhere. I have chosen 'Not in the scheme of generation' for sub-title to underline this; or, at least, to assist a case with which readers may or may not agree. This particular phrase –

like many other phrases and images in the poem – seems calculatedly ambiguous, yet in a manner not entirely like Eliot's ambiguities elsewhere.

C. B. Cox, writing chiefly of Eliot's earlier technique in *The Waste Land*, hit on the word 'contradictions' as an alternative to the more usual 'paradox' or 'ambivalence' when describing some recurring effects. If I am right, there is a usage peculiar to 'Little Gidding' for which the same word might be useful, though the actual effect is not the same. What I have in mind is that in many parts of this remarkable poem one encounters phrases which would be wholly consistent with a Christian (though not a dogmatic) interpretation, yet which leave open, also, alternative readings, equally valid, and perhaps in necessary balance with the main drift. I should make clear that the poem is, to my mind, in the widest sense 'Christian', and that I should stake this view, as will become apparent, chiefly on its tone. In place of the uncertainties, torments, aridities which haunted the earlier work, there is a serenity redolent of homecoming – of a final arrival, or near arrival, at the place of hope. Even so, innumerable details still offer other signals, and I cannot feel that this is not part of the poem's greatness, and of its final effect.

'Not in the scheme of generation' can serve as a model, to allow me later merely to point when I think the same technique is at work. The poet is about to arrive at the place of prayer, of *re*generation, and in an obvious sense the paradox is theologically exact. 'Generation' is the world of time, where there has been no redemption: 'not in time's covenant' is inevitably, it seems, the place to look for escape. As we learned in 'Burnt Norton', 'Except for the point, the still point, / There would be no dance, and there is only the dance': yet to reach the still point requires more than 'given' moments of vision, which beckon, but fail to welcome us home. The major theme of 'Little Gidding' is prayer and the forces surrounding it: 'Not in the scheme of generation' as we have encountered it *yet*.

On the other hand, the phrase is used to describe 'Midwinter spring' – an illusion of summer in winter, where 'transitory blossom / Of snow' mimes, for a moment, the 'voluptuary sweetness' of May. Even so, the warmth is missing ('In windless cold that is the heart's heat' rests upon 'frost', 'ice' in context); and 'Where is the summer, the unimaginable / Zero summer?' remains, in waking reality, 'Midwinter spring' precisely defined. As in the visionary moment in part I of 'Burnt Norton', the possibility of hallucination lingers. *Is* this midwinter visit, to the place of regeneration, a final arrival; or might 'Then a cloud passed, and the pool was empty' still haunt the tale?

II

The two central Quartets are set in locations deeply personal to the poet; and Burnt Norton was the scene of intense momentary revelation or vision, unexpectedly given. Little Gidding, in contrast, is a place of acknowledged pilgrimage, though not on any normal tourist-map of English shrines (unless Eliot's poem has now succeeded in putting it there). Travelling northwards from Cambridge, you can encounter the signpost, pointing left along a minor road, saying only 'Little Gidding'. In this poem, the place becomes symbolic of that moment in a man's life where the notions of death and conversion (metanoia) converge.

At Little Gidding a religious community led by Nicholas Ferrar flourished briefly during the English Civil War and its immediate aftermath. It achieved, in its moment, a reputation for holiness; but, as the world judges and as time measures, offered no historical continuity or perceptible sequel. As a Protestant community, it was outside Christianity's normal covenant and, for this reason perhaps, especially fitting to Eliot's scheme. The 'intersection of the timeless moment' is of God's choosing, whether it comes as unheralded insight or as the time of commitment; and now we are indeed presented not with one of those brief, numinous intimations which men may occasionally experience, but with the intensely personal moment of choice when, for some particular human pilgrim, 'the world's end' arrives.

Allusions to famous figures on both sides of the English Civil War flit through the poem. Charles, the 'broken king', and Milton the king-breaker are both caught up, 'United in the strife which divided them', and both fit therefore to offer 'a symbol: / A symbol perfected in death'. The context is deliberately widened, to include *The Divine Comedy* and Julian of Norwich's *Revelations of Divine Love* among many other Christian allusions. Meanwhile, the London of the Blitz (very specially, for this reader, of the 1944 doodle-bug period – though just possibly the special aptness of that weird summer is accidental, and the section was completed with the period between September 1940 and May 1941 in mind) recurs throughout, involving the poet in his highly pragmatic role as guardian against fire and bomb.

The first movement follows the pattern by now familiar, divided into two sections, the first of which has already been touched upon. The poet arrives at Little Gidding on one of those brief, vivid days in midwinter, when snow and frost offer an hallucinated vision, or parody, of midsummer blossom. 'Sempiternal' asserts the timeless and eternal aspect of the afternoon, 'sodden towards sundown' its enigmatic relation to time. It is its 'own season / ... Suspended in time'. This enigmatic quality is quintessential: 'windless cold' remains still the 'heart's heat', while 'glare' and 'glow', more intense than fire, are the 'brief' sun's trick, enacted on ice and water. A further contradiction is our first intimation of the main theme: 'no wind, but pentecostal fire / In the dark time of the year'. At Pentecost, a 'rushing mighty wind' was one phenomenon, while the flame that stirred the 'dumb spirits' of Christ's disciples from despair to joy (hard to discern from intoxication) was not winter experience: Whitsun is a spring feast, far from 'the dark time of the year' in calendar time – though yoked to it, symbolically, by the Good Friday experience, and the days of waiting, after Easter, for the promised general rebirth.

The remainder of this section is dominated more by the fear of illusion than by any true unfreezing. Negative concepts ('quivers', 'no earth smell', 'not in time's covenant', 'transitory blossom', 'neither budding nor fading', 'Not in the scheme', 'unimaginable / Zero') predominate, as if we have to wait a little longer to know whether this is one further optical illusion, or the 'long looked forward to / Long hoped for calm', authentic at last.

The second section of the movement is, with parts of the poem's third and fifth movements, including its actual conclusion, among the most visionary and unforgettable poetry in the world. It is also, in a manner carrying – for me, certainly – great conviction, the culmination of a rhythmic pattern which characterised Eliot from the first. I have in mind those circling, exploratory repetitions, effective and memorable from *Prufrock* onwards, which in the past had often mimed uncertainty, self-doubt, a ritual of death or of dreamlike detachment, and which now, unmistakably, have the sound of the Dove descending, or of a long-lost traveller at last coming home. From 'The Love Song of J. Alfred Prufrock' we recall the phrases 'Let us go', 'There will be time, there will be time', 'For I have known them all already, known them all', 'And would it have been worth it, after all', and 'This is not it at all', around which so much of the distinctive music weaves. In the somewhat harsher 'Portrait of a Lady', a similar effect is observable: 'my friends', 'Among the . . .', 'shall sit here, serving tea', 'You', and (again as in the first poem) 'after all'. Through most of the early poems, such circling rhythms add to the incantatory effects, plangent, self-torturing, bored, whistling in the dark (many such intimations). In *The Waste Land*, I fancy, there are fewer verbal effects of the kind, but structural juxtapositions serve a similar function; while in poems of the middle period we find two outstanding, if wholly contrasted, variants: the dreamlike and liturgical repetitions in that most elusive and Surrealist (though still bafflingly concrete) poem, *Ash Wednesday* ('Because I do not hope', 'And I renounce', 'only', 'At the first turning', 'Word', 'Although', etc.); and the blackly humorous usage throughout *Sweeney Agonistes*.

Now, in 'Little Gidding', the music weaves its way through incrementally more powerful, and stronger, phrases, which pick up the note of determinism that has dogged the first three Quartets as a question, and now finds, in the ultimate pattern of a divine initiative, some meaning consonant, in the end, with free-will and love: 'If you came this way, / Taking the route you would be likely to take'; 'It would be the same'; 'If you came'; 'It would always be the same'; 'Now and in England'. From the moment this section opens, the unrelenting enigmas of the opening yield to a powerful forward movement – a new circling, fated, purposeful, revealed after long searching, now too familiar for question; and, in context, assertions are made which – *if* we take *Four Quartets* as one whole – catch up doubt in truth and seeking in finding, opening the way to the key philosophic perception announced later – 'for history is a pattern / Of timeless moments' – and, also, to the assured and serene serenity of the close.

The phrase 'when you leave the rough road / And turn behind the pig-sty to the dull façade / And the tombstone' is accurate in its description of arrival at the chapel (at least, in the early 1940s: since then, Little Gidding has become a community again, though of a somewhat different kind). The cancelling out of 'purpose' presents itself, at last, not as blind drifting, or of mere determinism in a blind or Calvinistic cosmos dead to free-will, but as a transcending of the human quest which is also true fulfilment: no violation, whoever we are or whatever we expected, different though the pattern may be from our images and dreams. The perception 'Either you had no purpose / Or the purpose is beyond the end you figured / And is altered in fulfilment' picks up both the drift through time in 'East Coker', and the sombre bewilderment of 'The Dry Salvages – neither denying the validity of these images, nor implying that they could have been bypassed, yet suggesting that, when the 'end of the journey' is reached, there will be no sense of surprise or of violation: only a recognition that 'hints and guesses' of hope, however faint at the time, were, after all, true pointers.

Then, by a further marvel of poetic tact, Eliot reintroduces in this new atmosphere other images that, through his work, have been prevailingly fearful – urban loneliness; desert aridity; death by drowning – and assimilates them to the phrase 'the world's end', which I should have chosen as title for this section had I not also wanted, a little perhaps for personal reasons, to distance the intimations of finality in favour of the more familiar openness that is not wholly banished:

                    There are other places
Which also are the world's end, some at the sea jaws,
Or over a dark lake, in a desert or a city –
But this is the nearest, in place and time,
Now and in England.

'. . . the world's end': a major, and key, ambiguity. Do we think back
to *The Hollow Men?*

> *This is the way the world ends*
> *This is the way the world ends*
> *This is the way the world ends*
> *Not with a bang but a whimper.*

If so, the spell is unwound; yet 'the world's end' for many people will
still remain a derelict rubbish dump, loss of will, murder or suicide
(nor would I exempt myself or some dear to me from these
possibilities), just as it might be kneeling, at last, 'where prayer has
been valid' and uttering words that in varying degrees bind or
attempt to bind will to the freedom of faith.

These particular words of Eliot have pursued me since I first
encountered them, reappearing, in the past thirty-five years, on
occasions too numerous to list. One was underneath the Arches at
Charing Cross on a winter's night, looking at the old men bundled
up in newspapers, sodden with meths, unhelped by everyone in
London, myself included. Another was in Canada when, travelling
north of Montreal, through country outstanding in natural
grandeur, I caught sight of a religious house perched, it seemed
inaccessibly, on a distant peak at least 10,000 feet high. Again, I
remembered them in a nunnery in Oxford when meeting several
religious of undoubted integrity, who had none the less earned their
retreat, I suspected, more by evading their own tensions and
ignoring the tensions of the rest of us, than by any resolution, or
transcendence, that rang true.

These reflections, though personal, are also inevitable, and within
the announced law of the poet himself, in 'Burnt Norton':

                    My words echo
Thus, in your mind.
                    But to what purpose
Disturbing the dust on a bowl of rose-leaves
I do not know.

'There are other places / Which also are the world's end' requires
from each reader whatever images cluster, grow, 'fructify' over the

years. I cannot envisage that anything less than a lifetime's wrestling with hurt and darkness, accompanied by 'the intolerable wrestle / With words and meaning' of poetic discipline, could have produced such a phrase and the context required for them. Maybe the whole of *Four Quartets* is required for their fullness; and words from the conclusion of 'East Coker', where the meaning is different, may equally express one of the truths endemic to all three of the major poets concerning us in this book:

> a lifetime burning in every moment
> And not the lifetime of one man only
> But of old stones that cannot be deciphered.

The poem continues in a manner that might, in isolation, appear somewhat dogmatic, yet which depends on the mood created for its actual effect. I have an irresistible feeling that a highly personal moment is recorded (though one transferred to 'Little Gidding' for symbolic purposes), and that the numerous paradoxes of faith – the *via negativa* and the way of vision – which we have encountered meet, now, in a moment of surrender to God. The phrase 'you would have to put off / Sense and notion' is no longer remotely a call to superstition or unreason, but a definition of the moment when some leap of faith must be made. The word 'would' leaves choice open, to the last moment – even for pilgrims who have been drawn, and are on the verge of the place always sought for, if never envisaged like *this*:

> You are not here to verify,
> Instruct yourself, or inform curiosity
> Or carry report. You are here to kneel
> Where prayer has been valid.

So 'prayer' – a word which has occurred earlier in the Quartets, but always tentatively or surrounded with questions, emerges at last as the simple, lost key. In *The Waste Land*, the 'key' image occurred ('I have heard the key / Turn in the door once and turn once only / We think of the key, each in his prison / Thinking of the key'), but *The Waste Land* paused well among its ambiguities ('each confirms a prison' – fragments of West, East, ancient and modern 'shored against . . . ruins' in a still desperate search in desert terrain). Now, at last, prayer becomes not a complex idea but an act of will, a simple reality; and for a moment it escapes the poem as it escapes everything leading up to it; for, after all, a 'report' *is* carried by the poet on the other side now, of all that has gone before.

The lines about the dead have, once more, special resonance, at levels where the supernatural is scarcely needed to make them work. No one who has recalled words of lost friends – at the time little enough heeded – will miss at least some of the special poignancy lurking here.

So, 'the intersection of the timeless moment' is announced; and only in the last line is paradox (contradiction? ambiguity?) allowed back again: 'England and nowhere. Never and always.'

III

The second movement of 'Little Gidding' plunges us back, deliberately, into non-regeneration – a last, yet anguished visit to the waste land. Fine though it is, it strikes me as the poetic weak link in the poem, perhaps because both parts are less effortless than the rest in their final 'feel'. (I should add that my poetic assessment disagrees with many other critics, here as well as elsewhere; I have heard a critic I greatly respect describe the second part of this movement as Eliot's greatest poetic triumph.)

The first section follows 'The Dry Salvages' rather than the first two Quartets, though poetically it seems to me considerably inferior, in that it does not aim to be deliberate pastiche, intended to be kicked aside and restated, but is a valid lyric in its own right. The four elements, which have appeared throughout the Quartets as motif (as they did, earlier, in *The Waste Land*) are listed in turn, and their human violation made clear. 'Dust' is the image in the first stanza (reminding, again as in *The Waste Land*, both of the Christian hope that we were made from dust, return to dust and will be refashioned from dust at the Resurrection, and the 'fear in a handful of dust' symbolised by the Cumaean sibyl and her terrible fate: 'I want to die'). In the second stanza, 'flood and drought' once more recall *Waste Land* images, and death by water returns yet again as a frightening theme. The third stanza is an apocalyptic vision of earthly devastation brought about not by the Last Day, but by man's neglect of God – the self-created urban dust-heaps where fact and symbol meet.

Individual images have inherent power, and the piling up of concepts, though it can look heavy-handed on the page, reveals rhythmic subtlety when the passage is read aloud. I have a distinct impression that the one 'interminable night' of the London Blitz which is to be the literal setting for the rest of this movement is prefigured in this opening lyric as well. The lines

Dust in the air suspended
Marks the place where a story ended

take me back vividly to a moment in the summer of 1944. A flying-bomb had stopped almost overhead; I had rushed for cover in the usual way and started counting, to see whether it would dive straight down (about nine to twelve seconds) or glide on, to land some distance away (after about fifteen seconds, you deduced the second supposition). On this occasion there was an almighty crash after about seven seconds and, going out into the evening light, I have an ineffaceable memory of the great cloud of dust which rose from a neighbouring street, climbed above the housetops and, for what seemed like eternity, stayed quite still, before it then began, gradually, to drift further off, and disperse. Within it, one knew, was the transformed dust of houses, furniture, people – transformed in a moment; and I imagine that anyone who has experienced bombardment or explosion (probably a majority of living people, in one form or another) will recognise the sheer accuracy, and unanswerable power, of this one image.

The early 1940s were too soon for many people to worry about ecological damage, but earlier ravages of industrial revolution had been a theme of Eliot's as of other poets; and destruction by water has dominated one whole Quartet. In his final stanza, Eliot risks direct polemics more directly than usual, linking these ravages with neglect of the Christian faith. Personally, I find the tentative openings of 'East Coker' and 'The Dry Salvages' more authentic (because less localised; more open, and pagan) on this theme; but maybe the Quartets have now arrived at their openly Christian phase. 'The sacrifice that we denied' refers back directly to part IV of 'East Coker'; 'The marred foundations we forgot, / Of sanctuary and choir' could combine the erosion of spirituality with its literal symbol, the destruction of Coventry Cathedral in November 1940 (an event that took as strong a hold on the imagination of the period as did the almost miraculous preservation from fire of St Paul's, London, on 29 December 1940).

The whole lyric seems like a play of the elements which sustain life, turned to a dance of destruction. The opening image dramatises the suddenness with which roses can be burnt to dust, dust turn to senility, shabbiness. The poet contrives also to touch on the major stages of creation as understood by Christians (man made from dust; man fallen in 'hope and despair'; man redeemed on Calvary; man offered but spurning the Resurrection sacrament in visible churches). The effect is of a kind of cyclical vision of decay in the world of elements – linked to sin, judgement, the more bitter notes of 'wisdom' from the Old Testament; and in a tone preparing for the anger which, increasingly, is to be the dominant emotion of this movement. One result is that the lyric passes directly into the movement's second half, with no perceptible transition – except in rhythm, where an English measure approximating (distantly) to *terza rima*, and clearly designed to recall Dante's *Divine Comedy*, is used.

We know that Eliot took greater pains over this section than over most of his writing; and the effect of much labouring leaves its mark. A sympathetic reader can bring out many beauties of tone and diction, but a certain stiffness also recurs, especially, I think, in hints of the didactic. The ghost may be enigmatic, but he speaks like a pedant at times.

The opening finds us with Mr Eliot, on whichever night it is of the blitz. Such experiences are calculated to conjure up that timelessness brilliantly defined in the first movement of 'The Dry Salvages' – 'the recurrent end of the unending'; and the next image is the one I had in mind when saying that the Holy Spirit, as Dove, makes his first appearance seemingly as a doodle-bug. I have already acknowledged that this could be hindsight – though it does perfectly describe the appearance of the flying-bombs passing overhead before their engine had shut off, and when the jet trail showed, by night, as a 'flickering tongue'. On the other hand, an ordinary bomb or an incendary bomb from the winter of 1940 would fit the description: either way, this is not really Pentecost, but man's inhumanity to man miming it (the configuration of 'dove', 'flickering' and 'tongue' must equal Whitsun – though 'dark' is satanic parody, and 'the horizon of his homing' is the intended destruction of bombardment, not renewal by grace). 'Between three districts whence the smoke arose' would be normal observation as the raid continued, but moves subtly now towards the place of symbolic meeting: surely Hell, not Purgatory (and, indeed, it as if the first movement is now temporarily in abeyance, with the verse driving right back towards the waste land, and to the opening of 'Burnt Norton', where 'If all time is eternally present / All time is unredeemable').

And here happens the encounter with the drifting ghost, 'forgotten, half recalled / Both one and many ... / Both intimate and unidentifiable'. It is at this point that Eliot's critics have often tended to go slightly beserk in one way or another, as regards both the ghost's identity and the poet's role. Some have been determined to pin down the ghost and identify the unidentifiable – either as one sole figure of their own choice, or (with a bleak nod in the direction of 'compound') as the chief ghost, taking precedence over all co-presences. In contrast, other critics have piled up ghosts with abandon, leaving the poet either talking to an amalgam amounting positively to the Mind of Europe incarnate, or even, himself absorbed in the ghost, conducting a multiple-personality dialogue on the grandest scale. Grover Smith (whose *T. S. Eliot's Poetry and Plays: A Study in Sources and Meaning* will be known to all critical readers of *Four Quartets*) assures us that the 'double part' which the poet assumes 'forms the crux; everything depends on it. Unfortunately, there is little possibility of deciding what it means'. On the page preceding this daunting and, by his standards, unusual piece of pessimism, he offers us an amazing array of literary echoes that haunt the stanza (this is valuable, and I see no need to repeat it in full) but, when he arrives at the ghost, reminds us, pertinently enough, of 'that affable familiar ghost' (Shakespeare's Sonnet LXXXVI); of Mallarmé's 'Donner un sens plus pur aux mots de la tribu' (clearly very central); of Milton's 'instead of Fruit / Chew'd bitter Ashes'; of Swift's Epitaph; of Ford's 'a lamentable tale of things / Done long ago, and ill done'; of Yeats (naturally); of Johnson's 'Grief aids disease, remembered folly stings'; of quotations from *Measure for Measure* and *Hamlet*; and, very particularly, of the Brunetto Latini passage in *Inferno*, canto xv, where 'brown baked features' involve, he suggests, Brunetto's name (it is certainly one of the oddest touches), and 'the down-turned face' is again a phrase used.

At the risk of further complication, I must add that I have always been struck by the similarity between the ghost's words in the six lines starting 'But, as the passage now presents no hindrance', and the words of Count Guido de Montefiltrano in *Inferno*, canto XXVII, which Eliot had long ago used as an introduction to 'The Love Song of J. Alfred Prufrock' (rough translation: 'If I thought my reply would be to someone who would ever return to earth, this spirit would remain without further movement, but, as no one has ever returned alive from this abyss, if what I hear is true, I can answer you with no fear of infamy').

What are we to make of it? I think that 'intimate and unidentifiable', and 'forgotten, half recalled' are the chief clue (just as they may be to the 'unknown, remembered gate' at the conclusion of 'Little Gidding'). Eliot is surely encountering, in an eerie form, his own past: which clearly includes all those in life and perhaps especially in literature who have been his chief influences, together with his own dead self. I see no reason why Ezra Pound, who, though still alive at the time, was, in grim fact, suffering torments equal to Dante's imagination at its most infernal, should not be included; and surely the Eliot whom we know as author of all the earlier poems, long before Mr Eliot OM, churchwarden of St Stephen's, Gloucester Road, was born, must have his place? 'Too strange to each other for misunderstanding': *this* 'intersection moment' is not, I would suggest, the one with which the first movement ends and the later movements concern themselves; nor is it numinous visitation, or the courted emptiness which may prelude God's light and dancing. In tone, it is closer to the sleepless women of 'The Dry Salvages', but the bitterness is unmistakably personal, and deeply anguished. 'I am not eager to rehearse . . .' prefaces the whole story of life – everything that has been tormenting or mercifully forgotten, and which now *must* have forgiveness and purgation, unless it is to be, and stay, hell.

When this is said, I suppose I must declare some preferences, given the anarchy which follows if total inclusiveness (and therefore dilution) is let in. Mallarmé's words are the ones used to describe the poetic mission, and here alone despair maybe yields to a moment's sense of a life-task imposed and followed out. The passage concerning 'the gifts reserved for age' had been prefigured in the second movement of 'East Coker' as very personal experience, but no doubt sums up any honest man's self-assessment at the moment of death. Who would deny that evil effects often come, in this life, from good intentions; or regret that 'The paths of glory lead but to the grave'? Some people are perhaps insensitive enough for the first error, or stoic enough for the second; yet would even they doubt that human existence is the roughest of rides? If some Christians brood on God's final inquisition and their certain failure to meet it, others – perhaps all 'moderns', in the definition I am using – may wonder how God himself will dare look us in the eye. We are thrown back on the mystery of universal suffering and the certainty that either it will somehow be justified after this life, by greater goods not yet guessed at, or that it will be a mystery left for oblivion mercifully to hide.

Here the emphasis falls on bitter self-knowledge, too late to heal, too terrible not to lacerate; and, for a Christian, only grace and forgiveness (for God too?) will ever heal the intolerable sting. I tend to think that the obvious influence is Yeats, one of whose major themes this is. Yeats was recently dead. In their lifetimes, the two major poets went their own ways – Yeats for the most part uninterested or uncomprehending, Eliot, I imagine, refusing to acknowledge the one living poet writing in English who was beyond any margin of doubt his superior (his essay on Yeats made posthumous amends).

The section ends on the note which has prevailed throughout – unrelieved pessimism – except that the ghost's final words hint at the fire which will save from fire. The 'disfigured street' brings us back to war-ravaged London. And, though the 'blowing of the horn' will be the 'Raiders past' – that signal for which Londoners learned to wait all night for their moment of respite – the words 'valediction' and 'faded' remove hope even from this. We can be absolutely certain that, though Eliot accepted the OM, his true self bled at it: all the hope now is that every shadowy figure – that 'familiar compound ghost' we readers see in the mirror most notably – will rediscover what the first movement promised before this second intervened.

IV

The third movement, leaving behind the gloom of the second, opens
with a directly philosophic passage and then moves back to memories of the English Civil War and the brief flourishing of Little Gidding.

The opening reverts to previous themes and combines Western
and Eastern wisdom in classic form. The way of detachment has been
expounded before, especially in the third movement of 'The Dry
Salvages'; Krishna, and many Western mystics, would agree upon it.
The formula leads to the desert *positively* (the desert fathers form a
total contrast with urban deserts of modern emptiness), and can act
as a symbol for the withdrawn life of monastics and hermits, whether
under formal vow or as a choice of life by those ostensibly still living
in the 'world'. The way of 'attachment' we have heard less of, since it
is not Eliot's way, 'Indifference', the choice which Eliot associates
especially with the modern world, but also with all men and women
through history whose egocentricity has sacrificed everything to
personal need and acquisition, has been generally regarded in most
religious and moral traditions as a form of death, as much for those
who opt for it as for their victims.

It is now that the poem moves to another passage where I find the
special kind of ambiguity I have mentioned. For those following the
poem's Christianity, it may seem an obvious sequel to the opening
reflections; for others, it might seem a distortion of the very meaning
of 'love':

> This is the use of memory:
> For liberation – not less of love but expanding
> Of love beyond desire, and so liberation
> From the future as well as the past.

Until now, 'memory' has been an echo-chamber of 'What might
have beèn and what has been', pointing to 'one end, which is always
present'. Positively, it has been the place where numinous moments
can be remembered – yet, since all moments are isolated and past
and future are equally without redemption (perhaps without even
reality), memory has had no liberating potential. Here we appear, on
the surface, to break through into new light, new exuberance even,
as if 'past and future' are at last truly 'conquered', and united with
love. By the same token, 'history' is also released from the stasis in
which it has been previously immobilised, and is found to have
potentials for good or ill: 'History may be servitude, / History may
be freedom'.

The first famous reference to history, in Eliot's verse, was as early
as 'Gerontion', and it has always struck me as one of the first major

statements of some of the main themes as we know them, in the first
three Quartets:

> Think now
> History hàs many cunning passages, contrived corridors
> And issues, deceives with whispering ambitions,
> Guides us by vanities. Think now
> She gives when our attention is distracted
> And what she gives, gives with such supple confusions
> That the giving famishes the craving. Gives too late
> What's not believed in, or is still believed,
> In memory only, reconsidered passion. Gives too soon
> Into weak hands, what's thought can be dispensed with
> Till the refusal propagates a fear. Think
> Neither fear nor courage saves us.

This thought has no doubt haunted the second movement of 'East
Coker', the third movement of 'The Dry Salvages', and the second
movement of 'Little Gidding'. We have, then, to attribute to prayer,
and the discovery in prayer of new dimensions, this moment when at
last we really hear what the 'dead' have to tell us, in a new way:

> See, now they vanish,
> The faces and places, with the self which, as it could, loved them,
> To become renewed, transfigured, in another pattern.

But it is here that I find the doubts which beset me when reading
'Little Gidding' returning with some force. The concepts 'renewed,
transfigured' have great power, invoking the moment in Christ's
lifetime when his incarnate divinity was manifested to three chosen
disciples with supernatural light, prefiguring resurrection and grace.
At face value, they would validate all 'hints and guesses / Hints
followed by guesses' by establishing Incarnation, through the Word,
as a key to reality; and they also open the way to rebirth by water: the
counterpointing of the 'sea's jaws' with baptism.

Even so, the context is curious. For most Christians, 'love' will be
the nature of God, confirmed in Christ and therefore incarnate in
whatever human relationships most embody it. The poet does indeed
say 'not less of love', but the qualification 'but expanding / Of love
beyond desire, and so liberation / From the future as well as the past'
still suggests – to me, at least – a continued refusal to link desire with
love: and a continuation of the ultimate gnosticism, from Augustine
and other austere sources, which has made one always doubt Eliot's
ability to link sexuality, or even close human relationships, with
'love'. His theory of patriotism would appear to confirm this view.

No doubt, the opening out of narrow and exclusive patriotism towards a vision where one can accept the validity of all positive pride in race and nation, *is* 'liberation' – yet a special lòve of the native heath, going somewhat beyond the phrase 'of little importance / Though never indifferent' would sound warmer.

The introduction of one of the great Christian statements of hope, from Lady Julian of Norwich's *Revelations of Divine Love*, is a landmark, signalling that we have now moved to territory beyond even normal Christian hope – to a conviction of the love of God, shown in Christ, which will reconcile the whole universe, ultimately, in joy. This leads in turn to the beautiful, yet again obscurely ambiguous, return to Little Gidding, and the illustration of historical reconciliation in a concrete example, derived from the place.

How true does it ring, I wonder? I recall that in a lecture at Cambridge many years ago Enid Welsford suggested that one of the great disasters of history is this: most people pursue lives of indifference, which give them nothing either to love or to fight for; while those who do fight and love have more in common, if only they would recognise it – their commitment itself, in a word – than the things which separate them.

No doubt Miss Welsford's reflections were similar in kind to these: yet I recall thinking at the time that the Second World War had been a desperate battle between one of the bloodiest tyrants in history and forces who, in opposing him, were eventually led into evils, such as the bombing of Dresden, not unlike his own; and that to apply Miss Welford's undoubtedly important insight to *this* situation would be over-bland, to put matters mildly.

But what of the English Civil War? By comparison, the issues might seem to us, now, less redolent of good and evil – yet for the seventeenth-century actors this was not the case, for Charles as for his enemies. The battle between an absolutist monarchy, entirely depending on the Divine Right of Kings for sanction, and forces which were to introduce Protestantism, middle-class ascendancy and eventually democracy to the world, cannot be wholly assimilated to a war between differently motivated idealists. The poet says, rightly,

> We cannot revive old factions
> We cannot restore old policies
> Or follow an antique drum.

– yet the world we live in would have been incalculably different had not one side, rather than the other, triumphed. I doubt whether the fact of the Restoration greatly alters this view; or, if it does, then it is only to make the English Civil War a particular, rather than a general, case.

With this in mind, one wonders whether it is adequate to assimilate men as different as (say) Charles I and Cromwell, Marvell and Milton to phrases as generalised, and ultimately perhaps tired, as 'not wholly commendable', 'of no immediate kin or kindness', and 'All touched by a common genius'; or whether 'United in the strife which divided them' will carry any weight commensurate with Lady Julian's mystical utterance? I find the phrase 'Accept the constitution of silence / And are folded in a single party' singularly unconvincing, since it appears to merge two (at least) wholly different notions. All now are dead: as Donne says, 'It comes equally to us all, and makes us all equal when it comes'; but is Eliot's pun on 'constitution' truly justified, or does it yet again accept an implicit quietism, which sees little importance in events on earth, however they turn out, when these are placed against the backcloth of eternity?

If we are left with the symbol of 'a single party', it may be at the cost of draining all significance from the issues fought over, in favour of an insight that commitment itself, on whichever side, is what counts. Yet, if so, this is again less than satisfactory, in two ways which I cannot assimilate at all to 'perfected in death'. It would seem to deny the possibility of good and evil as real entities, fighting on the scene of history as well as that of eternity, in order to imply rather that, when the particular battles men fought are no longer relevant, then the principles which consumed them, too, are somehow vitiated – or even transmuted to the simple notion of 'good fighting good'. If imported into the present, this view suggests that our battles now, whatever these are, will one day seem equally meaningless: yet is this really true, when wholly opposite views of man, society, God himself, are involved?

Conceivably, an answer could be found by returning to 'East Coker', where the 'fight' is endorsed, yet once more raised to a rarefied and maybe impossible level:

> There is only the fight to recover what has been lost
> And found and lost again and again: and now, under conditions
> That seem unpropitious. But perhaps neither gain nor loss.
> For us, there is only the trying. The rest is not our business.

But here, Eliot seems to be thinking chiefly of the standards of goodness and truth exemplified in history by a tiny minority of saints and artists; and to focus attention on the quest for personal, rather than social, salvation. In 'Little Gidding', despite the associations of holiness in the place itself and the general theme of personal salvation, I feel that some deep discrepancy has been allowed in. The Civil War introduces, for better or worse, social issues that do not entirely lend themselves to moments of isolated significance, though this is to be their final use before the poem concludes. Eliot may not be attempting to 'summon the spectre of a Rose', yet his own prose writings, in works such as *The Idea of a Christian Society* and *Notes towards a Definition of Culture*, were an overt attempt to influence current culture in a manner inseparable from the unfolding of tradition and were frankly indebted to a mode of thinking which still links, however distantly, with one side rather than the other of England's ideological rending in the seventeenth century.

The section ends with a return, the second of three, to Julian of Norwich's motif, and to the attendant idea, now, of purgation:

> By the purification of the motive
> In the ground of our beseeching.

The 'gifts reserved for age' passage has explored, very bitterly,

> the shame
> Of motives late revealed, and the awareness
> Of things ill done and done to others' harm
> Which once you took as exercise of virtue.

But, once more, the individual soul's quest and its need for deliverance seem far more important to the poet than either the effects left upon others by past errors, or the inevitable influence of actions upon history as an unfolding pattern.

In so far as this passage fits the Christian meaning, then it does so by asserting that the inner battle for purity, and the perspective of history as a sequence of isolated moments directly relating to art as image and to religion as symbol, is the place where hope may be found. But, in escaping this context also and leaving unsolved questions, it possibly allows to non-Christian readers perspectives of their own. This effect (perhaps his intention also) is profoundly interesting, and in my judgement makes the poem greater, not less great, in a final view. The comforting notion that all paradoxes are taken up and resolved may please some readers; a continued unresolved openness could be more in line with the Quartets as a whole.

V

The fourth movement of 'Little Gidding' must function as a touchstone. Theologically, it describes the descent of the Holy Spirit at Pentecost, and seems finally to confirm the Christian intimations of 'pentecostal fire / In the dark time of the year'. The ambiguity of the event is theologically sound: there was terror as well as joy for the disciples and the world, as has been said, was 'turned upside down' by the ensuing phenomenon of the Christian Church, Militant.

Even so, Eliot's lyric embodies the element of contradiction in 'Little Gidding' remarkably. When read aloud, it has great rhetorical vigour, but no clear direction: the images, which should be of hope, are more like a nightmare.

Ambiguities abound throughout. 'The dove' is associated already with bomb and destruction, so that 'descending . . . / With flame of incandescent terror' evokes, for me, the most destructive moments of the London blitz. If so, then the image 'Dust in the air suspended / Marks the place where a story ended' returns, infusing 'The one discharge from sin and error' with sick irony and very decisively allying 'pyre or pyre', 'fire by fire' with despair, not with hope. The Whitsun theme is compromised, as before, by 'the tongues' − since once again Eliot uses the image in a capricious manner, which evades the scriptural challenge of a remarkable and universal gift of 'tongues', in favour of the suggestions of destruction associated with falling bombs.

Does the second stanza help? 'Who then devised the torment? Love. . . .'

Perhaps. The fact of torment needs no underlining, since all Eliot's poetry attests it, not by assertion only, but also by stirring our own most personal wounds. 'Love' made its appearance in 'Burnt Norton' − a swimmer, testing new water: 'unfamiliar Name' in Eliot then, as apparently now.

Why then go on with the image of human and jealous love at its most destructive: is the treacherous Nessus-shirt not 'love' in its terrible form? Hercules could escape this 'torment' only by immolation (why are we back with pagan references and contexts again?). The words 'intolerable', 'not remove' come from the same period as Belsen; the final couplet is a paradox that conjures horror on horror to any sensitive mind:

We only live, only suspire
Consumed by either fire or fire.

As I acknowledged earlier, the Christian interpretation remains open, provided that we strain a little to keep it so. Eliot has made casual use of other images (the Tarot, for instance) in past poems; why should we expect a more exact rendering of the intoxication, the joy, the new languages which Whitsun somehow demands? The fusion of love and terror is certainly not without precedent − particularly for a poet who can accept Dante's hideously sadistic Hell as God's handiwork without question; who can fuse Hitler's attempted destruction of London with the Holy Spirit, and identify the device of an insanely jealous woman with the Creator's 'refining fire'. There is no lack of stress on God's wrath, jealousy, punishment in the Christian tradition; arguably modern theology is itself eccentric in playing it down. The notion that the flames of Purgatory are the one alternative to the flames of Hell is impeccable Catholic theology: except that the 'flames of Purgatory' have often been interpreted less literally – more lovingly – than they are here.

For reasons best known to himself, Eliot is presenting the hound of heaven in his direst form, as if the Good Friday experience had really to be repeated by us all. Some theologians – by no means all of them Protestant – would identify the 'one discharge from sin and error' with part IV of *East Coker*, and claim that, mysteriously, Christ bore our stripes, in His body, on the tree. This lyric in contrast offers an 'only hope' which confirms an extreme dislocation of the Whitsun experience into the shape of human evil and hate.

By some Christians, even *this* could be justified: is Eliot saying, they could conjecture, that the Church is meant to suffer with Christ, for the world's redemption, and not merely to rejoice as a bride? If so, this is again orthodox, again fairly normal Christian experience – yet again, I would say, one part only of what Christians present as their 'truth'. Christ is reported as saying that he was going away in order to send 'another Comforter', who would be known by the fruit of love, joy, peace, visibly healing the world. These gifts were 'not as the world gives', and not incompatible with suffering; but they were to shine, they were to draw men, they were to be a light conquering darkness. Why, I wonder, is the Church's birthday presented in 'Little Gidding' with none of the charisma, only with the bleakness of 'intolerable . . . flame'?

I suppose I have said enough to revert to my original thesis, which is that doubt, as well as faith, is left open at this point. There will be those who expect at Whitsun not to be 'consumed' but to be 'consummated'. We have heard the word 'renewed, transfigured', yoked with the joy of Lady Julian: yet these remain unusual words in Eliot (just as *Revelations of Divine Love* is odd-man-out in a poet for whom Augustine, Aquinas, Dante, St John of the Cross, Pascal, Frazer, F. H. Bradley and the unknown author of *The Cloud of Unknowing* are more normal fare).

VI

The final movement of 'Little Gidding' is virtually Eliot's farewell as a poet and, if we put a question mark over ll. 3–12, it is possibly the most hauntingly beautiful passage in the whole of his work.

The opening lines have a teasing quality, which I have commented on before, in that they can become detached from context, with rich meanings of the most varied kind:

> What we call a beginning is often the end
> And to make an end is to make a beginning.
> The end is where we start from.

In education, 'The end is where we start from' could be an excellent guide, for purely pragmatic reasons: educators are aware of the immense riches of art, science, philosophy and speculation which man has accumulated, and could well see their task as matching children, from the start, with those gifts and loves most appropriate to their eventual fulfilment as men. More mysteriously, it may be true in religion, and even in certain human loves, that 'the end' beckons, at the start, as a prize to be cherished, nurtured, pursued, yet never doubted, since it is (or has been) already in sight.

In context, we shall be reminded of course of the two central Quartets – both variants on the theme – and of the particular resolution (one among several possibilities) that the Quartets are not to have.

But first there is a final visit to the question of language and art, in their relationship to creation, linking back with the appropriate passages in 'Burnt Norton' (part v, ll. 1–22), 'East Coker' (part II, opening of second section; part v, ll. 1–18), and 'Little Gidding' (the Mallarmé reference in part II). Perhaps the most important context of all is the opening of *Burnt Norton*, part I (ll. 11–18), where the phrases I have already commented on seem a perfect formula to describe *Four Quartets* in all but its few weaker passages – while this section of 'Little Gidding' sounds, in contrast, a little 'pedantic' itself. Eliot might almost be offering a few rules for 'classical' poetry – useful enough for beginners, but only dubiously convincing if they herald a final 'ordering' of this poem itself. Rather interestingly, it reminds me of the description of the rustic dancers in part I of 'East Coker' – though the verse there is finer; and any echo here may be intended or not (I have never been able to decide).

The next section is undoubtedly the moment of Christian resolution.

> And any action
> Is a step to the block, to the fire, down the sea's throat
> Or to an illegible stone: and that is where we start.

So, various moments of death are once more conjured up – King Charles, on the memorable morning on 30 January 1649, (Marvell's

words from the 'Horatian Ode' were no doubt in Eliot's mind);
Christian martyrs through the centuries, notably perhaps St Thomas
à Becket; the many dead at sea, who had haunted Eliot's imagination
from those very early days in Massachusetts; and the 'illegible stone'
retaining its secrets, along with our 'backward look behind the
assurance / Of recorded history . . . towards the primitive terror'.
Ends and beginnings: each scene recurs, vivid and isolated as it has
been throughout the Quartets, like a snapshot held in the memory.
Christian readers will inevitably think also of the Cross on Good
Friday, the empty tomb two mornings after; all readers will recall
certain personal moments of happiness, sorrow, vision, unexorcised
memory. Throughout the Quartets, the theme expounded so
powerfully in 'Burnt Norton' has been gathering substance; and
now, after the mysterious passage about the dead departing and
returning, we come to words which express with peculiar power the
vertical permanent relationship of each moment to eternity. Once
more we are in the chapel at Little Gidding, at the moment when this
Quartet opened; and, after the intervening development, in some
ways so puzzling, the serenity of tone once more attests insight, calm,
arrival:

> The moment of the rose and the moment of the yew-tree
> Are of equal duration. A people without history
> Is not redeemed from time, for history is a pattern
> Of timeless moments. So, while the light fails
> On a winter's afternoon, in a secluded chapel
> History is now and England.

Could this be followed? The lines have remained in my own mind,
since I first read them, ineffaceably – enacting what they say and, I
think, permanently influencing my own sense both of time and of
history. That they belong more with faith than with sight (or with
experience) is of course apparent, since bereavement and mortality
remain irrevocable as everyday fact. Yet I feel that Eliot is talking of
something more potent than Proustian moments or immensely
personal memories (potent though these are, in their own right); and
that if I am myself basically a religious person, believing in eternity,
it is more for these reasons, backed by the force generated in 'Burnt
Norton', than for any reason of a more structured or orthodox kind.
Though the insight is associated with a chapel, it transcends formal
religion; the very choice of Little Gidding – 'Not in the scheme of
generation' – ensured this effect.

Finally, we have the beautiful, isolated line – at last a voice
answering *our* searching – and the climax, where numinous echoes
recur, meet, and cohere for the last time.

If I have a minor criticism, it is of the poem's last three lines: I would rather it had ended with the third repetition of Lady Julian's words. Partly, this is because 'the tongues of flame' are still not, for me, Whitsun (in the terms of this poem); partly, because the final line has just a touch of Dantesque pastiche. Before this, there is a marvellous evocation of the last homecoming – a passage which has a parallel in English only, I think, in Vaughan's 'The Retreat'. The famous lines

> A condition of complete simplicity
> (Costing not less than everything)

are as justified, I think, as Yeats's 'All mere complexities' in 'Byzantium'. After a lifelong wrestling with anguish and doubt, Eliot is entitled to tell us that 'complete simplicity' is possible, and to announce the price. To some degree, of course, these final assertions must be taken on trust, since they depend entirely on the simple happening 'in the draughty church at smokefall' which we first heard of in 'Burnt Norton', though with no clue then to its ultimate meaning. As I realised when discussing that poem, Eliot had nine years further to travel before he ended 'Little Gidding', and it would be naïve to suppose that he himself understood at the time how *Four Quartets* would end (or maybe that *Four Quartets* would ever exist). The exploration we have been following is as absorbing, modern and honest as anything known to me; nor could the path to be travelled from 'Burnt Norton' to 'Little Gidding' have been bypassed.

Final Note

I have pointed to an openness in 'Little Gidding', which may or may not be accepted as one of its structural features; individual readers will test the notion for themselves. For some years I imagined that this final Quartet was intended to resolve all the paradoxes explored in the previous poems, by weaving them into a final movement where prayer and the Holy Spirit perform a final transfiguring of temporal anomalies from the realm outside time.

Since I first read the *Quartets*, my own religious views have evolved considerably, and doubtless this is true of all readers who regard 'exploring' – a major theme of the *Quartets* – as life's unending work. The directions in which an individual moves are not directly relevant to criticism, though how far his own critical judgements are affected, who is to say? I have become personally convinced (though this is not the place to argue it) that, while the ultimate 'greatness' of many works of art remains, for me, a constant, my interpretation of them, and certain nuances of judgement, have indeed changed. In his 'Ode on a Grecian Urn', Keats reminded us that works of art have foster-parents, as well as their creator; how far these alter not only a work of art in *its* time-scale, but a single reader in his own shorter one, is not easy to say. For Keats, the foster-parents can be named – 'silence and slow time' – and marvellously imaged; and this thinking is not alien to Eliot, though he early gave it critical formulation and a more formidable scope:

> No poet, no artist of any art, has his complete meaning alone. His significance, his appreciation is the appreciation of his relation to the dead poets and artists. You cannot value him alone; you must set him, for contrast and comparison, among the dead. I mean this as a principle of aesthetic, not merely historical, criticism. The necessity that he shall conform, that he shall cohere, is not onesided; what happens when a new work of art is created is something that happens simultaneously to all the works of art which preceded it. The existing monuments form an ideal order among themselves, which is modified by the introduction of the new (the really new) work of art among them. The existing order is complete before the new work arrives; for order to persist after the supervention of novelty, the *whole* existing order must be, if ever so slightly, altered; and so the relations, proportions, values of each work of art towards the whole are readjusted; and this is conformity between the old and the new. Whoever has approved this idea of order, of the form of European, of English literature will not find it preposterous that the past should be altered by the present as much as the present is directed by the past. And the poet who is aware of this will be aware of great difficulties and responsibilities.   ('Tradition and the Individual Talent' (1919), in
> *Selected Essays*, p. 15.)

This passage admittedly does concern itself with objective, if elusive, changes, and begs important questions in its own right. Why, I wonder, did Eliot confine himself to Europe (and then narrow this to England); would he have realised, or approved, the immense change which world, and negro, culture were shortly to bring? Again, he assumes some kind of critical consensus, seemingly allied to 'the Mind of Europe', which can already be seen to belong to a singularly narrow mould. Marxist or Islamic critics, or critics with other distinctive premises, would readily agree to the past's being 'altered' – often in ways far more drastic than Eliot seems to have had in mind. It is maybe odd, also, that Eliot does not allow for alterations relating to the inner journey of individual critics, through their own lifetimes – and to the possibility that the 'order of art' changes, also, against the 'order of life'.

I admire 'Little Gidding' almost as much as I did when I first knew it, but my attitude towards it has, with the passing of time, changed far more completely than I should have expected. Certain passages remain almost flawless as poetry, however one reads them; but I see the Quartet now not as a 'great Christian poem', but as the last, and perhaps most teasing, enigma that the poet left.

As will be apparent, 'Burnt Norton' strikes me (as it always has done) as his greatest poem, whether considered alone, or seen as the first movement of this most complex whole. Its exploration of 'time' probes a mystery that has never failed to fascinate me, and, considered purely aesthetically, transcends any other complete artefact that Eliot achieved.

The two central Quartets are simpler, yet full of beauty; I have picked the slow movement, 'The Dry Salvages', as personally the most haunting Quartet, in its quiet way.

This brings me then to a final comment, along with a question of poetic 'unity' that evades any answer I can find. If 'The Dry Salvages' had ended the sequence, leaving three Quartets, not four, to posterity, would the poem have seemed incomplete; or simply different? 'The Dry Salvages' would very evidently have left the work open-ended, though its fifth movement would have made a Christian resolution possible (I doubt whether the claim could go beyond this).

'Little Gidding' still leaves an open ending possible, if my analysis is accepted, but makes it far easier for dogmatic Christians to claim the whole work as 'theirs'. If so, then I think they are wrong: the poem is less 'dogmatic' than its creator even on the most 'Christian' reading (and, of course, never trust the teller, trust the tale).

We cannot be sure how far Eliot anticipated 'Little Gidding' when he wrote 'Burnt Norton': it is certain that he could not leap over the middle Quartets. We know also that, between 'Burnt Norton' and 'East Coker' he spent much time wrestling with *The Family Reunion*, which shares some of the first Quartet's images, but puts them to far different use.

However this may be, no one in his senses would regret 'Little Gidding', or doubt its crucial importance to the work we now have. Perhaps it is the final authentication of the insight that, though planned, works of art have their own dynamic, following laws of structure, art, language, and (of course) 'life'. Now that it exists, *Four Quartets* is a unity, a single poem, and not more elusive, after all, than most really great art. Whether its achievement of this status held larger elements of chance than is usual in such works, may therefore, be no longer critically relevant. Even so, Helen Gardener's account of the genesis makes fascinating reading, and is indispensable to anyone wanting further help of *this* track.

3 The Poetry of R. S. Thomas : What Resource ?

It is this great absence
that is like a presence, that compels
me to address it without hope
of a reply. It is a room I enter

from which someone has just
gone, the vestibule for the arrival
of one who has not yet come.
I modernise the anachronism

of my language, but he is no more here
than before. Genes and molecules
have no more power to call
him up than the incense of the Hebrews

at their altars. My equations fail
as my words do. What resource have I
other than the emptiness without him of my whole
being, a vacuum he may not abhor?

('The Absence')

I

Always the same hills
Crowd the horizon,
Remote witnesses
Of the still scene.

And in the foreground
The tall Cross,
Sombre, untenanted,
Aches for the Body
That is back in the cradle
Of a maid's arms.

('Pietà')

'Always the same hills'; R. S. Thomas's poems usually begin in a very distinctive manner. The first line does not appear to be the logical start of a particular thought, or even of a particular experience or event, but to be the moment when some profoundly meditated anguish, or image, forces itself into words. Immense silence of the hills, in the background. History, waiting still longer, for its dead centre. The Virgin, surely not weeping as she receives the Body. A man, brooding on life, and focusing on a brilliant lyrical or dramatic image, or startling statement, as some long notion intensifies and compresses itself towards form. The poem is precipitated, with unusual and brooding power, into the ambience where it then exists: language, submitting after long struggle, to will.

'Always': many of R. S. Thomas's poems home in upon a vivid image which is characteristically in, but not of, time. Some perception, arrested in time and space, acquires tragic or elemental colouring for the reader, momentarily before he senses, also, the consolation ('Dear parents, I forgive you my life'; 'Yes: that's how I was'; 'It will always win'; 'I want you to know how it was'). The consolation, coming as it does from some region of consciousness or creation wholly different from the often savage insight, is hard to pin down. Some long-built-up or pent-up force is precipitated, and the poem as a whole seems to be precisely the right weight, and length, to bear it. Only once or twice, as in the beautiful 'The airy tomb', does Thomas take a longer flight, floating more serenely above his sombre tale.

All of Thomas's readers recognise this tone – which one calls Welsh, or laconic, or lacerating, or ironically detached, or bitterly compassionate, or rarely empathetic, or universally human, for all these apparent contraries meet in it – only, it is never despairing, though the word 'despair' sometimes rings out unforgettably. There is pared down linguistic austerity, always reaching towards some apparent simplicity – though when Thomas encounters other people's attempts in this direction, they may wryly amuse him.

> Rose Cottage, because it had
> Roses! If all things were as
> Simple. . . .

Yet this search is also pre-eminently his own, the endlessly sought-after illusion of his kind of art. Kingsley Amis has written of it perceptively in words which, recognising the note of linguistic sparseness, draw attention also to the complex and vivid imagery that accompanies this: 'His imagery, thickly clustered as it frequently is, and made to proliferate and interconnect with great brilliance, is built upon a simple foundation of earth, trees, snow, stars, and wild creatures. To describe the effect of his work it is enough to say that he often moves to tears, and that certain lines of his impress themselves instantly, and perhaps ineradicably on the mind.'

'Pietà' is one of those rare short poems that keeps most of its secret, look at it though we will. One has to go to 'Western Wind' and one or two of the ballads, to 'The Sick Rose', and Blake's lyrics, to a rather rare species of poetry in fact, to find similar effects. It is precisely the kind of poem that the Imagists wanted to write, but somehow never could; the Imagist theories are fascinating, but where is even one Imagist poem that lives up to them? As Thomas himself has laconically noted, 'It seems that it is always easier for poets to evolve theories of language than to stick to them.' In 'Pietà' it seems that all the human emotions are transferred to objects apparently inanimate, and the real emotion, the grief beyond expression, to the Cross. The hills 'Crowd the horizon', suddenly very much present, yet still 'Remote' as they watch; and the scene remains 'still'. And then, as is Thomas's way, the strange note enters – an effect encountered also, though in a very different mood and with more conscious theological point, in the famous Good Friday hymn

> Crux fidelis, inter omnes
> Arbor una nobilis:
> Nulla silva talem profert,
> Fronde, flore, germine. . . .
>
> Dulce lignum, dulce clavos,
> Dulce pondus sustinet.

The instrument of death and torture has, as instrument of salvation, its own ineffable moment, and its own dereliction. For thirty years or so the Virgin has 'ached' with Christ, perhaps never more than at the foot of the Cross; for three hours his body has ached on the Cross, to the point of death. But it is not the Virgin, or Christ, who aches in this poem: it is the Cross itself, 'Sombre, untenanted' (marvellous word), which grieves, its purpose fulfilled now (*consummatum est*) and the tree, which went to make it, good now only for superstition, or decay, or burning, like any other wood in the world. It is not as if Thomas is telling us that human torturers suffer with their victims, but something far more elusive, more totally and inexorably Christian. If this weird and eerie paradox means anything, it means salvation ('salvation acquired by an increased guilt', as he writes in a later poem). *Rex tremendae majestatis*: and should the Cross which, in its destined moment, has been the death of the King, not ache in bereavement as the Body leaves it – for what created thing could fulfil such a role, and not take on something of the consciousness and pain? In this short poem, life passes into death; the Christ is dead, his voice which raised others will not raise himself; Easter morning is an infinity away. So, at the end, Christ returns to the beginning, to the arms of the maid. She has lost him in life, through the normal processes of adulthood, and perhaps in a way special also to herself in its pain ('Woman, what have I to do with you?' – John 2:4; 'Then one said to him, behold, your mother and your brethren stand outside desiring to speak with you. But he answered and said, Who is my mother? and who are my brethren? And he stretched his hand towards his disciples, and said, Behold, my mother and my brethren' – Matthew 12:47–50; 'And it happened as he spoke these things, a certain woman of the company lifted her voice and said to him, Blessed is the womb that bore you, and the paps that you have sucked. But He said, Yes rather, blessed are they that hear the word of the Lord, and keep it' – Luke 11:27–8; 'And if any man come to me and hate not his father, and mother, and wife, and children, and brethren, and sisters, yes and his own life also, he cannot be my disciple' – Luke 14:26). Again, she has lost him now in death. Her own paps no longer give milk, and if they could it would be useless. At the moment of *pietà*, the beginning comes full circle, and is *really* the end. It is the moment when Christ is totally human, and totally dead. All he has said and suffers remains now in the balance, in vacuum. Only the Cross feels and 'Aches' since it, at least, has had its moment and its grief, and is now finished with, whatever other end there might be.

'Pietà' is a poem which contains as many subtle intimations as does Michelangelo's carving. Everything that is not present in both – the incredible absences – contributes to the effect. ('There were days', Thomas writes in a later poem about the Holy Spirit, 'so beautiful the emptiness / it might have filled, / its absence / was as its presence.') Could the tone be described as neutral? Only, I would say, in the most literal sense. There is a longer extract I want to quote, from the same source as my previous shorter prose quotation, Thomas's pamphlet *Words and the Poet* (1964):

> One must take words as one finds them, and make them sing and here arises another question: Are words the poet's servant or master? We are familiar, no doubt, with Mr Eliot's pessimistic conclusions in 'East Coker', although he wins through to some sort of détente in 'Little Gidding'. I think that any practising poet would also agree that there can be no hard and fast rule in this matter. Most poets compose with great difficulty, choosing and

rejecting and altering their words, until often their finished draft bears little relation to what they began with. In this way the poet would seem to be the master, forcing the words to do the bidding of his conscious mind. Yet this, also, is a travesty of the position. Words have surprising resilience, and get their own way often by appearing to yield. The idea of the poet's eye 'in a fine frenzy rolling' and of the words flowing ready mixed with the ink off the tip of his pen is, of course, a fiction. Yet here again most poets could tell of periods of inspiration of varying length, when the words and lines did appear to come with agreeable ease. And although we have Yeats' words as a warning against being deceived by an appearance of ease, we also have it on Mr Vernon Watkins' authority that he said, too, that a poem is a piece of luck. This is a pregnant statement, but certainly one aspect of it has to do with words themselves – lucky finding or perception of the right word.

II

Dropped without joy from the gaunt womb he lies,
Maturing in his place against his parent's ageing;
The slow scene unfolds before his luckless eyes
To the puckered window, where the cold storm's raging
Curtains the world, and the grey curlew cries,
Uttering a grief too sharp for the breast's assuaging.

So the days will drift into months, and the months to years,
Moulding his mouth to silence, his hand to the plough;
And the world will grow to a few lean acres of grass,
And an orchard of stars in the night's unscaleable boughs.
But see, at the bare field's edge, where he'll surely pass,
An ash tree wantons with sensuous body and smooth,
Provocative limbs to play the whore to his youth,
Till hurled with hot haste into manhood he woos and weds
A wife, half wild, half shy of the ancestral bed,
The crumbling house, and the whisperers on the stairs.

('Country Child')

This takes us back to Thomas's early work, from *Song at the Year's Turning*. A whole life passes in synopsis, and the slow movement of the verse, strongly lyrical in beauty, co-operates with the suggestion of completeness in a sequence indebted to words such as 'Dropped', 'Maturing', 'slow scene', 'days', 'Months', 'years', 'Moulding', 'grow', 'unscaleable', 'Surely pass', 'crumbling'. Inside this sketch of a whole slow life, the four penultimate lines suggest the vivid immediacy of the one episode in different tempo – sexuality, lust, hasty marriage, followed again by long routine. What might have seemed wasted or humdrum strikes us rather as typical, and not undignified; the skeleton of life stripped bare. In balance with the sombre notes ('without joy', 'gaunt', 'puckered', 'luckless', 'lean', 'bare') there are other suggestions of richness (the common inheritance of 'grey curlew calls', 'an orchard of stars', 'sensuous body and smooth') and, amid these, the universality of the quest, 'night's unscaleable boughs' (an inescapable cosmic egalitarianism, for philosopher or fool); and the eternal round of birth, generation and death. Though austere, it is far from depressing; there is nothing here remotely like the *Waste Land* disgust. The tone is attuned to human isolation, but the overtones will seem either tragic, or religious, perhaps to different readers at different times.

If this 'country child' is not Iago Prytherch, he is at least kin to him, and Iago is the acknowledged centre of much of Thomas's self. 'A peasant' presents Iago as 'an ordinary man of the bald Welsh hills', who is also almost imbecile. Phrases such as 'half-witted grin', 'spittled mirth' prepare the way for these lines:

> And then at night see him fixed in his chair
> Motionless, except when he leans to gob in the fire.
> There is something frightening in the vacancy of his mind.

But who is frightened? Is it the cultured man, looking on, and perhaps judging Iago; or perhaps rather judging his own reactions to Iago, whatever these are? Or is it *Homo sapiens* – a wider concept – seeking the image of God in himself, and finding it here? The poem goes on, rather obliquely, to turn 'refined' and 'affected' into near synonyms (perhaps begging a question) and, inside this uneasy simplification, to allow to Iago 'naturalness', possibly in contrast to ourselves:

> His clothes, sour with years of sweat
> And animal contact, shock the refined,
> But affected, sense with their stark naturalness.

The poem culminates in the reminder 'This is your prototype' – but a prototype of deprived, uncultured man, or of man himself? The word 'naturalness' hangs over the question, acquiring its own question-mark. The qualities pointed to are resilience, perseverance, continuance of the stock against all discouragements of poverty and ignorance, and a stoicism which is even heroic:

Remember him, then, for he, too, is a winner of wars,
Enduring like a tree under the curious stars.

The word 'too' openly faces a reader with the choice of whether or
not to include himself. It he decides against, does he deny himself
'naturalness'; and is he asserting superiority of some kind, or the
reverse? ' . . . Curious', the qualification of the watching 'stars',
hangs poised over the human enigma also; 'winner of wars'. But, if
Iago is in any sense to be a primitivist ideal, this can only be against
the irony of a corresponding lower version of any 'civilised'
alternative.

In later poems about Iago, R. S. Thomas faces the underlying
problems in differing contexts. The poem 'Which?' turns the
questions upon himself. How far has his own depiction of Iago been
a distortion, perhaps influenced by role-playing ('was he a real man
. . .?'; 'Was he a survival / Of a lost past . . .?'; 'Could I have said he
was the scholar / Of the field's pages . . .?'; '. . . or nature's fool?')?
This is in *Tares* (1961), where the opening poem, 'The Dark Well', is
not only the most memorable of the Prytherch poems, but an
admission that this man has been of outstanding importance to
Thomas himself in the two spheres of his life that matter most, priest
and poet. Iago is both the man who, in his need, has drawn Thomas's
'slow / Charity' (not an automatic response, but a hard lesson and a
willed path) and who, in his inner life, apprehended by empathy, has
initiated the poet into tragic vision. The austerity of tone again
penetrates to a level where the personal merges with the religious,
without bypassing the crucial personal challenges:

They see you as they see you,
A poor farmer with no name,
Ploughing cloudward, sowing the wind
With squalls of gulls at the day's end.
To me you are Prytherch, the man
Who more than all directed my slow
Charity where there was need.

There are two hungers, hunger for bread
And hunger of the uncouth soul
For the light's grace I have seen both,
And chosen for an indulgent world's
Ear the story of one whose hands
Have bruised themselves on the locked doors
Of life; whose heart, fuller than mine
Of gulped tears, is the dark well
From which to draw, drop after drop,
The terrible poetry of his kind.

The twice repeated 'they' of the opening line surely includes city dwellers passing in cars, careless observers, the contented citizens of 'modernity' – all those who attract the poet's contempt, whenever they appear in his work. The 'me' of l. 5 must equally certainly be *close* to the poet himself, however we strive to avoid naïve identification. (Perhaps my use of the term 'R. S. Thomas' or 'the poet' instead of the now almost obligatory 'the persona' has already raised some eyebrows; in fact, R. S. Thomas does use personae, perhaps increasingly, and it is one of the matters that will be raised; at present, I am assuming a sufficient closeness of the poet to the speaker in the Prytherch poems for the distinction not to be crucial.) The sting in 'indulgent' is obvious, but the phrase 'fuller than mine' concedes to the inarticulate peasant an intensity of experience, which demands a Yeatsian awareness of paradox – 'terrible poetry' / 'terrible beauty'. In 'Affinity', from *Song at the Year's Turning*, the peasant's uncouth stupidity and squalor are presented in a manner suggesting the simple indictment of social injustice; yet the title, and the poem's direction alike, challenge us directly, if we think ourselves superior:

> Ransack your brainbox, pull out the drawers
> That rot in your heart's dust, and what have you to give
> To enrich his spirit or the way he lives?
> From the standpoint of education or caste or creed
> Is there anything to show that your essential need
> Is less than his, who has the world for church . . .?

And the moral (following the undefined 'essential', and the perhaps deliberately vague 'for church') is that an equation of 'superior' or 'inferior', worked out in social terms, simply disappears when we search for a common humanity:

> Don't be taken in
> By stinking garments or an aimless grin;
> He also is human, and the same small star,
> That lights you homeward, has inflamed his mind
> With the old hunger, born of his kind.

'The Hill Farmer Speaks' makes this assertion still more directly, offering to the farmer, unnamed in this case, the poet's gift of articulation and the poet's view of him, in order to culminate in one insistent statement:

> The dirt is under my cracked nails;
> The tale of my life is smirched with dung;

The phlegm rattles. But what I am saying
Over the grasses rough with dew
Is, Listen, listen, I am a man like you.

The poem actually called 'Iago Prytherch' (1958), carries the poet's
felt relationship to Iago still further. There is indeed guilt; yet not the
simple guilt that someone intent on social amelioration might
expect. The poet asks Iago's forgiveness for naming him – whilst
acknowledging also that, because of Iago's isolation and illiteracy, he
is never likely to know that poems about him even exist. There is the
plea for further forgiveness, for having 'made fun of you', and for
having 'pitied': yet the poem immediately asserts that these are not
true charges, but accusations 'gracelessly made' – presumably by
readers or reviewers of the earlier poems who have either simplified
Thomas's attitude into mere snobbery, or berated it for fooling
around with tragic universals when a Marxist critique and the
appropriate clichés are itching to get onto the page. The poem ends
with the poet acknowledging, as he often does, the failure of any
'word' to describe his feelings; thereby pointing either to a defect in
his own craft, or to a necessary defect in language (one of the themes
increasingly important in later volumes).

Fun? Pity? No word can describe
My true feelings. I passed and saw you
Labouring there, your dark figure
Marring the simple geometry
Of the square fields with its gaunt question.
My poems were made in its long shadow
Falling closely across the page.

A 'gaunt question' and 'long shadow'. Thomas is after all a poet of
images, believing these to go far beyond concepts. In discursive
language, communication is precise, and ambiguity offensive; but
all art belongs with those ambiguities of feeling, of sensibility, that
are built irrevocably into consciousness itself. Poetry and art may
indeed result in action, at second remove; but the action is not the
meaning of the art. There are moments when one senses that
Thomas *might* want some commitment from his reader; but even the
nature of this is not clear. Are the poems at one level a defence of
Wales, of Welsh nationalism even, and by the same token an attack
on England, or alien culture, or the 'modern' world? But we have
only to look at the multivalence, touching both poet and readers, to
realise that the effects are not to be contained in such terms.

It is perfectly clear that Thomas is unhappy with Iago's
predicament, unhappy too with himself and his putative readers;

and that the undercurrents are too deep and mysterious fully to chart. The poems have also however, their concrete lucidity, which for habitual readers is, more than anything, a distinctive tone. Thomas is one of those poets who is always and immediately recognisable, whether we chose to use the term 'poet' or 'persona' to describe this seal of his power.

We could say that Iago is certainly a victim, cut off from culture and poetry, and cut off too (but here is a *real* problem) from religion – or from the religion, at least, of a highly literate priest. We could say too, with some certainty, that Thomas does question his own 'refinement', and ours, if this runs to elitism – which he is honest enough to see as unavoidable temptation, and likewise as part of a truth.

Yet Iago has an elemental reality and power in his life which is in part to be envied; 'the machine' comes, to hill farmers, at best as a dubious friend. We might decide that this is not unlike Gray's ambiguous feelings for the 'unlettered dead' of his 'Elegy': he pities yet envies their ignorance, their solitude, their very unfulfilment – the mute Miltons, and the guiltless Cromwells alike. Yet the pity is tinged with guilt: what do his letters do for him? And, the paths of glory lead but to the grave. As for the envy, it may come from his heart, or it may come rather from weariness; it may be an envy as much for the death of these simple folk as for their once death-in-life. The poet more than half identifies with them, or wishes to, in their simplicity; yet draws back from the thought of really being unlettered and uncouth himself. Such conflicting reactions can be sneered at (and are, by some critics), but art of Gray's power, and still more Thomas's, evades such attack. The poems are after all (one returns to this) images, and stand or fall by their fidelity to the experience evoked.

The startling aspect of R. S. Thomas may be his deliberate refusal of the egalitarian challenge, which looms so much more directly in our time than it did for Gray. It is central for many great artists, at least since Dickens, and Thomas will not be forgiven, by some, for keeping it at the periphery of his vision, and his art. Should Pip have stayed at the forge, and avoided snobbery; or was he right to accept the great expectations, with their social risks? Should young people today accept grants, and go to universities; or should they keep their 'working-class culture', or its myth, beautifully intact? The case of Iago and his like may seem still more urgent, since, if we believe in art, how can we be reconciled to such a condition of life? If we believe in social justice, there is another strong challenge; which may (or may not) point in the same direction as the first. But if we are seeking the image of man, the image of God, the meaning of existence, then are the implications not bound to be of another kind? What has education to do with virtue, civilisation with resilience? Where shall we find the truest images of man's cosmic plight?

R. S. Thomas is not only concerned with poetic fidelity to mixed love-and-hate relationships (though the psychology of this is endemic in the depiction of his peasants, his parishioners, his country, his religion, and not least of himself). He is concerned still more basically with the present and future destiny of the poor forked creature, who might be a god in exile as well. Thomas has his great hatred of hedonism, garishness, vulgarity, modern urban culture – and the barren Wales of the hill farmers could have for him some touch of the gospel blessing of poverty, however disguised. It could equally be the place where religion has its deepest reality – as much in Iago Prytherch, Evans, Job Davies even ('Live large man; and dream small') as in the priest on his knees in long, bare vigils by the untenanted cross.

In the later poems, the religious questions are directly confronted, and perhaps *Pietà* and *Laboratories of the Spirit* are the best texts for the discussion of these. But in the early poems, from the first in fact, we are aware that the poet who might choose to ignore or despise much of the specifically 'modern' cannot evade our modern religious crisis of doubt. If our most serious need is for identity, meaning, apprehended divinity, then we all start today with the apparent absence of God. We cannot evade the findings of Darwin, Freud, Einstein, and their questions, we cannot evade the failure of discursive reason, and dogma, to satisfy the religious need. Perhaps, in the end, this may prove to be a blessing, and the recovery of doubt will be looked back upon as necessary prelude to the recovery of religion in its deepest sense. Maybe we need to get past episcopal bureaucracy, the creeds, the decaying remnants of Christendom, to come to the place where the religion of the East, of the Greeks, of Christ and the early Christians starts. The nails, the Cross, the empty tomb – those strange enigmas are a better clue perhaps – the first two of which, at least, recur in the imagery of Thomas's world. In 'The Airy Tomb', we read that

> each tick of the clock
> Was a nail knocked in the lid of the coffin
> Of that pale, spent woman, who sat with death
> Jogging her elbow

– and later, when her son is alone, 'But never a voice replied / From that grim house, nailed to the mountain side'. But the point hardly needs labouring. And, again in these early poems, R. S. Thomas faces the possible consquences of an empty universe more directly than

many more consciously intellectual moderns have always done. If
intellect leads nowhere, and sensitivity debilitates, is Iago not a more
viable, as well as accurate image than, say, the poet and his readers,
of 'man himself' – alone with the visible world? And what right have
we to think that virtue and beauty are in any sense 'natural'? (But, if
we cease to think them so, then the mystery of what they portened
may again appear.) The poem 'Valediction' begins with a sharp sense
that the poet has been deceived into thinking a peasant (not this time
Iago) naturally beautiful, simply because he works in beautiful if
bleak scenery. Later, he has been abruptly disabused of this view, by
some violence or treachery directed towards himself. He knows
(presumably) that the fault is partly his own, as it must be when
expectations are projected on to people for no better reason than
some wish or delusion in oneself. Yet he says that the farmer who has
'failed' him cannot make a merely Hobbesian plea on the grounds of
'nature': there is a 'human potential' which can be accepted or
rejected by all men, however humble they are:

> Unnatural and inhuman, your wild ways
> Are not sanctioned; you are condemned
> By man's potential stature. . . .

And, though this farmer, like Iago, has been denied the knowledge of
this 'potential' through literacy and art, he could still have learned it
from 'the grace that trees and flowers labour to teach'.

What exactly is implied here? Thomas is not a Wordsworthian
poet, and his 'nature' is not Wordsworth's; it is history, rather than
divinity, which he responds to most, in the bleak beauty of Wales. In
Christian terms, Thomas is not a poet of the transfiguration, of the
resurrection, of human holiness: despite 'Farm Wife', 'The Country
Clergy' and one or two poems where supernatural grace may be
hinted at, he more usually sees 'nature' spelled out in the peasants we
have been considering and their like. He is a poet of the Cross, the
unanswered prayer, the bleak trek through darkness, and his
theology of Jesus, in particular, seems strange against any known
traditional norm.

But, equally certainly, he is not a determinist poet, but a believer in
the free acceptance of life, whatever its offered terms. He always
avoids the naïveté of those who imagine that contact with nature, or
with culture or art or education or religion or any other single
influence, has an automatic power to ennoble, or even make good.
By the same token, R. S. Thomas is saved from the equally fatalistic
pessimism which may set in when those who start from this view
come to a point of disillusionment – as they surely must sooner or
later, for one experiential reason or another. Thomas's view, I take

it, is the more normal Pauline and Christian one, which is that things that are good, true, pure, lovely *tend* to work for good, if one chooses to be open to their influence and celebrate them, but that the choice whether to accept, or reject, the influence remains open. The mystery of good and evil is, after all, central; and in Thomas it is all the more impressive for not being identified with partly faked or superficial dilemmas such as pre-modern versus modern, civilised versus uncivilised, or even urban versus rural, but rather found in the inner tensions of the people he knows best.

It seems, then, that in finding in the Welsh peasants a 'prototype' of man, Thomas is making a universal statement, which may chime in with modern doubt, yet which equally has its roots in Christian paradox. This pared-down existence, in a land of ruined beauty belonging to the past, is more human than any educated sophistication. Or perhaps one should say, it is more truly symbolic of the human predicament, as educated sophistication now often understands it to be, than such educated sophistication is itself. Some such paradox does, I think underlie the other complexities; and explains why the social challenges do not emerge in any simpler form.

III

So we may turn to the poet; or, at least, to the poems where he seems to present himself most directly; or where we feel we have most directly tracked him down. I have already touched on the problems involved in this, particularly with a poet so rooted in his own country, his own situation, and his own tone. Of course R. S. Thomas *does* speak to us directly, and is not obsessively concerned to plead artistic detachment and disappear. On the other hand, he is a complex and – paradoxically in a poet, perhaps – a reticent personality, whose lucidity is clearly the product of highly wrought art. Often, he seems to be surveying his people, his themes, himself from an immense distance, even when remarkable empathy is also achieved. We recognise also that in poems so notably selected, distilled, refined, both in language and in evoked experience, any self-revelation must be very directly controlled by artistic form. R. S. Thomas is nothing like a 'confessional' poet, either in intention or by accident, and is not – I suspect – beyond laying false clues, with wry amusement, when in the mood. There is the further factor that, in recent volumes, he has become notably more experimental, so that it becomes increasingly difficult to regard any statement as unequivocally 'his'.

Among the earlier work, 'Twentieth-century Pharisee' should not be forgotten, as a piece of apparent self-satire which no one will swallow whole. We might next remember 'Sick Visits', a wonderfully accurate description of a geriatric ward, with a pastor visiting, where it is easy to believe that 'They keep me sober, the old ladies' is a statement fairly directly related to his own work:

> Some are like blonde dolls,
> Their joints twisted:
> Life in its brief play
> Was a bit rough.
> Some fumble
> With thick tongue for words
> And are deaf;
> Shouting their faint names
> I listen:
> They are far off,
> The echoes return slow.

Without them, he ends, 'I would have gone wild, / Drinking earth's huge drafts / Of joy and woe'. The Blakean echo here ('Man was made for joy and woe') seems highly personal; and we recall that Thomas quite often mutates well-known Christian formulae in a way which takes us close to his own sensibility. In 'A Blackbird Singing', for example, the resounding 'It seems wrong' of the opening records a feeling that total dualism would be almost more appropriate than the actual mingling, in the bird's song, of black and beautiful; and the phrase 'Love, joy and grief', describing the song itself, would *be* the fruit of the Spirit, as listed by both St Paul and St John, were it not for the substitution of 'grief' for 'peace'.

Still more personal, it seems, is 'Judgment Day' – marvellously bleak and austere, and infused with bitter self-knowledge:

> Yes, that's how I was,
> I know that face,
> That bony figure
> Without grace
> Of flesh or limb;
> In health happy,
> Careless of the claim
> Of the world's sick
> Of the world's poor:
> In pain craven –
> Lord, breathe once more
> On that sad mirror,
> Let me be lost

In mist for ever
Rather than own
Such bleak reflections.
Let me go back
On my two knees
Slowly to undo
The knot of life
That was tied there.

The profoundly serious pun 'Own / Such bleak reflections' suggests that the poem is a mirror, in which the poet catches sight of himself – as we might see our physical reflection, in a street suddenly, caught unawares. But the clarity is startling: is it not more usual to see images perhaps rose-coloured, perhaps unendurable, but seldom with this almost clinical mingling of the detached and penitent? I think this may be our vital clue; obviously, this is in no simple sense 'the poet himself'. His own bone structure – suitably Welsh – is far from graceless, and the charges 'Careless', 'craven' could not remotely be about *this* poet (or, if they should be, where does that leave the rest of us?). The truth is that true self-detachment is impossible, but moments of very unadorned self-knowledge are sometimes granted by God, as a necessary gift – the surgeon's knife, or the lanced wound. As always, in fact, the experience is universalised – the answer to Charles Wesley's plea 'Show me, as my soul can bear, / The depth of inbred sin', meeting at *this* point, the exact conjunction of God's measured gift and human stoicism. One step further, and such experience could carry us into the morbid territory that makes a Steppenwolf, or a suicide; but Thomas catches it at the moment when it is mercifully healing and *sane* – precipitating the kind of anguished prayer that is somehow taken and honoured, so that there is genuine catharsis.

Why does one know so certainly that this poem does not belong with modern absurdism, but with religious faith? No doubt because the poet survives, and there are other poems. I take this poem not as self-revelation simply, but as the calculated evocation of one of those moments (and they are not always apparent in Thomas) when the ubiquitous Cross is felt *as* a place of healing, after all.

The same balance is apparent, I fancy, in other poems which certainly relate to the poet's life, and might be mistaken for direct statements. One such is 'Ap Hew's Testament', which is admittedly deliberately distanced by its title. The grave and compressed consideration of 'the four people in my life' is unforgettable, again because of its universality. For everyone reading the poem, 'Father, mother, wife / And the one child' will be a different story, but the quality of comment – vividly dramatic through sheer compression –

has a granite-like ring of truth. It is perhaps because the poem so totally steers clear of distracting particulars, and of any explicit judgements, that its words 'echo thus in your mind':

> My mother gave me the breast's milk
> Generously, but grew mean after,
> Envying me my detached laughter.
>
> My father was a passionate man,
> Wrecked after leaving the sea
> In her love's shallows. He grieves in me.
>
> What shall I say of my boy,
> Tall, fair? He is young yet;
> Keep his feet free of the world's net.

The purification is clean, and akin to blessing. Any bitterness seems to be cauterised, by some stern will. A similar effect is encountered in the still briefer 'Gifts', from *Pietà*, where giving and taking with all possible generosity, and no illusion, is again distilled to quintessence:

> From my father my strong heart,
> My weak stomach.
> From my mother the fear.
>
> From my sad country the shame.
>
> To my wife all I have
> Saving only the love
> That is not mine to give.
>
> To my one son the hunger.

At the start, 'strong and weak' balance. But, then, if 'fear' and 'shame' might seem to balance with 'love', we find that 'love' is qualified. None the less, the nature of the qualification is elusive. The three penultimate lines are as mysterious as Marvell's 'Definition of Love' – a universal, against which each reader will test personal resonances; yet in the end I sense reconciliation, not bitterness, in the tone, and feel in the whole poem a power of life. '. . . the hunger' is that spiritual hunger which we hear of elsewhere – Prytherch's hunger, the poet's hunger in creation, the religious hunger for compassion. It is a richness of consciousness, amid enigma; and, when the elements of life are indeed purged alike of glamour and bitterness in this manner, the title, 'Gifts', seems to justify itself, and to have no irony.

I find this positive note almost everywhere, even when we might

least expect it. In 'The Minister', Job Davies is a pharisee and Walter
Llywarch a hypocrite; yet when the poet lends them his own voice,
for 'their' say, the respective poems are positive. Job Davies's poem is
called 'Lore'; and though the title here is certainly equivocal, the
main character of the man speaks of resilience and survival:

> Job Davies, eighty-five
> Winters old, and still alive
> After the slow poison
> And treachery of the seasons.
>
> Miserable
> Kick my arse . . .

The price of this particular survival is the actual 'lore', which the last
line embodies: 'Live large man, and dream small' – not the poet's
way, not *his* search, and *his* hunger, but a way of affirmation and
laughter all the same (reminiscent perhaps of Arabella, in *Jude the
Obscure*). And Walter Llywarch sticks in the mind, in the poem named
after him. His tone is more sombre, more petulant perhaps, nearer
to rejection of life than Job Davies's, yet the major image is by no
means without dignity:

> Walter Llywarch – the words were a name
> On a lost letter that never came
> For one who waited in the long queue
> Of life that wound through a Welsh valley

– and the ending balances laughter, of a kind, with despair.

In this context, I would finally mention two of Thomas's most
vividly dramatic poems – not dramatic monologue this time, but his
own observation (or 'the persona's observation', if that now seems
less misleading): 'On the Farm', and 'Meet the Family'. In the first of
these poems, three surly brothers, almost wholly dehumanised, are
balanced against the fragile beauty of 'the girl' – presumably a sister:

> And lastly there was the girl:
> Beauty under some spell of the beast.
> Her pale face was the lantern
> By which they read in life's dark book
> The shrill sentence: God is love.

In the second poem as I have listed them, though it was written
earlier, three very similarly wrecked men, 'John One', 'John Two'
and 'John Three', are described, and the final verse this time is

perhaps the direct environmental 'explanation' of their destruction:

> John All and his lean wife,
> Whose forced complicity gave life
> To each loathed foetus, stare from the wall,
> Dead not absent. The night falls.

Both poems end with an irony which is certainly typical of Thomas throughout his work – the first, irony held in check by the archetypal image, 'Beauty under some spell of the beast', and by the authenticity of the message the girl conveys, despite the savage thrust of 'shrill'. In the second poem, however, the culmination seems purely savage. The uncompromising directness of 'forced complicity', 'loathed foetus' culminates in an unanswerable, and unforgettable, conclusion. Taken at face value, the poem expresses unqualified bitterness – yet this, we may then realise, might be more appropriate to the people in the poem, than to any possible onlooker.

Even in the early work, no single poem suffices by itself; and the readers of Thomas, as of Yeats, will already be aware of subtle and elusive echoes set up between the poems, which become also part of the resonance of each when they are considered individually.

IV

This brings me to the second, and more difficult part of this chapter: an attempt to come to terms with the complex nature of Thomas's religious sensibility, as it moves increasingly into the foreground in his later work, and to define its centrality to his art itself.

I have written about 'Here' (from *Tares*) elsewhere, in a summarised account of a seminar in the University of East Anglia (now available in C. B. Cox and A. E. Dyson, *The Practical Criticism of Poetry*). That discussion discovered the multiple questions lurking under an apparently simple surface, and in particular, the possibility of two seemingly wholly different interpretations contained in the one artefact. If the images are taken as metaphor – and it seems that for most readers, this is the natural first response – you have a poem about 'man' coming to evolutionary, or possibly to adult, self-consciousness:

> I am a man now.
> Pass your hand over my brow:
> You can feel the place where the brains grow.

The 'brain' is the new feature, allowing the unnamed speaker to look back, seeing 'The footprints that led up to me'; and the rest of the imagery, powerfully organic and elemental, could be interpreted either as the human race coming to consciousness of itself as something more than animal, or as an individual becoming aware of himself as a unique being, something more than a child. But knowledge is suffering: the poem records strong perversities in the knowledge, hands that 'will not do as I say', prayers unanswered, inner will violated. Perhaps the head might have been (or might be) the original flaw – yet 'here', the place of the poem's title, ends with the strange, and apparently opposed assertion:

> It is too late to start
> For destinations not of the heart.
> I must stay here, with my hurt.

The 'destinations' of 'the heart', perhaps too late discovered or rediscovered, or perhaps recognised now as a possible evolutionary path which has not viably been taken, appear in conflict with the head and the 'brains'. Has the evolution of higher intelligence, of more sensitive awareness, brought to man only an increased awareness of the meaninglessness of his life?

Taken in this way, the poem might seem to affirm not religious belief, but bitter atheism; at the very least, an unhealed experience of the absence of God. It is undeniable that the major religious poems which have been written later can, and do, strike some readers in this light – chiefly, 'Pietà' (already discussed), 'Belfry' and 'In Church' (two haunting poems from the same transitional volume); and above all, almost the entire content of *Laboratories of the Spirit*, which, together with *H'm* and *Frequencies*, establishes him now without doubt, in my view, among the five or six greatest poets to have written in English in this century.

But, if we look again at 'here', allowing something like an optical illusion to happen, it offers back a startlingly different report. If the images are taken literally and not metaphorically, surely we have a poem about one particular man, in one place? The mysterious image including 'swift satellites' and the assertion 'the clock of my whole being is slow' could intimate darkness over the face of the earth. If so, the claim for special purity in the third stanza would be explained by virgin birth; the unmoving hands in stanza four by actual nails (never far from Thomas's imagination, as we have already noted); the cry 'Does no God hear when I pray?' as the special anguish of '*Eloi, Eloi, lama sabachthani?*', and the final stanza as the *consummatum est*: a destiny now accepted to the ultimate point of no return. On this reading, the opening stanzas turn inside out. 'I am a man now' means not, 'I am a man, no longer an animal or a child' but 'I am a man now, no longer God': the witness of the 'brains' meaning Incarnation. In fact, 'brains' are not really a distinguishing mark between man and the brutes, or between grown man and child (though the position and importance ascribed to them may be); certainly for Christ, the brains would be full awareness of the Word made *flesh*. The 'hurt' discovered 'here' is no longer a special anguish of our modern dilemma, but the mysterious task of salvation, foreseen before the creation itself. We have, in fact, a poem about Christ, at the moment when his death is upon him, and God appears to be absent from God.

To see this is to become aware that 'ambivalence' is at best a weak word to describe the poem, which is bifocal in a specially radical way. I do not think the effect can possibly be accidental (though this is not to say that it was necessarily 'intended', by the poet, in any crude sense). If images, differently interpreted, produce what at first seems to be a wholly different poem, the phenomenon cannot be ascribed to a mere trick in the use of language, or in the nature of words. Rather, the images do *in fact* work as they do, for readers who have any knowledge of Christian theology – almost as if witnessing to the Cross on their own. Is there something *in* the Cross ('the original fork / in existence', as it is called in 'Amen') which by its actual nature bypasses theology and, at the level of language and image, testifies to itself? 'I am a man now': the image of evolved man, alone in a creation where God is dead, is held in exact silhouette against the other image of Christ on the Cross, when God is absent. If the Christian religion has this paradox at its heart, perhaps it is not irrelevant to modern doubt after all, but simply an anticipation of it by 2000 years. And, if the revelation of love is 'Here', where the title directs us, then Christian faith and love have perhaps always been odder than naïve belief, or unbelief, would like to suppose. Such a vision is closer to Greek tragedy, to Hindu mythology, to agnostic doubt, even to atheism, than it is to middle-class churchgoing; it may well prove closer to the original New Testament documents, stripped of their deceptive familiarity, as well.

Thomas's own churches are often empty of worshippers, and this is no unmixed blessing, since when they come, as in 'Service', they may be merely the Cross for a private crucifixion of the priest:

> We stand looking at
> Each other. I take the word 'prayer'
> And present it to them. I wait idly,
> Wondering what their lips will
> Make of it. But they hand back
> Such presents. I am left alone

With no echoes to the amen
I dreamed of. I am saved by music
From the emptiness of this place
Of despair. As the melody rises
From nothing, their mouths take up the tune,
And the roof listens. I call on God
In the after silence, and my shadow
Wrestles with him upon a wall
Of plaster, that has all the nation's
Hardness in it. They see me thrown
Without movement of their oblique eyes.

We are to hear much, from now on, of the priest alone on his knees, praying without certainty and almost without hope, as the silence closes in, and only one sound remains:

There is no other sound
In the darkness but the sound of a man
Breathing, testing his faith
On emptiness, nailing his questions
One by one to an untenanted cross.

('In Church')

But the apotheosis of this development is the later volumes, and to these I shall now turn.

V

If we had Thomas's poetry to this point alone, he would still rank among the truly important moderns. But it is the three volumes of the 1970s (*H'm* appeared in 1972) which take him into a still rarer class of excellence. As the religious quest comes to the fore, and the dialectic between poem and poem reaches new complexity, he takes his place with the other two poets who have concerned us here, and with Wallace Stevens, among the very greatest creators of this century. Dissimilar though the four are, all have emerged as explorers of cosmic reality in its tenuous relationship to the structures of art. As creators, they are masters of imagery and cadence, tone and syntax – the crucial instruments of craftsmanship – and I think it no coincidence that, for many readers, all would count among prophets of modern consciousness itself.
    'Old men ought to be explorers'? – no doubt (though, unlike Yeats and Eliot, Thomas seems neither to age nor to complain of aging; he

might even regard such a preoccupation as trivial). Undeniably, as
they have developed, all have grown in stature, 'riding the echo' of
their language towards whatever shapes, or visions, appear. Yeats
searched through almost every religion, except the Christian, in his
quest for wisdom, pursuing incantation, invocation, occult
promptings, all ancient lore. As we have seen, the tension between
'lust and rage' and Byzantium never resolved finally – though
different readers will go on trying, tentatively, to balance them out.
T. S. Eliot opted for Christianity and adhered as a worshipper, but
Four Quartets remains mysterious and open, even after the Descent of
the Dove. In his prose, we find a different, sadder story; in the poetry,
we trust not the teller but the tale.

On the face of it, Wallace Stevens seems simpler than the others, as
he opts for a universe pervaded by beauty, and emptied of gods.
Man's verbal structures witness to what has been known, and felt, as
beauty – but these are fleeting epiphanies of consciousness, no final
entrée to 'realities' beyond. Like the mechanical 'tick-tock' of clocks,
if more subtly, they reveal men's patterns and rituals 'exactly as they
are'. The 'man with the blue guitar' will be looked to, by some, for
revelation; but beauty, and the inherent consolations, are all he can
give. As Wallace Stevens conjures religious notions away, with
unfailing courtesy, we may sense that there is more serenity – for
him, at least – in oblivion, than in all other ultimate human hopes.

R. S. Thomas may seem most akin to Eliot in his faith – running to
priestly commitment – yet, increasingly, conclusions akin to
Stevens's haunt his work. Even so the tone is harsher and angrier
than in Stevens (though never egocentric), and, however
uncompromising some statements, there are always others to
balance them out. If 'Petition', 'The Island', 'Remedies', 'The Fair'
and others seem a total rebuke to optimism, 'Via Negativa' may lead
us – however tentatively – a little way back. I return to the sense that
it is Yeats whom he resembles most of the four (if we look for
resemblances), far apart in tone and specific tensions though the two
are. Increasingly, Thomas sets up echoes between his poems, as Yeats
did, mutually enriching and elusive, to an almost equal degree. Does
he believe, does he not believe? – as in Yeats, so in Thomas, these
very questions seem futile – something left over from childhood, or
innocence, left far behind. I shall try briefly to define a personal
reaction to Thomas later; but first, 'The Kingdom', from *H'm*, seems
a good place to return to the verse:

It's a long way off but inside it
There are quite different things going on:
Festivals at which the poor man
Is king and the consumptive is

Healed; mirrors in which the blind look
At themselves and love looks at them
Back; and industry is for mending
The bent bones and the minds fractured
By life. It's a long way off, but to get
There takes no time and admission
Is free, if you will purge yourself
Of desire, and present yourself with
Your need only and the simple offering
Of your faith, green as a leaf.

This poem has something of the economy of Yeats's 'An Irish Airman Foresees His Death'. There are powerful contrasts which might signify mutual cancellation, or a strange fulfilment, since the driving emotion is at once apparent, and hard to pin down. 'It's a long way off': the opening phrase, later repeated, demands teasing clarity of utterance, though whether wistfulness, bitterness or mockery predominate, who is to say? Sufficient, no doubt, that the poem's first half rehearses the essence of the kingdom as Christ proclaimed it, in some ways enhancing its fairy-tale charm and uncancelled allure. That this vision resembles neither the Church of Christ in any of its visible branches nor any perceptible realities in the world that we know is likewise apparent, with a poignancy impossible to miss. Is the poem's indictment chiefly of the Church, or of Christ's original vision? A real question – yet, if the kingdom *is* impossible, how comes its power to haunt unnumbered lives (including Thomas's own?).

In the second part, the price of admission is again impeccably scriptural, though posed with a simple (or artful) directness that staggers the mind. Sunday by Sunday, such sentiments resound in hymns, ring out in scripture, are expounded in sermons: day by day they mock, or are mocked by, the Church. Note the extraordinary neutrality of the last lines, actively defying us – since, if we read them aloud, we have somehow to declare ourselves, like it or not: '. . . your faith, green as a leaf', 'the simple offering' – simple as curing the blind, mending the world, loving mankind. I recall one of my grandmother's favourite aphorisms, 'not as green as he's cabbage-looking' and wonder if this (doubtless Cockney) phrase ever reached Wales? The sting of this poem is surely its appearance of innocence, as its unanswered questions (savage indictment? – betrayed salvation? – pure nonsense?) tug at the mind. I am reminded of Dostoievsky's Grand Inquisitor, indicting the returned Christ from his own worldy wisdom: how dared Christ imagine that his terrible 'gifts' (love, freedom, healing) would remain in the Church, or meet real human needs? In the parable, Christ is dumb before his accuser, as in the original story: at the end, he kisses the old man's cheek. The kiss burns there, and the old man releases him from a second immolation; but the old man does not change his views.

At this moment precisely, the poem turns inside out, a perfect optical illusion (like 'Here' before it), so that for a moment one wonders how one could doubt the kingdom at all? The lost paradise, the promised eternity – are these not perpetual archetypes; and is not 'mending / The bent bones and the minds fractured / By life' a major reality – among surgeons, psychotherapists, day-to-day exercises of generosity and friendship – despite the mockery cast round it by the self-styled 'churches' of Christ? One recalls that Christ called his kingdom a leaven, not a political formula; and that leaven is hidden, has to be looked for, but does have its effect. Christ himself said that not all who say 'Lord, Lord' to him enter the kingdom; he pointed to children, casualties, outcasts when asked for a clue. Perhaps Wordsworth's 'Tintern Abbey' will also be recalled, and allied poems: notably Wordsworth's ascent, from admitted sublimity, to the yet greater reality: 'that best portion of a good man's life; / His little, nameless, unremembered acts / Of kindness and of love'. From here, a return to Thomas's poem is simple, and to the particular scriptural image that clearly lurks. Christ, confronted by a blind suppliant (Luke 18:41), asks a simple question, 'What would you have me to do?' The reply, 'Lord, that I might have my sight', is granted; and the first image the blind man sees is Love looking back at him.

Like other optical illusions, this poem can turn back on itself a few moments later, leaving us staring bleakly, again, at the 'to get / There' clause. A poem of faith, a poem of doubt, or something more elusive? – for readers of Yeats, the problem is familiar enough, if not in this guise.

I start from this poem since it may be a clue to the volume, where alternations of view seem often carefully placed. From man's disappointment, through necessary complexity, to God's disappointment: we can make the journey backwards, or forwards, or shuttle to and from. In 'Petition' we face this:

> Seeking the poem
> In the pain, I have learned
> Silence is best, paying for it
> With my conscience, I am eyes
> Merely, witnessing virtue's
> Defeat; seeing the young born
> Fair, knowing the cancer
> Awaits them. One thing I have asked
> Of the disposer of the issues

Of life: that truth should defer
To beauty. It was not granted....

But 'Via Negativa', though almost as bleak, at least embodies
traditional spirituality:

> His are the echoes
> We follow, the footprints he has just
> Left. We put our hands in
> His side hoping to find
> It warm. We look at people
> And places as though he had looked
> At them, too; but miss the reflection

– and this is followed, as if in counterpoint, by one of God's
soliloquies, in which the Creator laments the desertion, of himself,
by the being made in his likeness:

> I slept and dreamed
> Of a likeness, fashioning it,
> When I woke, to a slow
> Music; in love with it
> For itself, giving it freedom
> To love me; risking the disappointment.

('Making')

Looking at the volume, one can see a group of three poems together,
clustered near the centre, all of which – but with mounting savagery
– record God's terrible and inexplicable curse on man ('Ruins', 'The
Island' and 'He'). More spread out, there are groups that could spell
out man's disappointment with God, and God's disappointment
with man. Between these, there are new themes appearing – notably,
two poems of ironic intent concerning the Church obliquely
('Acting' and 'All Right'), and one concerning it very directly (the
title poem, 'H'm'), and poems in which 'The Machine' appears
almost as Frankenstein: a creation made perhaps to punish man, but
now running out of control of God Himself ('Once' and 'Other'). The
older theme of the Cross is less evident, though at least two poems
('Cain' and 'The Coming') add yet further perspectives to Thomas's
long fascination with this great symbol joining present and past.

But maybe it is the new savagery which dominates *H'm*, which
makes it Thomas's most memorable and most terrible volume to
date. The opening of 'Soliloquy' fuses Jehovah and Zeus, in images of
apocalypse:

> And God thought: Pray away,
> Creatures; I'm going to destroy
> It. The mistake's mine,
> If you like. I have blundered
> Before

while the closing poem is a rare mingling of violence, cynicism, and finally controlled laughter and compassion, in the image of an idiot riding a bumper-car at a fair:

>   This is mankind
> Being taken for a ride by a rich
> Relation. The responses are fixed:
> Bump, smile; bump, smile. And the current
>
> Is generated by the smooth flow
> Of the shillings. This is an orchestra
> Of steel with the constant percussion
> Of laughter. But where he should be laughing
> Too, his features are split open, and look!
> Out of the cracks come warm, human tears.

So, as men's machines kill Prytherch, Prytherch becomes still more evidently, at least by implication, man's image. But Thomas, as the 1970s progress, has new things to add.

VI

In *Laboratories of the Spirit* certain themes, perceptible earlier, emerge far more clearly – the limitations of language; the positive absence (or perversity) of God; flaws or apparent flaws in the very nature of creation, and salvation; the indissoluble union of God and Jesus, in a manner unknown to previous theology. This faith – if such it is – is not in any normal sense incarnational; even poems where the beauty of nature is acknowledged contain details which seem to forbid any direct leap to revelation. In 'The Flower', the 'riches' of 'the earth, the sea, / the immensity / of the broad sky' are acknowledged as both asked for, and granted; yet the poet turns away to another, invisible universe 'whose roots were not / in the soil, nor its petals the colour / of the wide sea', where his own lonelier and different battle for understanding is fought out:

>   its own species with its own
>   sky over it, shot
> with the rainbow of your coming and going.

And even in 'Good', the final poem, the old man who recalls life with contentment is surrounded by ambiguity of detail: a 'chill in the flesh', and a nature where 'The kestrel goes by with fresh prey / In its claws'.

'Sea-watching' presents a lovely image of the Holy Spirit, watched for through a lifetime, and wonderfully elusive:

> Ah, but a rare bird is
> rare. It is when one is not looking,
> at times one is not there
>   that it comes.

Thomas is not a poet of transfiguration, of the coming of the Spirit and the witness of holiness, in any obvious sense; his poems have few saints, though it is possible to believe, as I have already suggested, that the anguish and brokenness of the Welsh peasants is indeed a witness to the divine, if one has eyes to see in the great darkness of life. No: Thomas is now, as always, a poet of the Cross; and the Cross without the exegesis or piety of the ages to help it – more than ever facing us with its own starkness, as God's side of the dialogue. 'Poste Restante' opens with the possibility that the Cross itself might grind 'into dust / under men's wheels', just as it might shine 'brightly as a monument to a new era', and with this huge possibility open, his poem is a bleak record of the anguish of a priest *now*, compressed between its first line, 'I want you to know how it was', and its last, 'you, friend, who will know what happened'. Many poems, such as 'Emerging', 'The Hand' and 'The Combat', conduct a kind of imaginary dialogue with God – in which are faced such possibilities as God's own surprise at, and challenge by, 'the machine'; God's possible impotence or unwillingness as the explanation of unanswered prayer; God's dismay at his creation, or almost demonic laughter in the face of it. This technique, which we have encountered earlier, and which developed in *H'm*, is now central. The image of Wrestling Jacob is used more than once, always with ironic inversions. In 'The Hand', we are confronted with a silent battle between God and the hand he has made – the hand pleading its own need to be blessed, pleading God's own need for the works it will do:

> But God, feeling the nails
> in his side, the unnerving warmth
> of the contact, fought on in
> silence. This was the long war with himself
> always foreseen, the question not
> to be answered. What is the hand
> for? The immaculate conception

preceding the delivery
of the first tool? 'I let you go',
he said, 'but without blessing.
Messenger to the mixed things
of your making, tell them I am.'

The 'I am' of the Old Testament, taken up by Christ in John's gospel to the horror of his hearers, here receives a new irony. There are also, in this remarkable volume, shorter poems, such as 'The Word' and 'Which', that remind us of earlier volumes, both in style and content, yet which home in very directly upon the continuing preoccupation of *Laboratories of the Spirit*, so that they can seem, rather, almost parts of a much longer poem, to which most of these parts somehow belong:

A pen appeared, and the god said:
'Write what it is to be
man.' And my hand hovered
long over the bare page,

until there, like footprints
of the lost traveller, letters
took shape on the page's
blankness, and I spelled out

the word 'lonely'. And my hand moved
to erase it; but the voices
of all those waiting at life's
window cried out loud: 'It is true'.

('The Word')

The command; the exile; the reluctant honesty; and, with these themes now, compressed as always, a truly remarkable control of tone and speed. It is impossible to read this aloud without the sense that it is a slow movement, with subtle pauses – a poem far longer than it is, weaving tunes on a theme.

There are two poems in the volume which perhaps stand out, and which I cannot pretend fully to understand. 'Rough' and 'Amen' will be almost my last port of call in 'Laboratories of the Spirit, whether they turn out to be new departures, or a final summing up of the old. First 'Rough':

God looked at the eagle that looked at
the wolf that watched the jack-rabbit
cropping the grass, green and curling

as God's beard. He stepped back;
it was perfect, a self-regulating machine
of blood and faeces. One thing was missing:
he skimmed off a faint reflection of himself
in sea-water; breathed air into it,
and set the red corpuscles whirling. It was not long
before the creature had the eagle, the wolf and
the jack-rabbit squealing for mercy. Only the grass
resisted. It used it to warm its imagination
by. God took a handful of small germs
sowing them in the smooth flesh. It was curious,
the harvest: the limbs modelled an obscene
question, the head swelled, out of the eyes came
tears of pus. There was the sound
of thunder, the loud, uncontrollable laughter of
God, and in his side like an incurred stitch, Jesus.

I think we must accept that there is in this volume an element of experiment, of playing with notions, which has been a characteristic from the first, but only now fully declares itself. If I am right, each poem is a tentative whole, an autonomous creation, but the full effect depends upon dialogue. The result is not unlike that familiar in Yeats, as I have already hinted, though the two poets differ greatly in their religious vision.

Readers of Yeats are teased continually by poems which appear to work out a perfect if internally intricate statement of a theme or themes, but which then give place to other poems where different yet equally authoritiative effects are achieved. A tone of almost prophetic assurance overlays highly shifting and tentative explorations; no single poem can be paraphrased, and often a criss-cross of echoes and references seems the best approach to interpretation. In the growing body of art, we then become aware of coherence, individuality, a highly distinctive approach to life, which must in some sense correspond·to the 'poet's' explorations. 'Sailing to Byzantium' is followed by 'The Tower' – and, as we have seen, in the final ordering of his volume Yeats has even reversed the order in which they were written (while preserving 'The Tower' for title), perhaps because, if the second poem were read first, it might cause us to prejudge the calculated ambiguities of the first, starting from the wrong end. 'Lapis Lazuli' counterpoints 'The Circus Animals' Desertion', and in their complex way the two elaborate that simpler dichotomy, apparent in shorter but equally memorable poems, between a poet whose inspiration is at the same time 'the loveliest woman born', the eternal quest for beauty, and also 'an old man's frenzy', 'an old man's folly', 'lust and rage' dancing attention on old age; 'the place of excrement'.

Thomas's recurring themes are naturally different, but the best comment on his poems is often, in the same way, an interplay of echoes. The play of opposites moves between great tenderness and savage, yet always somehow unexpected, violence. The tone, though frequently an instrument to underline the violence rather than a check upon it, has also a deliberate extravagance that acts as warning. Clearly, any single poem is not the last word: and, if it were, the others would be impoverished rather than enriched. But, equally clearly, a poem such as 'Rough' could be the last word: no doubt, some men might discover in it a lucid, sufficient statement of the universe, as they know it.

What sort of God do we find in 'Rough'? He could be a monster, if moral judgements were made. But the moral judgements would have to be imported from outside, and where then would they come from? The God could be scientist experimenting, making a creation of horror. 'It was perfect': the notion of perfection is aesthetic; and perhaps an intellectual 'self-regulating machine' of some kind – perpetual motion? – is one of the oldest desires of ever-hopeful men, offended by transience. 'One thing was missing': this ironic comment, of obscure direction, falls into the poem. God inserts into creation the image of himself, made not of earth and air but of water and air – the water capturing the notion of reflection, but also distortion, in the last creature made. The 'one thing missing' proves to be the greatest killing-machine of them all. Note the word 'mercy' in this unpropitious context – presumably, squealing to be let off death, or, alternatively, to be killed painlessly. The scene seems fitter for a Hobbesian universe, where God is non-existent, and life a mere play of blind forces, than for a universe made by a monster. Perhaps the truly disconcerting factor is that God's response to the squeal, if that's what it is (though the parenthesis about the grass allows us to disconnect the two if we wish), is finally to throw in 'germs', which, presumably, bring a horrible death by physical disintegration – to whom? It is indisputable that in our own lifetime man threw a handful of germs into a world of unwanted rabbits, and produced symptoms akin to those described in this poem. If man treats the creation over which he has godlike powers in this way, might this be after all more the God that man makes in his image than the other way round? But at least there is a sign, thunder: followed by a strange conclusion. The God of the poem ceases to be the intellectual maker of a 'perfect, a self-regulating machine' and becomes himself instinctual, uncontrollable. The laughter of God may be purely demonic, but the consequence is apparent – not perfect mechanism after all, but a flaw, fatal to God: 'and in his side like an incurred stitch, Jesus'. 'Incur' is defined usually as 'a risk run' – often with the added suggestion of recklessness, or deliberate criminality. But it does have the secondary meaning of 'running up against': a consequence not to be evaded, given the course or direction; the courage needed for a difficult and dangerous undertaking. Whatever we make of God here and in the other poems, Jesus goes with him; and with Jesus go the nails, the Cross, the pain.

The only thing that seems remotely detached from disaster is the grass – 'green and curling as God's beard' (a deliberately unusual anthropomorphic variant) warming its imagination (what does grass imagine?) at man's cruelty. Grass is important to most of Thomas's people ('And the world will grow to a few lean acres of grass'). The peasants tear their living from reluctant, infertile soil, and the grass is there always, a consolation and a beauty so usual as to fade beyond the border of consciousness, perhaps because men who now 'operate on the earth's body' with their machines, for produce, still find the grass useless for food.

'Rough' would seem to suggest a creation flawed not accidentally, but in its inception. It is not a random but a planned artefact, but the creator is schizoid, or at least an amoral perfectionist whose energies have run out of control. The 'perfection' envisaged is of blood and faeces: man the image of God, or, possibly, God the image of man; and, at the heart, the inescapable God–man 'incurred'.

Now let us turn to 'Amen':

It was all arranged:
the virgin with child, the birth
in Bethlehem, the arid journey uphill
to Jerusalem. The prophets foretold
it, the scriptures conditioned him
to accept it. Judas went to his work
with his sour kiss; what else
could he do?

       A wise old age,
the honours awarded for lasting,
are not for a saviour. He had
to be killed: salvation acquired
by an increased guilt. The tree,
with its roots in the mind's dark,
was divinely planted, the original fork
in existence. There is no meaning in life,
unless men can be found to reject
love. God needs his martyrdom.
The mild eyes stare from the Cross

in perverse triumph. What does he care
that the people's offerings are so small?

A flawed creation; a flawed salvation? The two are linked: 'The
tree, / with its roots in the mind's dark, / was divinely planted.' So,
Jesus and the Cross again, as a constant: and this poem as far from
the sadness, piety and immense tragic meditation of thousands of
Good Friday sermons as 'Rough' was from the feast of the Nativity
and joyous welcome of God-made-man at Christmas.

The tone seems to signal something; but what? If we take the
poem at face value,. I suppose there are two kinds of men who might
accept it as a near total and final statement about reality – just as
there is one kind of man who might so accept 'Rough'. Such men
would normally be simple in their deepest responses to life and
possibly fanatical – doubtless, far less complex than such real-life
men as Schopenhauer, Hardy and Conrad. I suppose that in 'Amen'
a total sceptic might find room to say 'yes': someone determined, let
us say, to find in the Christian witness such a mixture of
contradiction and horror or both that he could lacerate believers
(and more secretly perhaps himself) with a QED. demonstration of its
impossibility, or its evil. (I am tempted to wonder what poet or
sceptic could write a more effective anti-Christian poem, if he
wanted to.) Or, if 'Amen' is not a deliberate mockery of the whole
story (and to read it aloud is to experience the difficulty of keeping
the *tone* appropriate to such an interpretation – though a certain
bitter anger, if not a hint of perverse satisfaction, seems equally
difficult to keep out of the reading voice), then might it not be seen,
rather, as the actual faith of a Calvinist or Jansenist – the perfection
of the theology of divine predestination and total depravity, which
manages to co-exist somehow for some 'Christians' with a belief in
God as Love rather than as a monstrosity, and which manages
somehow to worship God, not entirely through fear? It might be
possible to interpret the whole of history as a film made by God
before time started, with predestination to damnation as much a
feature for some men, in the divine drama, as it is for the villains of
an unsubtle human creation. The Judas of this poem might be
recognised as authentic, and not pitied, by some calling themselves
Christian; perhaps the terrible insight about the 'meaning in life'
would also give gloomy satisfaction to some, and not appal? Even so,
I suppose than even Calvinist readers might be thrown from their
assent by the end of the poem. If they get that far, will they further
accept Jesus as made in *their* image ('mild', 'perverse'), and will they
accept the final stroke, that even the world's neglect may please
Christ, since it leaves all the more of the suffering to him?

The poem cannot possibly (I would assert; but how do I set about demonstrating?) be anything of these kinds; so what is it? Another trial exploration, I suggest, on the very edges and outer boundaries of faith. 'It was all arranged': there is, in fact, that 'side' to the gospel; and, given that, perhaps the story cannot help coming out like this, if warped one way? Classic Christian theology had had to distinguish between God's 'foreknowledge' and 'predestination', between his power to bring good out of evil through the Cross, and his unconditional gift of free-will to the creature made in his own image; between a man tortured to death in Jerusalem in comparatively recent history and a God of infinite love who is to be apprehended in the same image. Perhaps R. S. Thomas is reminding us that theology does not remove the mystery; or perhaps he is reminding others that the mystery cannot, after all, be exhausted in *this* mode, though on the surface 'Amen' may seem simple and obvious. 'What else / could he do?' The question appears rhetorical, but in fact it simply hangs there – like the poem, which is an extension of it. The paradox of 'salvation acquired / by an increased guilt' pushes relentlessly towards the yet more excruciating paradox : 'There is no meaning in life / unless men can be found to reject / love'.

I am not sure that Thomas does not offer this poem as a temptation to the fashionable reviewers who still ignore his work, but might swallow this? It sounds profound, it sounds true; in fact, no doubt it is profound and true. But Christian prayer has trodden in anguish through such mysteries. Does the poet whose destiny is to 'kneel on' (see 'Moon in Lleyn') endorse such views, on his knees in the empty church? The destiny of priest and poet are inseparable, and no doubt he is forcing us to see the shocking simplifications in Christianity, partly because without these, we might not take it seriously? I think perhaps he shows that the shocking implications are the starting place for faith and devotion – the only starting-place, because a divide; on one side of which stand, perhaps, the respectable churchgoers (in church when fashionable, otherwise not so), along with the establishment as we know it; and on the other side of which are all of humanity's victims, all of its Christs? And between the two, at the dead centre, are the doubtful and tormented; wondering whether there is, in this strange religion, something that can only be mocked, only be shuddered at; or, rather, whether there is, in the Cross, a dark key, which happens to fit the dark mystery and exposure of human experience?

'Amen' seems to me a poem poised at a cross-roads. Either you do not come to it, preferring a view of life which bypasses the territory; or you go past it, to join those who kneel in prayer. But you cannot stop here: not unless you think the poem merely a smart joke (updated Shaw in verse, perhaps); or unless you feel that it is in fact the end: the way things irrevocably are.

But either of these views seems untrue to the poem, if one looks at it as it nakedly is. The prophets may have 'foretold', but they had no understanding of their message; they were as much in the dark as Caiaphas himself. And, of course, Judas did *not* have to betray Christ; the sour kiss might have come from any of the other twelve. Christ did not have to accept his destiny – just as he did not accept as it stood much that was 'written' in the Old Testament. And, naturally, the eyes were not 'mild' on the Cross, they could only be tortured; mild eyes belong to the parody crucifixes in comfortable, uncaring churches. The word 'perverse triumph' are mere shorthand for Good Friday meditation, which must bypass such words if salvation is at all to be reached. I would suggest that 'Amen', along with all these poems, should be read as an artefact; and the 'meaning' searched in, and through, the volume as a whole.

VII

After Christ, what? The molecules
Are without redemption. . . .

('Pre-Cambrian')

H'm was a volume chiefly bitter in tone; *Laboratories of the Spirit* charted new, and growingly philosophical, directions. Both pioneered strange dialogues of God with himself, which become one of the features of *Frequencies*. This latest volume abounds in 'anthropomorphisms of the fancy' (a phrase taken from it), yet 'fancy' is surely chosen with tongue-in-cheek. The vision of a deity more akin to Zeus than to Jehovah or Christ grows, even in poems when the Christian scriptures are invoked. As in the previous volumes, we encounter a God who may shrink from his creation, fearing it; or one who laughs demonically at the sufferings he chooses to cause. Flawed creation, flawed redemption, flawed religious traditions: and the suffering people afflicted further – with germs, fire or poverty – for the lot he has caused them to bear.

Frequencies contains slightly fewer poems as striking as 'Rough' or 'Amen', yet as a whole it may be Thomas's finest achievement to date. The cosmic explorations of the 1970s continue, as Thomas leads us now through more scientific terrain. The harsh détente with science, prefigured in the title poem of *Laboratories of the Spirit*, develops; there is even a partial, and ghostly, resurrection image, in one reference to the folded grave-clothes found in love's tomb. I have suggested that, though the technique resembles Yeats, the content seems closer to Wallace Stevens; but 'seems' remains the correct, and greatly distancing, word. Thomas has recently said that institutional religion is dead and fated to stay so; like all great moderns, he lives in the world where dogma is gone. The gain in realism and honesty is unquestionable, but, as he and the poets I have grouped him with all demonstrate, there is strain, as well as joy, in the personal quest. How *are* we to move through inner and outward enigmas, seeking myths for healing and loving, in this new and invincibly baffling terrain? For Thomas, Kierkegaard and Einstein emerge as key figures, as his creative energy renews itself, continually, in the unending fight. It seems likely to me (and the time has come for a tentative personal judgement) that comparative neglect, in his lifetime, has been the price that any great prophet must pay. In the future Thomas will emerge, more definitively than Eliot, as a pioneer of religious – even Christian – consciousness, when Christendom dies, and the grisly death-bed antics of the so-called churches cease to stand in Christ's way.

The poet of *Frequencies* exists between 'faith and doubt' (his own placing), needing now 'a faith to enable me to out-stare / the grinning inmates of its asylum, / the failed experiments God put away'. Yet his question – 'Why, then, do I kneel still / striking my prayers on a stone / heart?' – is far from rhetorical, invoking anguish, which has belonged with faith, throughout history, as well as with doubt.

The dialectic, still resisting synthesis, becomes in this later phase as teasing as religion itself. Though Thomas's earlier ambivalences yield to new ones, in appearance more sombre, we can never say 'here we have him', any more than the poet can say this of God the Spirit – or even of himself:

> All my life I tried to believe
> in the importance of what Thomas
> should say now, do next. . . .

Ironically, the poem which these words open ('In Context') discusses his former belief that he and 'destiny' were together working on some plan, however mysterious – destiny working on 'a big / loom',

> I with a small needle,
>   drawing the thread
> through my mind, colouring it
> with my own thought.

That belief is now swept away – in this poem, at least – with verbal precision that denies any appeal:

> Impossible dreamer!
> All those years the demolition
>   of the identity proceeded.
> Fast as the cells constituted
> themselves, they were replaced. It was not
> I who lived, but life rather
> that lived me. There was no developing
> structure. There were only the changes
> in the metabolism of a body
> greater than mine, and the dismantling
> by the self of a self it
>   could not reassemble.

What we have here is no solipsism of the feelings, however. Repeatedly in these later poems, R. S. Thomas strives to renounce 'the heart' for 'the mind'. The ambiguous balance he has always kept between the two, and the occasional swing from one to the other in quest of the least unreliable oracle, is a further link with Yeats. In *Frequencies* we are assured that the mind, too, has its solipsisms, even if – on the surface, at least – it is just now in the ascendant:

> Well, I said, better to wait
> for him on some peninsula
> of the spirit. Surely for one
> with patience he will happen by
> once in a while. It was the heart
> spoke. The mind, sceptical as always
> of the anthropomorphisms
> of the fancy, knew he must be put together
> like a poem or a composition
> in music, that what he conforms to
> is art. A promontory is a bare
> place; no God leans down
> out of the air to take the hand
> extended to him. The generations have
> watched there
> in vain.

> ('Emerging')

Thomas's 'mind' signifies no classicism or neo-classicism, reaching for universals, but the mediating of those dissolving insights of Hume, Kierkegaard, Eddington which our new science confirm. Maybe the mathematician is our hope, with his habit of using the impossible? Yet Thomas's God remains on guard, against all assaults. In 'The Gap', the first poem in *Frequencies*, God wakes, as if from sleep, but 'the nightmare did not recede'. He is haunted by the fear that man's language, a new Babel reaching insidiously upwards towards him, may one day jump the narrowing gap, and destroy his peace. But:

> He leaned
> over and looked in the dictionary
> they used. There was the blank still
> by his name of the same
> order as the territory
> between them, the verbal hunger
> for the thing in itself.

So God's decree for the gap 'No, no, no, / wider than that!' is fulfilled still, leaving him safe in the eternal silence which equally is his repose, and man's unquenchable torment. Note the word 'they' at the start of l. 3 above, with its hint of rooted distaste as well as resolute distancing. What can this be, if not a slap in the face for incarnational hope? Far from the 'Word' coming down, made flesh to reveal God's glory, we find men's own words monitored and blocked in their persistent upward assault upon God's inscrutable ways. On our side, the unending pain, love, bereavement, sacrifice, longing for knowledge and comfort; on God's side, the unending mockery of silence (and fear).

When the poet speculates, he knows that the material world is as strange as the spiritual, and as little likely to satisfy that ache for understanding which is part of our doom:

> I think he sits at that strange table
> of Eddington's, that is not a table
> at all, but nodes and molecules
> pushing against molecules
> and nodes; and he writes there
> in invisible handwriting the instructions
> the genes follow.

In this poem ('At It'), the poet says that, if he could, he would storm at the god 'as Job stormed, with the eloquence / of the abused heart'. But there will be no judgement, by man at least, in man's language: there will be no judgement at all, only

> The verdict
> of his calculations, that abstruse
> geometry that proceeds eternally
> in the silence beyond right and wrong

In the same vein, 'Play' underlines the folly of any hope that God's mind will meet man's in any perceptible commerce:

> Your move I would have
> said, but he was not
> playing. . . .
> As though one can sit at table
> with God! . . .
>   We stake our all
> on the capture of the one
> queen, as though to hold life
> to ransom. He, if he plays, plays
> unconcernedly among the pawns.

The almost throwaway words (in context) 'As though one can sit at table / with God!' glance back at the upper room, and maybe the poet priest's lifetime of Eucharists; yet are 'the pawns' really less than other pieces (were they entirely so, even in Prytherch days?). This image of play occurs again in 'The Game', which identifies God now with a shadow-show: 'It is the play of a being / who is not serious in / his conclusions.' This poem (one of the most characteristic) proceeds to consider further riddles that defeat human intellect as 'we are forced / into the game, reluctant / contestants', and ends with a more humanly pessimistic conclusion:

>   But the rewards
> Are there even so, and history
> festers with the numbers of the recipients
> of them, the handsome, the fortunate,
> the well-fed; those who cheated this
> being when he was not looking.

All those quotations come from the dark side of *Frequencies*, but the pattern always has two sides (maybe the enigmatic back of a tapestry will show, to practised eyes, more than the face?). Even 'Emerging', a poem whose opening, already quoted here, offers little positive, moves to a conclusion where other perspectives, in counterpoint, come into sight:

We are beginning to see
now it is matter is the scaffolding
of spirit; that the poem emerges
from morphemes and phonemes; that
as form in sculpture is the prisoner
of the hard rock, so in everyday life
it is the plain facts and natural happenings
that conceal God and reveal him to us
little by little under the mind's tooling.

And, looking again through *Frequencies*, we notice that, if the
assertions of God's absence seem as lucid as Wallace Stevens's, though
far angrier, there is a parallel possibility (perhaps the anger is always
its tribute?) of converse truths. Possibly 'The Porch' is one of the
strongest images, in the strand I have so far explored; and I want to
quote it, not simply as yet one further example of Thomas's extreme
beauty and economy, but for the multivalence unobtrusively built in.
The thrust of the apparent meaning needs little exposition; but note
that the first line at least implies *human* interest; that 'driven' does
not explain itself and is not necessarily inwardly motivated; that the
first line of the second half does not say there *was* no prayer, or
anything like it; and that 'kept his place / there for an hour' has
more of dignity than absurdism, in this place 'neither outside nor
in':

Do you want to know his name?
It is forgotten. Would you learn
what he was like? He was like
anyone else, a man with ears
and eyes. Be it sufficient
that in a church porch on an evening
in winter, the moon rising, the frost
sharp, he was driven
to his knees and for no reason
he knew. The cold came at him;
his breath was carved angularly
as the tombstones; an owl screamed.

He had no power to pray.
His back turned on the interior
he looked out on a universe
that was without knowledge
of him and kept his place
there for an hour on that lean
threshold, neither outside nor in.

Does this brief poem turn inside-out, like certain others, conforming to the effect of optical illusion remarked on before? If we toy with the possibility that 'A universe / that was without knowledge / of him' is the man's consciousness, not the universe's (as why should we not?), then maybe the 'forgotten' name is God's name for us all; and God might still be betrayed by men, not the other way round. So, against the bitter statements in 'Bravo!', 'Fishing', 'Pre-Cambrian' and maybe the majority of these poems, we can place hints more positive in kind. In 'Adjustments', there is the hope that God might yet be found obliquely, despite all the problems:

> We never catch
> Him at work, but can only say,
> coming suddenly upon an amendment,
> that here he has been.

'The Signpost' is an exquisite small poem about a town seen signposted, but never visited. It is left for ever, as a memory of sunlight unqualified for the mind. As image, this might seem half-way between Keats's 'little town / emptied of this folk, this pious morn' and Yeats's Byzantium – that resolute attempt (if we adopt this view for a moment) to create in time, albeit time past, a place where artistic, religious and philosophic verities may be monumental and safe.

'The Signpost' ends in a manner that is at once pure Thomas and pure enigma:

> It was best
> so. I need a museum
> for storing the dream's
> brittle particles in. Time
> is a main road, eternity
> the turning that we don't take.

It will be recalled that in Berkeley's universe (which we are surely permitted to conjure up, in so rich a context) whatever we do not look at does not exist. Admittedly, God continues to look, so there is some stability; though Hume was swift to cancel this mind-steadying notion as well. But, can we be sure that the things we do not see really are as we should have seen them; or might God's vision, or no one's, be truer still?

In 'Epiphany' we are faced with the possibility that Christ, 'Far / off from his cross in the wrong season' still 'sits at table / with us' ('Play' notwithstanding) – even though the royal presents are gone, and it is 'the fool's cap of our paper money' that we force him to wear. 'The White Tiger' (perhaps I was wrong to say there are fewer really memorable poems here than in *Laboratories of the Spirit?*) envisages that God may be as much our victim, after all, as other wild animals, forced into smallness, emptiness, perhaps even silence, by man's grossest affronts. The words 'you can imagine' keep open, as always, ambiguity: but their inclusion allows every indictment of God to be turned back upon man – and very particularly here, upon the man in the pew:

> you can imagine that
> God breathes within the confines
> of our definitions of him, agonising
> over immensities that will not return.

With this in mind, it is interesting to note that two or three times in *Frequencies* Thomas returns to old ground, always with some suggestion of hubris in his own former self. 'Gone?' is positively the last Prytherch poem; but, whereas earlier the contrasts were chiefly between the peasant's coarseness and the poet priest's 'refinement', along with complex uncertainties about which was humanly finer, and more fitted or likely to endure, this poem is on another track. Now Wales has been captured by the machine, the tractor, the global village of television and the universal idiocy of greed – so Prytherch, at last a memory for elegy, becomes definitive symbol of a better, if bleaker, lost world:

> But where is the face
> with the crazed eyes that through the unseen
> drizzle of its tears looked out
> on this land and found no beauty
> in it, but accepted it, as a man
> will who has need in him that only
> bare ground, black thorns and the sky's
> emptiness can fill?

The final poem in the collection, 'Pilgrimages', does something to heal, if not to resolve, much that has gone before it, in its images. The poet prays on still, after all, as he always has done:

> Was the pilgrimage
> I made to come to my own
> self, to learn that in times
> like these and for one like me
> God will never be plain and

out there, but dark rather and
inexplicable, as though he were in here?

Other images recur in the volume (for instance, that of the faithless
fatal female – often the church, sometimes Eve). There are also
personal poems as fine as any he has written, such as the bitter-sweet
'The Album', where the question 'Life, what is it?' attracts images
one will never forget.

VIII

I have attached my highest judgement of Thomas's status as poet to
his recent work, so perhaps I can end by returning, for a quotation,
to earlier days. It is rare for a reader to find images for his own
experience among alien people and places, and it may seem a
guarantee of unusual artistic authority when he does. 'The Airy
Tomb' is one of my favourite poems, and I will conclude by quoting
its final lines. The poet has rejected the notion that his hero, Twm,
must opt for marriage, and offers instead this final image, of Twm's
life and death:

> No, no, you must face the fact
> Of his long life alone in that crumbling house
> With winds rending the joints, and the grey rain's claws
> Sharp in the thatch; of his work up on the moors
> With the moon for candle, and the shrill rabble of stars
> Crowding his shoulders. For Twm was true to his fate,
> That wound solitary as a brook through the crimson heather.

Select Bibliography

In part 1 of this section, I list works, and editions, referred to in the text.

The number of works to which a writer on these poets is indebted is vast. In part 2 I list only works to which I am aware of the greatest debts. Many others, almost equally influential, are omitted. Readers who wish for more extensive bibliographies will find clues in a number of the works listed.

Part 1

The Collected Poems of W. B. Yeats, 2nd (complete) edn (Macmillan, 1950).

A. N. Jeffares, *A Commentary on the Collected Poems of W. B. Yeats* (Macmillan, 1968). [NB. This includes invaluable notes on every poem in the *Collected Poems* (above). It is indispensable, and I am assuming that all users of this book will read Jeffares's notes on the Yeats poems discussed here, as well as the poems, before looking at my own commentary.]

W. B. Yeats, *Autobiographies* (Macmillan, 1955).

——, *Mythologies* (Macmillan, 1959).

——, *Essays and Introductions* (Macmillan, 1961).

——, *Explorations*, selected by Mrs W. B. Yeats (Macmillan, 1962).

——, *A Vision*, 2nd edn (Macmillan, 1937). [NB. The first, and cancelled edition, referred to here but not used for quotation, was printed privately in 1925, and reissued in 1978 as *A Critical Edition of Yeats's A Vision (1925)*, ed. George Mills Harper and Walker K. Hood (Macmillan).]

T. S. Eliot, *Collected Poems, 1909–1962* (Faber and Faber, 1963).

——, *Selected Essays*, 2nd edn (Faber and Faber, 1934).

——, *The Use of Poetry and the Use of Criticism*, 2nd edn (Faber and Faber, 1934).

——, *To Criticise the Critic* (Faber and Faber, 1965).

——, *On Poetry and Poets* (Faber and Faber, 1967).
T. S. Eliot: Selected Prose, ed. John Hayward (Penguin, 1953).
——, *The Family Reunion* (Faber and Faber, 1939). [NB. Eliot's prose writings on culture and religion, which are referred to dismissively here, are not listed.]

R. S. Thomas, *Song at the Year's Turning* (Rupert Hart-Davis, 1955).
——, *Poetry for Supper* (Rupert Hart-Davis, 1958).
——, *Tares* (Rupert Hart-Davis, 1961).
——, *The Bread of Truth* (Rupert Hart-Davis, 1963).
——, *Pietà* (Rupert Hart-Davis, 1966).
——, *Not That He Brought Flowers* (Rupert Hart-Davis, 1968).
——, *H'm* (Macmillan, 1972).
——, *Laboratories of the Spirit* (Macmillan, 1975).
——, *Frequencies* (Macmillan, 1978).
[NB. The Hart-Davis volumes seem, regrettably, to be out of print. A number of poems from them are reprinted in R. S. Thomas, *Selected Poems 1946–1968* (New York: St Martin's Press, 1973), but some of the best poems have still, at present, to be looked up on the listed volumes above in libraries. No interim *Collected Poems* yet exists, though the time for one seems now overdue.]
——, *Words and the Poet* (University of Wales Press, 1964).

Harold Bloom, *Yeats* (Oxford University Press, 1970).
Nicholas Brooke, 'Crazy Jane and "Byzantium" ', *Essays and Studies 1974*, ed. Kenneth Muir (John Murray, 1974).
Richard Ellmann, *The Identity of Yeats* (Faber and Faber, 1954).
T. R. Henn, *The Lonely Tower: Studies in the Poetry of W. B. Yeats* (Methuen, 1950).
C. G. Jung, *Modern Man in Search of a Soul* (Routledge and Kegan Paul, 1961).
——, *Memories, Dreams, Reflections* (Collins, 1977).
Hugh Kenner, *The Invisible Poet: T. S. Eliot* (Methuen, 1959).
Frank Kermode, *The Sense of an Ending* (Oxford University Press, 1966).
Michael North, 'Symbolism and Obscurity in "Meditations in Time of Civil War" ', *Critical Quarterly*, xix, no.1 (Spring, 1977).
John Rechy, *The Sexual Outlaw* (Allen Lane, 1978).
Grover Smith, *T. S. Eliot's Poetry and Plays: a Study in Source Meanings* (University of Chicago Press, 1950).
Stephen Spender, *The Struggle of the Modern* (Hamish Hamilton, 1963).
Jon Stallworthy, *Between the Lines: W. B. Yeats's Poetry in the Making* (Oxford University Press, 1963).
——, *Vision and Revision in Yeats's Last Poems* (Oxford University Press, 1969).

—— (ed.), *Yeats: 'Last Poems': A Selection of Critical Essays* (Macmillan Casebook, 1968).

A. E. Waite, *A Key to the Tarot* (Rider, 1972).

Part 2

Bernard Bergonzi (ed.), *Four Quartets* (Macmillan Casebook, 1969).

Cleanth Brooks, *The Well Wrought Urn* (Dennis Dobson, 1947).

——, *Modern Poetry and the Tradition* (Oxford University Press, 1965).

C. B. Cox and Arnold Hinchliffe (eds), *The Waste Land* (Macmillan Casebook, 1968).

K. G. W. Cross and R. T. Dunlop, *A Bibliography of Yeats Criticism 1887–1965* (Macmillan, 1971).

A. E. Dyson (ed.), *English Poetry: Select Bibliographical Guides* (Oxford University Press, 1971). See especially the chapter on Yeats (pp. 345–59) by Jon Stallworthy, and that on T. S. Eliot (pp. 360–75) by Anne Ridler.

Helen Gardner, *The Art of T. S. Eliot* (Cresset, 1949).

Graham Hough, *The Last Romantics* (Duckworth, 1949).

Frank Kermode, *Romantic Image* (Routledge and Kegan Paul, 1957).

Louis MacNeice, *The Poetry of W. B. Yeats* (Faber and Faber, 1967).

F. O. Matthiessen, *The Achievement of T. S. Eliot*, 2nd edn (Oxford University Press, 1947).

A. Symons, *The Symbolist Movement in Literature*, 2nd edn (1908).

John Unterecker, *A Reader's Guide to W. B. Yeats* (Thames and Hudson, 1959).

Edmund Wilson, *Axel's Castle: A Study in the Imaginative Literature of 1870–1930* (Fontana, 1961).

Finally, the attention of readers is also specially directed to the following works.

Richard Ellmann and Charles Feidelson Jr (eds), *The Modern Tradition* (Oxford University Press, 1965). A substantial anthology of background texts, invaluable for students of 'the modern'.

The Variorum Edition of the Poems of W. B. Yeats, ed. P. Allt and R. K. Alspach (Macmillan, 1957).

W. B. Yeats, *Memoirs* (the original unpublished text of the Autobiography and the Journal) ed. Denis Donoghue (Macmillan, 1972).

Index